Robert Pringle, the chairman and founder of *Central Banking* journal, is a financial commentator, economics editor and entrepreneur. He has devoted his career to reporting and analyzing developments in the international money and capital markets and the international monetary system. His experience gives him a unique perspective on the dramatic changes that have occurred in global economics and finance and the problems that face the world economy now. He has held senior positions on *The Economist, The Banker* (as editor), the Group of 30 (a well-known think tank of which he was the first director), and at the WIDER Institute of the United Nations University. He has also served as a consultant to leading commercial banks and to governments on economic policy issues. He founded Central Banking Publications in 1990 and has built it into a leading source of independent information and commentary on the activities of central banks around the world. He has interviewed numerous central bank governors and has commissioned and published original work by many leading international economists.

'*The Money Trap* embodies an original, ambitious, bold, and provocative approach to the subject of the crisis and the monetary system ... A valuable addition to the literature available for policy makers, analysts, academics and participants in financial markets.' – Dr Y. V. Reddy, *Former Governor, Reserve Bank of India*

'This work is probably the most ambitious – and also relevant – attempt to explain the set of causes that led to the disasters of 2007 and following years. It proposes solutions based on economic literature and on the personal views of an author who has devoted most of his career to this fundamental subject. The analysis is fundamental not only for specialists but, more importantly, also for our society. It is a book that should be read by government officials, economists, students and citizens.' – Jacques de Larosière, *Managing Director of the International Monetary Fund (1978–87), Governor of the Banque de France (1987–93)*

'It is always very important to review history, particularly the history of past mistakes. By doing that, we can see how we should behave in the future when similar crises hit us. Robert Pringle's book does exactly that. It contributes greatly to our understanding of the present international financial system.' – Eisuke Sakakibara, *Professor of Waseda University, Tokyo, Former Vice Minister of Finance and International Affairs of Japan*

'This book cuts through all the carping and obfuscation to pinpoint the biggest burden on business enterprise: the lack of reliable money.' – Graham Bannock, *Co-author (with R.E. Baxter), The Palgrave Encyclopedia of World Economic History*

Also by Robert Pringle

BANKING IN BRITAIN

THE CENTRAL BANKS (*with Marjorie Deane*)

THE FUTURE OF CENTRAL BANKING (*edited with Claire Jones*)

THE GROWTH MERCHANTS: Economic Consequences of Wishful Thinking

THE CONTEMPORARY RELEVANCE OF DAVID HUME

The Money Trap

Escaping the Grip of Global Finance

Robert Pringle
Founder and Chairman, Central Banking Publications, London

palgrave
macmillan

First published 2012
First published in paperback 2014 by
PALGRAVE MACMILLAN

Palgrave Macmillan in the UK is an imprint of Macmillan Publishers Limited, registered in England, company number 785998, of Houndmills, Basingstoke, Hampshire RG21 6XS.

Palgrave Macmillan in the US is a division of St Martin's Press LLC, 175 Fifth Avenue, New York, NY 10010.

Palgrave Macmillan is the global academic imprint of the above companies and has companies and representatives throughout the world.

Palgrave® and Macmillan® are registered trademarks in the United States, the United Kingdom, Europe and other countries

ISBN: 978–0–230–39274–8 (hardback)
ISBN: 978–1–137–36690–0 (paperback)

This book is printed on paper suitable for recycling and made from fully managed and sustained forest sources. Logging, pulping and manufacturing processes are expected to conform to the environmental regulations of the country of origin.

A catalogue record for this book is available from the British Library.

A catalog record for this book is available from the Library of Congress.

TO

Alex, Otto and Harry
Freddy and William
Ben and Sam
Hamish

Contents

Acknowledgements

This book has grown out of my work as an economist, editor and commentator on monetary and economic affairs over the past 40 years. Ever since 1971, when I became editor of *The Banker*, I have stayed in close contact with the people and institutions that have shaped events, as well as the economists and other scholars who have influenced the climate of public opinion within which policy-makers operate. Later, as a member and founding director of the Group of 30, at the United Nations University World Institute for Development Economics Research (UNU-WIDER) in Finland and after 1990 as founder and editor of Central Banking Publications, I came to know well many of the leading financial statesmen of their time – and of ours.

They failed, didn't they? Or perhaps I should say, 'we failed' – our generation. Yes, there were achievements. And for much of the time, and in many ways, financial innovation supported broader economic progress. But at key turning points the financial mechanism screwed up; in J. S. Mill's metaphor, it became 'a monkey wrench' in the economic machinery. In that sense, the community of people involved in finance failed.

It would be some comfort if this could be seen as a 'learning experience', as if the world were a theatre for economic experiments. Some, including some central bankers, see it in that light and indeed claim that we are making progress. They seem to me rather like the surgeon who exclaims: 'the operation was successful', though the patient died. To judge by results – and what other test is relevant? – we have less practical knowledge and skill in how to drive the financial engine than we did half a century ago.

The fact that crises were predictable – and that plenty of early warnings were given – did not help to avoid them. The very first issue of *Central Banking* (Summer 1990) warned that 'we may have bought success in the fight against inflation at the cost of greater instability and risk in the industry of banking and money.' The article, which I wrote, asserted that a 'radical restructuring of banking' would be needed. Among other risks, there was a danger that bankers would become 'so powerful that they can demand ever greater privilege and protection – and in effect hold central banks and governments to ransom'.

In short, I was among those who warned of 'disasters to come', but was as shocked as anybody else when they duly arrived.

This book is my attempt to explain how all this came about, and how the world might avoid it happening again. On both these questions, I have come to very different conclusions from the majority of economists and commentators. It seems to me that no government is doing the right thing. Few of them, and only a handful of economists, are even pointing in the right direction.

I am grateful to all those who have given me their time over the years – the dozens of central bankers, government officials and others who shall remain nameless – to discuss international monetary issues as well as all those I have interviewed on and off the record.

Among those I ought to name are the following: Robert Aliber, Peter Bakstansky, Graham Bannock, Claudio Borio, Brendan Brown, Warren Coats, Haruko Fukuda, William Isaac, Tom Jupp, Allan Meltzer, Peter Urbach, Y. V. Reddy, Alessandro Roselli, Toyokuni Yamanaka, Judy Shelton and Frank Vibert, all of whom kindly read chapters or substantial parts of chapters of the book in manuscript and contributed valuable comments and information. The remaining errors are of course mine alone.

I would like to thank the participants in successive meetings of the Santa Colomba group for their contributions to the outstanding debates at the group's sessions and in particular thanks to the gracious hosts, Robert and Valerie Mundell, for their invitations to these memorable events at their wonderful home near Siena.

My thanks also go to Edmond Alphandéry, the founder and chairman of the Euro-50 group and Marc Uzan, founder and director of the Reinventing Bretton Woods Committee, for the many insights into the nature and recent development of the financial system afforded me by attending the various meetings of these groups. Likewise thanks to Christopher Rogers and William Lai for giving me the opportunity to moderate recent monetary conferences in Hong Kong and Tokyo.

My gratitude goes to all members of the advisory board of Central Banking Publications, and especially to Charles Goodhart, Steve Hanke, Otmar Issing, Andrew Sheng, Alexander Swoboda and Joseph Yam, for their support and valuable advice. I am grateful to Nick Carver, publisher of Central Banking Publications, for his dedication to and leadership of the company since its acquisition by Incisive Media in 2007, and to Matthew Crabbe, managing director of Incisive's Risk Division, for his understanding of the special nature of *Central Banking*'s readership and audience, both in print and online.

I want to pay tribute to Johannes Witteveen, former managing director of the International Monetary Fund, for his inspiring leadership of the Group of 30 when I was fortunate to work closely with him during its early years, and for his chairmanship of the advisory board of *Central Banking* from 1990 to 2007. Thank you also to those other outstanding financial leaders of our time, Sir Mervyn King, Jacques de Larosière, Masaaki Shirakawa, Jean-Claude Trichet and Paul Volcker, for their goodwill.

Looking back over many years as an economist, editor and financial commentator, I realize how much I owe my alma mater, King's College, Cambridge, and this seems an opportune moment to acknowledge my debt to it and to my former tutors and academic advisers, notably John Saltmarsh and Christopher Morris (History); John Goldthorpe and Michael Young (Sociology); and Nicholas Kaldor, Robin Marris and Joan Robinson (Economics). They instilled in me an abiding fascination with the history and performance of the international economy in its broader social context.

Any excess Keynesian bias left over from Cambridge was corrected in the bracing Alpine air of Interlaken, where I participated in seminars organized annually during the 1970s by Karl Brunner and Allan Meltzer, great teachers as well as great monetary economists, and in the first sessions of the European Shadow Open Market Committee, founded by them. It was at the Interlaken seminars, where we discussed the potential application of economics to sociological, political and ethical issues, that I first met James Buchanan. (I had already got to know Gordon Tullock and other pioneers of the Public Choice school.) Equally inspiring was the opportunity to meet Friederich von Hayek and discuss his views on money at the Institute of Economic Affairs in London (that must have been in 1976); Hayek had been a hero since my schooldays, when I had picked up and read my father's battered 1944 edition of *The Road to Serfdom*, with its ironical dedication to 'The Socialists of All Parties'.

I will always be grateful to Robert Skidelsky for contributing the Foreword. For Maynard Keynes's biographer to grace the opening pages of a book on international money is to give it the perfect start.

All that remains is to thank my wife for her patience during the long time it took to put this book to bed.

Preface

This book makes a case for radical reform of the global financial system based on a distinctive analysis of recent history. While the analysis has generally been well received, critics have said the proposals are too ambitious and radical, and cannot be implemented. The best way to make progress is by incremental steps, such critics say. Focus on measures that clearly improve matters in a specific field. Look at the ground at your feet, not at the heavens above! Well, if it were evident that real progress was being made, such criticisms might carry weight. But this is not the case. Current policies have not successfully allayed fears of further financial shocks. Markets remain fragile. Moreover, some of the measures that *are* being implemented are having the opposite effect to that intended. As I shall show, developments since the hardback edition was published have strengthened the need for radical reform.

Some of the key themes of the book are as follows:

- Financial instability has become *endemic to the world economy*. Since the early 1980s there has been an average of one such episode every three years, with several major cross-border bubbles. The relationship between these episodes and the international monetary regime requires much closer attention than it has so far received.
- Policies aimed at encouraging growth and reducing financial instability have been based on an *incorrect diagnosis* of the true nature of the economic problem.
- Academic and policy work on the international monetary system has become separated from work on the structure, functioning and regulation of the banking and financial system. We badly need *more joined-up thinking* about the interaction between exchange rate policies, monetary regimes and financial institutions.
- The same policy response, repeated after each crisis, merely lays the basis for the next one. In each cycle, rates are driven lower and lower, this time to near zero (White, 2013). Again, financial regulation is always tightened, and yet the view that lax regulation was a primary cause of the crisis is highly questionable.
- The reliance on monetary activism at the national level is misplaced, with diminishing short-term benefits and large potential long-term

costs. The failure of such policies reflects a *misguided view of how monetary policy* should operate in the economic system.

- Notwithstanding the continuing failure of policy, there has been little willingness to *reconsider monetary policy frameworks* in the wake of the crisis and few central bankers have voiced dissent from the consensus in favour of domestic inflation targeting. I argue that even when combined with a macro-prudential overlay, it will not be sufficient to tame the credit cycle. Indeed, such insular policies are bound to add up to sub-optimal policies for the world as a whole.
- The correct diagnosis points to flaws in the global financial system, with the central problem being the *absence of a real international monetary system* and associated lack of discipline on national policies and on players in the financial markets.
- Therefore a major effort is needed to build a new financial archi-tecture – or to change the metaphor, a new rulebook both for the official and the private sectors.

How recent developments strengthen the case for reform

Events since publication of the book in 2012 have strengthened its thesis:

- The suppression of market interest rates for extended periods has brought about conditions in which the monetary mechanism has been unable to perform its true functions in allocating capital resources. Interest rates can no longer serve as reliable signals to investors or borrowers. Thus, for example, company treasurers and investors cannot rely on using the US Treasury bond rate as a bench-mark for interest rates, as it is manipulated by the Fed and is hence not a true market rate.
- Although stock markets were strong between 2012 and mid-2013, many observers put this down to ultra-loose monetary policies by reserve centres rather than to a fundamental improvement in the outlook.
- Financial markets have become even more fragmented. It ought to be of deep concern to all who believe in the benefits of free movement of capital that politicians are increasingly resorting to measures of financial repression, as discussed in Chapter 11.
- There is growing scepticism about the efficacy of the entire approach to regulating banks (so-called Basel III and the Basel process).

Financial sector lobbying has held up the needed restructuring of the financial system.

- Measures such as 'quantitative easing' (money printing) combined with fiscal austerity have further increased levels of income and wealth *inequality*, which has been such a marked feature of the past 30–40 years. This because such measures boost the value of assets held disproportionately by wealthier individuals while reducing average real wages.
- There is no greater understanding of the true nature of the problem we face.

A climacteric of such dimensions, with a legacy of uncertainty and nervousness lasting a decade or more, evidently demands a full overhaul of the system that produced it. Otherwise there can be no assurance that it will not happen again. Reforms should enable the private sector financial system to perform its key social functions – above all, allocating scarce capital resources – better; and rebuild a proper official international monetary system that would provide an adequate framework for regulating monetary relations among nations and regions of the world. The foundation of a good international monetary system is to an appropriate monetary standard to serve as a reference point or reliable benchmark for national monetary policies (Chapter 13 surveys the main options). The key to building safer financial institutions is to put personal responsibility and risk awareness back at the heart of every institution and every user of services. The book argues that this is best achieved by (wherever possible) replacing loan contracts with equity contracts, where the parties assume upfront the risks along with possible rewards attached to ownership. Reform should be built on developments in financial markets; indeed, as suggested in this book, the globalization of financial markets, especially of equity markets, can be used to provide a foundation for a new monetary standard. Securities markets have huge potential, though they have a bad reputation in the crisis. New forms of financial intermediation should be encouraged and those mega-banks that are too big and complex to manage without posing unacceptable risks to society should be dismantled.

Since publication, popular demands for more radical reforms have persisted, fuelled by a constant stream of financial scandals (missselling of financial products, fixing of key interest rates, insider trading and so on). In my view many of the radical changes espoused either by those on the Left or on the Free-market Right would improve the system. In fact, they have quite a lot in common with each other and with the ideas discussed in *The Money Trap*. Break-up excessive concentrations of financial and political power; end too-big-to-fail institutions; stop the exploitation of public funds for private purposes; democratize the monetary system. Yet they have little chance of being taken up by mainstream political parties.

Since publication it has become even clearer why such proposals raise so much opposition. Real reform will call for the *sacrifice of some degree of apparent national autonomy in monetary and to some extent fiscal policies*. This sacrifice would be arguable in the interests of citizens as well as promoting sound banks and commerce. But it is not in the interests of national politicians who naturally wish to be able to continue to offer programmes and make promises to their electorates that they can finance as a last resort by virtue of their control over national money.

Counterproductive policies

Governments continue to adopt policies that are making a bad situation worse. For example, regulators tell banks to hold more capital in relation to their assets (loans and investments on their books), i.e. raise capital assets *ratios*. Yet in advancing this policy, governments and regulators ignore its effect on the incentives facing bank managers, whose pay is typically linked to the achievement of specified rates of return on equity capital. Not surprisingly, managers have tried to achieve the higher capital ratios partly at least by reducing assets and restraining new lending rather than by raising new capital, which would reduce the rates of return on equity. Arguably, the insistence on raising capital ratios has restrained demand and impeded recovery. This is emphatically not to argue, however, that it was wrong to try to strengthen banks in this way, given the risks that weakly-capitalized banks can pose for the economy, as the crisis showed. Rather, such policy dilemmas point to flaws in the system itself.

This is just one example of the way that official policies have reflected a mistaken, partial analysis of the problem. So when people say 'Calm down, Robert; we are getting there', it makes me rather frustrated. Not only are many of the measures arguably taking us farther away from a solution, but they are also imposing high costs on the economy; among these is the ever-spreading web of controls over financial institutions and markets. Historical experience, for example in the period 1945–60, shows that such a 'collectivist' approach to monetary matters is unlikely to produce desirable or efficient results.

The mistakes reflect the faulty and superficial analysis of the problem – that the pre-crisis was fundamentally sound and needs to be patched up. This criticism is not an 'extreme' view held only by a few radicals on the anarchist Left or the libertarian Right. Sir Mervyn (now Lord) King, who retired as Bank of England governor at the end of June 2013, bluntly pointed out that 'none of the underlying causes of the crisis have been removed'. (The remark was made in 2011 but there is no reason to think that he has changed his mind.) I know several other senior officials who privately harbour deep fears for the future but cannot say what they think publicly. Driven by mistaken ideas and fearful of renewed financial turbulence, governments reach for bad policies and controls. That is how the money trap operates; it lures governments, financiers and consumers into acting against their true interests. *The Money Trap* was written in an effort to show that these ideas need to be changed, to expose the sectional interests that they serve, and to provide signposts to a deeper understanding of the underlying problem in our financial system. I hope that this new paperback edition will engage the interest of a wider audience so that public opinion can help to push policy-makers to address the real problems.

Reaching escape velocity?

Nobody who read the book when it first came out should have been surprised that the so-called economic recovery has been set back repeatedly by new shocks. As always, optimists point to a few bright spots. Once again, hopes centre on the US, but there too growth has repeatedly disappointed expectations. Recovery has been weaker than after previous recessions. A good idea of the lasting impact of the Global Financial Crisis is shown by the way that US families on average have made up only 45 per cent of the decline in their net worth since the peak of the boom in 2007. The wealth of the median US household fell by 39 per cent between its peak in 2007 and 2010, with poorer families suffering disproportionately. As a recent survey showed that families that were younger, had less than a college education and/or were members of a historically disadvantaged minority group suffered 'particularly large wealth losses' (Boshara and Emmons, 2013).

Most of the rebuilding of wealth that has taken place in the US is due to gains in the stock market, primarily benefiting wealthy families. Current forecasts of 3 per cent growth in 2014–15 depend heavily on buoyancy of the housing market being maintained. The world's leading economy also remains uncomfortably dependent on an asset price boom to lift demand – i.e. it remains caught in the credit cycle, and on persuading consumers to take on more debt. Other major economic problems facing the US, such as the fiscal crisis and how the Federal Reserve, the US central bank, will withdraw its exceptional support, known as 'quantitative easing', remain to be solved. In the troubled euro area, the efforts of debtor countries to regain competitiveness vis-à-vis Germany continue to rely heavily on austerity. Unemployment remains very high and (in all countries except Germany, which is benefiting from several years of holding its costs down and so is super-competitive) longer-term prospects for the area remain uncertain. The European banking and financial system continues to need the support from the European Central Bank (ECB) and depends on government guarantees to retain public trust. Meanwhile, in Japan, where the central bank has taken somewhat rash measures in an attempt to resuscitate the economy from the grip of the dreaded deflation, GDP growth is projected at less than 2 per cent annually for the foreseeable future. At the same time, several large developing countries, including Brazil, China, India and the Russian Federation, are experiencing a slowdown.

Looking to the future, economists agree that *unresolved risks* could again derail the global economy. Officials often refer to these as 'headwinds'. These headwinds include damaged banking and financial systems that impede firms' access to credit – difficulties worsened by an excess of regulatory initiatives. Surveys show, for example, that European companies still have great difficulties obtaining loans, with interest rates charged by banks for loans to small enterprises often prohibitively expensive. The absence of a strong revival in capital investment is a telling symptom. Indeed, there is growing evidence that the Global Financial Crisis has done permanent damage to the long-term health of many economies, including emerging markets. As the OECD puts it, 'the rate of potential growth has become more uncertain since the onset of the global crisis' (OECD, 2013).

With the OECD again forecasting 'disappointing' global growth, there is an urgent need to get banks functioning again properly. But present feeble and unimaginative reforms do not provide realistic prospects of achieving that.

What should reforms aim to achieve?

It is time for a change in the terms of the debate. The financial system plays such a key role in society, and has such a pervasive influence on the nature of work and leisure activities, that it must fit in with the social values we hold and aspire to. So let us step back for a moment from the economic outlook and put it in a broader context. What kind of society do we want?

As soon as this question is raised, ethical issues such as fairness, proportionality, honesty, and inter-generational equity come to the fore. Economists assume that our overriding objective should be to 'recover' and resume economic growth – as if a given, quite fast, rate of growth were 'normal'. Yet the traumatic experience of the crisis has raised questions about the purpose of economic growth itself. They note that in some countries, a high proportion of young people face the prospect of being unable to find permanent employment for 10 years or more. Are they being in some sense 'punished' for their parents' addiction to consumerism and the pursuit of monetary gains at any cost? When thinking of ultimate ends, what life is for, only a fool would imagine that growth holds the answer – yet some of us may feel we succumbed to the belief that it does.1 Such is the view of various church leaders and others. More important are the criticisms made by several recent commentators of the current obsession with growth of GDP, however measured, as the chief goal of economic policy.2 Values that many attach to other possible goals – preservation of stability and social order, the values embodied in traditional cultures, enjoyment of the arts, linguistic diversity, fairness, leisure, the natural environment and 'the good life' – are not simply luxuries to be afforded only after a decent material standard has been achieved, especially if the hell-bent pursuit of consumption destroys or undermines such values in the process. Nor are they goods to be preserved for the enjoyment of elites. In other words, there are trade-offs. Many people may, for example, give a higher priority to reducing disparities of wealth and income – inequalities that have soared in many countries in the past generation – over and above the aim of increasing GDP.

Reform needs to address such legitimate worries. The ideas that dominated policy-making immediately after the Global Financial Crisis – of going back so far as possible to business as usual – were misconceived because the financial system we had during the build-up to the Global Financial Crisis was not only inefficient and crisis-prone but also deeply unfair. It allowed certain elite groups to skim the cream from the top of the money supply. The pre-crisis financial system made it easy for corruption of various sorts to flourish and for politically powerful interests to hold society to ransom. What is so telling, even bizarre, is that measures aiming to restore growth and refloat the banks have further increased inequalities of income and wealth. If we have a financial system that can survive only by squeezing middle- and lower-class incomes and by allocating all the gains from social activity and economic progress to the super-wealthy, then that is as morally indefensible as it is economically suicidal. Yet that is what is happening. This is why I subtitle the book 'Escaping the Grip of Global Finance'. What has also become clearer since the book was published is that the shift to collectivism embodied in current government policies is, ironically, likely to make it even easier for the rich and powerful to cherry-pick the best of the available products and services. Without realizing it, people from the Left who call for stronger State control are playing into the hands of the sectional interests that they claim to detest.

Thus a good monetary system should allow economies to grow slowly, or not at all, if that is what people want. The present system needs endless growth – with regular bouts of inflation – to survive. It encourages the build-up of debt at every level. Under the reformed system outlined in Part IV, which is based so far as possible on equity (or equity-like) claims, debt would become much more expensive and people would prefer risk-sharing contracts. We should realize that it is incredibly expensive for an institution to promise nominal fixed-value contracts like deposits when the counterpart assets are inherently unstable and of uncertain future value. That is one of the key lessons of the financial crisis that everybody seems determined to ignore. That is why, historically, bankers rely on the State for support – not only as lender of last resort but as the monopoly supplier of risk-free assets. The interaction of central banks' insular monetary policies with banks profit-maximization and floating exchange rates must inevitably lead to periodic cross-border as well as domestic debt-fuelled booms and busts, unless the banks are made safe by draconian regulation – a cure that could be worse than the disease. This regulation, again, is inevitably national, encouraging financial protectionism.

Yet, events have shown that we cannot escape the implications of globalized markets and should not turn our backs on the opportunities they offer. The success of global trade and investment in raising many hundreds of millions of people out of poverty through market mechanisms – even if supplemented with a strong dose of 'state capitalism' in many parts of the world – is not to be gainsaid. This makes it all the more urgent to solve the financial challenges that lies behind repeated episodes of extreme financial instability. A proper monetary mechanism should, as the old saying goes, oil the wheels of commerce. When it malfunctions, as the philosopher J.S. Mill said, it throws a monkey wrench into the economic machine. That is exactly what has happened.

Reforms advocated in this book would reduce concentrations of financial power, reduce the pressures to build up debt, make unnecessary measures that have increased social and economic inequality, deregulate finance and go far to democratize the world of money and banking. The analysis has indeed been strengthened by recent developments. In this book, I show how the crisis developed (Part I), the efforts of governments to find ways out of the trap (Part II), the key challenges that must be addressed by any reforms aimed at setting up a better monetary system (Part III) and the road to possible solutions (Part IV). I have little to add here to the first part, as it is mainly historical scene setting, or to the exposition of more radical policy options, though I take the opportunity to reply to some criticisms (those interested in following the debate on the proposals advanced in the book are invited to visit the website at www.themoneytrap.com).

We now look at the implications of recent developments – since the hardback edition was published – for the analysis and proposals.

What are central banks for?

Since publication of the hardback edition, the debate on this topic – What should be the objectives of central banks? – has come into the open (see Chapter 5). Defenders of inflation targeting have not given up the fight, and indeed are still a majority. But they are on the defensive, and governments have grown impatient. Following the Global Financial Crisis, central bank opinion has diverged. Some say that central banks should continue to be responsible only for price stability, and that giving them further responsibilities carries the danger of undermining their commitment to that overarching goal; this is the view of Germany's central bank, the Bundesbank. Others say that they should keep their eyes not only on inflation control but also on 'financial stability', a concept that is difficult to define precisely but means essentially reducing risk in the financial system; i.e. designing and implementing a regulatory regime that makes banks less liable to fail and less costly, to taxpayers and society, if they do fail. The central banks in the US, the eurozone, the UK and many other countries have been granted added responsibilities and instruments to promote financial stability. Yet they have also become closer to governments. George Osborne, UK chancellor of the exchequer, wrote to the governor of the Bank of England only a few weeks after the legislation giving effect to the reforms was passed saying that 'at this stage of the cycle', it is 'particularly important... that the committee takes into account, and gives due weight to, the impact of its actions on the near-term economic recovery'. This is typical of the new tone that finance ministers are adopting towards their central bankers – much more intrusive and assertive than they were pre-crisis.3

Do the new responsibilities change the focus on inflation control? Some central bankers think that monetary policy instruments – notably interest rates – should be reserved exclusively for maintaining price stability, and that other tools should be used to achieve financial stability. Others believe, however, that the full panoply of weapons, including interest rates, should be available if necessary to stop emerging bubbles in house prices or other assets. The arrangements introduced by the major financial centres differ but they share certain characteristics. In practice, governments have given central banks a large degree of responsibility for both price and financial stability, and extensive new powers to implement the second function. There is a fair degree of confusion about many organizational aspects of the new set-up. Central bankers admit in private that it will be a challenge to make them workable and effective in practice.

What is clear is that the new regulatory set-up gives unelected central bankers/regulators huge discretionary powers over the private sector. True, in some circumstances they will need political sanction to proceed with a measure they might wish to take, but in many cases they will be called on to take decisions that will have life-changing implications for individuals and firms. Whether they can in practice be held properly accountable is an open question.

After the reforms have been implemented, central banking will in future have more to do with financial stability than with monetary policy. National central banks' obligations will be to ensure maintenance of the peg to the international currency standard – and eventually convertibility into international currency units (Ikons) at a fixed, internationally agreed, price. This should become a more or less routine business, leaving more resources to deal with financial stability issues – and driving through structural reforms to banking and finance.

Giving governments and banks new alibis

If central banks risk becoming instruments in a new kind of centralized 'planning' mechanism, the new arrangements also give governments a bigger say in the affairs of central banks, while granting them at the same time a politically convenient 'alibi' – i.e. the freedom to blame central banks/regulators when a big bank or other financial group gets into trouble. As many banks – especially in Europe – still carry a load of bad debts on their books at the start of this new regime (covered up by access to cheap central bank money) banking in fact badly needs further structural reform. But no politician dares to confront that reality. At the same time, the banks also have a new alibi – they can say, when the next crisis hits, 'the regulators have made a hash of it – again!' Thus, expect banks to comply meticulously with the regulations while paying even less attention to building their own defences. If a bank management has a choice between doing what is needed to put the bank on a genuinely sound footing and complying with regulations on pain of severe penalties, which will they choose? In the old days, banks made provision for possible future bad debts of two kinds – general provisions needed as buffers to ride through a future general business downturn, and specific provisions for anticipated bad or doubtful loans to specific borrowers. Some banks managed to survive for a hundred years or more using rule-of-thumb methods to calculate how much money should they set aside for each risk. They were conservative and risk-averse, as the penalties for failure were expected to be humiliation and effective bankruptcy. In a future crash, the banks as well as public and the government will be able to point their fingers at central bank/ regulators. This puts their credibility generally, including in monetary policy matters, further at risk.

If the effects of bad decision-making could be brought home to individual bankers, they would build adequate defences and instil a culture of risk awareness throughout their institutions. Structural change to make individual bankers responsible for their mistakes is the very minimum of what is needed – where the 2011 Vickers Commission in the UK, the 2012 EU Liikanen Report and Paul Volcker, ex-chairman of the Fed, have pointed the way. I do not believe it would go far enough, but it would be a start. Regulations aimed at changing behaviour will not work in the long run without changes to an industry's structure.

Monetary debate sidelined by the euro

Moving to the debate on the future of the international monetary system, this has got nowhere. It has been completely sidetracked by the problems of the eurozone. The origin of these problems is clear enough as explained in Chapter 6. At the time it was planned and launched, the eurozone was far from meeting the conditions for a single currency area, where economic efficiency demands that different parts of a region share a single currency. These conditions are usually considered to include a high degree of capital and labour mobility, price and wage flexibility, and automatic fiscal transfers to regions adversely affected by recessions. Governments went into the euro project aware of the risks, their ears buzzing with warnings. In that sense it certainly was launched too early; closer economic and political integration should have preceded monetary union. But political factors dictated the timing – France wanted a say in monetary policy rather than obediently follow the German policy (the old Deutschmark), while Germany needed French support for re-unification. But their bargain left a lot of work to do to make the single currency viable. The past few years have seen agonizingly slow progress in forging the conditions necessary for such a union. Reforms will doubtless continue to be made at this snail's pace, with decisions taken in the heat of battle and amid clashes among national governments and parliaments. The big countries of the Union will, I believe, persevere with this as a political project of the utmost importance for Europe.

However, this obsession with the euro means that institutions such as the IMF whose job it is to look after the international monetary system and contribute to the debate on it had their energies diverted. It was a mistake when, at German insistence, the IMF was dragged so deeply into the bailout programmes for Greece and other countries. Another unfortunate side-effect has been to turn many economists and informed observers against all proposals for wider monetary cooperation. So it is necessary to point out again that the reform of the international monetary system proposed here would be very different from the experiment being undertaken in the eurozone. The key is to provide a more stable and reliable international monetary standard than present arrangements, based as they are on unreliable national currencies, are able to do. The plan does not propose forcing countries unwillingly into a straitjacket.

The IMF's mantra

In so far as the IMF has concerned itself with the problems of international money outlined in Chapter 7, it has too often relied on a simple mantra. Christine Lagarde, the managing director, put its view in 17 words:

> 'The financial system can work if each of its members follow the right principles for their economy'

This statement, at a G20 meeting in 2013, shows that the Fund remains focused on the national policy level. This tends to divert attention from the faults of the international monetary system itself. Indeed, this predisposition helps to explain why the Fund got its analysis and prognosis breathtakingly wrong in the crucial period before the Global Financial Crisis. The argument of *The Money Trap* is that the errors it made at that time and since the crisis (its outlook has repeatedly been proved too optimistic) are not accidental; they result from faults in the underlying analysis. The story of the years leading up to 2007 is precisely that each country followed the IMF's advice and did what it deemed the right thing. Just as the central bankers with their inflation targets set policies couched in terms of domestic objectives, the IMF repeatedly examined the policies of major countries and found them, with a few qualifications, satisfactory. So it was left, post-crisis, without a convincing or distinctive contribution to public understanding of how the crisis occurred. The Fund has not been able to take a holistic view of the dynamic relationship between major public and private players as components in an interacting system. The nearest it has come to this is in the more recent work on so-called 'spillovers' (assessments of the effects of a major country's policies on other countries and on global financial markets), which are summarized in the managing director's 'global agenda' reports, but in practice these have mainly enumerated the risks facing developed and emerging market economies – with some platitudes about policies needed – and have had little impact.

This reluctance to face systemic challenges may be partly a result of the pressure put on the IMF by major members, especially the US – pressure revealed by post-mortem evaluations after the crisis (IMF, 2011). But it is also that the Fund simply reflected, rather than challenged, the prevailing ideology. Despite all the heart-searching, it does not appear as if much has changed. First, the US Treasury does not want the Fund to get involved in what it views as speculative work about the future of the international monetary system, because it feels (wrongly, in my view) that the present system is in US interests. Second, the IMF, like the central banks, remains in thrall to the prevailing ideology of monetary and economic management, despite the clearest possible evidence that the crisis has called into question all the intellectual underpinnings and assumptions on which this ideology is based.

This is a background factor that helps explain why the Fund has lost – we have all lost – the old language international monetary cooperation – and with the loss of language, can it be long before we lost the habits that go with it? Under the Bretton Woods regime from 1945 to 1971, when the IMF policed countries' exchange rate policies, the Fund developed a distinctive language – the language of 'adjustment', 'liquidity' and 'conditionality' as well as mutual assistance – the idea of the Fund as a self-help club – a place where you can go to advice on how to help oneself. This enabled the institution not only to build up a corpus of economic expertise, but also to reduce the politicization of international monetary relations. In the past 10–15 years, international monetary relations have become, as in the 1930s, a free for all, in which might is right. Lacking the language to develop a systemic analysis, the IMF acts as an honest broker between strong political and national interests. It tries to avoid finger-pointing; it tries to avoid putting Japan, China or any other big power in the dock. Its message is: 'Let's calm down.' Talk of the prospect of currency wars is 'overblown', according to Madame Lagarde. Where the old language used impersonal terms to identify and press for the adjustment of policy in each country needed to promote the objective of the common good – the dogma of market-determined exchange rates has degraded the language and habits of international cooperation. It is replaced by power politics. Hence the repeated outbreak of – yes – competitive currency depreciations, which are often disguised forms of protectionism. So the Fund tends to approve whatever the big boys, above all the US but also increasingly China, believe from time to time is in their interests.

But it is not just pressure from member countries. At a deeper level, the problem is that the Fund shares the prevailing illusion that more policy activism, especially by the managers of money, can help, if it is the right kind of 'activism'. It should be pointing out what is missing from current debates, namely the contribution that a proper international monetary system itself could provide. For example, as discussed in Chapter 7, history shows that a good system can accommodate large and persistent global imbalances without causing the periodic collapse of banking and financial systems. It does so by nudging countries to follow policies that are in the general interest by agreed, universal rules, and thereby inducing stabilizing private capital movements. With rules, private agents such as multinational corporations and financial institutions do a lot of the work needed to reconcile different countries' differing endowments, preferences and objectives, and the associated international payments imbalances, by their interaction through decentralized markets. Without such rules, there are too many easy arguments for currency manipulation – which is often in the short-term interests of local politicians, as it facilitates finance of their pet spending projects.

In the past two years, the entire G20/IMF process, which started off trying to reach a consensus on the need to mend the system, has run out of steam.

The convenient Chinese scapegoat

The problem of global imbalances, as discussed in Chapter 8, while undeniably an important issue, has also become another distraction – offering yet another scapegoat for monetary policy. Policy-makers and some bankers hold that China, Germany and other surplus countries with excessive savings had a large responsibility for the financial crash, by (in the case of China) forcing low interest rates on the US, fuelling the preceding asset boom and the US external deficit (and in the case of Germany forcing peripheral eurozone countries into deficit and debt). This hypothesis remains, to say the least, unproven. The criticisms of it have not been convincingly answered (See Borio and Disyatat, 2011). On this latter view, analysis confined to national account concepts like savings and investment throws no light on the cross-border flows that actually finance credit booms. It diverts attention away from the monetary and financial factors that have been the main cause of repeated financial crises. It is the financial decisions of market participants that determine financing flows, not the *ex post* distribution of savings and investment. Financial institutions create purchasing power by extending credit. In the build-up to the Global Financial Crisis, there is no evidence that the US current account deficit was 'financed' by an increase in global savings. The roots of the Global Financial Crisis should be traced rather to a global credit and asset price boom, fuelled by central bank monetary policies and commercial bankers' aggressive risk-taking, following financial deregulation, and facilitated by the lack of any international discipline or sanction on irresponsible policies. The system lacks a mechanism to prevent the build-up of unsustainable booms in credit and asset prices that lead to serious financial strains. Another conclusion follows: even if the scale of current account imbalances were to be permanently reduced, whether in the euro area or at the global level, that would not make the financial system or the global economy any safer. By the same token, a strong global financial system would accommodate large and long-lasting imbalances on current account, which are indeed a natural accompaniment of international economic development.

I should just add that this is not to say that excessive trade surpluses and deficits are not a problem; under the current monetary system they clearly are. They fuel protectionist pressures, and cost jobs. But they did not cause the financial crisis. Policies based on a faulty diagnosis will not be effective in preventing another crash. Talking about them is just another excuse for failing to face up to the real issues.

The reserves time bomb ticks away

No progress has been made in defusing yet another demanding issue – the reserve currency time bomb. This is one of the four key challenges that, as explained in Chapters 8–11, a proper reform of the system would have to meet (the others being global imbalances, making banking safe, and managing international unsustainable 'bubbles' in currencies, property prices and other asset markets like stock markets).

The accumulation of costly reserves has continued. Capital, which should in general flow from rich countries to emerging markets (where it would normally earn a higher return), has instead continued to flow from poor to rich countries – with a high proportion of reserves still invested in US dollar securities. Yet at the same time, the foundations of the dollar's global reserve currency role continue gradually to weaken with the deadlock over the US budget talks and as the US authorities continue policies of dollar depreciation. What has become clearer in the past two years is that, as the time bomb ticks away, it is already having other undesirable effects. There is pressure on central banks to not only accumulate more reserves but also raise earnings on their reserves. How can they do this safely at a time of low interest rates? In their search for more income, central banks are starting to behave more like the commercial financial institutions – like the banks over which they have newly extended supervisory powers. More of them are pursuing profit opportunities and playing the markets in search of yield. In many jurisdictions, governments rely on central banks to make a regular contribution to the public purse, and this has been increasingly challenging for many of them in the post-crisis world of near-zero interest rates on traditionally safe assets such as government bonds of countries with the highest credit ratings. By stepping in to support, or if necessary, to replace some very important financial markets, some central banks are also acting as market makers. By using new weapons to direct credit to particular types of borrowers, they are in effect making credit decisions. In Europe, ECB liquidity is supporting Europe's banking system. They are highly leveraged and definitely too – important-to-fail.

In the pursuit of revenues for their owners (i.e. governments), central banks have turned to riskier assets. A survey conducted by *Central Banking* reveals that more than one-third of participating central banks either invest, plan to do so or have long-run intentions of making equity investments (Carver and Pringle, 2013). The Swiss National Bank, Czech National Bank and the Bank of Israel are among the central banks to have confirmed they have such holdings. It is true that a few central banks have dabbled in equities for many years, but this is now becoming much more widespread and extensive. In an environment of near-zero interest rates and downgrading of credit standing of sovereign borrowers, central banks, like other investors, have conducted a 'search for yield' and are ready to take on new risks. They also want to diversify away from traditional reserve currencies. Investing in a portfolio of global equities provides a return at an acceptable risk, relative to alternatives. I expect this trend to go further. Yet it marks a potentially dangerous blurring of the line between public and private sectors. It means that central bank portfolio managers will be tempted to act in such ways that exacerbate market volatility and herding behaviour, potentially adding yet more fuel to asset bubbles.

Banking reform stalls...

How about the reform of banking? As already mentioned, *The Money Trap* argues that the private and the official sectors of the global financial system have to be analysed in an integrated way. Analysis should focus on the results of their interaction. Every international monetary system of the past has been accompanied by a distinctive species of private finance that 'fits' into the wider monetary mechanism of commerce and investment. This is true whether we look at Medieval and Renaissance bills of exchange, the first 'banking houses' of Florence, the British country banks of the 18th century, free banking and joint-stock banking under the gold standard, the overseas and Commonwealth banks of the sterling area, the state-led banks of Germany, France, Japan and other countries that industrialized after Britain, or the big US multinationals such as Citibank, Chase and Bank of America that financed and serviced the vast growth of American commercial interests and foreign direct investment in the mid-20th century. The narrow focus of most analysts on either the banking system or the international monetary system, treating them as if they belonged to separate worlds, is bound to lead to major policy errors and lack of understanding. This approach leads governments to miss the wood for the trees – and gives them yet another pretext for ignoring the real problems.

Banks' wounds have gradually been healing, with the US again in the lead, but only thanks to sustained (and expensive) official support. You don't have to be a financial genius to make a profit when you can borrow from the local central bank at near-zero interest rates for years on end and invest in government bonds at 2–4 per cent without taking any risk. Yet there are many institutions that need official succour. Let them go and they will crash again – that is what everybody fears but cannot say openly. Meanwhile, the financial system is falling more under the control of state agencies. The crisis has redrawn the lines between the market and the state – to the advantage of the state. We are entering a new age of collectivism. Given present political realities, that is likely to last for a considerable time. Of course, that is not the official story you will hear from government ministers or from central bank governors. The party line is that the new regulations promote and support safe, sustainable, consumer-friendly financial institutions and markets. Yet in reality this is largely a smokescreen for a return to a larger measure of state direction. Certainly the 29 'mega-banks' now called 'G-sifis' (global systemically important financial institutions) are being gagged in red tape. As explained in Chapter 10, this is to continue with the same approach as before. This approach has created banking organizations that are too-important-to-fail, households that have to be lured into increasing debt to keep the economic machine ticking over, and governments that likewise succumb to the temptation to increase borrowing when things appear to be going well.

Regulation without end or aim

The new regulators have no clear objective. There is no common-sense definition of 'financial stability'. In practice, political pressures are likely to define it in a way that will be totally counterproductive: that is, as the *absence* of bank failures. This is a recipe for freezing the existing structure of finance just when it should be totally overhauled. Little progress has been recorded even in areas in which there is widespread agreement on the nature of needed reforms. These include authority to manage the failure or impending failure of a banking institution (so-called 'resolution authority'); reform of money market mutual funds; progress toward consistent international accounting standards; any meaningful reform of the credit rating agencies; and consumer protection in the form of meaningful disclosure requirements. The lobbyists, ideologues and self-interested political funders have all combined to complicate, stall and derail any reform that's meaningful. Thus, there will need to be another dramatic and serious event causing real pain before any consensus and progress toward reform can be made.

No wonder Paul Volcker impatiently dismisses the entire effort: 'It's a recipe for getting nothing done. This really is a disaster,' the *Wall Street Journal* quotes him (23 May 2013) as saying. He is frustrated that three years after the passage of the Dodd–Frank law, regulators still haven't agreed on a way to implement a still-controversial provision, known as 'The Volcker Rule,' which is designed to force commercial banks to stay away from trading for their own accounts.

The 'balkanization' of banking

Among the further disturbing features of these measures are, first, as mentioned above, the wide latitude being granted for regulatory discretion, which history shows often leads to the abuse of arbitrary power; second, the new opportunities for high-profile regulators to secure well-paid positions in the private sector, a trend that is bound to compromise independence, and third, the weakness of the boards of big banks. Typically, bank boards have no means of disciplining the CEO (Johnson, 2013). Moreover, as recent developments have demonstrated, the inherent difficulties of implementing such a complex regulatory apparatus naturally leads regulators down a slippery slope to more *repression*. This is reinforced by the tendency for countries to act unilaterally in an attempt to defend their markets and public finances. HSBC Chairman Douglas Flint has warned of the costs of more countries acting unilaterally on regulation:

> 'This puts at risk globally consistent regulation and also risks 'balkanizing' firms' capital and liquidity resources,' adding 'This risks a retreat from globalization and greater financial exclusion – neither consistent with the pursuit of growth.' (Bloomberg, 24 May 2013)

'Structural' measures, such as splitting retail from investment banking, do offer a prospect of real change if they can be driven through the armies of lobbyists employed by the banks to stop them. Yet as a thoughtful paper by two IMF officials, José Viñals and Ceyla Pazarbasioglu, shows that subjecting a global institution to different structural measures in different countries and jurisdictions would create further complications. Resources taken up with checking whether institutions are complying with the 'multiple rules' may drain resources needed to monitor risk and 'could increase the cumulative costs of these national initiatives.' (Vinals and Pazarbasioglu, 2013). Structural reforms offer no magic bullet.

Another complaint of many bank non-executive directors (Neds) with whom I have talked is that bank board members have to spend an inordinate amount of time educating regulators about how their banks actually operate. To quote from one of my interviewees in 2013:

Our regulators have never been bankers. They are civil servants. Their assessment of the riskiness of bank assets and strategy can often be questioned.

Others comment that these regulators enjoy their 'power', and treat everyone as guilty until proved innocent. So bank boards are forever concerned about 'pleasing' the regulators and spend far too much time second-guessing what would or would not get their approval. In such a climate, bank boards and regulators become preoccupied with complying with regulatory requirements rather than with making sure the business is on a sound footing. If the hundreds of new supervisors being recruited by regulatory agencies the world over were really good at assessing risk and judging the quality of management, staff and strategy, they should be working for banks! They would make a bigger contribution to society employed by financial intermediaries, with the personal risk attached to their decisions, rather than second-guessing the judgements of others.

'New banks' flex their muscles

People say my proposals for new kinds of banks are 'unrealistic'. Yet can they be more unrealistic than the calls one often hears to 'simplify' financial regulation? This is not going to happen. All the signs point to ever-greater complexity and ever-higher costs. That is why I argue in Chapter 10 that the long-term answer should be not to squeeze the financial system in a icy grip but rather to nurture the development of new species of financial institutions. We need firms based, as good financial intermediaries have always been based, on a culture of risk awareness, competitive markets and an ethic of personal responsibility. In the current environment, it is too much – and too late – to expect the mega banks to relearn old lessons. The rot has spread too far. The needed changes can best be achieved by different types of enterprise and financial intermediation – involving more reliance on securities markets, encouragement of equity issues even by SMEs, partnership-type legal structures, mutual organizations, cooperatives – all of which had a long and, in general, honourable history in many countries before they were swept aside by the craze for mega banks.

This is part of the future conjured up in the concluding chapters of this book. Happenings of past two years have not been entirely negative. Innovations have been taking place in finance. Changes that may have appeared barely conceivable when the book first appeared are starting to appear less unrealistic. Far-reaching developments are already under way in the markets. Technological changes, new forms of lending and deposit-taking (often internet-based), and the invasion of banks' turf by other institutions have put them on the defensive. In the end, many experts believe that such forces, in conjunction with regulatory burdens, will force the mega-banks to yield the central place they have enjoyed in the financial system – if they were not protected by the regulators! This process is more advanced in the US than in Europe or Japan. US securities markets have for many decades been much more diverse and varied than those in Europe. Bond finance has stepped in to take over a larger share of banks' traditional lending activity. Everywhere, tighter regulation on banks, higher capital ratios and de-leveraging (mainly by asset reduction) at major banks are creating opportunities for new credit intermediaries. In the EU, pension funds and insurance companies are increasing their corporate lending.

Look at what is happening in Europe. As EU banks cut an estimated E5 trillion from their balance sheets, European borrowers are increasingly turning to private equity groups (many US based) such as KKR, GSO Blackstone, Ares Management, International Capital Group, EQT Partners and CVC Capital Partners. Many 'private equity' groups (which operate in a similar way to the leveraged buy-out firms of the 1980s) are raising new funds to provide working capital for firms using a variety of investment strategies (Chassany and Sender, 2013). It is often high-cost finance, but the point is that the risk and reward are tied tightly together; unlike banks with passive depositors and taxpayer-funded safety nets, those bearing the risk invest with their eyes open and the firms are not too-big-to-fail. If banks' share of funding for European companies were to fall from 80 per cent towards the US average of 20 per cent, many mega-banks would have to change out of all recognition or go out of business. At the same time, treasuries of large manufacturing and other non-financial corporations are actively seeking to diversify sources of finance away from their former over-reliance on banks. The seizing-up of the banking system during the Global Financial Crisis was a wake-up call – not only in Europe but also round the world.

To clear the way for the growth in such alternatives to banks, obstacles to increased non-bank credit should be removed. A priority is to improve the quality of information and disclosure on corporate finances, so as to enable potential creditors and funders to assess the credit risk more accurately than they have done in the past. Poor risk assessment by banks was one of the main factors triggering the Global Financial Crisis. Equally, regulators should be encouraged to leave room for these competitors to banks to grow. Yes, there are dangers in shadow banking. But the answer is to ensure tough discipline by the markets; a few well-publicized demonstrations that firms, which cannot control their risks adequately, can and do fail would do more than any amount of regulatory overkill to usher in a new era of responsible finance.

An international currency unit – reply to criticisms

In Part IV, I explain how a new banking system must be accompanied and supported by a reformed international monetary system.

Thank you to the people who have commented on the proposal for a new type of global monetary standard. I believe the system will need a strong anchor. After reviewing several of the leading candidates, I outline a proposal for a real-asset backed currency unit. This is a revival and elaboration of the proposal made by my friend the late Wolfram Engels, who was a professor of economics at Frankfurt University from 1968 to his death in 1995, and with whom I worked (Engels, 1981, p. 266). It has not won many followers as yet, but I am content to let it stand along with others as a candidate for the eventual world monetary anchor. I take this opportunity to restate my view that several of the other candidates, including gold, could also provide strong anchors.

I would also like to respond to two fundamental criticisms of the proposal for an investment currency, which I call the Ikon. The first is that it would be pro-cyclical, tightening monetary conditions when markets fall and increasing the money supply and output when markets rise (Taylor, 2012). This is a misconception. Let us assume that money is issued by a currency board that is entirely passive and committed to keeping the index of stock prices within a narrow range, just as the HKMA fixes the Hong Kong dollar to the US dollar. It only buys or sells at the initiative of the public. In this case, if the equity index drops, then the monetary unit will have a greater value in the market and banks will buy cheap money units from the issuer. The money supply rises, encouraging output. Alternatively, one can visualize a central bank version with a similar result. Assume that instead of targeting CPI (inflation), the central bank targets an equity index. If equity markets fall below the target, then the central bank will purchase cheap stocks thus increasing the money supply. This gives the same result as in the currency board version but it operates through monetary policy rather than a market driven passive policy. One thing the scheme will certainly not do is increase the volatility of stock market or other asset prices, as money will be defined in such a way that its market value is constant. The legitimate question that arises is of course whether constancy in terms of such tradable assets, or a subset of tradable assets, is 'worth' greater volatility in real value (in terms of CPI inflation). On this, it is worth remembering that during the gold standard, there were also large swings in terms of money's purchasing power value – fluctuations lasting up to 30 years. But what mattered was that prices and the value of money held constant in the long term. Under an Ikon standard, prices would fall gradually, money incomes would remain constant or rise slowly and the *real value of money would increase* in the long term.

Second, the proposal can be criticized on the grounds that it is not an anchor at all – that it suffers from the fallacy John Law's scheme of 1705 for paper currency based on land values and the 'real bills' doctrine. Law proposed in *Money and Trade Considered* (1705) that the banknote issue be secured by and bear a fixed ratio to the market value of land. The real bills doctrine, which originated with Adam Smith, promised to gear money to production via the short- term, self-liquidating commercial bills of exchange. It was supposed to ensure that output generates its own means of purchase and money adapts passively to the legitimate needs of trade. Such proposals were exposed by Henry Thornton (1802). The basic mistake in such schemes is to relate the supply of money to a value that *reflects* inflationary pressures, and cannot therefore limit or restrain them. Prices can shoot upwards without limit. But the Ikon proposal would tie the monetary unit to a thing, an object, i.e. a number of shares, through an index. In this it is like the gold standard, where money is defined in terms of an ounce of gold.

Another line of criticism comes from those who see the dollar-centred system being replaced by a multi-polar, multi-currency arrangement. It is claimed that allowing external surpluses and deficits to create claims and liabilities in the same currencies would promote more effective currency adjustments and therefore external adjustments. Related to broader reserve allocations is of course also the development of local bond markets that would help capital markets developments and thus reduce dependence on external financing. This is a worthy aim – it was already a well-worn theme when I wrote a paper on Asian bond markets in 1987 (Pringle, 1987). It is conceivable that a multiple currency system would make for a more stable system. But it is inherently a transitional system and likely to lead to various inefficiencies, bubbles and destabilizing cross-border capital flows.

Meanwhile, if governments and central banks of the major powers cooperate to reduce such instability, they will in the process in effect be evolving a new standard. Thus it is necessary and urgent to define an idea of the desirable end-state. We need a focus for our efforts – an idea of our ultimate destination. Of course, it is true that economic and political *power* is becoming more 'multi-polar' , reflecting the rise of China, India and other emerging markets; but that is not a good reason for wishing a *multi-currency reserve* system on the world. To insist that the present or something akin to it will continue for the indefinite future is also unrealistic – in fact, crazy. It is more realistic to articulate the concept of a genuine one-world monetary system, I believe such a system would be far superior in theory and practice (see pp. 153–55 and 224–25).

In my view, finding the most suitable anchor for money is the biggest challenge to modern monetary economics, though it is one that is pretty much ignored by economists, with the honourable exceptions of those whose ideas and proposals I discuss in Chapter 13 (with further references in Chapters 14 and 15). The much-touted multi-currency or multi-polar schemes will not be an adequate successor to the dollar; by nature, they cannot provide the global benchmark required. So the world remains on what I call (p. 271) the seesaw between one currency, the dollar, in long-term decline and another, the euro, which does not fulfil the conditions needed to serve as an international currency. When major governments are eventually forced to coordinate monetary and exchange rate policies, the best *interim measures* pending a full overhaul remain those outlined (on pp. 280–85) for a North Atlantic Currency Area and a New Creditor Standard. But there are very few candidates for *the anchor itself*: basically, there is gold, an SDR standard, a commodity standard – and the Ikon.

The outlook

Six years after the outbreak of the Global Financial Crisis, it haunts us still. Reforms have been made, banks are said to be safer and stronger, yet doubts continue to be expressed. As one American economist put it, the relatively modest changes that are being introduced are 'unlikely to be enough to prevent future financial shocks from inflicting large economic harm':

> I worry that the reforms we are focusing on are too small to do that, and that what is needed is a more fundamental rethinking of the design of our financial system and of our frameworks for macroeconomic policy. (Romer, 2013)

Exactly. The reforms are far 'too small'. It is disturbing that long before the US economic recovery has reached full capacity operation, Ben

Bernanke, chairman of the Fed, already in mid-2013 felt it necessary to warn banks of the dangers of taking excessive risks, and of possible credit bubbles (Bernanke, 2013). The dangers are not just of generating inflation and bubbles but also of distorting the entire allocation of capital and monetary flows geographically, and between sectors of the economy and social classes. Money is being directed towards large firms and high-income people, notably people with stocks and real estate, while little is going to the average household, or small businesses. Wall Street benefits hugely from the Fed's efforts, being in a position to take maximum advantage of ultra-low borrowing rates; traders hang on every nuance of the Fed's policy and messages, with billions at stake. Forward guidance is virtually an open invitation to financial specula-tion. Against this sombre background, the thesis of this book takes on added punch:

> 'The erosion of confidence and trust in the financial world, in the financial authorities that oversee it, and in government generally is palpable. ' (Volcker, 2013)
> 'We should establish a global mechanism to manage the current increasingly divided currency exchanges', said Robert Mundell, Nobel Laureate in economics (China news agency, 9 June 2013)

Will such reforms become practical politically? Repeated experience of crisis leading to slow growth and continued high unemployment would eventually produce growing pressures for change. But an intellectual effort is also needed to prepare the way. Otherwise change could be of a destructive, backward-looking and insular kind. The stakes are high.

Failure to diagnose the problem and address it adequately is having far-reaching geo-political ramifications. It is contributing to a rise in nationalistic sentiment, especially in East Asia, the Pacific and Europe. Americans point the finger at China. Tensions grow in Europe, with the real possibility of the UK leaving the EU, which British politicians often blame for making the UK's economic problems worse. Meanwhile, continued austerity in vulnerable countries of the eurozone might still trigger a political backlash in southern Europe. The spectre of the inter-war period stands as a continual reminder of the terrible effects that mistakes in such an apparently technical and arcane area as mone-tary policy can have.

The challenge is to write new rulebooks for international money and finance. This can be achieved only by governmental cooperation. Without such rules, the world is at risk of missing unique opportunities presented by financial globalization for enhancing wellbeing and for promoting international cooperation. The lack of appropriate rulebooks is also leading to an insidious erosion of the foundations of social and political order. That is the true moral of the crisis. Only when such rulebooks are in place will money and finance again be able properly to fulfil their classic – indeed, indispensable – functions in society. We are tempting fate.

Notes

1. I am not referring to the disputes about how to measure it correctly; there is continuing debate about this, but most studies come to the conclusion that GDP growth per head as conventionally measured remains among the best measures of overall material improvement.
2. See for example, Robert Skidelsky and Edward Skidelsky (2013).
3. The UK Treasury claimed that the letter was in line with the *new remit for the Bank of England's monetary policy committee (MPC)*, which was timed to coincide with the start of incoming governor Mark Carney's period in office in July. The new remit also asks the MPC to give 'due consideration to output volatility' and to deploy 'unconventional instruments to support the economy while keeping inflation stable'. But many observers took the view that it all added up to less independence for the Bank of England.

Bibliography

Boshara, Ray and William Emmons, 'After the Fall: Rebuilding Family Balance Sheets' Federal Reserve Bank of St. Louis , Annual Report, 2012, Published May 2013.

Borio, Claudio and Piti Disyatat, 'Global imbalances and the financial crisis: Link or no link?', BIS, Working Papers No 346, May 2011.

Caprio, Jerry, Jim Barth, and Ross Levine, *Guardians of Finance*, MIT, 2012.

Carver, Nick and Robert Pringle, *RBS Reserve Management Trends, 2013*, Central Banking Publications, 2013.

Chassany, Anne-Sylvaine and Henny Sender, 'Forced into the shadows', FT, 7 June 2013.

Eichengreen, Barry, 'Our Children's Economics' in *Project Syndicate*, 11 February 2013) Ferguson, Charles, *Inside Job: The Financiers who pulled off the Heist of the Century*, One World, 2012.

Graeber, Debt: The First 5,000 Years, Melville House, 2011.

IMF, Independent Evaluation Office, *IMF Performance in the Run-Up to the Financial and Economic Crisis IMF Surveillance in 2004–07*, IMF, 2011.

Issing, Otmar, 'Central banks – Paradise Lost?' Mayekawa Lecture, Tokyo, May 2012.

King, Mervyn, 'Do We Need an International Monetary System?' Speech, 11 March 2011.

Pringle, Robert, 'International Financial Trends in East and South-East Asia', National Centre for Development Studies, Australian National University, 1987

Rogoff, Kenneth, 'Blaming the Fed', *Project Syndicate*, 3 February 2013.

Romer, David 'Preventing the Next Catastrophe: Where Do We Stand?' *IMF Direct,* May 2013.

Skidelsky, Edward and Robert Skidelsky, *How Much is Enough: The Love of Money, and the Case for the Good Life*, Allen Lane, 2012.

Taylor, Michael, 'Review of The Money Trap' , *Central Banking*, Vol XXIII No 1, August 2012.

Thornton, Henry. An Enquiry Into the Nature and Effects of the Paper- Credit of Great Britain (1802): and Speeches on the Bullion Report, May 1811. Edited with an introduction by F. A. von Hayek. New York: Rinehart & Company, Inc., 1939.

Vinals, Jose and Ceyla Pazarbasioglu, *Banking on Reform: Can Volcker, Vickers and Liikanen Resolve the Too-Important-to-Fail Conundrum?* IMF, 2013.

Volcker, Paul, 'Central Banking at a Crossroad, Remarks upon Receiving the Economic Club of New York's Award for Leadership Excellence', 29 May 2013.

White, William, 'Comments by William White on the Presentation by Lord Adair Turner', INET Conference, April 2013.

Foreword

Lord Skidelsky

The main economic function of the international *monetary* system is to provide the global public good of monetary stability. Equally, the main function of *international financial regulation* is to provide the global public good of financial stability. The provision of both kinds of public goods failed comprehensively in the crisis. The results include crippled economies, bankrupt governments and zombie banks. What went so terribly wrong and, more important, what can be done?

Incentives were skewed. A good international monetary system – normally defined to include mechanisms for ensuring adjustment of imbalances as well as adequate liquidity – benefits everyone. In the absence of a good system, all parties suffer. Everybody therefore has an interest in making the system as good as it can be, given the political and economic constraints of the time. But the fact that there is a common interest in establishing and maintaining a good system does not, in itself, bring one about, and plainly has not done so. It does not pay the major players – companies, banks or individual governments – to provide such a service. Their short-term interest lies, rather, in preventing any strong public rules from being agreed.

Historically, the public good of price stability was provided by basing international money on gold or, from 1950 to 1971, on exchange rates fixed to a stable currency such as the dollar, which at the time was of course itself linked to gold. These were supported by capital controls and by segmented, cartelized, but stable, banking systems. In the years leading up to the global financial crisis and recession, governments and central bankers were well aware that, since the breaking of the historic link with gold in 1971, and the liberalization of finance, the public goods of reasonably stable prices and financial stability would not be provided quasi automatically. The monetary disorders of the 1970s – the result of abandoning fixed rates – drove the point home. They therefore deliberately set out to create substitutes for these. It was hoped, and believed, that inflation targeting and central bank independence would provide adequate price stability, while rules governing capital adequacy, banks' own risk management policies and an increasingly elaborate bank supervisory structure would provide financial stability. Of course, it was recognized that exchange rates would continue to fluctuate, but it was assumed that in general such movements would serve to bring payments towards equilibrium and that cases of prolonged over- or undervaluation of currency values would be fewer than they had been under fixed rates. Similarly, it was recognized that banks would get into difficulties from time to time, but it was expected that these would be confined to isolated cases, and that knock-on effects to the broader financial system could be contained. In general, there was a widespread belief that we had made considerable progress in understanding the dynamics and the weaknesses of financial markets.

The global financial crisis and recession starting in 2007 blew these comforting assumptions away. It turned out that we did not know more about the financial system – or, rather, that what we had learnt was not useful knowledge. At least it was not useful in protecting the public interest. Financial innovations and mathematically sophisticated risk management techniques benefited private interests, and the system as a whole turned out to be highly efficient in promoting the private ends of financiers – but to the detriment of the public good. All the defences that central banks and regulators had erected – after taking the best academic advice they could find – were demolished like children's sand-castles before an incoming tide. Never had financial experts received such a shock; never had their public prestige suffered such a blow; and never had so few got so rich so quickly at the expense of the many.

The enormity of the financial cost, the devastating economic damage and the outrage felt by the public have fed a violent reaction – and a demand for political action that has yet to run its course. There is a widespread feeling that the responses of the G20, of individual governments and of the private sector are inadequate. We feel we are living on the brink of another disaster. Is this because governments have missed some key strands in the analysis?

That is the question pondered by Robert Pringle in this thoughtful book, which takes an original and integrated view of the global financial system. He argues that what has been missing is an understanding of the connections between dysfunctional international monetary and financial structures, economic and monetary policies, the political influence of the over-mighty 'princes of finance', and the repetitive recurrence of crises. This is what he calls the money trap. On this analysis, it was the systematic under provision of the public good of monetary and exchange rate stability, the lack of anything that could be called a system – meaning a set of rules and conventions governing relations between states and between the public and private sectors – and above all the lack of an international monetary standard that in retrospect were the underlying causes of the succession of financial crises. (There was ample warning, in the shape of several big waves of cross-border currency and banking crises before the big one hit, but we failed to take heed of these warnings and to prepare adequate defences.) And one key weakness was that governments, regulators and central banks did not take sufficiently into account how easy it has become for the rules to be influenced by powerful private interests.

The book argues that the current efforts of central banks and governments to extricate their economies and the world economy from the continuing financial crisis are likely to continue to fail. Essentially, they are obstinately trying to return to 'business as usual' and fail to measure up to the full dimensions of the crisis. What business, traders, investors and governments need is a firm structure of public policy – and a standard to cluster expectations around.

The book begins by explaining how we got into the trap (Part I); this is followed by a critical examination of various efforts being made to get out of it (Part II). Major challenges that a new regime would have to address are analysed in Part III. The author focuses on the need for a stronger (but voluntary) international monetary standard and reviews various options, including rehabilitating the dollar standard, and various proposals by distinguished economists such as Richard Cooper, Ron McKinnon, Allan Meltzer and Bob Mundell. The author then contributes his own ideas. This standard would set the unit of account for a new international money and reserve currency.

One among many difficult questions he tackles is how such a monetary standard gains credibility; here one must look to the lessons of history. Unfortunately, from the author's own review, it is apparent that few of the conditions for setting up a new system seem to be fulfilled. Yet, whatever the obstacles, I believe he is on the right track when he insists that market disorder will eventually force politicians to take the big step of thinking in such global terms. Otherwise we shall simply go on with the closed cycle of policy errors, constantly at risk of slipping back into recession. By contrast, if a firm and unshakeable public policy structure were in place internationally, then it would be much safer to conduct expansionary fiscal and monetary policies.

Granted the undoubted benefits of international monetary stability as a public good, it should be feasible to develop for the twenty-first century an arrangement that encourages governments to take actions that are in the general interest without at the same time binding them fast to rules that deny them sufficient discretion and scope to respond to domestic political and economic requirements. Given the enormity of the damage inflicted by lack of such a common standard, Robert Pringle argues that we have to go on searching for a solution to this familiar dilemma – one Keynes struggled with throughout his life. If it were possible to reach an international standard, one which did not bind countries to deflationary policies, but did provide an anchor or reference point against which to measure national policies, I think Keynes would have been in favour of it.

As in the 1940s, and as again in the 1960s, we cannot in the 2010s rely on central bankers to lead the way forward. As always, they are bound to the present system, for reasons explained in this book by an author who has followed central banking closely for many years. Like Keynes, he is deeply suspicious also of the views of most central bankers, dominated by conventional thinking – the status quo. True, the content of these conventional opinions differed – then, slavish adherence to the gold standard; now, slavish adherence to floating exchange rates and inflation targeting. But the stubbornness with which they defend the status quo has not changed.

As I pointed out in my recent book, *Keynes: The Return of the Master,* Keynes's vision of harmony had national and international dimensions: a clearing union for international payments would bring to an end global macroeconomic imbalances, automatically creating a more plural world. After eliminating imbalances, currencies would become more stable. Today, as during the tribulations of the Second World War, Keynes's vision points to an emerging world order.

The weaknesses of existing international monetary arrangements are clear enough. They include volatile capital flows that can easily destabilize small economies as well as cause asset booms and crashes even in the largest economies, a net flow of capital from emerging to developed countries as reflected in the high-cost accumulation of excess reserves by emerging countries, wide swings in major exchange rates that still fail to ensure external balance; the lop-sided adjustment pressure bearing more on deficit than on surplus countries, a haphazard supply of global liquidity and the lack of an international lender of last resort in times of financial crises.

A contribution of this book is to tie in discussion of the monetary system, as usually understood, with the parallel topic – usually discussed separately by different groups of experts – of banking. Robert argues that a reliable and trusted international monetary standard would also provide the firm policy benchmark needed to deal with the particular dangers of modern financial instruments and techniques. These subjects must not be kept, as they still often are, in separate boxes, but integrated.

The Money Trap also differs from the majority of books and articles on the financial crisis and recession (which he terms GFC), in spending as much time on possible solutions as on analysis. If official policy is fundamentally on the wrong track, it is not helpful just to argue this without also putting forward alternative ideas. His reform proposals, albeit offered in a questioning and tentative spirit, are founded in a discussion of the ideas of monetary thinkers of the past and the present, and the ideas he advances for discussion are fleshed out. Here he focuses on what would be the features of a good international monetary and financial standard – one that would command voluntary adherence, which would be the respectable, modern monetary system of the future.

This book is a plea for action to defend the open, multilateral trading and financial system, and to preserve the enormous benefits derived from globalization. In the process, monetary autonomy will have to be limited (though this autonomy is partly illusory anyway). It would not be handed over to some international committee of bureaucrats, but sacrificied voluntarily, managed as it was under the classical gold standard. Only by embracing a modern version of an impersonal standard for money can the benefits of financial and economic globalization be retained.

The author's idea of tying international money – the agreed international unit of account – to the productive forces of the entire world economy through what he calls the market portfolio – essentially a diversified equity basket – is admittedly ambitious, and clearly some way from being politically feasible. The reader does not have to accept that idea to be persuaded by the argument that the logic of this seemingly never-ending crisis demands a more radical reform of the world monetary and banking systems than anything yet attempted or even imagined by governments.

A Note on Abbreviations

GFS

This refers to the Global Financial System, which we use as the unit of analysis to help understand the dynamics of the world economy and as the object of reform efforts. The GFS comprises, first, what is usually called the international monetary system and, second, the commercial network of banks, investment banks, other financial institutions, asset managers, capital and money markets. It embraces the rules, norms and structures governing the behaviour of decision-makers in both the public and private sectors. These are best thought of as integral parts of one structure. The need to take an integrated view of the interlocking elements in the GFS is a theme of the book.

GFC

This stands for the financial crisis and recession, the epicentre of which was in the US, originating in the sub-prime mortgage market, which started to cause shock waves around the world in August 2007 and then turned into a global systemic financial crisis with the collapse of Lehman Brothers in September 2008, followed by a steep global recession in late 2008 and all of 2009. Recovery was then interrupted by the linked outbreak of sovereign debt crises in the US and, even more virulently, in the eurozone in 2010–12. Although some developed economies (such as Australia and Canada) continued to perform relatively well, and while many emerging markets managed to maintain relatively fast growth, the world economy as a whole was expected to continue to show weakness through 2012–13. Unemployment remained at very high levels in many countries. The term GFC is used to denote the entire experience.

G20

The G20 was established in 1999, in the wake of the 1997 Asian financial crisis, to bring together major advanced and emerging economies to stabilize the global financial market. Since its inception, the G20 has held annual Finance Ministers and Central Bank Governors' Meetings and discussed measures to promote financial stability and to achieve sustainable economic growth. To tackle the financial and economic crisis that started in the summer of 2007 and spread across the globe in 2008, the G20 strengthened its cooperation, and G20 Summit meetings of heads of government were held in Washington in 2008, in London and Pittsburgh in 2009, in Toronto and Seoul in 2010, in Cannes in 2011 and in Mexico in 2012. The chairmanship rotates among members. The G20 is made up of the finance ministers and central bank governors of 19 countries and the European Union: Argentina, Australia, Brazil, Canada, China, France, Germany, India, Indonesia, Italy, Japan, Mexico, Russia, Saudi Arabia, South Africa, Republic of Korea, Turkey, the United Kingdom and the United States of America. The managing director of the International Monetary Fund (IMF) and the president of the World Bank, plus the chairs of the International Monetary and Financial Committee and Development Committee of the IMF and World Bank, also participate in G20 meetings. Together, member countries represent around 90 per cent of global gross national product, 80 per cent of world trade (including EU intra-trade) as well as two-thirds of the world's population.

Introduction

What is the 'money trap'?

The world economy is held back by deeply flawed monetary arrangements. These suit neither the ageing societies of the West and Japan, nor the younger economies of Asia, Africa and Latin America. Policy-makers of whatever political persuasion find that their room for manoeuvre is severely limited. They are paralysed by fears – fear of deflation on the one hand, and inflation on the other, fear of markets, fear of further shocks. It is a soft trap – a money trap, as discussed further in the chapters that follow. Yet it clearly has very real and painful effects. As it squeezes the life out of business and trade, the world suffers repeated recessions. Clearly, at some point policy-makers will have to act decisively to release the global economy from this trap. This book argues that policy-makers will be able to act effectively only on three conditions: first, that they have a correct analysis of what has gone wrong with world money – how we got into the trap; second, that they act at the right level, which is that of the global financial system as a whole; and third that they have the guts to face down their over-mighty subjects – the princes of private finance. Those are the main lessons to be learnt from examining the underlying causes of the difficulties that beset the world economy.

Whether one looks at the plight of banks and other financial institutions, or of over-indebted governments or at the participants in gridlocked money markets – all are plagued by radical uncertainty, not just about their immediate future, but about the viability of their whole way of operating. The very survival of banks and central banks, as we have known them, and of money markets, or of reserve currencies, is in doubt. At a minimum, the way they operate is changing in ways that policy-makers and economists are struggling to understand.

Is it not obvious that governments, banks and international institutions are indeed trapped? Whichever way they turn, they bump up against seemingly immovable constraints. However much they talk in optimistic terms about solving this or that problem, cooperating more closely, implementing reform programmes and so on – whether at the national level, or in regional groups such as the euro area, or on the wider international stage – few are taken in. In fact, the public senses that policy-makers do not themselves have confidence in their own prescriptions for a troubled world. Few sets of policy choices are both economically viable and politically feasible, as graphically illustrated in the accompanying figure (IMF, 2011). They are caught in the money trap.

Strategically, there are two options – two ways out of the trap: to suppress finance, or to harness it. There is a real risk of governments choosing the first option, out of sheer desperation. Yet to go for extensive state controls would be a major strategic error, and risk causing long-lasting damage. It might even set the world on the wrong path for generations to come – a path leading to greater poverty, social unrest and possibly even armed conflict. What governments should do is to harness the energies and power of the global financial system for the global good. Yet designing a good harness for global finance requires, as a prior condition, reaching a broad consensus on the analysis of the problem – what has gone wrong and why. This book presents a distinct view of the process that led the global financial system into the trap, of what governments have been doing to find a way out and the major challenges any reformed system would face.

Why recoveries have been weak

In order to gain a hearing for reforms of a scale that is needed, it is important that governments should first acknowledge the deep structural flaws in current arrangements – indeed, that they are the trap. We can perhaps brush aside the usual objections from so-called practical men who typically dismiss proposals for radical changes on the grounds they are 'unsound' or politically unrealistic (if such changes take place nevertheless, these people will say they were in favour of them all along). Yet it is important to understand the seductive attractions of the old model – and that the bait in the trap still looks succulent. Policymakers naturally prefer to work with arrangements with which they are familiar. So it is essential to demonstrate how and why these have led to disaster. In fact, efforts to go back to business as usual go a long way to explain why recoveries are so weak. Those whose readiness to take risks is needed to get a sustainable recovery going and reduce unemployment have not had sufficient confidence in the direction of policy. They watch policy makers caught in the trap illustrated in the diagram from the IMF – measures that are economically desirable are often not politically feasible, and the room for manoeuvre has been shrinking.

One might say, 'We all know the system is broken – just give us the solution!' It is true that many people might feel something is basically flawed, yet governments go on following policies that can work only if the old system is still functioning. So it is necessary to show in some detail why the old model is kaput. To do this, it is necessary to get down to the nitty-gritty of banking, finance and the international monetary system, to show how the relationship of governments to markets has become deeply dysfunctional.

At the same time, new proposals must, if they are to stand a reasonable chance of success, be grounded in market and political realities. They must meet the interests of societies as we know them, not as we would like them to be. That is why we also have to analyse the changes taking place in global markets. A new global order needs to take into account – even perhaps be based on – emerging global financial markets. Often portrayed in the media as monsters, and seen by governments as run by alien 'speculators', these markets can indeed be destructive, especially when powerful players can bend the rules of the game to suit them. But global finance is also potentially a massive force for good. Only through decentralized market processes and the finance that facilitates market exchange is it possible to satisfy individual wants within a democratic social order. But ever since John Locke it has been recognized that some social needs can be met only by collective action. Markets can function properly only within an appropriate framework. Such a framework still has to be developed for global finance. A few introductory remarks might be useful to show where the author stands on a number of issues touched on in this book.

First, money and finance have become emotional subjects on which passions can run high. As the financial collapse and ensuing recession have wreaked havoc with public and private finances, and will take many years to repair, this is understandable. It is important to recognize this as a political and moral issue, not just a dry technical issue to be left to

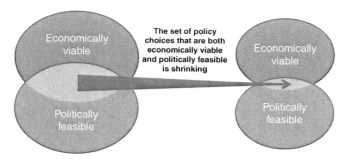

Figure 0.1   The available set of policy choices is shrinking

specialists, still less to market operators. At the same time, it is desirable to avoid the 'blame game'. Certainly there was plenty of blame to go round, and the public were right to be angry at the greed and reckless-ness of some bankers and financiers – and at the errors of public policy. A good monetary order would make it harder for actors to abuse the system for private gain and should provide better incentives and disciplines for public policy-makers as well. But pointing the finger at particular indi-viduals or groups would not help to get us out of the money trap.

Secondly, while taking account of the fact that the future of finance is a major political issue for governments and electorates throughout the world, it is not helpful to frame the issues primarily in terms of the familiar debate between 'Left' and Right', still less in party political terms. There has been a strong tendency, especially in the US, to politi-cize the debate in this way. Economists have taken up positions along the political spectrum. Their messages then become predictable. Again and again, economists on the right or those of a free-market disposi-tion point to what they regard as excessive regulation, government restrictions on business and large public debts as obstacles to recovery. Economists on the left call continually for greater 'Keynesian' stimulus, tighter financial regulation and tighter controls on 'laissez-faire capi-talism'. The reason that this politicization was so depressing is that to most fair-minded observers it seemed obvious that neither set of reme-dies measured up to the dimensions of the challenges we faced. If I may take this opportunity to state my own position, it is definitely more on the 'free market' side of the divide, yet I also believe that decision-makers, whether in the private or public sectors, need to be constrained and guided by firm 'constitutional' structures – and also that simply mouthing free-market mantras hardly advances the debate. What is at stake is the public good of international monetary stability.

Thirdly, this financial and economic problem should not be viewed, as it has been by some commentators, as merely a symptom of an assumed and inevitable 'decline of the West'. Yes, China and other emerging econ-omies have grown rapidly in recent decades, and may continue to do so. It is important to take this into account, as this book does, in thinking about the future of the world's monetary arrangements. But it is equally important to bear in mind that, historically, Europe has been a dynamic, restless, ambitious and hugely successful part of the world, though with an unfortunate tendency to engage in civil wars. The US is a unique, remarkable and thriving economy – the most productive the world has ever seen. There is no sign of an end to its ceaseless innovation – the pipeline of upcoming technological advances and patents remains full.

Japan (for this purpose part of 'the West', though frequently misunderstood by Western commentators) has in many ways the world's most enviable standards of living, of urban civility and technical prowess.

Fourthly, this book does not view the challenges to governments, when dealing with the global financial system (GFS), as part of a 'crisis of capitalism'. Capitalism will continue to evolve as it has done for many centuries. Versions of capitalism have been adopted by every country. These differ so much from each other that it becomes questionable how useful it is to bundle them all under one label.[1] It is, however, certainly true that how the financial crisis is addressed and eventually resolved may have far-reaching consequences for the development of capitalism – and possible implications of different solutions for society will be explored.

The GFS as the unit of analysis

The principal argument of this book is that action should be directed at a higher level than it has been so far, that is at the level of the GFS as a whole. The way in which the parts of the system interact is malfunctioning. What needs to be reformed are the crucial mechanisms that govern this interaction – such as the exchange rate system, the reserve currency system, the production of international money, the rules of the game for markets and market players and the whole relationship between money, markets and states. Symptoms of this disorder can be seen in many areas of the world economy – notably in the problems of global imbalances, of the reserve currency system and in the difficulties that have met efforts to reform banking and finance. Yet official action has been directed largely at national or regional levels, when what is needed, but so difficult to elicit, is a truly international response.

The argument will be that, at the core of the problem, is the lack of a respected international monetary standard and of appropriate rules of the game. So we need to examine not only international standards of the past that have worked – notably the gold standard and the dollar standard – but also the views of classical and contemporary scholars on what makes for good international money. This will show that there are indeed rich resources of experience and expertise to draw on as we try to navigate out of the current dilemmas. The world economy has also suffered badly from the lack of a system of rules to coordinate the actions of governments as well as private institutions. We shall argue that these faults are the main reason for the repeated crises of the past 40 years, culminating in the rolling financial crisis and recession (which we will abbreviate to GFC) that started in 2007 and in 2012 showed no sign of ending. The author appreciates fully that this approach is not widely accepted. Indeed, his main motive for writing this book is to persuade readers of the merits of this approach. (While it is certainly the case that the problems that came to the surface in GFC had in many cases domestic origins, it is essential to investigate how they link together internationally.) The right analysis and approach is logically and politically prior to any consideration of suitable remedies. In short, he hopes to show that the GFS is the appropriate unit of analysis and the object of reform efforts.

Plan of the book

This book presents a narrative, an analysis, a review of a number of options for reform and some recommendations. Working backwards, the author's policy recommendations grow out of the preceding review of options, which emerges out of the debates on these topics among central banks and economists and the challenges that the GFS must adequately manage. These in turn emerge from the historical narrative, which is necessary to show how the GFS got into this mess. That brings us back to the money trap in which policy-makers are entangled. To help readers track the twists and turns of the argument, each chapter has an italicized introduction and conclusion.

The book is organized in four parts:

Part I: In the Trap
Part II: Searching for Ways Out
Part III: Four Key Issues
Part IV: The Power of Global Finance

Part I: In the Trap

While the causes of GFC will be debated for many years to come, it is desirable to reach a broad consensus on how it came about if we are to avoid repeating the mistakes that led up to it and to construct a basis for reforms to the GFS. Part I therefore outlines the conditions that led to GFC, why many players still hope to go back to 'business as usual', how the pressures for reform are building and whether the conditions for reform are fulfilled. A final chapter describes how the world economy fell into the money trap.

Chapter 1 shows how recurrent financial crises and economic weakness have been the product of the operation of the GFS, that is, the rules, norms and structures governing the behaviour of economic agents. It presents one of the main themes of the book: that analysis of the traditional 'international monetary system' has to be integrated with an analysis of banking, finance and financial markets. Anticipating the more detailed treatment in later chapters, it also outlines how the demand for more comprehensive reforms has grown as familiar policy-making models struggle to cope.

Chapter 2 discusses the structure of incentives presented by the GFS to agents and shows how it led the leading players into making disastrous policy errors. The system did not help any of them reach their true, longer-term objectives. But is renewal practicable? To answer this, it is useful to consider the conditions for the birth and survival of an international monetary order, that is, for a change in the 'monetary constitution'. This is the subject of Chapter 3.

Chapter 4 discusses the record of the last proper international monetary system, the so-called Bretton Woods regime, and the advent of flexible exchange rates among leading currencies in the early 1970s. An era of rules, controls and relative financial stability was succeeded by an age of rapid innovation, policy experimentation and growing financial instability, culminating in GFC. That was how the world became trapped.

Part II: Searching for Ways Out

In an implicit acknowledgement that governments and market players were indeed trapped, a search for alternative policy models and structures got under way. This process, which proceeded by way of trial and error, is viewed as taking place at national, regional and international levels.

Chapter 5 outlines options available to, and efforts being made by, governments to improve domestic policies, focusing on monetary policies. The options are ranked in terms of the degree of discretion that each of them allows national policy-makers/central banks. I argue that the direction taken by major governments and central banks following GFC – to bolt on a 'macro-prudential' systemic risk arm to the existing monetary policy apparatus – was unlikely to be satisfactory in the longer run.

Turning to regional solutions, in Chapter 6 the efforts of European political and financial leaders to create 'an island of monetary stability' in an unstable GFS are discussed. It is argued that these cannot succeed within the current GFS, and that a lasting solution to the problems of the eurozone would necessarily involve a wider reform of the international system.

Chapter 7 looks at what governments are doing at the international level to prevent a repeat of GFC and spur sustainable growth. It focuses on the reforms to the international monetary system and banking regulation pursued through the G20.

It is essential to reach a view on the scope and limits of what might be done at these three levels for another reason: if a wider GFS reform proves not to be feasible, then governments will inevitably be thrown back into doing what they can at such levels, as second best or third best solutions.

Part III: Four Key Issues

This part discusses challenges in four major areas of the world economy that present arrangements have not been able to deal with efficiently and that a reformed GFS would need to manage.

Chapter 8 looks at the specific challenge of continued global payments imbalances: what are the views of qualified observers, and how might a reformed monetary system improve outcomes? It argues that the role of global trade and current account imbalances in causing GFC has been exaggerated. It was, above all, a product of a dysfunctional monetary and banking system.

Chapter 9 draws on the large literature on reserve currencies to discuss the seemingly never-ending growth of reserves and the threat that this poses. What is the future of the dollar, euro, the Chinese RMB and other currencies – with or without a move to a new GFS?

Chapter 10 focuses on the core problem of the banking system. Grievous mistakes were made in managing the crisis, but these were not accidents. They were the natural result of actions taken in response to previous episodes. So should it be a surprise when the financial sector reforms being put in place following GFC are again proving insufficient? They are not coming close to removing the sources of systemic instability.

Chapter 11 places the relationship between the state and the markets in a longer-term perspective. It argues that financial innovation is likely to remain a constant feature of the GFS, and that in the absence of a stronger order or monetary constitution, proposals to fix markets by regulation are unlikely to succeed. We need to renew the GFS.

In each of these controversial areas, existing policies would not satisfy the key condition needed to spur sustainable growth: whether they restored confidence in the direction of official policy. That could only be met by reform directed at the GFS itself.

Part IV: The Power of Global Finance

In the concluding part, I will argue that there is a wide range of resources to draw on in the search for better solutions – including a rich repertoire of ideas. The fundamental questions involved have been pondered by some of the greatest economists and other students of society.

Chapter 12 describes the classic contributions from Fisher through Keynes, from Rueff to Hayek and Triffin and shows how many strands in the contemporary debate have their roots in such classical proposals. Chapter 13 surveys and assesses selected proposals by contemporary economists and outlines the conditions for reaching agreement and making the transfer to a new or reformed standard. Chapter 14 discusses what might be the features of a future GFS combining a real monetary standard with a new model of private finance. It introduces the concept of a new type of money backed by real assets, the Ikon. Chapter 15 sums up the prospects for the GFS, the dangers involved in a failure to reform it, and the longer-term political pressures for change. It also offers proposals to create a strong framework for international public policy, which is the essential condition for lasting recovery.

If the analysis presented in the book is anywhere near correct, then the need for a profound change in existing monetary arrangements will persist. True, a recovery would enable governments to shelve proposals for real reform for a few years, but without such a reform to the GFS the underlying obstacles to sustainable growth would not have been removed. We would still be stuck in the money trap.

Note

1. See, for example, various publications by John Gray, especially *False Dawn*, and *The End of the Free Market* by Ian Bremmer.

Bibliography

Bremmer, Ian, *The End of the Free Market: Who Wins the War between States and Corporations?* Portfolio, 2010.
Gray, John, *False Dawn: The Delusions of Global Capitalism*, Granta Books, 1998.
International Monetary Fund, *Global Financial Stability Report*, September 2011, IMF, Washington DC.

Part I
In the Trap

1
Into the Danger Zone

Many of the underlying causes of economic weakness and high unemployment were due to faults of the global financial system (GFS), yet governments and central bankers were loath to acknowledge this.

A monetary failure

The failure of the world economy to recover fully from the financial crisis and recession was a monetary as well as a real phenomenon. Why did the climate for international business, trade and investment remain hostile? Why, years later, were many economies struggling to emerge fully out of recession? With governments desperately seeking to reassure financial markets that they could and would service their debts, the deterioration in the soundness of banks and other financial institutions was particularly alarming. Before GFC, there had seemed no reason to doubt the creditworthiness of most of the world's major financial institutions, or governments' capacity to control a financial panic if one should break out. Of course, banks had from time to time got into difficulties, currencies had swung around wildly and the so-called Asian crisis in 1997–98 had shown the damage that such financial panics could inflict on an increasingly global scale. It is also true that economic history is pockmarked with financial panics. But until GFC it was thought that we were learning how to manage such difficulties. International institutions such as the IMF and World Bank had accumulated expertise through learning from such experiences and advising governments around the world in a wide variety of different circumstances. Economists studied them exhaustively; whole libraries of scholarly books were devoted to them. We seemed to be making progress. But

GFC and the stuttering recovery from it sent a different message. Almost, it seemed, out of a clear blue sky, a storm had descended that laid waste to wide areas of the financial landscape. No bank, it seemed, could be relied on to stand on its own feet. Governments' resources – their balance sheet strength – were drained in fighting the collapse and the recession that followed. Efforts to repair private and official balance sheets were a drag on demand. Another recession was feared, and that would cause another wave of sovereign and commercial defaults and more losses for banks.

Because banks and other financial institutions are central to the running of a capitalist economy, this deterioration in their soundness generated fear. Like a new virus, this rapidly spread to all parts of the global economy, speeded by advances in communication. The 24-hour news machine ensured every businessman and woman in the world could reasonably ask: is my business safe? Savers asked: are my investments safe? What can I do to protect myself and my family? Whom can I trust? Businesses and households everywhere became ultra-cautious.

Lack of trust in money and monetary institutions was at the root of GFC and of the anxiety of senior officials about the prospects. On 6 October 2011, Mervyn King, governor of the Bank of England, said it may be the worst crisis ever; and a few days later Jean-Claude Trichet, then president of the European Central Bank (ECB), said, 'it is a historical event of the first magnitude, the worst crisis since the Second World War.'[1] A deeper slump had been averted by dint of extraordinary expenditure of money to sustain demand, and the only way to service the interest on that borrowing was to maintain growth; yet, given the lack of confidence, where was the demand to come from?

Governments twisted and turned this way and that. One favoured remedy after another was tried – banking reform, new regulations, fiscal stimulus, monetary stimulus – while the cries of rival groups of advisers almost drowned out reasoned debate. All to no avail: the diagnosis was monetary failure, something as life-threatening to the economy as heart failure is to a human being.

The underlying problem

This book treats these controversial topics from a distinct angle, that of the GFS as a whole. The general approach can be stated simply: a few years ago, around the start of the new millennium, the process of economic and financial globalization reached the limits compatible with existing international monetary arrangements. Fixing parts of these arrangements, such as raising bank capital requirements or introducing so-called macro-prudential risk oversight (see Chapter 10), would not solve the problem, as they treated symptoms rather than the real causes of stress. That was the mistake leading nations were making; essentially, they were attempting to return to 'business as usual' – recycling the set of policies and style of policy-making and institutional set-up that they had worn to death over the previous half-century. Numerous initiatives were taken to reform regulation and other bits of the policy apparatus but these fell short of the major recasting of arrangements that was needed to restore confidence. Finance would escape from these attempted constraints. Banks would always be one step ahead of the regulators. This excessive flexibility of the finance system is what has led us into so much trouble – or at least had been a major contributor to it, as is argued in more detail later. Within the existing GFS, governments could respond only by applying yet tighter restrictions – higher capital ratios and so on – which would actually cramp the recovery rather than control the bankers. So recovery would stall, or even go into reverse, and this was indeed happening.

True, some areas and countries of the world economy seemed to be able, for a time, to shrug off what was happening in the West. China and India, in particular, continued to bowl along at high, albeit more moderate, growth rates. Much of the rest of Asia and some other emerging economies were also doing well. Yet the longer the problems of the GFS continued to weigh down the West, the harder it was for these areas to retain dynamism. There were limits to their resilience. They would be severely impacted in time by loss of export markets, volatile capital flows and exchange rates, and the higher cost of finance – to mention just a few of the links connecting 'the West' with 'the rest'. The world economy as a whole was being cramped by the GFS.

These links pointed to some of the basic faults within the GFS itself. The interaction between credit expansion, capital flows and volatile exchange rates had been a key factor in the build-up of successive international financial and economic booms and busts well before GFC (including the developing countries' debt rescheduling of the 1980s and the Asian crisis of 1997–98). GFC demonstrated how that same mechanism was undermining the financial systems at the core of capitalism, in the US and Europe.

Regime change would be necessary. But it was not even on governments' radar screens. Nor was it on the agenda of the G20. Could one not expect, after such a cataclysm – the equivalent of a Richter scale 9 earthquake and tsunami – that leading nations would at least make an attempt to design a new set of defences, a better sea wall? In the monetary field, the most famous of these took place after the Second World War, when agreement on an international monetary order was reached at Bretton Woods (see Chapter 3). But this was not the only example of constructive engagement at the international level; when the Bretton Woods regime broke down in the early 1970s there followed sustained international attempts to construct a new order better adapted to the economic circumstances of the time. Not all such attempts succeeded, and the failures as well as successes will be analysed in subsequent chapters. But in 2008–12, in the aftermath of the near collapse of the GFS and the worst recession for 70 years, there was no comparable effort. This was on the face of it surprising. As will be argued in more detail later in this book, the US, Europe, China and other major powers had ample reason to be dissatisfied with the functioning of the system. Many smaller countries were already highly discontented. Above all, it was no longer clear that the US benefited so unambiguously from the dollar's role as the leading reserve currency that it would automatically be expected to veto any such fundamental review of the system.

Governments' feeble response

The G20 discussed a wide range of reforms designed to put the GFS back together again,[2] but the proposals were at best limited changes to existing arrangements. Essentially, governments and the international institutions were sending the message that the system had been developing along the right lines, but that further improvement was being hampered by a few factors, notably a lack of political will. More 'political will' was needed to lift international cooperation onto a higher level. If this could be achieved, then the international institutions such as the IMF would have the authority needed to make the system function satisfactorily. That would require endowing the international community through the IMF and the G20 or a successor body with greater influence on the policies of important economies. In the circumstances of 2011 this was code for measures to reduce the fiscal deficit of the US, and to increase domestic demand and exchange rate flexibility in China. These were seen by most western governments as designed to ensure that China's growth relied less on exports and more on domestic consumption

But few observers expected that countries would be prepared to show the political will – that is, sacrifice perceived sovereignty – needed to make a real difference. At that point, governments ran out of ideas. The political imperative was to resume growth, even though the defects in the GFS, left untreated, would ensure that such growth could only be short-lived. With unemployment remaining high in advanced countries and the need to absorb the millions entering labour markets in emerging markets, recovery and growth were, naturally, the priorities. What the exercise led by the G20 group of leading countries amounted to in practice was a massive, coordinated, fiscal and monetary stimulus. No country by itself was large enough to give the world economy the injection it needed to kick-start demand; and none was prepared to risk the deterioration in its external payments that would take place if it acted alone. So they agreed on a collective heave – but this too soon ran out of puff.

The reasons for the narrow focus of reform and the lack of drive behind it lay elsewhere. The GFS, especially when oiled by official injections of cash, suited the short-term interests of major players (analysed in Chapter 2). So governments put about the dangerous half-truth that GFC had very little to do with faults in the international monetary system (the reality being it had a great deal to do with faults in the GFS). So they proposed only limited reforms to make existing arrangements work better, including reductions in budget deficits, and even greater exchange rate flexibility (while many senior officials had little confidence in the sustainability of the system, they could not voice these doubts publicly).

Lack of imagination – or lack of courage?

There was also a lack of intellectual courage. Economists, stunned by the ferocity of the financial hurricane, generally retreated to well-established positions. In this they behaved like governments. The same applied to professional financial regulators and central bankers. They pulled their familiar ideological and professional clothes more tightly around them. Central bankers declared their confidence in their monetary policy regimes. Regulators said that what was needed was, of course, better regulation – and they could be entrusted to deliver it. Bankers said that they accepted the need for new regulation and higher capital (the costs of which would be passed on to customers), but that they would regard tougher measures as vengeful and warned that this could prompt them to relocate from London and New York to more friendly jurisdictions. To the bemusement of the public, governments were reduced to pleading with bankers – employees of the very same institutions that the public had bailed out at vast cost – to reduce the size of their bonuses: and could you, please, increase lending to small businesses?[3] What these responses had in common was a domestic focus.

Behind the political failure of nerve, behind the failure of ideas, behind even the growing infiltration of politics by finance, yet another factor was involved: the globalization of finance itself. This continually ran ahead of the extension of political agreement on 'rules of the game' that would be necessary to harness it and make it serve the public good. This had been a constant theme of the growth of international banking and finance since the freeing of financial markets from postwar controls during the 1960s and 1970s. It was what lay behind the power of financial lobbies on issues such as remuneration. To see the situation from the bankers' point of view, if their competitors in other countries could pay their executives what even they (privately) thought were excessively generous pay packages, they would feel obliged to follow suit.

If there was one professional group to whom, it might be hoped, one could turn for an objective, internationalist view of systemic problems, it would be central bankers. Traditionally, they formed in many ways a separate caste, with their own ethic of public duty and responsibility. Distanced from the pressures of day-to-day politics, with a privileged, bird's-eye view of their financial institutions and those of other countries, with traditions of discreet cooperation and backed by economics research departments, surely they could be relied on to draw attention to defects in the operations of GFS. After all, they were specialists in analysing financial system stability.

Why most central bankers have tunnel vision

Yet central bankers' enthusiasm for reform was distinctly circumscribed – with a focus on the need for regulatory change and 'macroprudential' oversight (the need to take a view of the financial system as a whole). An analysis of the political economy of central banks suggests the reason for this. Despite what many would see as major policy errors in the run-up to GFC, and their failure to manage it well, central banks emerged from it with additional powers. They were the key players in official plans to strengthen the oversight of payments, banking and capital markets. Their greater responsibilities necessarily came with greater accountability to governments and/or parliaments. That might have been inevitable when committing public funds to support the banking system required the authority of political leaders.

But the interconnections between politicians, civil servants and central bankers became even closer in the aftermath of GFC. These changes were making them even more wary than usual of rocking the boat. Thus when they talked about the international monetary system, their focus was limited; in essence, it often amounted simply to telling China to revalue its currency.

Unfortunately, the central banks' cherished independence predisposed them to support key features of the existing GFS. The policy-making model followed by leading central banks – using the power to set a short-term interest rate to influence monetary and credit growth – depended crucially on the maintenance of flexible exchange rates. Any change in the GFS that reduced the flexibility of exchange rates would mean giving up monetary policy autonomy, and with it the prestige that went with a fully fledged central bank Thus central banks such as the Federal Reserve, the ECB, Bank of England and Bank of Japan, occupied roles that in effect prevented them from supporting any change that might one day result in a move to a fixed or heavily managed exchange rate system. More than that, they were instinctively hostile to any suggestion even of closer exchange rate coordination, on the grounds that this would jeopardize their ability to fulfil their mandates, all of which were couched in terms of purely domestic and often narrowly defined objectives.

Therefore the interests of one of the most respected sources of 'independent' comment and analysis of monetary affairs were rooted in the structure of the existing, flawed, international monetary system. The big central banks were unlikely to be on the side of proposed reforms that questioned their twin pillars of domestic inflation targeting and preserving flexible exchange rates, at least for major economies. They were unlikely to sponsor or commission research that could lead to such a conclusion – and given their massive weight in academic research projects on monetary issues, this was another hidden obstacle to academic discussion, at least in the US (see White, 2005), added to which was the fact that central bankers were used to operating the status quo – at most, making procedural changes to improve the effectiveness of the existing system, notably in the field of monetary operations. To a naturally conservative breed of policy-makers, it had the additional advantage of familiarity. Just as, during the 1960s, central bankers and the IMF fought hard to keep the old fixed-rate, gold-linked Bretton Woods system – frowning on media discussion of devaluation or flexible exchange rates – so in the 2000s they would fight to the bitter end to defend a flexible exchange rate system.[4]

Yet there was a deep irony here. The multiple objectives and complex mandates that governments imposed on the central banks following GFC were going to be extremely difficult to achieve and bankers were well aware of it. The pursuit of price stability by itself could be made consistent with the GFS, and could in principle be achieved by independent central banks (though in the process of achieving it they would stoke up other problems, but that is for a later chapter). By contrast, as I will argue more fully later (see Chapters 5, 10 and 11), achievement of their added financial stability mandate was inconsistent with the existing GFS – and many of them suspected that also. To anticipate an argument advanced later in this book, finance had become too international and too fast-moving for any national central bank to monitor, and central banks were nowhere near reaching agreement on adequate international oversight (such as cross-border bank resolution and bankruptcy regimes), partly reflecting the far-reaching financial and political difficulties in reaching of agreements on how to share the burden of rescue operations. In fact, central banks could deliver on their new responsibilities for financial stability and macro-prudential oversight *only within the structure of a different and much stronger set of international rules.* Anticipating this, several commentators called for a move to a global bank supervisory structure.[5] But this move too could succeed only once the GFS itself was reformed. In short, the central banks had taken on mission impossible: many of them knew or suspected it, but none could speak in favour of the big changes needed for them to have a better chance of achieving their new or modified mandates.[6] Maybe they thought it was a government decision, and therefore they were in no position to complain.

But ideas were changing...

Although the dominant strand in the response to GFC was a retreat to familiar ideological positions, there were encouraging signs of a shift of ideas. The crisis prompted international institutions and economists to revisit some of their positions on policy issues. Attitudes towards exchange rates, for example, were in flux. Whereas in 2004 economists at the IMF strongly advocated greater flexibility of exchange rate regimes, by 2011 some appeared to be less certain that this was right. Not only did the IMF no longer make much effort to persuade small, open economies to adopt floating exchange rates, but there were also signs that the views of economists who had long considered that excessive emphasis had been put by the majority on the role of exchange rates in the adjustment process were gaining ground.[7] It was true that the IMF remained sceptical of moves to hard pegs or currency boards; and countries could choose their exchange rate regimes. But, as in the case of attitudes to capital controls, they had become less dogmatic. This more pragmatic approach may be partly explained by the growing influence in the debate of emerging market economies, most of which were attached to fixed or heavily managed exchange rates. Indeed, it is probably true that a growing number of commentators had come to agree with the late Tommaso Padoa-Schioppa, a leading European economist, in his scepticism regarding the doctrine of floating (Padoa-Schioppa, 2010, p. 10). As one report stated: 'Large, lasting swings in currency values can cause serious distortions in the system and in the allocation of resources.'[8]

In the longer term, as governments adjusted policies to changing circumstances, a shift in attitudes seemed in prospect on other aspects of the functioning of the system as well. Emerging markets again responded by building up reserves at a rapid rate, while in 2009–10 low interest rates in the developed countries spurred a big rise in capital flows to emerging markets. The upward pressure on their exchange rates caused by this surge of hot money was countered in some countries by capital controls on inflows. There were growing fears of competitive depreciations and Brazil's finance minister warned of 'currency wars'. There were also fears that the build-up of reserves mainly denominated in US dollars would in the long run undermine confidence in the dollar's reserve currency status (See Chapter 9).

The weaknesses in the international adjustment process were all well known: excessive accumulation of reserves, ineffective global adjustment, financial excesses and destabilizing capital flows. These, surely, were symptoms not just of remedial defects but of systemic faults. After reviewing such weaknesses, a report by a group of former leading monetary statesmen, referred to above, called for a 'meaningful, comprehensive reform':

> Most of the problems...are not new, but the consequences of not addressing them are increasing and inhibiting the realization of the full benefits of globalization. As long as problems in the international monetary system are not addressed, an increasingly integrated world economy becomes more and more vulnerable. A muddling through approach therefore is an increasingly inadequate response. Any meaningful comprehensive reform will require taking near-term steps within a longer-term vision. (Palais Royale Group, 2011).

Yet were the conditions for successful regime change likely to be met? Monetary history supplies several examples of disastrous major international monetary policy decisions, and few successful ones. The decision by the UK and other leading powers to go back to gold at the wrong parities in 1925–30 is widely regarded as a prime example of the former, Bretton Woods in 1944 as an example of the latter (see Chapter 3). The effort of the Committee of 20, an official body set up in 1972 to prepare a draft of a reform of the international monetary system, ended in failure, and led to a period of great instability. This crucial question is discussed in Chapter 4.

...and so were geo-political realities

Rapid geo-political changes seemed likely to reinforce pressures to reform the system.

First, the fraction of the global economy represented by China and other emerging markets was increasing dramatically – with some forecasters indicating that their share of global output could rise from approximately 30 per cent in 1990, to one-half in 2011 to nearly three-quarters by 2050. China was forecast to overtake the US as the world's largest economy during the 2020s. In terms of contribution to growth, in the decade to 2011 emerging markets already accounted for 70 per cent of growth in the global economy (Goldman Sachs, 2011) Second, emerging markets would also account for a rapidly increasing share in global international financial flows. Third, they would have a much bigger voice in the IMF. And the IMF did respond. In November 2010 it approved a package involving a large shift of voting power to emerging markets and developing countries, an all-elected, more representative Executive Board, and a doubling of IMF quotas to $755 billion. The top ten shareholders would be the top ten economies in the world, namely the US, Japan, the four biggest EU economies (Germany, France, the UK and Italy) and the four original BRIC countries – Brazil, Russia, India and China. In all there would be a shift of 6 per cent of quota shares to the emerging market and developing countries. But this was nothing compared with what the emerging markets would soon be in a position to insist on.

Emerging markets were becoming more forthright in their criticisms of the monetary system. When additional funds were needed, they insisted it should be on their terms. Traditionally, criticism of the IMF focused on issues to do with conditionality. These conditions were often viewed as a package – the 'Washington Consensus', focusing on liberalization of trade and the financial sector, deregulation and privatization of nationalized industries. Critics complained that such conditions were attached without regard for the borrower countries' individual circumstances and that the prescriptive recommendations by the World Bank and IMF failed to resolve the economic problems within the countries.

But, increasingly, emerging markets were challenging from a different angle – the lack of discipline on the reserve currency centres, notably the US. While much of this could be dismissed as mere rhetoric, there was little doubt that some capitals – notably Beijing – were positioning themselves for a long-term challenge to existing international monetary arrangements, and gathering considerable support from countries that were suffering from it. In March 2009, Zhou Xiaochuan, governor of the People's Bank of China, called for replacing the dollar as the world currency and for the creation of an international reserve currency that would be 'disconnected from individual nations': 'The outbreak of the current crisis and its spillover in the world have confronted us with a long-existing but still unanswered question, i.e., what kind of international reserve currency do we need to secure global financial stability and facilitate world economic growth, which was one of the purposes for establishing the IMF?' (Zhou, 2009).

This question had become more severe due to the 'inherent weaknesses of the current international monetary system'. Zhou said that 'the crisis again calls for creative reform of the existing international monetary system towards an international reserve currency with a stable value, rule-based issuance and manageable supply, so as to achieve the objective of safeguarding global economic and financial stability' and repeated his warnings the following year: 'The current global financial crisis and economic recession, the most severe since the Second World War, has alerted us to the necessity to accelerate the reform of the international monetary system' (see his Statement to the International Monetary and Financial Committee, Twenty-Second Meeting, 9 October 2010).

In 2011, in the midst of Europe's sovereign debt troubles, Chinese economists pushed for disciplinary action over sovereign debt, with the IMF setting limits on the ratio of sovereign debt to GDP. Many leaders from other emerging markets, such as Russia and Brazil, also criticized the dollar reserve-currency standard and called for a shake-up.

Exploring the case for reform

Despite signs of a shift in attitudes among some economists and these powerful voices from emerging markets and some developed countries, such as France, the weight of institutional, professional and academic opinion in the West remained in favour of keeping the basic features of the status quo. They thought that action had to be focused at the national level. One veteran of the monetary conference circuit neatly summed up the negativism of official positions as follows:

> In fact, this crisis demonstrates more than ever that national level is the only level that matters. No one is ready for a global financial regulator, for a global central bank, for a global single currency. So we will need to live with a patchwork of cooperation which is going to be more and more complicated to manage. That transition will be complex as we don't really have a global financial macro theory to understand the episode of the last 12 months. (Uzan, 2010)

However, this 'complex transition' makes it all the more important to explore the case for deeper reform and what would be involved in it. In this book, I argue the case for the following propositions:

- The monetary policy regimes in use by leading countries and economic areas in the years before 2007 contributed to the build-up of imbalances that precipitated the crisis.
- Monetary policies under the existing GFS were inherently inward-looking, as they were directed at national interests and lacked a common framework of reference.
- The monetary policy regime did not favour expectations of stable relationships between different countries' price and cost levels as there was no common unit of account.[9]
- Expectations of big exchange rate swings fuelled booms that led to busts.

And looking to the future,

- In the absence of reforms to the GFS, the world economy will be denied the benefits that it could and should derive from the public good of monetary stability.
- Market suspicions surrounding both major reserve currencies – the euro and the dollar – will persist.
- So long as the existing GFS remains in place, each country would look after the stability of its own banks, shunning agreements that might require it to share the costs of rescuing cross-border banks.
- The capital and regulatory requirements imposed on financial institutions will force such institutions to retreat from global finance.

- Under the existing GFS, the euro area and dollar area economies will be subject to repeated external shocks from wide fluctuations in exchange rates between the euro and the dollar.
- The major emerging market economies, notably India and China, will be denied what they needed above all, a stable international monetary environment.
- Smaller emerging markets will from time to time be overwhelmed by volatile capital flows, encouraging the erection of capital controls that endangered trade.
- Households and corporations, seeing that governments and financial authorities had not responded adequately to the challenges, and still burdened with excess debt, will be cautious in their spending, keeping a lid on growth of demand.

The risk is that these forces would interact with each other to keep the world economy from achieving a full and sustainable recovery, with a recurrent risk of protectionist measures, or else that governments, desperate to create jobs, would kickstart demand by ever larger monetary stimuli, undermining confidence in their ability to control inflation and retain high credit ratings in capital markets.

The intellectual challenge is to gain a standpoint from which to analyse the operation of the GFS as a whole. This book tries to establish that some of the biggest problems were caused by the interaction of the official international monetary system with the commercial banking system and markets. To reach such a standpoint, it would be necessary to bring together diverse spheres of discourse: for example, to discuss the future of the financial structure it would be desirable to be familiar with the discourse among experts in banking, financial market regulation and supervision. Some of the issues that needed attention – such as the oversight of macro-prudential systemic risk – had long been studied by economists, practitioners and financial historians specializing in these fields. These groups had their own journals, international conference circuit and close personal and professional ties. Equally, to discuss monetary reform it was essential to be familiar with the numerous past debates on the international monetary system. But the economists, officials and commentators specializing in issues to do with the international monetary system formed a distinct group, being interested in exchange rate issues, governance of the IMF and related themes. It was true that a few individual economists crossed borders and contributed to debates in both specialisms, yet there were not many of them.

When governments lost credibility

Urgency should have been lent to demands for a comprehensive review by the blatant inadequacy of official responses. In September 2011 the IMF had to report that the global financial system had entered a dangerous phase and that some of the progress made in recovering from GFC had actually gone into reverse. In January 2012 the IMF further cut forecasts for world recovery, saying prospects had dimmed and risks to financial stability had increased further; there would be hardly any dent in very high levels of unemployment. Indeed, at every level, and in all major economic zones, governments and official agencies were struggling to remain in control.

At national level, central banks were fighting to retain the credibility and relevance of their monetary policy regimes – and their independence – under intense political pressure to stimulate demand. In the US, the Fed resorted to several rounds of monetary injections known as quantitative easing (QE), in the face of strong opposition from some respected economists.[10] With bank lending picking up, and reserves boosted by QE, there was uncertainty whether the Fed could, if needed, withdraw the monetary stimulus in time to avoid accelerating inflation. True, there were also experienced economists on the other side, but the mere fact that there was so much disagreement about the proper course of policy and uncertainty eroded confidence. Much the same applied to the ECB and Bank of England.

Meanwhile, the euro area was hit by a series of existential shocks, with the bail-outs of Ireland, Portugal and Greece followed by a collapse of bond prices of all other eurozone countries except Germany testing the fabric of the entire euro project. Eurozone countries that had abused the era of cheap money during the boom had suffered a serious loss of competitiveness. Being part of the currency union, they could improve competitiveness only through falls in nominal wages. To bring this about unemployment had to rise sharply. With unemployment already exceptionally high and rising social and political tensions, the eurozone had plainly a long way to go to develop the federal type of fiscal and bank regulatory system – and proper monetary policy – needed to accompany a monetary union (see Chapter 6). In the meantime, the strains in the eurozone – and fears that it might even eventually break up – hung like a dark cloud over the world.

In short, policy-making models that had enjoyed a long record of seeming success and only a few years earlier seemed capable of delivering lasting price stability, with economic stability and growth, were seen to be floundering. Central banks were fighting simultaneously on two fronts – the fear of deflation and a possible downward spiral of prices and output, and the fear of reigniting inflation. It seemed unlikely that there would be any way out of this dilemma for some time. Ominously, the way the GFS worked gave governments and central bankers no alternative. That was the money trap.

Yet major governments admitted the need only for limited reforms to elements of the GFS, and seemed unable to view it as a whole. Chapter 2 explains how this myopia developed.

Notes

1. Mervyn King interview on Sky News, 6 October 2011, and Jean-Claude Trichet interview in the *Financial Times*, 13 October 2011.
2. These are described in more detail in Chapter 7; in 2011 the IMF launched a website called 'Reforming the international monetary system'.
3. On 28 September 2011, the Bank of England's recently formed Financial Policy Committee asked banks faced with falling profits (and under official pressure to improve capital and liquidity) to cut dividends and bonuses to staff rather than reduce lending. In the US, regulators rejected a proposal by Bank of America to raise its dividend to shareholders. Such official direction marked a return to state dirigisme that would have been difficult to imagine at any other time since the end of the immediate post-Second World War period 50 years before.
4. When Arthur Burns, then chairman of the Federal Reserve, who opposed the US action to suspend gold convertibility of the dollar in August 1971, was overruled by President Nixon, he noted in his private diary: 'What a tragedy for mankind!' He feared that this action, the floating of the dollar, would be followed by trade wars, currency wars and political friction as occurred in the 1930s and 'chaotic financial markets'. After the action, which everybody hoped would be temporary, he warned Nixon that postponement of efforts to rebuild the international monetary order (fixed exchange rates) would probably lead to a wave of protectionism and restrictions of all kinds. But he noted that Nixon's calculations were entirely concerned with domestic politics and how any decision would affect his re-election chances (Ferrell (ed.), 2010, pp. 49, 52 and 55).
5. See, for example, John Eatwell and Lance Taylor (2000), who proposed several years before GFC, 'a bold and necessary solution to the financial crises that threaten us all – a World Financial Authority'. Numerous publications by leading financier George Soros also supported the calls for a world regulator.
6. At least while they held office. It was striking that after leaving office several very distinguished central bankers did protest, such as Thomas Hoeing, who had been President of the Kansas City Fed for many years until his retirement in 2011.
7. This group includes, for example, the following international economists: Alexandre Swoboda, Hans Genberg, John Greenwood, Ronald McKinnon and Steve Hanke, as well as Robert Mundell; see Bibliography, Chapters 9, 10 and 13.

8. See 'Reform of the International Monetary System: A Cooperative Approach for the Twenty-First Century'. A report of the Palais Royale Initiative, otherwise known as the Camdessus report. February 2011.
9. Richard Cooper described the desiderata of a good system as follows: 'The proper role of a monetary system, national or international, is to provide a stable expectational environment for the wealth-producing sectors of the economy and for the public generally' (Cooper, 1988, p. 336).
10. Allan Meltzer, the historian of the Federal Reserve System, commented in February 2011: 'Throughout its modern history, the Fed has made several of the same policy mistakes repeatedly. Two are prominent now. It concentrates on near-term events over which it has little influence, and neglects the longer-term consequences of its operations. And it interprets its dual mandate as requiring it to direct all of its efforts to reducing unemployment when the unemployment rate rises. It does not have a credible long-term plan to reduce both current unemployment and future inflation, so it works on one at a time. This is an inefficient way to achieve a dual mandate. It failed totally during the Great Inflation of the 1970s. I believe it will fail again this time' (Meltzer, 2011).

Bibliography

Cooper, Richard, 'Towards An International Commodity Standard?' *Cato Journal*, Vol. 8, No. 2 (Fall 1988), p. 336.

Eatwell, John, and Lance Taylor, *Global Finance at Risk: The Case for International Regulation*, Polity Press, 2000.

Ferrell, Robert H. (ed.), *Inside the Nixon Administration: The Secret Diaries of Arthur Burns, 1969–1974*, University Press of Kansas, 2010.

Goldman Sachs, 'The BRICS 10 Years On', Global Economics Paper 208, December 2011.

Meltzer, Allan, 'Ben Bernanke's '70s Show', *Wall Street Journal*, 5 February 2011.

Padoa-Schioppa, Tommaso, 'The Ghost of Bancor: The Economic Crisis and Global Economic Disorder', Louvain-la-Neuve, 25 February 2010.

Palais Royale Group, *Reform of the International Monetary System: A Cooperative Approach for the 21st Century*, February 2011. A group convened by Michel Camdessus, Alexandre Lamfalussy and Tommaso Padoa-Schioppa, and also comprising Sergey Aleksashenko, Hamad Al Sayari, Jack T. Boorman, Andrew Crockett, Guillermo de la Dehesa, Arminio Fraga, Toyoo Gyohten, Xiaolian Hu, André Icard, Horst Koehler, Guillermo Ortiz, Maria Ramos, Y. Venugopal Reddy, Edwin M. Truman, and Paul A. Volcker.

Uzan, Marc, 'The Way Forward', in *Building an International Monetary and Financial System for the 21st Century: Agenda for Reform*, Marc Uzan (ed.), eBook published by the Reinventing Bretton Woods Committee, 2010, www.rbwf.org

White, Lawrence, 'The Federal Reserve System's Influence on Research in Monetary Economics', *Econ Journal Watch*, Vol. 2, No. 2, August 2005, pp. 325–54.

Zhou Xiaochuan, 'Reform the International Monetary System', People's Bank of China website, March 2009.

2
Why Players Need a New Rulebook

This chapter traces how the global financial system (GFS) developed in such a way as to frustrate rather than facilitate the long-term interests of players, whether in the public or private sectors. It became too flexible and open to inappropriate influence.

How the GFS misled major participants

A good GFS should make it possible for participants to achieve their legitimate interests while also channelling the results of their pursuit of self-interest to the service of the community. Adam Smith's invisible hand always did need a proper structure of rules and ethical behaviour – and stable money – to function properly. Yet in the course of the years from the 1970s onwards the GFS developed in such a way that it frustrated players from achieving their key longer-term objectives. These players included financial institutions, multinational corporations, other businesses involved in international trade and investment, and individuals, whether as taxpayers or investors. We first look at the point of view of some major players and then discuss what went wrong.

Naturally, banks and other financial institutions used opportunities provided by the system to expand their businesses and develop new markets. In the repeated crises of the period, however, many went out of business, others survived only by dint of state aid, while the survivors faced the prospect of hostile legislatures and publics, with the real prospect of being forcibly broken up. Although legacy banks hoped to continue as independent commercial enterprises, and behaved as if they were back in a 'normal' market setting, in fact the measures needed to support the banking system during GFC and the succeeding tensions in sovereign bond markets had changed their status permanently. Nor could the authorities simply announce that in future banks would be expected to stand on their own feet, when in fact everybody knew that governments would guarantee them if required to. Many if not all, so-called systemically important financial institutions had in effect become, without intending or even realizing it, wards of the state. That had not been part of their strategic plans.

Turning to governments, GFC left the finances of most developed country governments in a parlous state, as a result of both its direct and indirect costs, forcing radical retrenchment on their economies. In this it resembled the experiences that many developing countries had suffered in the past century; the cost of a fiscal injection taken in an effort to prevent a deflationary depression or directly to rescue banks turned out to be so high as to endanger state finances. Why did they prove so vulnerable? In view of the turbulent history of finance from the early 1980s on, governments had had plenty of warning; contrary to the impression sometimes given, the years up to GFC saw the publication of numerous reports on financial panics and the measures needed to avoid them. But no adequate safeguards were put in place – and there was no fundamental review of the GFS. Instead, governments relied on regulation. But as a result of the pressures of market players and the prevailing set of economic ideas, regulation had to be 'market friendly' and left room for regulatory arbitrage. Governments also welcomed booming revenues from taxation of the financial sector (which in both the UK and US at one point accounted for 40 per cent of all corporate profits and tax revenues). They ended up turning a blind eye to activities of questionable social value and to excessive risk-taking. Safety nets placed under the system did not prevent a collapse of business activity and tax revenues. This had not formed part of governments' game plan.

Meanwhile, in the private sector, multinational corporations and smaller businesses, as well as consumers, took on debt in the good years and then, after GFC, faced the prospect of servicing it in much less favourable circumstances. The process of cleaning up debt-laden balance sheets was likely to take years to complete.

Faustian pact

Nor had the GFS served emerging markets well. Post GFC, fiscal consolidation and the need to reduce leverage in the corporate and household sectors in the developed countries doomed western economies – their main export markets – to slow growth. Their financial institutions suffered less than those of the advanced economies, but this was because many of them had recent memories of the catastrophic effects of financial panics. The defensive measures that had been taken by these countries – cleaning up their banks, ensuring capital was adequate and building up exchange reserves – protected their financial institutions, partially at least, from the direct effects and contagion of GFC. Others, such as China, had never fully joined the global financial system, sheltering behind a wall of capital controls. Yet a GFS that permits only those with recent memories of disaster or huge foreign currency reserves and capital controls to survive can hardly be described as a great advertisement for free enterprise.

GFC did little to increase respect for the models of financial market liberalization and regulation espoused by international financial institutions. Some of the countries to escape relatively unscathed, such as China and India, had retained more highly regulated banking and financial markets (and in the case of China a non-convertible currency), despite being urged for years by international institutions, the US and others to liberalize their markets more rapidly. The lesson they were likely to draw was that integration with global markets should continue, but very slowly, under careful monitoring and laser-sharp supervision.

Unfortunately, international institutions and their major shareholders were slow to appreciate the profound challenges posed for the whole GFS. When addressing remarks to emerging market governments, spokesmen continued to give the same kind of 'advice' they had been giving for years before – that governments should adopt more flexible exchange rates, implement autonomous monetary policies, open their markets and focus on sound domestic policies in order to operate more independently of the system. As regards unwanted volatile capital flows, the advice was that they should adopt 'good practices' as recommended by the IMF and World Bank, so that they could manage such problems while remaining open to outside investment (see Zoellick, 2011) This was another illustration of the desire of leading players from developed countries to go back to the *status quo ante* – or as close to it as they could get – and of their seeming inability to grasp the true dimensions of the challenges.

To understand what went wrong, one needs to analyse the ways in which the GFS had developed and the parts played by the major institutions in it. Why did they persist in courses of action that would become so self-defeating? The principal actors in this modern tragedy – perhaps all or most of us, for householders were implicated as well – had entered into a Faustian pact. We would test the limits of the system, enjoy the ride and see what happened. Anyway, we hoped, if it all ended in tears, we might come out of it well individually. Nobody thought about the interests of future generations and how they would suffer from our mistakes and wrong-doing if it all came unstuck. But in order to ensure that the reforms discussed in later chapters address this issue, it is necessary to see in some detail how this came about.

The Janus face of finance

In the course of this and subsequent chapters we will have occasion strongly to criticize the role of the major financial institutions and markets in contributing to instability. It is therefore important to recognize the positive roles played by these in supporting global growth. That is what makes reform of global finance so difficult to design – there is always the risk of throwing the good out with the bad.

Though pockmarked by financial instability, the period from the mid–1970s to the 2000s witnessed an explosion of demand for financial services. This can be attributed to multiple factors, including the spread of market economies, privatization, the rapid growth of international trade and cross-border investment and the re-entry into the world economy of economies such as Russia, China and India. The demand for financial advice, from individuals saving for their retirement right up to multinational corporations wishing to raise funds to exploit a new technology, expanded at exponential rates. Mounting accumulations of financial assets controlled by individuals, corporations and official agencies around the world needed to be managed. Repeated waves of technological innovation readily found financing and contributed to surges in productivity growth. Financial institutions globally responded to this unprecedented combination of circumstances with alacrity. They made a big contribution to the growth of the world economy. In the process, the private financial sector helped to raise living standards and widen economic freedoms.

However, there were negatives to set against these successes. This period of unparalleled global economic growth also witnessed rising inequality, many civil and international conflicts, episodes of terrible famines in some parts of the developing world, irreversible environmental damage and much religious intolerance. Whether in the final analysis the positives would be judged to outweigh the negatives of this record would depend not only on how it all turned out but also on how future generations would evaluate this period, when 'we' become history. We cannot tell because we do not know how their values and criteria of judgement will differ from ours – that was one reason why committing them to pay interest on our borrowing was questionable in a moral sense. In many countries, the sins of the current generation have left future generations to face an awful choice between default and depression as they struggle to service our debts.

The money game

Having given finance its due, what went wrong? To attempt to answer that question, we cannot avoid a little history. The GSF traces its origins back to two developments: the official part goes back to the Bretton Woods agreement of 1945, while the private part took shape with the rise of international money and capital markets in the economic boom of the 1960s, following recovery from the Second World War. These financial markets facilitated the growth of an international bond market, accompanied by a rapid extension of international banking, which previously had been held back by a regime of capital and exchange controls and state allocation of resources in Europe and Japan, and by bank regulations in the US. A growing number of banks, led by the Americans and closely followed by Japanese, set up foreign branches, initially to cater for their main corporate customers. Dozens of banks that had never set foot outside their home markets joined the few old-established international banks, such as Bank of America, Chase Manhattan and Citibank, and the British overseas banks such as Chartered, Standard, Barclays DCO and Hongkong and Shanghai Banking Corporation (all these famous names of banking or their successor organizations were to survive GFC, though in some cases only with government support).

Banks financed their overseas activities increasingly by borrowing short-term, and often were able to offer customers better services and lower borrowing rates than had been available from local banks in the locations where they established branches. The latter had formed cartels to fix deposit and lending rates, a practice sanctioned by the authorities in an attempt to avoid a repeat of the banking crises of the 1930s. Throughout the world, as late as the 1960s the very idea of free competition for deposits was anathema, as was any discussion of flexible exchange rates. The lesson drawn from the currency wars and banking collapses of the 1930s was that floating exchange rates and competition for deposits led quickly to chaos. At the time, finance in the UK and US was strictly compartmentalized, with the main deposit or clearing banks accounting for the bulk of financial bank intermediation, but not venturing into merchant or investment banking (which engaged in underwriting, mergers and acquisitions and corporate finance).

Banks and other financial institutions of the City of London were regulated but not supervised in the modern sense. Regulation simply meant that an institution, such as a foreign bank, entering the UK, had to obtain permission to accept deposits and make loans and banking licences but were then free to do what they wanted. British banking remained largely unsupervised. The Bank of England used its traditional channels – the discount market firms, representatives of which would visit the Bank every day wearing their top hats – to keep up with the latest gossip going around the City. And the Bank was privy to the real profits of the big banks – which at the time, banks did not have publicly to disclose; bitter experience had proved that banking was an exceedingly risky business, characterized by huge swings in profits, which would scare depositors if they were made public. There was somewhat more detailed supervision of banking in continental European countries and in the US, again reflecting their economic histories.

Each of the big banks of the UK, continental Europe, Japan and America had its own individual way of doing business, as shaped by its history. Employment was generally lifelong and it was virtually unheard of for somebody to move from one bank to another, still less for a bank to try to poach an employee. Although to an outsider or a customer there might seem to be little difference between one clearing bank and another, as interest rates were fixed by the cartel, the bankers themselves perceived large differences in style, corporate behaviour and what we should call culture.

The quarter century after the end of the Second World War saw occasional individual bank failures but no systemic bank crises or panics, at least in developed economies. What were the sources of that stability? The fixed exchange rate regime and indirect link to gold (through the dollar) helped to keep inflation low. Despite the growth of new financial markets towards the end of the period, banks relied mainly on stable sources of funding – mainly retail deposits – and maintained quite high capital ratios. Competition was limited, and banks diversified in their business models and loan portfolios. The range of bank business models and cultures made for a more resilient structure. Moreover, self-regulation had teeth. The City and its various specialized sub-sectors were like villages. In each village, everybody knew everybody else. Outsiders were carefully scrutinized before being admitted, and the penalties for failure and for unethical behaviour – if you were found out – were swift and sure.

The authority of official institutions (though in the UK lacking statutory foundation) was absolute: the Bank of England in the UK, the Federal Reserve and the Securities and Exchange Commission (SEC) in the States, and the supervisory authorities in continental Europe.

Players kept a proper distance from each other, with a clear distinction between the public and private actors. Their respective roles were well understood. Public policy was run by governments, not central banks, though the latter were useful, as we have seen, in keeping an eye on their financial institutions and markets. There was little interchange of personnel between public and private sectors; although occasionally civil servants – usually when approaching retirement – joined the board of a financial institution, it was rare for a banker to join the civil service (after all, few bankers even had university degrees, a *sine qua non* of admittance to the civil service).

The international monetary system proper consisted of the commitments that governments had entered into vis-à-vis each other, including acknowledgement that a country's exchange rate policy was a matter of international concern. These commitments were formalized in the articles of the IMF, World Bank and OECD and in the rules governing trade. They were designed to protect and preserve the open trade system, and provided for a gradual liberalization of the extensive controls over capital movements, all monitored by an international policeman, the IMF. If countries wished to change their exchange rate, they had to apply to the IMF, and prove that their payments were in 'fundamental disequilibrium'. These rules in turn set limits to a country's freedom to run independent monetary and fiscal policies. On the other hand, a member country was assured of support – though temporary and, beyond a defined limit, with conditions attached – from the international community in case its external payments went into deficit. As was often said at the time, IMF facilities gave countries time to adjust 'but not time to waste'. The IMF monitored the system to ensure the rules of the game were followed (lessons to be learnt from the Bretton Woods era for the reform of the GFS are discussed in Chapter 3).

Gradual erosion

In reality, this set-up did not work as smoothly in practice as hoped and eventually broke down (see Chapter 4), but it did enshrine – and, within limits, hold countries to – a common set of aspirations and rules. There was an internationally agreed set of arrangements for the financing and adjustment of payment imbalances embodied in the articles and procedures of the IMF. You followed rules appropriate to your station. These rules set the framework within which market operators – corporate treasures, investors, importers and exporters – ran their businesses. Governments in turn also agreed to comply with a set of rules, the most important of which were rules governing maximum fluctuations of their exchange rates round a fixed 'par value' and rules providing for exchange rates to be changed in certain conditions and with international agreement. Meanwhile, private sector institutions made markets, provided services for customers, managed funds and served as financial intermediaries.

As these pillars of stability and the supporting economic ideas were dismantled from the early 1970s on, so market players had more scope to pursue short and even medium term profit opportunities. This applied both at the national level, where financial innovations like hire purchase/instalment credit firms started to challenge the functions of the regulated deposit banks, and at the international level. The growing US payments deficit and inflationary pressures, linked to the financing of the Vietnam War, put the fixed exchange rate system under strain, while economic opinion moved towards favouring flexible rates. As the US would not change the dollar price of gold, the structure was unsustainable (see Chapter 4). Whether it could have lasted longer if the gold price had been adjusted remains a matter of speculation – just as a similar adjustment in the 1920s might, some economists claim, have prolonged the classic gold standard. The price of this greater freedom was greater instability in the environment in which firms operated, placing a premium on trading, short-term results and taking big bets on markets, such as foreign currency and bonds.

The period of international financial instability started with the inflationary monetary expansion of the 1970s that followed the move to floating exchange rates. Several crises followed:

- 1981–86   Developing countries/Latin American debt
- 1985–86   US Savings and Loan Scandal (not systemic but might have been)
- Early 1990s Nordic banking crash
- 1991–2000 Collapse of Japan's bubble and lost decade
- 1997–98   Asian and Russian financial instability
- 2007–   GFC

In addition, there were several systemic banking crashes in developing countries.

How the turbulence changed the behaviour of players

Three initial observations may be made about this history. First, while the episodes differed in many ways, there was one common factor: each was preceded by extremely loose monetary policies, which would not have been possible within the constraints of a more disciplined set of rules. They all showed the truth of the old adage that the best way to avoid a crash is not to have a boom. Consider a few examples. The debt problems of the 1980s were created by the easy money and low rates of the 1970s, followed by a sudden rise in US interest rates in 1979–81, which made it impossible for Mexico, Brazil and other countries to service these bank borrowings. The US Savings and Loan episode, where a bank run was headed off by the Federal Deposit Insurance Corporation (FDIC) and the Federal Reserve, was also caused by easy money policy, a property boom and faulty deregulation.

The underlying cause of the Nordic banking crash was another property boom financed by easy money and capital inflows. The Japanese crash followed a credit-fuelled asset bubble that had been created largely by the central bank's interest rate cuts, designed to offset the deflationary impact of the appreciation of the yen following the Plaza Accord of September 1985. The dollar fell by 40 per cent against the yen, and in a bilateral agreement in September 1986 Japan agreed to further expansionary fiscal measures. More oil was poured on the fire when the Bank of Japan cut rates in response to the US banking crash of 1987 (illustrating how measures to correct market fluctuations often cause distortions elsewhere). House prices doubled in ten years to 1990 in Japan, just as they did in the US and UK in the ten years to 2005. In Ireland they soared by over 500 per cent between 1994 and 2006 – with the price of an average second-hand house rocketing from €82,773 to €512,461.[1] The 1997–98 Asian episode was also driven largely by the monetary policy cycle in developed countries. Interest rates were held down to encourage growth, which prompted a massive capital inflow to emerging markets driven by a search for yield, coupled with the attempt by several Asian countries to stabilize their exchange rates and liberalize their capital accounts.

Secondly, the episodes of extreme instability tended to become larger, more catastrophic in their effects on the real economy, and more global. The less developed countries' debt problems of the 1980s threatened a number of leading US and some European banks, and caused a decade of slow growth in Latin America. The Nordic, Japanese and

Asian episodes, though all systemic, were seen as regional problems, though with the growing risk of contagious effects. GFC was the first fully fledged systemic banking panic of the globalized GFS. Thus while governments of the 1980s and 1990s could adopt national solutions to banking crises, in the twenty-first century any effective solution demands an international approach.

Thirdly, there was also a pattern in the way in which these episodes were resolved. This was to foist more of the costs of the clean-up onto taxpayers and less onto banks and other financial institutions. This reached a climacteric under GFC.

These trends reflected and contributed to changes in the ways in which the global players pursued their interests and in the relationship between them and official sector bodies like central banks. For instance, the abolition of exchange and capital controls throughout the advanced economies in the late 1970s and early 1980s opened the window for bankers to offer their services and trade in financial instruments across borders. Bankers could help governments postpone adjustment of payments positions by borrowing in the new markets – see Chapter 11 and Part II. Taken together, different rates of monetary expansion in leading countries, allied to freedom from exchange controls, produced fertile grounds for property and asset bubbles and large fluctuations in exchange rates between major currencies – all offering attractive opportunities for banks and other market players to make trading profits. This was how the absence of an international monetary system combined with an elastic financial system triggered repeated financial crises. (For a further analysis of bubbles and crashes see Chapter 11.)

In such ways, incentives facing private financial institutions were gradually twisted in favour of short-term results, with an emphasis on trading revenues, as well as growing investment in lobbying to secure 'light-touch regulation' (see Chapter 10). In the City, the influence of US investment banks became stronger (well described in Augar, 2000).

A cycle of empty reassurances

The stakes were raised by the response of the official sector. George Soros has described how a 'super-bubble' grew through a series of mini-bubbles in an arc from the early 1970s right through to 2007.[2] After every cycle, the pattern of response from governments was similar. There was jockeying for position between the many international regulators over who did what next, often resolved by creating yet another level of decision-making, followed by the creation of a raft of official programmes, usually embracing IMF credit facilities, additional capital/liquidity buffers, early warning systems and calls for 'close international cooperation'. Right-wing commentators often criticized these measures as simply jobs for the boys – essentially ways of picking the pockets of taxpayers. And so they were, sometimes. But there was more to it than this. The succession of weak-kneed responses was all that the international institutions – including the Bank for International Settlements (BIS), financial regulators, as well as the IMF – could do, trapped as they were between the power of large (government) shareholders on the one hand and the pervasive, seductive lobbying of the big financial institutions on the other. And they had to calm markets, didn't they? They had to pretend to be in control.

After each cycle, all these measures to support the system would be underpinned by a new burst of easy money from central banks that gave a lifeline to struggling institutions – and started the next credit cycle. When asset prices began to rise, institutions scrambled to get into the act and load up on assets and debt fast – laying the basis for the next crash. Yet the official story was always that regulators were learning from each episode. Spokesmen would repeatedly reassure markets and citizens that – this time – they had got an adequate apparatus in place – or would have soon. This extract from a speech by Stefan Ingves, who was then at the IMF, is typical of its kind. He was looking back, in 2002, on the lessons learned from the Nordic banking collapse of the early 1990s:

A lot of international attention has been devoted to banking crises and how to prevent one or deal with one, once it occurs. Triggered by the Nordic crises and the Mexican crisis of the mid-1990s, the G-10 established a working group to come up with recommendations for how to strengthen national financial systems…. By mid-1996, the IMF's Managing Director, Mr. Camdessus, predicted that the next major international crisis would have its origin in the banking sector and called for better international banking guidelines; and instructed IMF staff to develop such guidelines.

This, of course, was outside IMF's traditional turf and did not move far. But it did trigger the Basel Committee on Banking Supervision to develop the Core Principles for Effective Banking Supervision in 1997, which subsequently have become accepted worldwide as a minimum standard. (Ingves, 2002)

That conveys the flavour of such official stories. As usual, prevention would be better next time:

> Accordingly, IMF surveillance therefore has been expanded to include the financial sector under the so-called Financial Sector Assessment Program (FSAP) which feeds into the IMF's traditional Article IV surveillance process. The FSAP does not focus only on the banking sector but also on the broad financial infrastructure that provides its underpinnings (e.g., accounting, bankruptcy and foreclosure rules, payments systems, etc.) and on other subsectors of importance for financial stability, such as insurance and pension schemes. (Ingves, op cit)

Market players knew the regulators had to speak like that – and discounted it. It's always the same story. (Similar speeches were uttered after the next, bigger crash ten years later.) In 2002 Ingves even specifically referred to the need to adopt a 'macroprudential' approach – showing that claims in 2009–12 that this was a new box of tricks were bogus. In reality, good bankers and good central bankers had always been aware of the distinction between risks affecting an individual bank and systemic risks well before GFC. But Ingves was not to be put off his stride:

> There is also a race under way to find the 'holy grail' of macroprudential indicators and early warning signals that will signal major problems and weaknesses and allow prevention of major financial sector crises. This is an elusive task, which remains highly country specific. (Op cit)

The 'race' may have been 'under way' among these bureaucrats, but it would lead panting bankers straight over the cliff yet again. Each episode, and each new layer of regulation, was invariably followed by an unprecedented burst of financial innovation. Clever investment bankers were quick to exploit the fleeting opportunity for mega-profits, before the next inevitable crash. So, a few short years later, came the biggest and most destructive banking panic of all time, which yet again took the IMF completely by surprise. So much for all those early warning systems.

And the official response to GFC? Surprise, surprise, it followed the same pattern as the response to the Nordic and Asian crises ten years before – new international bodies, new codes of conduct, agreements on higher capital, to be phased in judiciously so as not to jeopardize the recovery – and a reluctance to probe the underlying causes of the dysfunctional system. This latter was discouraged by major shareholders, notably the US. This dreary repetition of a response made familiar from previous cycles explains the widespread sentiment in 2010–12 that governments, central banks and regulators were not on top of the situation, and that GFC was not yet over and could mutate to more virulent forms. These official measures had in truth done nothing to put the GFS on the right tracks. It remained slippery, flexible and permissive. It had a liability to sudden storms. It was by turns indulgent and threatening.

During the long global economic expansion leading up to GFC, government ministers, regulators and central bankers failed to appreciate the implications of these profound changes in financial markets and that regulation could never make up for the absence of an international monetary standard and for the lowering of ethical behaviour. The headline message from the IMF itself was one of stout optimism. Central bankers held to the view that as long as chosen measures of domestic prices remained reasonably stable (inflation and inflationary expectations of around 2 per cent a year), the market should be allowed to function with minimal interference. Whenever anybody questioned them about financial stability, central bankers would wave their mandate in your face: 'our job is to provide price stability – go and talk to somebody else about financial stability', one was told (see Chapter 5). Yet these new regulators were simply not up to the job of disciplining powerful private institutions, at a time when all the incentives were towards maximizing short-term returns. Regulatory rules were plastic, the structure of official oversight liberal and credit supply elastic. The cover story was that the 'science' of risk management was making such progress that bankers and regulators finally had quantitative measures of risks and so could control the sum of risk-weighted assets across an institution's balance sheet – with a separate calculation applied to trading activities. It was thought that regulatory requirements had to 'go with the grain of market forces', otherwise they would be running the risk of being stricter than actually necessary on economic grounds and/or of being circumvented.

The finance lobby

Gradually, an incestuous relationship developed between big financial institutions and governments. True, finance had always been close to government – the state and financial interests had been bound closely together throughout history. This was tolerable so long as it was discreet, conducted according to well-established rules, and worked without great overt cost to the public purse. GFC showed these assumptions to be no longer valid. The use of private influence to gain public favours became gross and indecent, as numerous examples from the US, UK, Ireland, Greece and other countries showed; the balance of power shifted decisively towards finance and away from the state – and the cost had become crippling. Again, governments on both sides of the Atlantic seemed at a loss as to what to do. Whereas a previous generation of political leaders had no compunction in breaking up big banks, forcibly separating their functions or even nationalizing them, this time they seemed paralysed by indecision and fear of the consequences.

One of the pioneers who developed this political economy view of events was Simon Johnson, a former chief economist at the IMF (see Johnson and Kwak, 2010). In an article published by *Bloomberg* on 19 February 2011, Johnson commented as follows:

> Who are the government sponsored enterprises today? Which entities are too big to fail, in the eyes of lawmakers and regulators, and therefore are receiving implicit, no-cost government guarantees?
>
> The answer is our largest bank holding companies such as J.P. Morgan, the second-biggest U.S. bank in terms of assets...
>
> Who has an incentive to increase debt relative to equity in really big ways? Again, it's the largest banks. The executives in these companies are paid based on their return on equity – and the easiest way to increase that is to add leverage. Of course, this increases returns only when times are good. It also increases the potential losses when markets tumble. In other words, greater leverage increases risk.

On the analysis advanced in this book, the most recent, most costly and damaging of all financial crashes occurred, like previous ones of the past 40 years, because of structural faults in the GFS itself. Underlying these faults was a change in attitudes towards money itself: the use of money as a tool of policy undermined respect for money. The real lesson is that when money is dethroned from a lofty constitutional plane, and becomes subject to the whims of official policy-makers, it inevitably becomes a plaything of the private sector. As a result, instability becomes endemic. As pointed out above, none of the institutions or players intended to produce the collapse. But the rules, structures and incentives in place led them collectively to produce disastrous results for society, though some individuals gained considerable rewards for themselves privately. Although in principle this broadly based market structure should have been able to coordinate the actions of the major players, it proved incapable in practice of doing so. Although in theory the development of new market tools should have diffused risks and allowed them to be borne by those most able and willing to shoulder them, in practice it magnified risk and left the public sector to pick up the bill.

The severity of the financial crisis and the depth of the recession put the record of the previous 40 years in a different light, tilting the balance towards the negative side and underlining the need for fundamental reform.Obviously, the financial market rulebook needed to be rewritten. But the players couldn't do that without a lead from the rule-makers – governments.

Notes

1. See the entertaining account by Fintan O'Toole, *Ship of Fools*, 2009. O'Toole documents how warnings from a few economists and the IMF were completely ignored and portrays a political establishment riddled with corruption. As early as 2001, the IMF studied the Irish property bubble in the context of others and concluded that it would inevitably collapse. Yet such warnings were rebuffed not only by the government but also by many economists: 'The overwhelming majority of Irish economists either contented themselves with timid and carefully couched murmurs of unease or, in the case of most of those who worked for stockbrokers, banks and building societies and who dominated media discussion of the issue, joined in the reassurances about soft landings' (p. 123). Bertie Ahern, then prime minister of Ireland (Taoiseach), responded to one critic by urging him and people like him to kill themselves: 'I don't know why people who engage in that ("cribbing and moaning") don't commit suicide' (p. 122). Another crash caused by an unsustainable credit boom fuelled by capital inflows and false reassurances was Iceland. The way in which eminent economists painted rosy pictures of Iceland's economy just before the crash has also been documented (see Aliber and Zoega, 2011).
2. George Soros address at INET conference, King's College, Cambridge, 2010.

Bibliography

Aliber, Robert Z. and Gylfi Zoega (eds), *Preludes to the Icelandic Financial Crisis*, Palgrave Macmillan, 2011.
Augar, P., *The Death of Gentlemanly Capitalism*, Penguin Books, 2000.
Ferguson, Niall, *The Cash Nexus: Money and Power in the Modern World 1700–2000*, Allen Lane, The Penguin Press, 2001.
Ingves, Stefan, 'The Nordic Banking Crisis from an International Perspective', Seminar on Financial Crises, The Banking, Insurance and Securities Commission of Norway, Oslo, 11 September 2002.

Johnson, Simon, and Kwak, James, *13 Bankers: the Wall Street Takeover and Next Financial Meltdown*, Pantheon, 2010.

O'Toole, Fintan, *Ship of Fools: How Stupidity and Greed Sank the Celtic Tiger*, Faber and Faber, 2009.

Zoellick, Robert, 'Monetary Reforms for a Multipolar World', *Financial Times*, 18 February 2011.

3
How Monetary Systems Are Born

To succeed, an official effort to reform the GFS should be undertaken when conditions are appropriate. The question is: under what circumstances are new systems born? We should learn from history.

Since the Industrial Revolution there have been only two international monetary systems that could claim to be global in reach, and in which a given standard of value was recognized internationally: the classical gold standard, usually dated from 1880 to 1914, and the Bretton Woods period 1945–71.

The classical gold standard

The classical international gold standard came about through an unplanned evolutionary process. In the seventeenth and early eighteenth centuries England was on a silver standard, so that changes in the ratio between gold and silver came about by changes in the gold and not silver parity. An early foundation happened in the 1690s when gold became overvalued relative to silver and Isaac Newton, Master of the Mint from 1699 to 1727, inadvertently failed to correct this, though he strongly believed in the silver standard. Soon, 30 times more gold than silver was coined in England. London became the centre of the gold trade, and attracted gold from the new discoveries in Brazil, as well as from other sources. Plentiful supplies of gold and its attractive price in London brought Gresham's law into operation, with the 'bad money' – gold in this case – driving out the old silver coinage, opening the way for gold to become dominant (see Chown, pp 63–66).

The standard developed along with rapid changes in money and banking markets. Increasingly paper money was used, and then fractional reserve banking developed, enabling a huge increase in the money supply to take place on the gold reserve base – as Keynes put it, 'turning a stone into bread'.[1] Foreign governments and traders built up sterling balances in London, and with the development of the discount market, a high proportion of international trade came to be invoiced and settled through bills of exchange drawn on London. As growth of Britain's GNP and trade accelerated, it became the dominant economic and trading power. The prestige and power of the British Empire and the Royal Navy – plus the pound sterling, which was considered as reliable as gold – facilitated the development of a global system of foreign lending and capital exports from Britain. The Bank of England learnt how to operate the system so that, sustaining a credit structure on a narrow gold base, there was no danger of being forced off its commitment to convertibility. That remained the sole aim of monetary policy until 1914.

It was the confluence of all these factors that produced the classical gold standard, which became the world's monetary system when other countries voluntarily adopted it. As indicated by Keynes's jibe in 1923 about the gold standard being 'already' a barbarous relic, gold had only comparatively recently – a mere 40 or so years before – come to be seen globally as the most advanced of all monies (Keynes, 1923). That is one reason why Germany, France and the US joined the international gold standard – as a symbol of modernity, to show that they, too, were part of the emerging GFS.

Being a member of the gold standard club had other attractions. It brought access to global capital markets, a commitment to free trade, an end to messy particularist restrictions on trade, such as had crippled the German economy until the coming of the customs union (*Zollverein*) in the mid nineteenth century; it meant, in a word, being part of the modern world. Did it depend on a hegemonic power? Not really. It did not involve subordination to Great Britain politically, commercially or financially. True, countries on the so-called periphery of the system suffered from more shocks than those at the centre – the system's method of dealing with shocks being to pass them down the line – but a country on the periphery would hope to graduate to higher rungs on the ladder. For the first time, governments and commentators sought to position their country in relation to the international finance and trading system. There was growing realization of what we would now call international interdependence, and a number of conferences debated what was then a new topic – the international monetary system.[2] Then, quite suddenly, what seemed to be a coordinated move to gold took place: Germany in 1871, Sweden, Norway and Denmark in 1873, France, Belgium, Switzerland, Italy and Greece in 1874 and the US in 1879. By the end of the nineteenth century, all the major countries except China had shifted to gold. The pound sterling/gold standard was the world's unit of account *and was expected to be so indefinitely.*

That is a key point. Habits, familiarity and what economists call 'network effects' all conspire to give huge advantages to the sitting incumbent, that is, the dominant financial centre and its currency. They can be destroyed – quickly by war or slowly by the rise and fall of empires and financial centres. The migration of the dominant centres of finance and banking from the late medieval period through the Renaissance cities of Venice and Florence to northern European cities like Amsterdam and London is a familiar story. But at the time participants not only expect the structures to endure but also believe that it is in everybody's interests to ensure they do.

The death of the gold standard

The outbreak of war in 1914 led to the gold standard being suspended in most countries, with the important exception of the US.[3] During and after the war prices rose rapidly, more in Europe than in the US. After the war political chaos and currency instability, including hyperinflation in Germany, meant that immediate resumption was out of the question. Germany's introduction of the gold mark in 1924 following the successful stabilization of its currency started an international trend. The UK returned to gold in 1925 at the old pre-war parity, despite the fact that the UK had suffered much higher inflation than the US in the intervening period, and this move was followed by France and many other countries. Keynes warned against the dangers for Britain, and the Swedish economist Gustav Cassel warned against the dangers for the world. They were both proved right. The return to gold by most countries caused a scramble for gold, the erection of protectionist measures and reduction in money supplies. These forces pulled the world into deflation and the Great Depression of the 1930s. Other influences were of course at work. There was, for example, the growing role of central banks, especially the foundation of the Federal Reserve in 1913, which created a powerful rival to the Bank of England. Central bankers were beginning to develop ideas about how they might follow monetary policies in their country's individual interests, while leaders of the newly powerful movements of the Left throughout Europe tended to view the gold standard as the symbol of a free-market, laissez-faire system that would stand in the way of building socialism. Nationalists viewed membership as putting roadblocks to autarchic policies. The whole nationalist fervour of the times was against it.

The birth of Bretton Woods

The monetary constitution eventually agreed at Bretton Woods built on the foundation of the fixed dollar price of gold established by Roosevelt in 1934, but was also shaped by political, economic and intellectual influences. The architects of Bretton Woods were convinced of the superiority of political over market mechanisms for the framing of the international monetary order. A high degree of confidence was placed in the collective wisdom of governments. The advocates of Bretton Woods and its central institution, the International Monetary Fund, argued that this was preferable to the approaches tried in the inter-war period. However, some economists later maintained that the proposals and the arguments deployed in their favour were based on a misreading of the 1930s. Was the Fund set up to deal with problems that had never existed or whose causes were misunderstood?

The most influential of the economists writing on the experience of the 1930s at that time was Ragnar Nurkse. In his book on the *International Currency Experience*, published in 1944, he made the case against floating, which inevitably led to destabilizing speculation, while devaluation often worsened the trade balance: 'If currencies are left free to fluctuate, speculation in the widest sense is likely to play havoc with exchange rates…' (p. 137). The devaluation of sterling in 1931 had led to competitive devaluations; and these in turn led to exchange controls and restrictions of trade by bilateral agreements. Thus Nurkse proposed a system of internationally agreed, fixed but adjustable exchange rates – changes in parity being allowed only in cases of structural disequilibrium.

However, re-examination of the episodes used by Nurkse, especially the French floating rates of 1922–26, finds no evidence of destabilizing speculation (Eichengreen, 1992). In addition, there is little evidence for the view that competitive 'beggar-thy-neighbour' devaluations were common in the 1930s (Eichengreen and Sachs, 1985). On the contrary, most devaluations were accompanied by expansionary monetary policies. Countries that remained on the gold standard were more inclined to impose trade restrictions, and countries that abandoned the gold standard freed up monetary policy, giving scope for stimulating the economy (Eichengreen and Irwin, 2009). The breakdown of the gold exchange standard may have owed more to attempts by the US and France to accumulate excessive shares of the world's stock of monetary gold than to structural flaws in the system (see Bordo, 1993). This re-examination of the historical record raises the question whether the Fund and the Bank were actually founded on a misinterpretation of the historical experience. It is a fascinating example of the influence that ideas about the past can have on the institutions that shape the future. As Bordo states, 'One wonders how the [Bretton Woods] system would have been designed had the architects been freed from misperception' (Bordo and Eichengreen, 1993).

But what mattered was that the plans accorded with the dominant strands of thinking among commentators at the time, and that the US and UK governments were ready for them. They may have been first formulated in the fertile brains of Keynes and White (see below), but they were subject to wide public debate and had to be passed through Parliament and Congress. Opposition was brushed aside as obscurantist. Central bankers became objects of particular scorn and obloquy. In a famous passage, Keynes (Moggridge, 1980, p. 413) disposed thus of the Bank of England's alternative proposals for a sterling bloc:

> I feel great anxiety that, unless a decisive decision [sic] is taken to the contrary, and we move with no uncertain steps along the other path, the Bank will contrive to lead us, in new disguises, along much the same path as that which ended in 1931. That is to say, reckless gambling in the shape of assuming banking undertakings beyond what we have any means to support as soon as anything goes wrong, coupled with a policy, conceived in the interests of the old financial traditions, which pays no regard to the inescapable requirements of domestic policies.

Public opinion had become convinced of the need for a large measure of state control; and the US and UK governments, though their respective national financial positions were widely different, were persuaded of the need for an international system of rules governing monetary affairs. The Bretton Woods institutions – which later came to be symbols of conservatism for many left-wing critics – were products of the age of European socialism and the American New Deal. They betrayed signs of their origins – such as their ambivalent attitudes to financial markets – long after the world that had brought them into being had passed away, along with its collectivist outlook and interventionist habits.

Political influences

In 1940–41, when discussion started in Britain and America on the shape of the post-war settlement, it was assumed that the overriding political imperative after the war would be to put Europe back on its feet. Although nobody anticipated the Iron Curtain or the formation of a political bloc in East Europe by the USSR, many feared that extreme socialist or communist parties would come to power in Europe. The Allies needed a plan that would effectively counter communist propaganda about the inevitability of the collapse of capitalism. It should also be able to counter Nazi propaganda, which contained criticisms of the 'decadent' western economic system – criticisms that were taken seriously by some intellectuals in the West.

In 1945, America emerged from the war with a dominant position in the world economy, accounting for the bulk of world economic activity, and two-thirds of its monetary gold. Europe was totally dependent on the Americans. The great fear was of spreading deflation and high unemployment. How could Europe pay for the essential imports it would need to repair its devastated factories, transport and communications? Fortunately, America was ready – indeed, determined – to use its new status as the world's major creditor and only superpower, and to exploit the opportunity afforded by the aftermath of war to shape a new system.

As a wartime ally, Britain was listened to. Indeed, modifications were made to the IMF's articles in the course of the negotiations, which had the effect of making the system more flexible. Without the input of a debtor nation, it is doubtful whether the articles for the IMF would have been workable. It is certain that they would not have been as adaptable as they had to be to allow the Fund to survive into the very different world of the 1960s, let alone the 1990s. The articles allowed the management of the Fund considerable discretion and flexibility.

There were close links between pre-war and post-war monetary arrangements, notably the dollar price of gold, which remained at $35 an ounce, as set by Roosevelt in 1934. Insight into the intellectual influences shaping the Bretton Woods institutions can be obtained through Keynes's writings. Interestingly, Keynes's first essay on the post-war world, written in 1940, was a response to German propaganda for a 'new order'. Germany's proposals had been made by Walther Funk, who was both Minister for Economic Affairs and President of the Reichsbank for most of the war years. Apparently provoked by suggestions that Britain should counter Funk's propaganda by preaching the virtues of the gold standard, Keynes said that 'If Funk's plan is taken at its face value, it is excellent and just what we ourselves ought to be thinking of doing.'

Keynes and White

Keynes's first considered proposals were made in September 1941. In two memoranda he reiterated that after the war governments must above all avoid returning to the discredited laissez-faire system (see Moggridge, 1980, p. 22). The lessons of the inter-war period must be learned. The interval had, he stated, been 'an intensive laboratory experiment' in all the alternative false approaches to the solution: 1. freely floating exchange rates; 2. liberal credit arrangements between credit and debtor countries flowing from the mere fact of an unbalanced creditor-debtor position; 3. the theory that the unlimited free movement of gold would automatically bring about adjustments of price levels and activity in the recipient country that would reverse the pressure; 4. the use of deflation, and still worse of competitive deflations, to force adjustment of wage and price levels; 5. the use of deliberate exchange depreciation, and still worse competitive devaluations; 6. the erection of tariffs, preferences, subsidies and so on to restore payments balance by restriction and discrimination.

The basic failure of the gold standard, Keynes argued, had been to throw the burden of adjustment onto the debtor – that is, on the weaker and generally the smaller countries. Of course, he was viewing the system from the perspective of Britain's new status as an impoverished and deeply indebted country. The metallic standard had, he argued, worked successfully only in two periods: first, in the sixteenth century when the flow of silver from new mines forced strong, creditor countries that first received the silver to take the initiative in price adjustment; and second, in the Victorian age when the 'peculiar organization' of the City of London immediately translated a flow of gold into changes in foreign lending and investment rather than movements in internal prices and wages. Keynes concluded that the architects of a successful post-war system must be guided by these lessons. In addition, it was essential to continue with controls on speculative short-term movements of capital; otherwise, 'loose funds may sweep around the world disorganizing all steady business.'

Harry White, the US Treasury official who was to lead the US delegation at the Bretton Woods Conference, had produced a plan of his own by the end of 1941. Originally a highly disciplined system, in which members surrendered the right to vary exchange rates and had to abolish all exchange controls, it was nevertheless designed with the same purposes as Keynes's: to prevent the disruption of foreign exchange and the collapse of the monetary and credit systems and to assure the restoration of foreign trade after the war. As in the UK, Americans were strongly influenced by a specific interpretation of the inter-war period, and in particular the view that currency chaos was responsible for the Great Depression.

The Roosevelt administration believed that finance should be the servant of the political process, not its master. Yet in Congress many hankered after the gold standard, and White was forced to water down several of his more radical ideas. Nevertheless, 'the primary aim of the Treasury planners was not to restore a regime of private enterprise but to create a climate of world expansion consistent with the social and economic objectives of the New Deal' (Gardner, 1969, p. 76).

White's proposals envisaged liberal overdraft facilities to member countries to make sure they would be able to eliminate restrictions on current account transactions. America's plan stressed the desirability of moving quickly to freedom of international payments – whereas the British assumed that tight exchange controls would be necessary for an indefinite period.

US determination the key factor

The proposals evolved by the American and UK governments, advised by Keynes and White, were presented at an international conference at Bretton Woods, New Hampshire, in July 1944; articles were drawn up and agreed, and on 27 December 1945 a sufficient number of countries had ratified the articles for the international treaties to come into force. However, it was a close thing. The agreement nearly broke down over the American loan of 1945 (Pressnell, 1987, p. 324), and in particular the demands – regarded as unrealistic by the British – for an early general move to convertibility.

The US made clear that it had considered granting the special loan partly to ensure convertibility.[4] The Bank of England opposed acceptance of the Bretton Woods proposals (Pressnell, 1987, p. 267), partly because of its opposition to long-term borrowing from the US.

At this stage Keynes was leading the intellectual battle for multilateralism in trade and payments. In the end, American determination was the key factor.

The Bretton Woods agreement was a central building block in the great era of institution-building following the Second World War. The institutions that it set up were intended to help the world move from an era of conflict and war which had been fomented by the previous system to an era of peaceful cooperation. In the distinctive institutional forms in which those aspirations were embodied, they were, from the start, fundamentally American. In essence they were exercises in the American art of constitutional innovation.

They might have gone even further. Both the Keynes and White plans contained proposals for a world currency – *bancor* and *unitas*, and Keynes argued passionately in favour of creating real international money with symmetrical obligations on creditor and debtor countries (Howson and Moggridge, 1990). But America could get what it wanted by giving international legitimacy to the dollar-gold standard that already existed. Thus although proposals were in fact written into the original version of the Fund's articles that would require countries, including the US, to act symmetrically to keep currencies within 1 per cent of the agreed par values against gold, the US did not need to intervene in the foreign exchange markets and did not intend to do so – others would have to keep their par values within margins by intervention. So the US inserted a gold clause (Article IV, 4 (b)), according to which a country that was buying and selling gold freely was deemed to be satisfying its exchange rate obligations (see Mundell in Bordo and Eichengreen, 1993, p. 604). In short, the dominant power did not want to be subject to the same obligations as the agreement would require of others; such a dilemma would also face proposals for a global currency in the future. (The *bancor* is discussed further in Chapter 12.)

The ideals of the founding fathers

Just as the US Constitution is seen by Americans as the foundation of the world's first truly democratic society, so an international constitution for monetary and economic affairs could mark the start of a new world order built on the principles of the United Nations Charter. Put another way, just as the establishment of the classical nineteenth-century gold standard can be viewed as Britain's effort to export its domestic monetary system, which had long been based on gold, to the rest of the world, so the Bretton Woods system, and its institutions, was an attempt by the US to export its liberal trade and payments system. The system was to be exported in a way suited to America's traditions, and that meant the creation of institutions in which free and nominally equal partners would come together, as the states did in the US Constitution, to create a system *de novo* – apparently out of nothing except the exercise of their own free will. It was a bid to give the world a new start, to do away with age-old great-power rivalry, and in 1945 the plans passed through America's normally isolationist Congress on a high tide of idealism and soaring hopes for a better world.

For Americans, it was natural to assume that the best way to ensure international cooperation in future was by creating a club which members could join only if they undertook to follow the rules. Bretton Woods was intended to be much more than just an exchange rate system. It provided a framework – a constitution – assigning member nations certain rights and requiring of them certain obligations. Every club needs a rulebook, and in America that meant a written, legally binding constitution with a set of agreed articles which new members are required to sign. The International Monetary Fund was designed to be such a club. Countries would apply to join, undertake certain obligations while they are members and can apply to leave at any time.

In that sense, Bretton Woods was – and was intended to be – the very antithesis of the way in which great powers normally obtain the cooperation of others. Americans saw it as completely different, in its whole spirit and way of working, to any previous system, such as the classical gold standard, Britain's sterling area, or France's franc area, let alone Germany's pre-war bilateral trading agreements with neighbouring countries. They had been based on power relations. America's was a free, open and universal system, in which all members were supposedly equal (though the US was more equal than others, as we have seen). In fact the most important principle and rule of the system was that members should treat each other equally, that is, by the principle of non-discrimination.

The major international financial institutions of the Bretton Woods period were the product of a very particular set of circumstances, and could not have been set up at any other time. They reflected the ideals of their founding fathers, notably a shared determination to avoid a return to laissez-faire in international monetary relations – still less a return to the gold standard. Permanent institutions were needed to secure monetary stability and promote development through a partnership of the public and private sectors, especially large American corporations.

Attempted reforms – a hypothesis

What lessons can be drawn from this experience and from the other, less successful efforts at reforming the system during the past 100 years?

What are the conditions for successful reform? James Boughton, the historian of the IMF, sums up his conclusions from a survey of twentieth-century efforts at reform as follows:

> The central lesson that emerges from these efforts is that successful reform in response to a crisis requires three ingredients: effective and legitimate leadership combined with inclusive participation; clearly stated and broadly shared goals; and a realistic road map for reaching those goals.[5]

My hypothesis also requires several conditions to be fulfilled for a new order to be brought into being, but I would phrase them somewhat differently:

- First, the existing or previous system has to be viewed as flawed and weak;
- Second, there has to be a clearly articulated view of the main elements of a better system;
- Third, there has to be a broad political consensus among major governments involved on the desirability and feasibility of the reforms;
- Fourthly, the architecture of a new system must appear sufficiently attractive to induce countries to join and fulfil the conditions of membership

Thus, the path to providing the public good of international monetary stability leads from discontent with existing arrangements, via diagnosis, vision and consensus to leadership.

In the case of Bretton Woods, there was a universal desire to break from the flawed non-system of the 1930s. The clearly articulated concept or vision of the main elements of a better system was provided by Keynes and White, while the broad political consensus among major governments involved on the desirability and feasibility of the reforms required to inaugurate a new order was provided by US leadership and British input. Finally, the reforms were adjusted to recognize the special position of the dominant power.

But the obvious lesson to be drawn from comparing the establishment of the classical gold standard with that of Bretton Woods is an acknowledgement of how very different they were. One was unplanned, organic, working with markets, largely self-regulating, without an official institutional infrastructure and without overt use of hegemonic power. The other was planned (though building on the foundations of a system in existence with the fixed gold price), quite hostile to markets, with agreed rules and central institutions to police them and with more overt application of hegemonic power. Yet both systems provided in quite different ways the umbrellas for remarkable expansions of world trade and investment, globalization and an over-arching financial order. Both provided, above all, global monetary standards.

The case for a global standard

In the 2010s, 70 years after the ideas for the Bretton Woods system began to take shape, and as a world in distress again started dreaming of a better system, unfortunately only one of the above pre-conditions for reform was in place: discontent with the existing regime (and that was not universal – some central bankers and economists still defended it). There was a half-formed diagnosis linking it to the faults of the global financial system and the global economy, but even that was not widely shared. Any vision of a new and convincingly better regime was yet to be articulated and there was no consensus on how to proceed.

Yet there is another lesson from this history. It shows the benefits of universality: both the gold standard and Bretton Woods provided global monetary frameworks to go with global markets and liberal trade. As the systems were credible, and were expected to endure, capital flows tended to be stabilizing, and there were no *systemic* financial panics – none that brought the entire order into question. Governments, banks, capital markets, households, all adapted them-selves to the system's written and unwritten rules. They were binary systems – you either belonged to the club or you did not. There was no negotiation on the standard. Both structures put international money in a constitutional realm beyond the reach of the governments even of powerful countries. These global standards denied countries adhering to them the so-called benefits of monetary sovereignty, while leaving them considerable latitude to pursue their own ends in arguably more important areas like politics, foreign policy, culture and social structure. As we contemplate the debris that GFC has left in its wake, that is the key point to hold on to. Steil and Hinds (2009, p. 10) put the point in a nutshell: 'Monetary sovereignty is incompatible with globalization, understood as integration into the global marketplace for goods and capital.'

Both the classical gold standard and Bretton Woods regimes were the official parts of viable GFSs. In other words, they succeeded in containing and harnessing the power of markets and in providing a framework and rules of the game for markets and governments. In both eras, individual nations were persuaded to join a system that disciplined their own actions in the hope of gaining collective benefits for the public good. They both became respectable systems. As noted above, gold in its time was seen as a symbol of civilization, of modernity. Bretton Woods represented for its architects a new era of international cooperation. Admittedly, as a system for coordinating behaviour of freely choosing agents, Bretton Woods was a pale shadow of the gold standard. It relied on controls over many aspects of finance and could not provide a framework for free global money and capital markets. But for its time it represented a strikingly successful attempt to create a global monetary order that left room for the growth of commerce and international exchange – and for the survival of capitalism in a socialist age. It should be emphasized that both were voluntary standards – and were all the stronger for it. Countries and their governments 'owned' the economic policies necessary to join the club of advanced nations – and to remain a member. They were meritocratic hierarchies. Countries climbed a ladder to full membership. To enter the club, you had to be dressed appropriately.

One may speculate whether geo-politics will play a decisive role in establishing and maintaining a future monetary order, or whether one will emerge, like the gold standard, from gradual evolution and accident. Doubtless political leadership and market evolution may both play crucial roles – and they may have to be brought together. Domestic electoral pressures on leaders to do more to reduce unemployment and get economies moving again were steadily growing. As already noted, rising powers were pressing for reform. Meanwhile, preparatory work should be put in hand. Another lesson of history is that there is no one pattern or model of how this public good can be provided. One can be quite eclectic and pragmatic about the choice of routes to the destination. It should not be beyond the wit of man to use existing technology and the astounding globalization of financial markets to create an international order appropriate to the twenty-first century. A vision of a new GFS needs to be articulated in anticipation of a political push for action.

To prepare the ground, the next chapter assesses the achievements of Bretton Woods and the era of experimentation and nationalism that succeeded it. That era left a legacy of problems that any new GFS would have to solve.

Notes

1. Keynes provides the memorable phrase that captured this process when he advocated the establishment of an international currency in the early 1940s: 'The substitution of a credit mechanism in place of hoarding would have repeated in the international field the same miracle already performed in the domestic field of turning a stone into bread.' (See 'Proposals for an International Currency (or Clearing) Union', in *Activities 1940–1944*, p. 114.)
2. At the International Monetary Conference in Paris in 1867, gold was called 'the modern metal', and it was agreed that gold coins, of an acceptable fineness, equivalent to five francs, would be accepted as legal tender in all the participating states.
3. In principle Britain retained the old gold parity during the war, and there were no legal restrictions on the export of gold, but the pound was not in fact convertible and the German U-boat threat stopped gold exports; these were banned when the war ended and the U-boat menace was removed. The US briefly suspended the gold standard between July and December 1914.
4. 'So apprehensive were the Ministers that they came very close to suspending negotiations. The Chancellor believed that to do so over Bretton Woods should provide "a clear and limited issue", to Britain's rather than the USA's advantage; and he began to consider how he would announce the crisis to the House of Commons' (Pressnell, p. 323).
5. See James Boughton, 'A New Bretton Woods?' *Finance & Development*, March 2009, http://www.imf.org/external/pubs/ft/fandd/2009/03/boughton.htm

Bibliography

Bordo, Michael, 'The Bretton Woods International Monetary System: An Historical Overview', NBER Working Paper No. 4033 (Also Reprint No. r1774), issued March 1993, in Michael Bordo and Barry J. Eichengreen (eds), *A Retrospective on the Bretton Woods System*, NBER, University of Chicago Press, 1993.

Boughton, James M., 'A New Bretton Woods?' *Finance & Development*, IMF, March 2009.

Cassell, Francis, *Gold or Credit? The Economics and Politics of International Money*, Pall Mall Press, 1965.

Chown, John F., *A History of Money*, Routledge, 1994.

Davies, Glyn, *A History of Money from Ancient Times to the Present Day*, University of Wales Press, 1994.

Eichengreen, Barry, *Golden Fetters: The Gold Standard and the Great Depression: 1919– 1939*, Oxford University Press, 1992.

Eichengreen, Barry, and Douglas A. Irwin, *The Slide to Protectionism in the Great Depression: Who Succumbed and Why*, NBER Working Paper No. 15142, 2009.

Eichengreen, Barry, and Jeffrey Sachs, 'Exchange Rates and Economic Recovery in the 1930's', *Journal of Economic History*, Vol. 45, 1985, pp. 925–46.

Gardner, Richard N., *Sterling-Dollar Diplomacy: The Origins and the Prospects of Our International Economic Order*, McGraw-Hill, 1969.

Howson, Susan, and Donald Moggridge (eds), *The Wartime Diaries of Lionel Robbins and James Meade, 1943–45*, Macmillan, 1990.

Keynes, J. M., *A Tract on Monetary Reform (1923)* Vol. IV, *The Collected Writings*, Macmillan, Cambridge University Press, 1971.

Keynes, J. M., *Proposal for an International Currency (or Clearing) Union*, in Vol. XXV, *Activities 1940–44; Shaping the Post-War World: The Clearing Union*, edited by Donald Moggridge, Macmillan/Cambridge University Press, 1980.

Nurkse, Ragnar, *International Currency Experience: Lessons of the Interwar Period*, League of Nations, Geneva, 1944.

Nurkse, Ragnar, 'The Gold Exchange Standard', abridged from *International Currency Experience*, in Barry Eichengreen (ed.), *The Gold Standard in Theory and History*, Methuen, 1985.

Pressnell, L. S., *External Economic Policy Since the War:The Post-war Financial Settlement* Vol.. 1 *Peacetime History*, HMSO Books, 1987.

Steil, Benn, and Manuel Hinds, *Money, Markets and Sovereignty*, A Council on Foreign Relations Book, Yale University Press, 2009.

Tanzi, Vito, *Government versus Markets: The Changing Economic Role of the State*, Cambridge University Press, 2011.

4
World Money without an Anchor

This chapter discusses how the Bretton Woods monetary standard established itself in pratice, why it collapsed and the dangerous era of monetary nationalism and experimentation that succeeded it.

An international standard

In practice, the Bretton Woods regime illustrated the advantages of having an international standard with stable exchange rates – and some of the possible disadvantages. The regime depended on highly specific conditions and was in any case flawed from the outset. However, one design fault, the lack of a global currency, was filled initially by the US dollar, which was as good as gold (which is why this period is often called 'an anchored dollar standard'). The price of gold at $35 an ounce served as the lynchpin of the system and a residual link between the world of fiat currencies and the historical attachment of currencies to precious metals. Whether it actually constrained US policy is debatable, but it provided continuity and a background presence, as the gold price had remained unchanged since 1934. Gold was still keeping an eye on the dollar. Economic performance was good – especially by comparison with the inter-war period. A number of positive developments – successful currency reform in Germany, agreement on international rules governing trade, the Marshall Plan and rapid economic growth – paved the way for the resumption of convertibility on current account by the main European countries, which took place in 1958–59. Through the pegged rate system, all countries benefited from access to the US market and that of the dollar area. The IMF had a clear role as policeman of the system and of the rules that countries had agreed to live by. The US remained committed to the international order it had done so much to create.

By comparison with other post-war periods, notably the disasters following the First World War, it was a successful period. True, it was a very constrained kind of capitalism. Controls over capital movements remained widespread. Moreover, the 'high' Bretton Woods system proved short-lived. The first of a series of dollar crises came as early as 1961, and this was followed by several sterling crises and the winding down of the sterling area. As financial markets developed, and with them increasing flows of 'hot money', it became clear that the pegged exchange rate system itself was coming under increasing strain. Above all, with inflation rising in the US and UK, the most important weakness of the system became apparent: there was no mechanism for keeping the world price level stable, so that the fulcrum of the entire structure – the gold price peg – would be bound eventually to come under attack.

The obvious solution was to raise the dollar price of gold, and if this had been feasible politically, the system might have endured and the crazy inflation of the years after 1971 avoided. The whole of subsequent financial history would have been entirely different. And although raising the gold price was ruled out by the US for political reasons (a feared loss of prestige), when the breakdown came, the US and other countries searched vainly to find a successor – a new international order with an agreed set of rules. There was a widespread and ultimately a justified fear that floating exchange rates would lead to a return to currency wars. Yet, despite the best efforts of the Committee of Twenty, which was supposed to negotiate on reform of the system, political differences proved irreconcilable and the world resorted to floating rates. Although the darkest forebodings were not realized, the change did usher in a period of high inflation and monetary nationalism.

Let us now briefly revisit the early days of the Bretton Woods period and consider its record. The prime achievements of the Bretton Woods treaty were, first, to prevent the US from relapsing into isolationism by giving it a permanent stake in the future of the world economy; secondly, to provide the world, for a time, with a monetary anchor; third, to open the vast US market and that of the dollar area to all members of the IMF. The agreement reached in 1944 had clear and achievable goals, and a roadmap to achieve them. There was a determination to avoid the errors made after the First World War. American leaders, including the founders of the IMF and World Bank, as well as the Marshall Planners, believed they could transform political problems into technical ones that were in principle solvable once (bad) old 'European' ways of doing things had been superseded and old habits of class conflict had given way to modern American methods of scientific management and corporative collaboration (see Hogan, 1987, p. 19).

This boundless optimism was reflected in the expectations that American leaders held of the IMF and World Bank. For example, from the start, the US Administration wanted the IMF to push for policy reforms in other countries. As a result, the IMF started early to develop a policy on conditionality, clearly in response to domestic pressures in the US (see Gardner, 1969). But the US placed too many hopes on the IMF during the period of transition – and the Marshall Plan was launched to do what might have been regarded as the Fund's job. Two other developments that would be important later in the story took place in the early years. First, the Fund moved rapidly to establish par values for currencies, as laid down in the articles. Second, there was a Mexican crisis – the first of many – which was important for stimulating one of the key figures in the history of the Fund, Jacques Polak, to pioneer the Fund's distinctive approach to payments adjustment: the Monetary Approach to the Balance of Payments (see Boughton, 2011). This was to have far-reaching implications for the Fund's approach to payments adjustment and exchange rate management.

Lessons of Bretton Woods

The principal features of the system were described by Robert Solomon (1982) in his history of the international monetary system. In brief, the articles provided for a permanent international institution, the IMF; fixed (but adjustable) exchange rates; convertibility, though controls on capital movements were permitted; and access to finance. The Fund would be able to lend to countries in deficit, out of its holdings of gold and currencies arising from subscriptions by its members in relation to their quotas. Many of the ideas that had dominated early proposals for the post-war system were embodied in the new set-up; in particular, there was provision for orderly changes in exchange rates; respect for the maximum national policy autonomy consistent with the discipline of the system; and an acceptance of continuing government controls over money and capital markets.

But the key to the benefits gained from this regime derived from the fact that it embodied an international standard – the par value for the currency of all major countries, expressed in terms of the rate against the US dollar. The bargain struck at Bretton Woods was that countries traded their independence to set exchange rates, in return for being able to call on the international community, in the shape of the IMF, to finance temporary payments deficits and, in the case of the World Bank, also development capital. Developing countries belonging to the system were to make increasing use of the financing facilities of the Fund and Bank, but perhaps more important was the widespread conviction of the desirability of maintaining a fixed rate of exchange. This provided international discipline on national policy-makers. As a former Fund official later stated, 'Given the stability of US prices from after the Korean War until the mid-1960s, the fixed exchange-rate system greatly intensified the pressure that the weaker industrial countries put on their politicians to deliver more conservative fiscal and monetary policies' (Finch, 1989, p. 6).

That was also true of some low- and middle-income countries. Though critics maintained that the system introduced undue rigidity into exchange rates, the notion that there was an international standard did provide policy-makers with a benchmark of financial respectability. With the world on the dollar-gold standard, during the 1960s, inflation in developing countries on a year-to-year basis never rose above 16 per cent (that was in 1964).

A major lesson to be carried into the twenty-first century is that an international regime can, at least for a time, exercise a discipline over governments. The institutions of Bretton Woods were strongly supported by other agencies, in particular the Organization for Economic Cooperation and Development (OECD, which was originally set up, as the Organization for European Economic Cooperation, to recommend how aid under the Marshall Plan to finance post-war European reconstruction should be distributed among recipients). In conjunction with the OECD, the Bretton Woods institutions facilitated a gradual dismantling of restrictions on trade and currency controls; in 1957–58 the leading industrial countries made their currencies convertible on current account. Spurred by successive cuts in tariffs, international trade grew rapidly. This provided buoyant markets for developing countries' exports. The IMF made its mark orchestrating stabilization plans to restrain inflation and ballooning payments deficits, although it could not prevent countries from adopting programmes that would inevitably produce such problems. Indeed, it can be argued that the IMF, by helping newly independent countries to set up the financial infrastructure and policy-making institutions of a nation-state – including a central bank – created conditions that eventually undermined the discipline it sought to impose. But it worked for some countries, including the developed countries of Europe and Japan.

The undermining of Bretton Woods

Several factors combined to undermine the foundations of this era of relative price stability. One was the weakening of the dollar standard itself, as a result of a gradual acceleration of inflation in the US following the long economic expansion during the Kennedy years (1961–63), culminating in the inflationary financing of the Vietnam war under President Johnson (1963–69). Another was the gradual development of international capital and money markets which fostered the growth of capital mobility; this had many effects but one was to enable governments that had access to the markets greater freedom in managing their exchange rates without necessarily having to borrow from the IMF. A third was the development of central banking: the number of central banks rose from 55 in 1950 to 109 in 1970 (see Pringle and Horakova (eds), 2011).

The spread of the central banking habit was to prove a handicap for many countries. Often, in developing countries, monetary emission came to depend almost entirely on the whim of the ruler, except in those few countries, mainly in East Asia, where an entrenched bureaucracy was partially insulated from the centre of political power. Another severe problem was that central banks came to be saddled with a wide range of quasi-fiscal and other responsibilities. The capacity of the corruption that was unfortunately all too common in many developing countries to inflict macro-economic harm was expanded by the availability of central bank credit.

The gradual growth of foreign exchange reserves did give countries that could accumulate them a degree of freedom, however. External reserves came to be viewed as part of the apparatus of the nation-state – along with having one's own currency and central bank. Once central banks were established, they all had to have net external reserves (at least as an objective), and that implied developing a reserve policy. This was another area where discretionary policy replaced automaticity. The idea was to give more leeway for the pursuit of independent economic policies for full employment and growth. But, as in other areas of policy, for many developing countries this hope proved illusory: in some cases excessive monetary creation led to loss of reserves and external depreciation, while in others prudent policies led to an accretion of foreign reserves that caused increasing money supplies and inflation.

Yet while America was banker to the world and the 'anchored' dollar was its monetary standard, countries were content to invest surplus funds in New York; a large proportion of world trade was invoiced and settled in dollars; and when long-term capital flows revived in the 1950s and 1960s, they were dominated by outflows of investment from the US.[1]

The balance sheet

As the global economic boom fostered by the success of Bretton Woods continued in the 1960s, major problems were faced by some large advanced countries in surplus, notably Germany and Japan. During the 1960s, both countries repeatedly experienced large capital inflows, increasing their money supplies. Monetary growth in Germany doubled from 6.4 per cent in 1969 to 12 per cent in 1971 and the German inflation rate increased from 1.8 per cent in 1969 to 5.3 per cent in 1971. Indeed, it was this pressure on the money supplies of surplus countries as a result of the flight from the dollar, caused by US inflationary policies, that was to force Germany to usher in the era of floating exchange rates by cutting its link with the dollar in February 1973. The problems of countries in chronic deficit also progressively weakened the system, though in this case the assistance to the UK before and after the devaluation of sterling in 1967 boosted the prestige of the IMF. It demonstrated its ability to influence the economic policies of a leading industrial country – so long as the country was a debtor and not a creditor.

This period also saw a successful exercise in international cooperation in the creation of the Special Drawing Right (SDR) in the Fund to remedy one of the 'design faults' of Bretton Woods – its failure to provide for an international currency. The SDR was created originally as 'a supplement to existing reserve assets', but was later promoted to the role of prospective 'principal reserve asset in the international monetary system' by the Second Amendment of 1978. The SDR itself is simply a bundle of currencies, with the weight of each currency reflecting factors such as the relative size of the economy and its international trade. The weighting is changed periodically. The dollar has always had a large role in the basket, making it unsuitable for those countries that wished to diversify reserves out of the dollar. The IMF can issue new SDRs only with the approval of member governments – approval that some countries have generally been reluctant to give, so that the SDR remained only a small proportion of world reserves.

Membership of the IMF and World Bank grew rapidly in the 1950s and 1960s so that by 1971 nearly all countries outside the then Soviet bloc and other communist countries were members. By joining, each country committed itself by international treaty to abide by the articles of the Fund, maintain a par value (fixed exchange rate) and follow its code of good financial conduct. Transitional arrangements (originally developed in response to Britain's difficulties in moving promptly to convertibility after the Second World War) were found to be also convenient for the new members from developing countries, virtually all of which enforced payments restrictions and/or multiple exchange rate policies. Nevertheless, the obligations to forbid discriminatory currency practices and other rules of the Fund were taken seriously and the Fund maintained pressure on countries to work towards acceptance of Article VIII, which prohibits members, subject to certain exceptions, from imposing restrictions on the making of payments and transfers for current international transactions.

Although the monetary system assisted the process of economic development during this period in several ways, it contained the seeds of its own downfall. And for each of the benefits, there was an accompanying 'problem'. This can be seen in three key areas of inflation control, adjustment to payments imbalances and international investment flows. First, as long as inflation was kept to moderate levels in America, countries that pegged their currencies to the dollar 'imported' American price stability. On the other hand, as already noted, many newly independent countries set up their own central banks, frequently on the advice of the IMF and with its technical assistance, and these often came under the control of local politicians; excessive monetary expansion fuelled inflation and currency depreciation. Secondly, the IMF's readiness to help countries that experienced difficulties in financing payments deficits demonstrated that the 'international financial community' was ready to help. However, fixed-but-adjustable exchange rates invited speculative attacks on particular currencies deemed 'suspect' (i.e. likely to devalue) and these grew in ferocity as the financial markets began flexing their muscles in the late 1960s. Finally, the system did allow for a revival of long-term international investment, but most of this was channelled through governmental bodies such as the World Bank. There was widespread suspicion of and hostility to US and other foreign investment, which were widely viewed as instruments of US economic imperialism; so private investment was strictly controlled by governments. Exchange controls remained the rule rather than the exception. Even in Europe virtually all countries – with the notable exception of (then) West Germany – maintained controls over capital movements.

Five-star performance for some

The period from 1950 to about 1970 was later seen by many as a Golden Age. The rapid growth rates recorded by Europe and, above all, by Japan, were then matched by a record-breaking period of expansion in the US, ushered in by President Kennedy's tax cuts of 1962. International trade was buoyed by successive rounds of tariff reductions and the volume of international aid for less developed countries also rose rapidly as Cold War rivalry made industrial countries more conscious of the need to promote economic development, and rising wealth made them more able to afford such assistance.

Economists agree on the principal factors involved in this successful performance by industrial countries. The commitment to an open system of world trade and payments made by the leading countries under US leadership in the 1940s, and later endorsed by West Germany and Japan, was crucial. The Marshall Plan provided an early boost – as much by the push it gave to improved policies as by its injection of cash. The Korean War in 1951–52 led to a worldwide, if short-lived, boom in commodity prices, which raised incomes of many primary-producing countries, increasing the market for Western exports. Business confidence had been bolstered everywhere by the unequivocal commitment of the US under President Eisenhower (the general who had led the Allied D-Day landings in Europe in 1944) to the security of the part of Europe that had not fallen under the control of the Soviet Union – a commitment dramatically underlined by the Berlin airlift of 1961 and President Kennedy's 'Ich bin ein Berliner' speech at the Berlin Wall in 1962.

The international monetary system was an important part of this stable framework. European countries benefited greatly from their ability to maintain undervalued exchange rates against the US dollar, at least during the critical years of post-war reconstruction in the early 1950s. The German currency reform of 1949 laid the foundations for what was to become Europe's dominant currency a generation later (administered by a nascent central bank called the Bank Deutscher Länder, trans-formed into the Bundesbank in 1957). France devalued from time to time to maintain its competitiveness; and the devaluation of sterling in 1949 left the UK with a highly competitive exchange rate, although the benefits were squandered by expansionary economic policies.

The US was able to take a benign view of the increasing competitive-ness of European exports and its own move into deficit (at least on some measures of the balance of payments) because of its initial overwhelming strength, not only of its trading position but also of its international balance sheet. In 1950 the US had 60 per cent of the world's stock of gold, 70 per cent of the stock of foreign investment and 40 per cent of its GDP. Even without the Bretton Woods agreement, other countries would naturally have used the dollar as their benchmark and anchor.

That exchange rate system disintegrated when the dollar no longer provided a firm fulcrum for it. America followed increasingly inflationary policies, the impulses from which rippled out into the world economy through the fixed exchange rate mechanism. Countries such as Germany and Japan, confronted with repeated tidal flows of capital and rising reserves, lost control of their money supplies and suffered increasing inflationary pressures. Eventually they broke loose and many others followed.

Interestingly, however, this was not at the time perceived to be the main problem. The most popular explanations of the system's growing difficulties posed the issue in terms of a growing lack of international liquidity and the 'inherent contradiction' of a system that relied on the national currency of the US to serve as the source of new liquidity (it was this perceived problem that had led to the creation of the SDR in 1970). In other words, the problems were defined in terms that made them in principle soluble by the exercise of a sufficient degree of collective management and economists' ingenuity. Yet the US was not ready to submit to any such collective discipline – an unwillingness confirmed in the early 1970s by the failure of negotiations on the reform of the system, when the US rejected the 'asset settlement system' (a kind of substitute gold standard) proposed by the Europeans.

The fall of Bretton Woods

The basic problem was the acceleration of US inflationary pressures, which were faithfully reflected in the gold market. The role of the gold market in the breakdown of fixed rates was a reminder that the system set up at Bretton Woods still had its roots in the old world of international finance. Since the mid-1960s, the US had tried to drive gold out of the system, but the dollar lost its battle with gold. President de Gaulle's call for a return to gold in 1965, though plainly politically motivated, was based on an accurate diagnosis – largely the work of Jacques Rueff, the French economist, discussed in more detail in Chapter 12 – that the Bretton Woods system was doomed.

When the requirements of the system came into conflict with America's perception of its national interest, the US reneged on its treaty obligations under the IMF. Certainly, the resurgence of nationalist attitudes among deficit as well as surplus countries conflicted with the 'Bretton Woods' assumptions – shared by most economists in the 1960s – that the world was moving towards a system of 'rational' collective management. The way President Nixon chose in August 1971 to announce the end of gold convertibility, flanked by protectionist measures and wage-price controls, was an apt herald of the new era – aggressive, nationalist and flirting dangerously with protectionism. As noted, Arthur Burns, America's leading central banker, was appalled – and central bankers the world over were shocked.

The implication of the fall of Bretton Woods went beyond the transition to floating rates among the leading currencies (which came about in 1972–73). The sense of an international community of financial authorities was weakened, as were the obligations of countries to the Fund. Countries were cast adrift without a compass to guide them, especially in the field of monetary policy. Many of them had yet to develop the political maturity, financial markets or economic expertise which could allow them to manage this freedom successfully. The next 40 years were to be kind to those who could cope – and tough on those who could not. The gates had been opened to a range of new inflationary pressures; and those inside each country who saw the need to pursue sensible monetary policies no longer had the support of an international system with its par values and treaty obligations to defend them from the demands of political leaders for easier financing.

The dollar-based international monetary standard under Bretton Woods had provided 25 years during which the world economy grew steadily without a systemic banking or financial crash. By most standards, this was a magnificent achievement. In particular, it had provided Europe with currency stability. American expansionary policies provided the demand, and the financing, through growing payment deficits. Before turning to reform options, it is important to understand how governments first stoked up inflationary pressures and then, under political pressure, tried to bring them under control and to protect their countries from the worst of the turbulence during that period.

Monetary policy experiments

The era that succeeded the end of the dollar peg to gold was one of monetary experimentation. Fortunately, while its heart had been torn from its body, much of the infrastructure of 'the Bretton Woods system' survived – the IMF and its articles, countries' obligations under them and much of the structure of international cooperation. But with the advent of flexible rates among major currencies, the fabric of international cooperation became more loosely structured. Many governments repeatedly misused their new power to manipulate money. They all got into difficulties as a result. At the same time, removal of controls over capital movements and rapid financial innovation fostered the growth of global money and capital markets – and the potential for huge speculative cross-border flows. In sum, the period did confirm some of the fears expressed about floating exchange rates in the 1930s and 1940s and by most economists right until the middle of the 1960s – in particular that exchange rates would become highly volatile.

The original insights of the advocates of flexible exchange rates, if subject to adequate monetary control, did represent progress. They were needed to break away from the bad habits and assumptions of the previous regime. It should not be forgotten that the high tide of Keynesianism, which coincided largely with the Bretton Woods era, was accompanied by severe restrictions on freedom, controls on financial markets and a top–down 'the state knows best' view of the world. This dogma obliged policy-makers to assume that individuals would not learn from their mistakes, and that they could be tricked – especially that they would always confuse money with value. As soon as people cottoned on to that, they rejected this patronizing, elitist view. Where the advocates of floating went wrong was in predicting that exchange rates would adjust smoothly to inflation differentials, that there would be less scope for currencies to become grossly undervalued or overvalued, the capital flows would be equilibrating, and that they would enable countries to follow independent monetary policies – and all of this would lead to a more harmonious international monetary system.

With the advent of floating rates, the IMF could no longer act as arbiter of exchange rates and guardian of sensible monetary policies. The floating regime did not bring monetary policy independence, but it did seem to bring independence from the IMF. This was recognized in the Second Amendment to the Articles which came into force in 1978 and allowed a country to choose any exchange rate regime it wished, except a link to gold.[2] This sense of an international community helping each country to follow good economic policies dissipated.

The negative aspects of the transition started to become more prominent. Even as the markets themselves became global, they seemed less able to perform their function of channelling financial flows towards socially beneficial ends. Countries started to export their problems.

Increasingly, if not deliberately, governments adopted a narrow interpretation of their interests – one often driven by the exigiencies of the
electoral cycle. Bankers were influenced by this mood. The excesses of
markets went unchecked, and as mentioned in Chapter 2 governments
also benefited from new borrowing opportunities.

Mad money

The world then entered a decade of unprecedented inflationary excesses
in the major industrial countries, record peacetime inflation and an
international borrowing spree by developing countries – all of which
ended in tears (see Pringle, 1977, for a contemporary polemic). This
was a period without a monetary standard – there was no consistently observed criterion to guide monetary policy choices (which
authors such as Mason, 1963, view as the defining characteristic of a
monetary standard). The new era started in June 1972 when Britain
floated the pound, followed in March 1973 by joint floating of six EC
currencies (Germany, France, Belgium, the Netherlands, Denmark and
Luxembourg).[3] Immediately, constraints on monetary and economic
policy that had been built into the fixed rate system were dissolved.
Countries would have to exercise self-restraint, but just when self-
discipline was needed, along came the oil shock, in the last quarter
of 1973, involving steep and sudden increases in the oil price, large
increases in the cost of living and massive payments imbalances. This
made it extremely difficult to sell the need for restraint to politicians
or the general public. They could now do what they liked! UK inflation
soared to an annual rate of 25 per cent in 1975.

Very quickly, there was a real danger of competitive depreciations and
trade restrictions. IMF managing director Johannes Witteveen proposed
an 'oil facility' where, in effect, countries receiving large windfall gains
would recycle these, through the Fund, to countries experiencing a
sudden deterioration in their payments. This proposal was supported
at a meeting of the Committee of Twenty in Rome in January 1974. The
only condition on use of the facility was that countries should avoid
recourse to restrictions on imports or on payments. This was a valiant
attempt to resist the forces of economic and monetary nationalism.[4]
But the mood music had changed. The idea of a partnership between
the Fund, representing the community of nations, and a member state
in difficulty, had given way to a confrontational atmosphere. The Fund
was coming to be seen as just another source of financing. In fact, the
standby agreements with Britain and Italy concluded in early 1977 were

to be the last such agreements between the Fund and developed country members for many years. Worse was to follow. The Fund's treatment of Asian countries after the collapse of the bubble of the mid 1990s confirmed their view of the Fund as an enemy, to be shunned at all costs. It was a club no more.

When in 1978 a new oil price increase contributed to another wave of inflationary pressures in the world economy, again, the question was, 'to finance or to adjust?' By this time, because of the 'recycling' of oil money to countries in deficit, the aggregate debts of non-oil developing countries and debt service ratios were far higher than during the first oil shock. Concerned about the build-up of debt, banks confined their lending increasingly to short-term maturities. Ideologically, this period also marked the end of the 'high' Keynesian era. Countries had learnt from the mistakes they had made in the first oil shock. They started to cut back on borrowing and on monetary growth. Nevertheless, there were enough new players coming into the banking system, enough liquidity from the Fed and enough optimism in the markets about the prospects for developing countries, to support an unwise increase in indebtedness. The first great bubble of the flexible exchange rate era, fuelled by cross-border flows and financial innovation, was about to burst.

It was easy, with the benefit of hindsight, to label this lending and borrowing as unwise. Yet, in the circumstances of the time, it was well-nigh impossible for developed country governments, or bankers, to say 'no'. The concern was rather how to ensure smooth adjustment and further financing. Indeed, the question discussed by the economic commentariat was this: could banks make *sufficient* funds available for oil-importing countries? The feeling was that, in the new world of markets, if market forces could deal with a challenge, they should be allowed to. So, let the markets take care of the problem.[5] However, under floating rates and with capital mobility, they couldn't.

Paul Volcker's historic change in monetary policy in October 1979, shortly after he became chairman of the Federal Reserve, was designed to halt the inflationary process that had taken hold in the US. Interest rates would be allowed to rise to whatever level would be needed to enable the central bank to regain control of the money supply. It was a turning point in twentieth-century history and arguably saved capitalism. But, like Nixon's closing of the gold window and imposition of US tariffs on imports eight years before, it was, and indeed had to be, an exercise in monetary unilateralism – one country acting alone, no matter what the implications for others, and no consultation.

It came after the system had become unstable as a result of the advent of floating in 1973 and the inflationary madness that followed it. It was unexpected. It represented a lurch from permissiveness to discipline, desperately necessary, but highly damaging to the governments and their creditor banks that had made plans on different assumptions. The debt-financed growth they had enjoyed or financed turned out to be built on sand. It was an early example of the way that the absence of an international system led participants in markets into a trap – and it took them ten years to get out of it.

It was the monetary regime that caused the threat to the world's banking system and the lost decade of growth in Latin America. Even with the benefit of hindsight, would it really have been preferable for the countries to have refrained from increasing their overall indebtedness in the late 1970s and early 1980s in the face of the oil shocks? That would have involved an abrupt forced adjustment of their economies and dreaded deflation. Then, as now, everybody wanted to avoid that, and the discussion at the time was on finding ways to help countries borrow more. Thus, given the circumstances of the time, over-borrowing and default were unavoidable. The causes of the debt problem of the 1980s were credit expansion and financial innovation of the 1970s – the huge rise in bank lending to developing countries following the success of the syndicated loan model of bank lending – together with a long period of easy money from the Federal Reserve. The US followed policies it had to for domestic reasons, ignoring the effects on the outside world and – because of interdependence – on itself. But that was precisely the nature of the trap. The sub-prime property bubble more than 30 years later was fuelled by exactly the same mix: financial innovation and huge cross-border flows on the back of easy credit. The money trap opened – and again everybody fell in.

But what subsequent volatility showed was that the instability of the 1970s and 1980s was not simply part of a process of learning to live with a new exchange rate regime. It was an inherent feature of such a regime. (See also Chapter 11 on how flexible exchange rates and capital mobility produced successive waves of asset price bubbles from the 1970s through to 2007.)

Monetary policy lessons learnt?

After a fitful attempt at policy coordination in the late 1980s (the so-called Plaza and Louvre Accords) ended in recriminations, and following the debacle of Europe's exchange rate mechanism (with sterling being pushed out in September 1992 and the whole system collapsing in July 1993), a new generation of independent-minded central bankers decided to focus on something they could achieve, or thought they could: domestic price stability. That was naturally flanked by a renewed focus on domestic aims and the domestic economy. Indeed, in pursuit of their aims, international policy coordination could easily be an obstacle rather than a help.

In theory, under flexible rates adjustment of different countries' payments positions and levels of inflation should occur naturally through changes in relative currency values in the markets. No committees of officials or central bankers would be needed. In this market regime, countries could choose what combination of exchange rate stability and independent monetary policy suited them best; if they wanted their currency to hold its value close to that of another (as, for instance, the French authorities wished in the ten years to 1995 to keep the franc closely aligned with the D-mark), that was their choice – a decision that set narrow limits to their monetary policy. In practice, however, the interaction of politics and markets didn't work in a way that allowed monetary policy-makers such freedom of choice; and what they got was a succession of booms and busts.

For example, look what happened after Deng Xiaoping's sweeping economic reforms in China in the 1980s, the fall of communist regimes in Eastern Europe in 1989–90, the dissolution of the former USSR and its replacement by 14 independent successor countries. Commentators heralded a new age of triumphant global capitalism. Yet in practice virtually all former communist countries promptly fell into the trap of monetary nationalism, descending into hyper-inflation – a disastrous experience that would sour these people's attitudes towards capitalism for a long time. The IMF could do nothing effective to help. (Luckily, China itself, whose people had traumatic memories of the hyperinflation following the Second World War, kept credit under strict control and from 1994–2005 wisely kept a fixed exchange rate to the US dollar.)

A new monetary standard of a sort did develop. Under pressure of public opinion, governments changed tack. This began a hopeful period, leading some to believe that national monetary sovereignty was compatible with economic integration. Throughout the world, governments in the new market environment became conscious of the need to gain credibility for their monetary policies. One such means, pioneered by the New Zealand government in the early 1990s, was to grant greater independence to a central bank and charge it with the task of reducing or eliminating inflation. Large hopes were placed on it and it accorded well with developments in monetary theory. The prestige and successful record of the independent Bundesbank was a background influence and it was given real muscle during the planning for European Monetary Union. As outlined by the Delors Committee and subsequently developed by European Central Bank governors into the statutes of the European Central Bank, this required all countries that wished to enter the final stages of EMU to grant full autonomy to their central banks.

Disillusion – and despair?

Following the breaking of the dollar's link to gold, the international community needed to find a framework – above all, a monetary standard. But few people were aware of the necessary connection between a viable international order and achievement of their domestic objectives. Keynes himself, while being a champion of active monetary policies, would surely have seen through the illusion that floating exchange rates would allow each country on its own to achieve these objectives for itself, even given the right domestic policy framework, such as central bank independence. The experience of monetary experiments in the period from 1973 to 2007 should have persuaded impartial observers of the falsity of this illusion. Meanwhile, the influence of private sector institutions on public policy grew, and as banks developed many new financial instruments, especially derivatives, they could feed the growth of a shadow banking system largely obscured from the view of regulators. Banks stepped up investment in lobbying activities.

Luckily, the global economy was at the time, for various deep-seated reasons, growing on average at such a healthy rate that (given sufficient time) it was able, following the regular booms and busts, to refloat the financial sector. But the recovery after each collapse required more and more state support. Official policy was always to support the banks when they were threatened; few noticed how banks' behaviour changed when they understood that they could rely on such a safety net. The market came to count on the state, not for a stable framework as under the Keynesian Bretton Woods period, but for direct support. Governments were quick to issue guarantees against risks and it is true that there is a role for governments to help in reducing risks and protecting their economies from instability. Stable monetary policies, well-capitalized banks, relatively low household debt and loan-to-deposit ratios and a cushion of foreign reserves can, given the appropriate set of international rules, provide a degree of protection.[6] But even then they had limits: low and stable inflation was not itself a guarantee of protection. Yet, instead of doing that, governments increasingly resorted to the worst way of managing risk – by providing blanket guarantees to commercial intermediaries. Finance ministers were aware such guarantees were foolhardy and courted further catastrophes, but saw no option. That is how they too were driven into the money trap.

At the end of this period, which we have portrayed as one of monetary experimentation, yet another experiment was about to begin – CBI+IT+MPT (Central Bank Independence, Inflation Targeting and Macro-Prudential Toolkit). But the banking system of the West was badly damaged, and the fabric of international cooperation was under enormous strain. To quote the distinguished economist, Axel Leijonhufvud,

> No big exogenous shock set the current crisis in motion. What this almost certainly means is that the occurrence of crises is an endogenous property of the world financial system as we have let it evolve over the last twenty-some years. (Leijonhufvud, 2007)

Leijonhufvud added that the experience would doubtless induce some regulatory changes: 'But it is safe to assume that they will be of marginal significance – which means that we have other crises coming down the pike towards us.' How right he was.

Part I of this study has shown how the GFS functioned under two classical international monetary standards and how it deteriorated when there was no such standard. It showed also how the behaviour of public authorities as well as private banks and other agents changed so as to produce growing financial instability. Part II describes how governments started a search for a better world and assesses the results.

Notes

1. Excluding the large part of the world that was at the time under various forms of communist or socialist rule, notably the former USSR, Eastern Europe and China.
2. The asset that had served as the universal anchor for currencies and for the monetary system since the Industrial Revolution was banned, mainly because of political pressure from the US.
3. Further moves within the European Community to create another managed or fixed rate system are discussed in Chapter 6.

4. Thirty-eight years later, Johannes Witteveen suggested a similar scheme to help solve the crisis in the eurozone economies, and IMF resources were greatly increased to put it in a position to help struggling euro area economies: 'In my time as managing director of the IMF (1973–78), we successfully created an "oil facility" in 1973 to overcome the Opec surplus problem and resulting deficit problems. We also created a "supplementary facility" in 1977 that proved crucial to our response to the Latin American debt crisis. Why not now create a new "debt facility" to give struggling sovereigns headroom to work out their borrowing issues?' See *Financial Times*, 22 August 2011.
5. This was, after all, the start of the Thatcher-Reagan duumvirate – Thatcher being elected Prime Minister of the UK in May 1979 and Reagan President of the US in November 1980.
6. See *Weathering the Financial Crisis: Good Policy Or Good Luck?* By Stephen Cecchetti, Michael R. King and James Yetman, BIS Working Papers No. 351, August 2011.

Bibliography

Bagehot, Walter, *Lombard Street: A Description of the Money Market*, first published 1873; new edition with an introduction by Hartley Withers, Smith, Elder & Co, 1912; online source: Johnstone and Hartley Withers (eds), London, Henry S. King and Co. Comments include editorial notes and appendices from the 12th (1906) and the 14th (1915) editions, see www.econlib.org

Boughton, James M., 'Jacques J. Polak and the Evolution of the International Monetary System', *IMF Economic Review* Vol. 59, 379 –99, June 2011.

Capie, Forrest, *The Bank of England: 1950s to 1979*, Cambridge University Press, 2010.

Cecchetti, Stephen , Michael R. King and James Yetman, *Weathering the Financial Crisis: Good Policy Or Good Luck?* BIS Working Papers No. 351, August 2011.

de Vries, Margaret Garritsen, *Balance of Payments Adjustment, 1945 to 1986: The IMF Experience*, IMF, 1987.

Finch, C. David, *The IMF: The Record and the Prospect*, Issues 175–78, International Finance Section, Dept. of Economics, Princeton University, 1989.

Gardner, Richard N., *Sterling-Dollar Diplomacy: The Origins and the Prospects of Our International Economic Order*, McGraw-Hill, 1969.

Hogan, Michael J., *The Marshall Plan: America, Britain and the Reconstruction of Western Europe, 1947–1952*, Cambridge University Press, 1987.

Leijonhufvud, Axel, 'Bubble, bubble, toil and trouble', Vox EU, September 2001.

Mason Will E., *Clarification of the Monetary Standard*, The Pennsylvania State university Press, 1963.

Morse, Jeremy, 'Address', dated 7 June1974, *Finance and Development*, IMF, September 1974.

Pringle, Robert, *The Growth Merchants: Economic Consequences of Wishful Thinking*, Centre for Policy Studies, 1977.

Pringle, Robert and Martina Horakova (eds), *The Central Bank Directory*, Central Banking Publications, 2011.

Proposals for an International Clearing Union, HMSO, Cmnd 6437, April 1943.

Solomon, Robert, *The International Monetary System 1945–1981*, Harper & Row, 1982.

Part II
Searching for Ways Out

5
Improving National Policies

In an implicit acknowledgement that governments were indeed in a trap, a search for alternative policy models and structures had already got underway. A variety of remedies were applied at national, regional and international levels. Here we outline options available to governments at the national level, some of which were being tried out in practice.

Introduction

Because of the faults of the GFS, nations and regions had to fend for themselves and had to make do with second- or third-best solutions while maintaining the level of cooperation required to achieve these limited, and mainly defensive, aims. How successfully they did this would determine the fate of the economy in a possibly prolonged and turbulent period of transition.

At the level of day-to-day monetary policy, policy-makers were clearly in the money trap. This was illustrated by the dilemmas facing the Bank of England's monetary policy committee (MPC). The consumer price index of inflation rose to 3 per cent in December 2006, and stayed above the government-set target of 2 per cent for the next four years (with two temporary dips back down to 2 per cent); equally consistently, the MPC projected that it would fall to within its target range in the future. Yet in 2011 it rose well above 5 per cent, though it was expected to fall through 2012 and into 2013 as the effect of temporary factors raising it waned and 'downward pressure from slack in the labour market persists'.[1]

So for a full five years, the MPC, which had been set up to represent society's interest in ensuring low inflation, had felt unable to raise rates even though inflation remained significantly above target. Indeed, the MPC repeatedly took action intended to *boost* demand. Granted, the period had witnessed the worst recession for 70 years and the near collapse of Britain's banking system. Decent men and women, charged with keeping inflation within target, could not be expected to take action to fulfill their mandate at the cost of worsening real economic activity in such circumstances. Nevertheless, it was no good pretending the policy-making model was working fine: in this case, it was not the MPC that was at fault, but its beguiling model.

This underlined one of the problems that continually recurred under inflation targeting – a difficulty facing any regime of monetary activism; it forced a central bank to take risks either with inflation (and its credibility) on the one hand or with the real economy (and its independence) on the other. Even if central bankers preferred not to see the situation in that light, other people did. Either way, they were continually at risk of undermining the credibility of their strategy. Again, the markets seemed to take a mischievous delight in destroying one monetary policy regime after another. This is what it meant to be in the money trap.

Leading options

Below is a list of policy options open to national governments looking for ways of improving national policy management. All except the last are changes that they could make on their own volition, without needing international agreements. Broadly, the options can be ranked in terms of the degree of discretion each afforded to national policy makers/central banks to pursue independent monetary policies, starting with the option allowing most discretion. The first four would involve changing the mandate and operating procedures of central banks in more or less radical ways; the last four would involve the abolition of the central bank as a discretionary policy-making body.

1. Add financial stability duties with minimal change to monetary policy framework.
2. IT-plus: integrate financial stability into the monetary policy framework itself.
3. Target nominal GDP.
4. Target broad money.
5. Target base money.
6. Align your currency with that of another currency.
7. Fix the exchange rate or adopt a currency board system.
8. Join a currency union.

Among practical central bankers, only the first two approaches were under serious discussion. The first one involved no change in the monetary policy framework strictly speaking – that is, policies to ensure financial stability would be added to the central bank's responsibilities but would involve different instruments and methods that would not impinge on monetary policy-making at all, or only in a minor way. This seemed to be the approach favoured by the Bank of England, the Fed and Sweden's central bank among others. These central banks looked not to monetary policy but rather to new policy tools to assure financial stability, such as changing leverage, liquidity or capital requirements. They wanted to keep the interest rate weapon exclusively to ensure price stability, a view that at least recognized the prime importance of having a monetary rule.

Yet in practice not only had many central bankers come to the view that monetary policy needed to look beyond horizons of one to two years and pay greater attention to asset prices and the balance of risks to the outlook; in reality this was no more than a recognition of what they had already been doing. Central banks had been pursuing objectives other than price stability in their efforts to revive economic activity, build confidence in financial system, stop a collapse of credit and encourage lending to small- and medium-sized enterprises. The longer the recovery from GFC remained weak, the less relevant the existing inflation targeting framework appeared.

But the biggest objections to the first option were deeper. First, as economists such as Otmar Issing (2008), former chief economist of the ECB, often pointed out, inflation-targeting regimes usually excluded any systematic role for money and credit. This was ironic, as both the Fed and the Bank of England had resorted to policies that relied entirely on boosting money supplies for their effect. Secondly, it was clear that excessive expansion of money and credit had played a role in the boom that preceded the bust of 2007–08. If economists such as Claudio Borio of the Bank for International Settlements (BIS) were right to say that 'the boom did not just precede but *caused* the subsequent bust'[2] was it right for pure inflation-targeting central banks to persist in their old monetary ways? Thirdly, such an approach continued to leave national monetary conditions at the mercy of international conditions. Exchange rates could be dominated by capital flows, moving far out of line with the needs of the domestic economy.

Thus there were examples both of excessive devaluation putting upward pressure on domestic prices and costs – and therefore threatening the credibility of the regime – and of excessive appreciation as demonstrated by the case of Switzerland, which in summer of 2011 was forced to peg to the euro in a desperate effort to cap the relentless appreciation of the Swiss franc and the threat to its export and economic competitiveness.

Problems with IT-plus as the leading option

The second of the two leading candidates to replace old-fashioned inflation-targeting was what we call 'inflation-targeting plus' (IT-plus). Under such a regime, central banks would keep the inflation-targeting framework to set a ceiling on inflation but explicitly make room to allow for a tightening if there were signs of an asset boom or other dangerous imbalances – even if inflation were low and stable. This would in theory allow central banks, in that irritating phrase, to 'lean against' the build-up of imbalances, if necessary by raising interest rates when the forward indicators pointed to the need to do so. They would supplement this with use of macro-prudential policy tools.

To support this point of view, central bankers cited research suggesting that it was possible to construct indicators of incipient asset booms that would predict financial crises, economic weakness and disinflation over horizons that varied between two and four years ahead.[3] These forward indicators were based on deviations of credit trends and asset prices from historical averages.[4] Some economists argued that asset markets can indeed be valued objectively, allowing policy-makers to nip a boom in the bud before it became dangerous.[5] Economists pointed to many indicators that, it seemed, would enable policy-makers to spot imbalances.[6]

But if the authorities raised interest rates in a bid to curb an asset boom, that action might in reality do more to restrict real output than to curb the rise in the prices of assets. It was indeed this fear that had often stopped policy-makers from intervening to stop booms in the past, notably in the years preceding the great stock market crash of 1929 and again in the boom in 2002–07 that preceded GFC. Then there was the unpredictable effect that such action might have under a floating exchange rate regime on the country's exchange rate. Raising interest rates could easily lead to a rise in the exchange rate, as funds were drawn from overseas, attracting an inflow of 'hot money', which could flow out again when confidence or asset prices fell, causing further complications for policy-makers.[7]

This approach also seemed politically naive. Would governments sit idly by while central bankers stopped an economic upswing in its tracks just because they wanted to play safe – whenever they detected faint signs of a boom? Surely politicians would in practice be unlikely to give central bankers carte blanche to follow such unpopular policies.

In sum, 'inflation-targeting plus', where the control of inflation could be overridden by other objectives, would surely be a weak and unreliable framework, at a time when markets urgently needed clear, robust rules. It would suffer from an inherent credibility deficit. Inflation-targeting can only build credibility if the central bank selects targets it can hit, and then succeeds in its aim. The independence of the central bank would be brought into question, as policy would inevitably be subject to intervention by governments – understandably so. Allowing central bankers the operational independence needed to keep a lid on inflation was one thing; giving them *carte blanche* to intervene in banking, stock markets, currency markets and the property markets even when inflation was under control – just because they thought they could spot some early signs of a boom – would be quite another. Moreover, under such a regime, policy-makers would also be vulnerable to lobbying by vested interests, such as the finance industry, consumer groups and industrialists.

The inflation-targeting regime which this proposal would modify was more than just one operating framework among others. It provided the system's key price rule.[8] Tampering with it would undermine the only monetary rule – the only putative monetary standard – the central banks had come up with to replace the discipline of the international dollar-gold standard under Bretton Woods and previously the gold standard.[9]

Target nominal GDP

The notion that monetary policy should aim to ensure steady growth in domestic output, measured in current prices, was first put forward during the 1970s and enjoyed a renaissance after GFC. Some economists believed that if a regime of targeting nominal GDP growth had been in place in 2008, at the height of the financial crisis, both the US and UK would have embarked more quickly on stimulatory monetary policies. After Lehman Brothers collapsed, the Federal Reserve elected to hold rates at 2 per cent, whereas they should have cut rates and started on more direct measures to boost the money supply. Fed policy was much tighter than the Fed thought at the time – you have to look only at the sharp rise in the dollar and fall in the dollar price of gold in the third quarter of 2008. But the Fed had its eyes focused on the rate of increase of consumer prices, rather than the expected course of output, which was already in the midst of a precipitous fall. Equally, in the build-up to GFC, the Fed might not have panicked at the fear of deflation in 2002, after the collapse of the dot.com bubble, if it had targeted nominal GDP; as real growth continued to sustain nominal growth figures, adjusting monetary policy to nominal growth would have indicated that there was no need to cut interest rates in an attempt to get prices back up to the implicit 2 per cent target. They might not have held interest rates so low for so long in 2002–06, during which years the asset boom and other ingredients of the 2007–10 crisis, especially leverage of financial firms, increased markedly.[10]

Communication of policy-makers' intentions to the public might be easier under a nominal GDP framework. It was odd when in 2010–11 central bankers were reduced to arguing that they had to try to raise inflation; after all the sermons about the evils of inflation, what was the public to make of it? Nominal GDP targeting would not require central bankers to make estimates of the extent of the output gap – the gap between actual and potential output – which proved to be one of the most difficult aspects of practical policy-making under inflation-targeting. If central banks targeted monetary policy in an attempt to meet a certain level of GDP, then the private sector might behave in a way that helped achieve these goals – it would tend to increase spending when demand fell below target as there would be an expect-ation that the authorities would in any case act to lower interest rates. GDP targeting might also offer a way out of the liquidity trap, when a central bank cannot cut nominal rates further because they are already close to zero. If growth and inflation fell below target, and markets assumed the central bank would act to maintain nominal growth, long-term rates would automatically fall.

Problem solved? Unfortunately not. This option was vulnerable to many of the same objections as the first one discussed above. It also relied on central bankers and official regulators using the wide degree of discretion afforded them wisely, resisting inevitable political pres-sures to turn a blind eye to the next mini-boom and generally behaving in a saintly way. But even if we had such saintly and sturdily indepen-dent guardians, the cards would be stacked against them because of the implications of financial and economic interdependence. Because each country or region would continue to decide its monetary and economic policy for itself – and because its policy stance in the absence of an international standard would be determined by domestic factors above all – capital flows and exchange rates would remain volatile. Because of interdependence, efforts to tighten monetary policy would be offset by capital inflows. Also, forecasts of GDP would remain highly uncertain, leaving too much room to discretion. For example, in the autumn of 2008, forecasts of GDP did not immediately decline. Such forecasts would always take time to produce and digest, and when policy is in crisis mode, with day-to-day decisions of vital importance having to be decided in the heat of the banking panic, it is hard to believe that shifting the target of monetary policy from inflation (with discretion) to GNP targeting (with further use of discretion needed because of the uncertainty of past estimates of GDP let alone forecasts) would make much difference.

Critics of GDP targeting also pointed out the risks involved in relying on a single instrument, the interest rate, which affected different elements in the economy at different times, with unknown and variable time lags. To raise interest rates in response, for example, to a rise in incomes due to a credit bubble might cause real output to decline much more quickly than the underlying rate of inflation, so that policy would be unstable. Inflation indicators were more up to date and reliable than estimates and forecasts of nominal GDP, although central banks' forecasts of inflation two years ahead have also frequently proved wide of the mark. Altogether, nominal GDP targeting could not offer a firm platform for policy-makers.

Target broad money

The 'broad money' school had its greatest influence in the great battle against inflation during late 1970s and early 1980s, but still had its supporters a generation later. Some advocates of targeting broad money held that it should be the key target for monetary policy as it was the main determinant of nominal national income in the long run. A milder version held that empirical data showed there was merely a close association between broad money movements and inflation over the long run (without necessarily insisting that changes in money 'cause' changes in activity). Other economists of a monetarist persuasion remained eclectic. Many favoured looking at all monetary aggregates, analysing the reasons for the growth in any specific aggregate and obtaining what information one could from it. Thus when the newly appointed management of the European Central Bank was deciding on its monetary policy strategy in 1999, it found that narrow monetary aggregates (currency in circulation and overnight deposits) had the best correlation with economic activity, but nevertheless decided to make broad money aggregate (M3) the focus of the so-called monetary pillar and the one supposed to provide an anchor for prices (using it to set what they called a 'reference value'). They argued that this approach clarified the responsibility of the central bank for determining the monetary 'impulses' to inflation.[11] Significantly, however, the ECB stopped short of setting a monetary objective as such, because of the difficulties that the Bundesbank (their model in these matters) had had in following such an objective and in communicating its policy to markets, the media and the public.

Those who believed that money *causes* changes in national income and prices claimed that the basic mechanism involved was simple enough: if the supply of money exceeded demand, households and companies would find they had excess money balances in relation to their holding of other assets. They would tend to reduce them by spending more – on investment and/or consumption, and possibly also by buying longer-term and less liquid financial assets. If the demand for money exceeded growth in supply, they would find that their holdings of money were below what they felt comfortable with, and reduce their spending. Proponents of broad money dismissed monetary base targeting on the grounds that the base was too small a fraction of the money supply to motivate decisions to spend or save.

However, there were reasons to be sceptical. While monetary variables were important (even causative) factors in the movement of prices and should be monitored by the central bank, both the demand and supply of broad money were subject to unpredictable influences, making it unwise to use it as the fulcrum of policy.[12] Financial innovation led to the creation of large 'money-like' liabilities and assets that were not counted in official measures of the money supply; and history was one of more or less continuous innovation – indeed, the growth of a large shadow banking sector was one of the features of GFC. (Many predicted that owing to the increase in regulation, and resulting incentives to avoidance, it may be an even larger feature of the next boom and bust.)

Notoriously, it was the unreliability of the link between broad money and demand that led the UK to abandon monetary targeting in the 1980s. Year after year, growth in broad money was rapid, but year after year inflation remained subdued. Easier access to bank credit led to rapid monetary growth (lending creates deposits) but there was no evidence of higher inflation for some years – it may have been concealed, rather in the way that happened in the 2000s. As Gerald Bouey, former governor of the Bank of Canada, put it, 'We didn't abandon monetary targets;

they abandoned us.' Thus even policy-makers sympathetic to a monetarist approach, while continuing to pay attention to money supply
statistics, concluded that they should not be taken at face value. You
had to go behind the statistics and examine why demand for money
balances by different sectors of the economy might change. All this
took the discussion a long way from the simple mantra of monetarists
to 'control monetary growth'. Again, a large dollop of discretion was
likely to be unavoidable. That was its Achilles heel.

Monetary base control

Free market economists would generally prefer policy regimes that
required policy-makers to follow rules rather than giving them scope
to use their discretion. This preference was based on their general political philosophy – for a society based on laws and distrust of arbitrary
power[13] – but also it reflected their observation that discretion had often
been abused by monetary policy-makers (as described in Chapter 4),
and was easily subject to political manipulation. As a result, discretionary policies tended to have an inflationary bias. But such economists
often disagreed about the nature of the rules that should be followed.
Even within the monetarist camp, which embraced those who believed
that the money supply had an important role in determining nominal
national income and the price level, there were strong disagreements
about which monetary aggregate mattered most and which to target.

Some pinned their hopes on a rule that would bind the authorities
to target the monetary base, otherwise known as high powered money
(or M0). Monetary base comprises banknotes in circulation plus bank
reserves, that is, cash in bank vaults plus deposits with the central bank.
It is the purest form of money under a fiat money regime, the most
liquid part of the money supply, and is always acceptable in final settlement of debts. It is also the only part of the money supply that is, in
principle, fully under the control of the authorities – though, as we shall
see, central bankers insist that in practice it is not.

This approach traces its origins back to the gold standard, when
gold was the monetary base.[14] Fractional reserve banking, where banks
can extend credit to a multiple of their reserves, developed under the
gold standard (Keynes's 'turning a stone into bread' again – see note
1 to Chapter 3). Banks found by experience that they had to keep a
certain fraction of their deposits in reserve in the form of gold so that
they could at all times be ready to pay gold on demand. Gold was the
ultimate regulator of the system; when the general level of prices was

low, gold was scarce, and this encouraged mining of new gold, bringing of gold out of private hoards and an expansion of the monetary base. Under monetary base control without gold, rules would be mandated that mimicked the operation of the gold standard – thus, for example, the monetary authority could be required to produce a given average annual increase in the monetary base.

A system similar to this has been tried from time to time.[15] In the US, it was used by the Federal Reserve under Paul Volcker in 1979–82 to break the back of inflation by allowing a sufficient rise in interest rates. In Germany, a version of it was practised by the Bundesbank for around 15 years from 1973, producing an enviable combination of low inflation without a property or asset price boom. In Switzerland it also met with some success, though the Swiss illustrated the difficulties of this approach to monetary policy encounters in small open economies. (In practice these regimes often targeted what is called narrow money, but this had a close correlation with the monetary base.)[16]

Under a monetary base system, the central bank ensures that the monetary base grows in the long term at a rate consistent with the growth of the economy's productive potential, plus an allowance for a low or zero inflation rate. In practice, the central bank would target bank reserves at the central bank, that is, the reserve component of the monetary base, adjusting this to take account of any shifts in holdings of notes and coin by the public. The central bank can change the quantity of reserves it supplies to the banking system through a combination of open market operations and other operations in government bonds, but also possibly in other assets.

Only possible for some?

Narrow money targeting works best where banks have to keep quite large reserve requirements with the central bank (say 10 per cent of bank deposits and other short-term liabilities outstanding). If the reserve requirements are fixed at a low level and applied only to a narrow range of monetary-type instruments, then changes in demand for reserves might be dominated by random movements rather than underlying changes in demand.

It would be essential that political circumstances allowed monetary policy-makers to take a long-term perspective, possibly involving a period of several years of falling prices and rising unemployment. Only if a country can summon up the political will to sit through such periods can this route offer a solution to the conundrum. Many commentators ruled it out on such grounds, quite apart from theoretical reservations. But historically, as under the gold standard, cyclicality of the price level has helped stabilize activity in the long term. If households and businesses see a dip in prices in a recession, but expect prices to rebound further ahead, then they are likely to boost spending in the present. The system relies on built-in incentives, rather than government activism, to act as stabilizers. These, over time, should spur recovery and lead to growth of bank lending and the acquisition of other assets by banks and thus to a recovery in the broad money supply. Again, one had to remember that the monetary policies tried in the past 40 years repeatedly produced crippling booms and busts that resulted in depression and high unemployment.

The main difficulty of monetary base control was different. It would really not be possible for such a system to be adopted one country at a time – unless that country was very large. Like the gold standard, from which it is derived, it should be a universal standard. Otherwise a country (or countries) following such a rule would be swamped by the monetary spillovers from larger countries following normal central bank discretionary policies. As Switzerland found in 2011, a smaller country following prudent monetary policies with a floating exchange rate could easily find itself overwhelmed by monetary excesses emanating from the volatile monetary policies of central banks of the large currency blocs. So the real question was whether such a monetary regime might in time be adopted by one of the two big currency areas: the US or euro area. If adopted, such a regime would give a competitive advantage to the bloc concerned, encouraging investment because of the new credibility of its policies, and this might induce others to follow.

Fix the exchange rate to another currency

The final options open to individual countries all involved a large sacrifice of (presumed) monetary autonomy and discretion. But the evidence suggested that many countries were willing to trade these for greater stability of the exchange rate.

At a time when the world's monetary arrangements were dominated by the dollar and euro, these major currency areas exercised a gravitational pull on other currencies. Small, open economies naturally tended to orient their exchange rates to one or another of these large blocs. This could involve either fixing the exchange rate against, or 'shadowing', one of these. This involved following the monetary policies and inflation rate of the centre country or managing the exchange rate against a basket of currencies. Most baskets had large weights for the dollar and the euro.

A good illustration of the gravitational pull of the major currencies was given in Steve Hanke's account of China's experiments with various exchange rate regimes since Deng Xiaoping's opening up of China from 1978 onwards:

> Since China embraced Deng Xiaoping's reforms on 22 December 1978, China has experimented with different exchange-rate regimes. Until 1994, the renminbi was in an ever-depreciating phase against the U.S. dollar. Relatively volatile readings for China's GDP growth and inflation rate were encountered during this phase. After the maxi renminbi depreciation of 1994 and until 2005, exchange-rate fixity was the order of the day, with little movement in the RMB/USD rate. In consequence, the volatility of China's GDP and inflation rate declined, and with the renminbi firmly anchored to the U.S. dollar, China's inflation rates began to shadow those in America. Then, China entered a gradual renminbi appreciation phase (when the RMB/ USD rate declined in the 2005–08 period). Without a firm dollar anchor, China's inflation rate picked up, relative to the U.S. inflation rate. And, yes, the volatility of China's GDP picked up ... '[17]

Currency boards would guarantee that the market value of the currency they created and issued was equal to its fixed posted value, which would be an exchange rate for some other currency. The required supply of such currencies would be regulated by the market via the central bank's commitment to buy and sell its currency for the foreign anchor currency at the fixed posted price.

Some economists believed that the only way forward was to make the US dollar once again the pivot of the system. One way to achieve this would be for the US to take into account feedback from the rest of the world in setting monetary policy. (These options are examined in Part IV.)

Under floating exchange rates, strict and sustained monetary control was difficult to achieve for any but large, developed economies. The institutional requirements – including central bank independence and developed foreign exchange markets – were demanding. Even for large developed economkes, exchange rate volatility frequently complicated economic management. When speculators were willing to exploit interest differentials and exchange rate trends in the short term – while ignoring longer-term risks – their investment flows added to the volatility of the foreign exchange markets. For example, after 2000, because of zero interest rates and a weakening yen, financial capital poured out of Japan into a variety of neighbouring countries. But when the credit crunch of 2008 arrived, Japanese speculators could not renew their yen credits in Tokyo and had to sell foreign exchange assets to get back into yen, so the yen shot up in the foreign exchange markets. The same switchback experience was suffered by many 'smaller' currencies.

Central banks run out of options

Before GFC there was a widespread assumption that if central banks stabilized inflation in the short term, and financial regulators did their job properly, the economy and the financial system would broadly take care of themselves. Indeed, with the credibility of the policy regime assumed to be established, central bankers were ready to take risks with inflation to counter incipient deflationary tendencies. Thus in 2002–07 monetary authorities, scared of deflation, were willing to take the risk that their ultra-loose policies might encourage aggressive risk-taking, increased leverage and stretched private-sector balance sheets. They let real interest rates fall to extremely low and sometimes negative levels – the lowest since the 1970s – further encouraging over-borrowing and lending. This relaxed approach plainly did not succeed in the long run; indeed, temporary success seduced policy-makers into actions that had the long-term effect of worsening the eventual crisis and bringing about the near-collapse of the financial system. Yet it seemed unavoidable at the time. That, again, was the money trap.

If the approach to monetary policy during the boom did indeed not merely precede but caused the near collapse of the world's financial system in 2008, one would have surely expected that the intellectual approach and operating framework that guided policy-making during that period should at least be questioned.[18] After all, it was the central bankers of the US, Euro area and UK who were in charge of policy as we all marched over the cliff. Not a bit of it. They showed no inclination at all to trade it in for a new model. They successfully pinned the blame on such factors as China's payments surpluses, lax bank regulation and poor risk management by the private sector. In fact, governments not only turned a blind eye to central banks' roles in these disasters, but showed how much they loved them by giving them lots of shiny new policy tools to play with.

Central bankers debated how to use them. Some wanted to keep their interest-rate weapon for use only in the pursuit of price stability, sharpening their new tools to fight the war on financial instability. Indeed, defenders of inflation targeting such as Lars Svensson, deputy governor of Sweden's central bank, were quick to see the risks of confusing policy both at the theoretical and practical levels (Svensson, 2011; 2012).[19] Others were not so sure, and said they would *normally* keep interest-rate policy to price stability objectives but, *in certain perhaps undefined circumstances*, might have to use it for financial stability objectives. Normally, they pointed out, the policy settings designed to achieve each of these objectives would point in the same direction. But if there were a conflict – an asset boom with rapid technological progress and with consumer prices falling, for example – 'we' would know what to do: we would raise interest rates for financial stability reasons. Or would 'we' pump up demand as our ancestors did in the 1920s to maintain price stability, and end up with a crash and a Great Depression? They called it 'state-dependent' inflation targeting. Others argued for a generally tighter stance for monetary policy to guard against the build up of booms (Woodford, 2012).

Whatever tactic they tried, one thing was certain: the markets would have a field day testing official policy-makers' reactions to one set of circumstances after another. One suspects the markets would find one to which monetary authorities had no answer. Such a feeble framework would never be able to overawe markets. Yet for any official policy to 'work' at all, the state had to be able to set up a structure that was robust against anything the markets could hurl at it. It also had to be simple enough that individual consumers and even investment bankers could understand it. That was the way to instill confidence, and to engineer a lasting recovery. Instead, the course followed by central banks in practice – aggressive and prolonged monetary stimulus – carried many dangers. 'A rising tide lifts all boats' is not the dictum of a good central banker, but it's what they did. Covering everything up in a sea of liquidity tended to postpone necessary recognition of losses by banks, postpone needed real adjustment to changing circumstances and damage the balance sheet of the central bank.

To sum up, for countries that wanted, and were able to maintain, flexible exchange rates, in principle the best anchor for their prices and financial system would be through the central bank's control of narrow money. It is the national policy option most in accord with the monetary philosophy that is advocated in this book – as something separable from the day-to-day policy-making level, a policy-making sphere that should be given a distinct constitutional status. This rests on the expectation that, once economic agents have learnt that the system would not bend to their short-term interests, they would adapt accordingly. This would imply that monetary policy could not be used as a policy tool to lean against the build-up of imbalances, or for short-term stabilization policies. Using policy first to stimulate, and then to stop, booms had made money itself less and less reliable. As the wise regulator and economist Andrew Sheng remarked, a financial crisis was the inevitable outcome of the 'fiat money feedback loop' without a hard budget constraint: 'The crux of the global fiat money crisis is how we can impose the hard budget constraint on shadow banks creating global fiat money when the tools are mainly national' (Sheng, *Central Banking*, Vol. 22, No. 1, August 2011, p. 66). It would mean a readiness to allow the general level of prices sometimes to fall – and possibly for an extended period – as well as to rise. In short, successful use of that option to secure greater stability in the long run at the national level would demand high levels of political discipline, and the ability to take a long-term view. Realistically, this option could be adopted only by a large currency area or group of countries.

Inflation targeting is in my view a superficial, naïve concept. It may have its crude uses in some circumstances, such as bringing inflation down from a very high level (as it did in countries like Israel, Chile and Peru in the 1990s, with other success cases including the Czech republic, Mexico and Poland). But stability of consumer or retail prices capture only a fraction of what is traditionally meant by sound money, or the value of money. This is far broader concept, one not easily definable, if at all, in terms stretching over four our five years, let alone two. It allows for prices to move around, and for the general level of prices to go down as well as up. It means among other things stability of expectations over the long term, say 20 years. It brings in the role of asset prices, and for many, traditionally, it implies maintaining the external as well as internal value of the currency (as in the case of the mandate originally given to the Deutsche Bundesbank, for example, see Chapter 6). Inflation targeting is the attempt by the manipulators and issuers of fiat money to mimic the properties of real money. But everybody knows that the so-called long-term frameworks will be cast aside as soon as short-term political needs require it. What started off as a monetarist idea, to place monetary policy out of the hands of politicians, the idea that was behind the original impetus to give central banks operational independence, gave way to its polar opposite – the Keynesian idea of monetary activism. By maintaining zero interest rates – or as close to them as possible – and promising to hold such rates beyond the horizon of expectations, the issuers of fiat money made it suffer the ultimate indignity – being spurned even when offered free of charge. The *reductio ad absurdum* of this approach was when people suggested that the risk of a double-dip recession could be avoided if the inflation target was replaced by a price level target say of 15 per cent above existing prices – to be maintained even if the economy recovered and even if there were no margin of spare capacity – and never mind the effect on long-term expectations (Crafts, 2011). If 15 per cent, why not 50?

Finally, all attempts to rehabilitate confidence in currencies of the main reserve centres would have to face the fact that the balance sheets of the central banks that issued the currencies had been torpedoed below the water line by GFC and the fallout from it – by repeated recessions, bank bail-outs, quantitative easing and the accumulation of poor-quality paper. Moreover the finances of the governments that stood behind the central banks were in even worse shape. In the case of the ECB, markets asked: did any government stand behind it?

Ultimately, there was only one answer that should be given to the question: 'Central banking post-crisis: what compass for uncharted waters?' The proper answer was clear: money itself should be the compass. But to enable it to serve this crucial social function, a new monetary constitution would be needed.

The search for a better world could not succeed if confined to the options available at the national level. Only the US and, assuming it would sort out its internal difficulties, the euro area, had genuine freedom to choose and the potential capacity to set up a monetary standard for the world. In the next chapter we see how the euro fared in the crisis and the lessons that could be drawn.

Notes

1. Inflation Report, August 2011, p. 8.
2. C. Borio, 'Central Banking Post-Crisis: What Compass for Uncharted Waters?' in R. Pringle and C. Jones, 2009.
3. C. Borio and M. Drehmann, 'Financial Instability and Macroeconomics: Bridging the Gulf', paper prepared for the Federal Reserve Bank of Chicago conference *Financial Stability, Monetary Policy and Central Banking*, Chicago, 24–25 September 2009.
4. Bank for International Settlements, 79th Annual Report, Basel, 2009.
5. See, for example, Andrew Smithers, *Wall Street: Imperfect Markets and Inept Central Bankers*, Palgrave Macmillan, 2009.
6. R. Barrell, E. P. Davis, D. Karim, I. Liadze, *The Impact of Global Imbalances: Does the Current Account Balance Help to Predict Banking Crises in OECD Countries?* NIESR and Brunel University, April 2010.

7. See Philip Turner, 'Central Banks and the Financial Crisis', in *Perspectives on Inflation Targeting, Financial Stability and the Global Crisis*, BIS papers, No. 51, March 2010.

8. Nor were all economists convinced that monetary policy did contribute to the asset boom anyway. Adam Posen is one who challenged this, claiming that economic research showed no relationship between easy monetary policies and property or real estate booms (speech, October 2010). Like others (Svensson), he favoured sticking to IT.

9. It should be made clear that here the term 'inflation-targeting regime' is used in a broad sense to include those central banks such as the Fed that did not at the time have publicized numerical targets but operated frameworks that shared many of the characteristics of those, that did have such targets. Another complication was that most central banks were also under instruction to support growth and employment. At the Fed, this was enshrined in its dual mandate; at most other central banks it was subject to the overriding objective of the inflation target.

10. The case for nominal GDP targeting was clearly put by Scott Sumner in a publication of the Adam Smith Institute:

     Nominal GDP targeting provides a way to address both inflation and output stability, without placing the central bank in the confusing situation of having to aim at two separate targets. Consider a country where the trend rate of output growth is roughly 2.5 per cent. A 4 per cent NGDP target would insure a long-run rate of inflation of roughly 1.5 per cent, with modest short-term variation in response to real economic shocks, such as a sharp increase in energy prices. For instance, suppose oil prices rose sharply. Under strict inflation-targeting, non-oil prices would have to fall to offset the increase in oil prices. If nominal wages are sticky, the fall in non-energy prices might lead to much higher unemployment. In contrast, NGDP targeting would allow a temporary period of above 1.5 per cent inflation, along with somewhat lower output, in order to cushion the blow on the non-oil sectors of the economy.

11. See Chapter 6; and Otmar Issing, *The Birth of the Euro*, Cambridge University Press, 2008, p. 107.

12. See *Bank of England Quarterly Bulletin*, Vol. 47, No. 3, pp. 476–88: 'In practice, central banks implement monetary policy through changes in interest rates rather than changes in money supply; their models tell them that aggregate demand is determined by expected real interest rates, with no explicit role for money.'

13. See Hayek's *Road to Serfdom* for a classic general statement of the evils of arbitrary power.

14. The monetary base consisted of gold coin in circulation, banknotes backed by gold, plus deposits of the banks with the clearing house or central bank convertible into gold or banknotes.

15. See Brendan Brown and Robert Pringle, 'Why Monetary Base Control can Offer Stability', *Central Banking*, Vol. 22, No. 10 (August 2010) and Brown (2011) for fuller accounts of this approach.

16. In practice, many advocates of narrow-money targeting assume a clear and stable link between the monetary base (notes and coin and bank reserves at the central bank) and narrow money. Both schools also share an insistence

on a longer-term policy orientation; the success or otherwise can be judged only over a period of, say, 10–20 years. Now, it is of course true that central banks have not in practice controlled the money base directly. Thus, base targeting in Germany was really a form of monetary aggregate targeting. The money stock was controlled indirectly, through the demand side. Nor did the Fed target base money or M1 through the supply side: to do so would have risked disrupting the actual supply of notes and coin and thus retail spending. But these central banks made quite clear that they were willing to tolerate short-term volatility in interest rates so as to reduce demand abruptly if need be.

17. Steve H. Hanke, 'America's "Plan" to Destabilize China'. This article appeared in the November 2010 issue of *Globe Asia*. It can be downloaded from the Cato Institute's website at http://www.cato.org/pub_display. php?pub_id=12492

18. See Claudio Borio in Robert Pringle and Claire Jones (eds), *The Future of Central Banking*, Central Banking Publications, 2011.

19. Svensson puts the point clearly:

> Importantly, monetary policy and financial-stability policy should not be confused with one another. Confusion risks leading to a poorer outcome for both policies and makes it more difficult to hold the policy-makers accountable. Trying to use monetary policy to achieve financial stability leads to poorer outcomes for monetary policy and is an ineffective way to achieve and maintain financial stability. (Svensson, 2012)

Bibliography

Bank for International Settlements, 79th Annual Report, Basel, 2009.

Barrell, Ray, E. P. Davis, D. Karim, I. Liadze, 'The Impact of Global Imbalances: Does the Current Account Balance Help to Predict Banking Crises in OECD Countries?' NIESR and Brunel University, April 2010.

Borio, Claudio, 'Central Banking Post-Crisis: What Compass for Uncharted Waters?' in *The Future of Central Banking*, Robert Pringle and Claire Jones (eds), Central Banking Publications, 2011.

Borio, Claudio and M. Drehmann, 'Assessing the Risk of Banking Crises – Revisited', *BIS Quarterly Review*, March 2009(a).

Borio, Claudio and M. Drehmann, 'Financial Instability and Macroeconomics: Bridging the Gulf', paper prepared for the Federal Reserve Bank of Chicago conference 'Financial Stability, Monetary Policy and Central Banking', Chicago, 24–25 September 2009(b).

Brown, Brendan, *The Global Curse of the Federal Reserve: Manifesto for a Second Monetarist Revolution*, Palgrave Macmillan, 2011.

Brown, Brendan and Robert Pringle, 'Why Monetary Base Control can Offer Stability', *Central Banking*, Vol. 22, No. 1, August 2010.

Crafts, Nicholas, 'Fiscal Stimulus Is Not Our Only Option: Look to the 1930s', *Financial Times*, 16 November, 2011.

Hanke, Steve, 'America's "Plan" to Destabilize China', *Globe Asia*, November 2010 and Cato Institute, website: http://www.cato.org/pub_display. php?pub_id=12492

Hayek, Friedrich von, *The Road to Serfdom*, George Routledge, 1944.

Issing, Otmar, *The Birth of the Euro*, Cambridge University Press, 2008.

Posen, Adam, 'Monetary Ease and Global Rebalancing: Debunking the Japanese Scare Speech to the Economic & Financial Institutions Research Group Queen's University, Belfast', October 2010.

Pringle, Robert and Claire Jones (ed), *The Future of Central Banking*, Central Banking Publications, 2011.

Smithers, Andrew, *Wall Street: Imperfect Markets and Inept Central Bankers*, Palgrave Macmillan, 2009.

Sumner, Scott, *The Case for NGDP Targeting: Lessons from the Great Recession*, Adam Smith Institute, 2011.

Svensson, Lars E. O., 'Monetary Policy after the Crisis' Speech at the Federal Reserve Bank of San Francisco, 29 November 2011, www.larseosvensson.net

Svensson, Lars E. O., 'Comment on Michael Woodford's paper "Inflation Targeting and Financial Stability"' Sveriges Riksbank Economic Review, forthcoming. PDF.

Turner, Philip, 'Central Banks and the Financial Crisis', in *Perspectives on Inflation Targeting, Financial Stability and the Global Crisis*, BIS papers, No. 51, March 2010.

Woodford, Michael, 'Inflation Targeting and Financial Stability' Sveriges Riksbank Economic Review, 2012, Vol 1.

6
A Solution for the Eurozone

Was there a regional alternative to the absence of a proper international standard? The answer was 'No' – the Eurozone itself needed international support.

The true destiny of the euro

The dollar, which acted as the indispensable global currency hub for half a century, showed recurrent bouts of nerves from the 1970s onwards and by the end of the twentieth century its foundations were visibly crumbling. Given the absence of an alternative international monetary standard, governments naturally had to consider what options were available to discipline economic and monetary management. In Chapter 5 we looked at various strategies open to individual countries and found that few of the candidates proved to be attractive. The best would be a strict type of narrow money control, but this would be difficult to implement, especially for smaller economies, because domestic monetary conditions could be swamped by external flows. GFC showed up the weaknesses of flexible exchange rates with inflation targeting, while the central banks' adoption of 'IT plus' (inflation-targeting with a macro-prudential toolkit to assure financial stability) would risk weakening the anchor for prices. On the other hand, trying to find stability by fixing exchange rates or adoption of a currency board would be likely to be beneficial only so long as there was a good external anchor to link to. The rolling recessionary crisis after 2008 showed there were no such reliable external currency anchors in sight. Central bankers were in charge of ships that had neither anchors nor compasses on board.

In this chapter we look at an alternative route to regaining monetary control with stability – regional cooperation. The lead here was of course taken by the European Union in establishing the euro, so that is the focus of this chapter. But the success or failure of the euro experiment would plainly have a massive influence on the development of the international monetary regime.

The dream of the founding fathers of European monetary unification was to create 'an island of stability' in a turbulent world. Whatever the achievements of the euro project, this aim was not achieved. This is not to deny that countries in the eurozone could possibly have suffered even greater turbulence if they had still had their national currencies in 2007–09. But being part of a single currency without a common fiscal policy introduced new sources of strain that put into question the cohesion of the eurozone itself. To save the euro area from break-up, the European Central Bank was obliged to adopt measures that went far beyond its original mandate and beyond any conception that had been held previously of its proper role. Governments continued to fight to prevent weaker peripheral countries from defaulting, or even leaving the euro.

It was possible to take a hopeful view of the longer-term effects. If sufficient political will were found in such a crisis – and maybe it could be forged only in the heat of such a crisis – to centralize fiscal policy, supervision and debt management at a federal level, and if countries accepted the permanent sharing (or, otherwise interpreted, loss) of sovereignty that would go with such centralization, then the euro area might emerge stronger. For a time, in 2010–11 economic recovery in France and Germany held out the prospect that the euro area could grow its way out of the crisis. Efforts were made to strengthen banking stability, and to guard against the build-up of financial imbalances in future. If these efforts were successful, then there would be grounds for greater optimism; on a consolidated basis, euro area public finances compared well with those of the US, Japan and the UK. But these reforms, though necessary, would not create an island of stability, because they would not address other fundamental causes of the instability.

The message of this chapter is simple: to realize the aims of the founding fathers, euro area governments need to help build a new GFS. They had been too narrowly focused on internal European affairs – natural, perhaps, as the institutions of monetary unification were built up – in the conviction that strong European institutions following sound policies would protect Europe from storms originating overseas. But that turned out to be an illusion. In future they needed to be more involved in the wider process of international monetary reform. Among the euro area governments, only France had attempted to place reform on the international agenda, as will be discussed in Chapter 7, and this initiative had failed to gather sufficient support from other countries to gain real momentum. That had to change. It was time for governments and federal institutions of the euro area to develop a constructive policy towards the future of the international monetary system and policies towards banking and financial markets – what we have called the GFS. The true destiny of the euro was to be a stepping stone towards – maybe even a foundation stone of – a new international order.

An island of stability?

The impetus behind monetary unification in Europe had always been defensive. Right from the outset, Europe's long and arduous journey towards economic and monetary union (EMU) had been spurred more by external instability than by a desire to create a European rival to the US dollar. As a result, European integration proceeded by fits and starts. Whenever the US Federal Reserve adopted an easy money policy to stimulate the economy, and the resulting flood of short-term capital threatened European monetary stability, interest in European monetary integration rose.

Even as early as the 1960s repeated bouts of dollar weakness sparked flows of capital to the then Deutsche Mark (DM) bloc, facing Germany with the choice between absorbing the flows at the cost of increasing its money supply and inflation, or revaluing the DM in agreement with the IMF. It was shortly after the DM revaluation of November 1969 that the European Community launched a programme aimed at deepening and widening European integration, including commissioning of a report on EMU from Pierre Werner, prime minister of Luxembourg. Again in the early 1970s, a surge of 'hot money' into the DM provoked bitter criticism of the US, criticism that served only to highlight Europe's limited room for manoeuvre. The US meanwhile urged Germany to revalue its currency again (just as it was later to indulge in 'Japan-bashing' and 'China-bashing' with the same aim of securing appreciation of their currencies).

In October 1970 the Werner report proposed a plan to create EMU, including a federal political structure, within a decade. However, French President Pompidou opposed such a sacrifice of national sovereignty; he was also suspicious of Britain's commitments and ties outside Europe, both with the US and to countries of the overseas sterling area (Britain was at this stage negotiating to join the European Community under the strongly pro-European prime minister Ted Heath and it was expected to participate in the EMU project). In Germany, the Bundesbank feared that the set-up would be inflationary – so it was dropped.

In 1973, Germany and France led the move to floating exchange rates reluctantly and as a last resort, not out of conviction. Indeed, the move was accompanied by efforts to keep the core currencies of the European Community together – initially by a joint float, and then by a currency 'snake' and later, following yet another bout of dollar weakness, by the European Monetary System (EMS). This was inaugurated in March 1979 following a meeting the previous summer between Chancellor Helmut Schmidt of Germany and President Valery Giscard d'Estaing of France. Both the snake and the EMS were seen as creating zones of monetary stability in Europe. Both systems came unstuck for the same reason – nothing short of complete and irrevocable fixing of exchange rates would be credible in markets. Thus the founding fathers of the euro concluded that only full monetary unification would do the trick: European monetary cooperation and integration built around flexible exchange rates was never considered to be a serious option. The architects of the Maastricht Treaty in 1991, like those of Bretton Woods nearly 50 years earlier, feared that floating or flexible rates would be objects of speculation, and likely to be disruptive. With memories of the 1930s still vivid, they also feared the long-term political consequences.

Why did the leading countries of continental Europe take such a different view of exchange rates from the US and the UK, which by the mid-1970s were converts to the case for flotation? It is simplistic to attribute this, as British and American commentators often do, to ambitions for political dominance. The attitudes had roots in each country's monetary and economic history. France's support for fixed exchange rates in Europe was a legacy of its financial conservatism, shown in its long-standing wariness of credit creation, its historical emphasis on high levels of bank liquidity and prudent bank regulations, its attachment to large gold and foreign currency reserves, and its scepticism of 'international monetary cooperation' as preached by the US and Britain – when that often meant little more than pleas to hold their currencies in its reserves. It had from time to time lapsed from its own strict standards, with spells of high inflation and external depreciation weakness, but, as Fred Hirsch pointed out in the 1960s, these only seemed to make it more determined to make amends when it could – 'to store up, so to speak, a pile of virtue, both physical and spiritual, against the next fall from monetary grace'.[1] Such attitudes dovetailed with France's perception of its national interest, and with the analysis by Jacques Rueff, to make France the leading critique of the gold exchange standard in the 1960s.[2] For France, historically, a fixed exchange rate was a natural discipline on governments.

The convergence debate

In a portentous victory, France also won the debate on the process and mechanism through which economies joining EMU would 'converge' sufficiently to be consistent with lasting exchange rate stability. As a natural part of its approach, the French took the view that fixing exchange rates would itself force or induce convergence. The so-called economist position, shared by most German economists, was that this was putting the cart before the horse – without prior convergence of national monetary policies and inflation rates, any attempt to fix rates would simply be blown apart by markets. Many went further, insisting that EMU should be preceded by political union.[3] The dominance of the French view on this issue was reflected in the design of the EMS and the Maastricht Treaty of 1991. Subsequent crises would test it to the limit – and in 2011–12 the jury was still out.

Germany's willingness to embrace monetary union also had roots in the past. The origins can be traced back to the public's demand for monetary stability after the Second World War, a demand satisfied by the success of the Bank Deutsche Länder (BDL), a quasi-central bank set up by the Allies in 1947, the governing structure of which was modelled on the Federal Reserve. The currency reform and introduction of the Deutsche Mark, again planned by the Allies, followed in 1948 with Ludwig Erhard, later Minister of Economics and Chancellor, receiving the credit for its enormous success. The BDL maintained a fixed exchange rate with the dollar, as required under Bretton Woods rules, and delivered price stability in the context of rapid economic growth, an undervalued exchange rate and falling unemployment. Soon Germany was experiencing an export boom and its *Wirtschaftswunder*, and when the BDL was succeeded by the Bundesbank in 1957, its articles reflected the overwhelming public demand for an independent central bank, which was set the objective of 'safeguarding the currency'. Significantly, the central bank's articles did not spell out whether it was the internal or external value of the currency that was to be maintained; objectives that economists usually view as separable were by then deeply interconnected in the public mind and lay at the heart of what was coming to be called Germany's 'stability-oriented culture'.

It was this mind-set that Germany carried into the process leading to the Maastricht Treaty of 1992 with its 'convergence criteria' – conditions for members of the EU to enter the final stage of EMU – and establishment of the euro. It did so, toughly, by insisting that if other countries wanted Germany to lead the way to EMU, they would have to subordinate their exchange rate and monetary policies to those of the Bundesbank. German public opinion would accept EMU only if the ECB was modelled on the Bundesbank. Many senior Bundesbankers were also sceptical of the Maastricht Treaty and made little attempt to hide their doubts – putting pressure on other European partners to agree to Germany's terms.[4] Then, in the 1980s and 1990s, a series of exchange rate crises threatened to pull the single market apart. For Germany, it was vital that Europe's markets at least remained open to free movement of goods, services and capital; as the area's greatest exporter and surplus country, Germany had the biggest stake in it. If the choice in the end was between free floating and a common currency, the clear advantages of a common currency were sufficient to sway the doubters.

Thus, both approaches to convergence implicitly anticipated that there would be further crises stemming from defects in the design. The difference between them was that some (the so-called monetarists, though this has a different meaning from what is usually meant by that term and so is avoided here) gambled that the drive towards greater cohesion would overcome such difficulties, while others (the so-called economists) feared or in some cases hoped that the crises would doom the entire project.

Early weaknesses were never remedied

One of the questions to be settled related to exchange rate policy. Who or what body would set the exchange rate policy for the single currency (called the euro from 1995)? In the end the ECB had the whip hand. After the ECB was set up, spokesmen made clear that 'Mr Euro' was none other than its president. Yet such a set-up was bound to cause tensions, as exchange rate policy is generally considered to be a political, or even constitutional, prerogative of the state, because the state has to define the monetary unit used by residents (for example, to pay taxes). Then there was the uncertainty about which countries would be in the first wave. The markets and most observers expected these to consist of Germany, France, Austria, the Netherlands, Belgium, Luxembourg and Ireland. But there was enormous political pressure to include others, and, as the decision would be taken by qualified majority voting, considerable scope for political manoeuvring.

A question mark still hung over Italy. Most Italian leaders demanded Italy should be in the first wave – with the exception of Antonio Fazio, then governor of the Bank of Italy, who said it would be too risky for Italy. Others, such as his predecessor Carlo Ciampi, warned that if Italy was not in the euro club, it would become even more difficult for it to fulfil the Maastricht criteria. The smaller countries clamoured to be in. The Portuguese government argued that it was unacceptable to exclude a country that fulfilled all the criteria laid down by Maastricht, as Portugal planned to do. Finland was equally determined. Yet of the inner group expected by the markets to enter EMU, neither Austria nor Belgium nor even France was likely to pass the government deficit test (3 per cent of GDP was set as the 'reference value'). Italy was planning a deficit of 4.5 per cent in 1997. The Maastricht criteria would have to be fudged if the project was to go ahead (as they were in the cases of Italy and Belgium, whose public debt-to-GDP ratios were well above the criteria); as Issing put it later, 'a major effort at interpretation and ultimately a political decision were required to enable their entry.'[5] This reached its *reductio ad absurdum* when the Greek government, advised by Goldman Sachs, the US investment bank, fiddled the data about its government debt to gain entry.[6]

That was why governments stressed the need for a framework to ensure fiscal discipline after the launch of the single currency. In the absence of such discipline, the tension between decentralized fiscal and centralized monetary policy would undermine the whole project. Yet, in the absence of a federal European government, it was already being questioned whether the ECB could bring sufficient pressure on national governments to curb their deficits. Legal sanctions built into the Treaty seemed unlikely to do the job. Agreement had not been reached on the German proposal, dating back to 1995, for a 'stability pact'. Such a counterpart to monetary union was seen to be essential but the German proposals were softened under French pressure, renamed the Stability and Growth Pact at the Dublin Summit in 1996 and later breached by both Germany and France. As Issing (2008) acidly commented, 'In so doing, the three largest EMU countries, including the country that originally pushed the Stability and Growth Pact through against stiff resistance, took an axe to one of the pillars of monetary union.'

Price stability was not enough

On average, the ECB delivered on its mandate: its primary obligation was to maintain price stability, interpreted as an inflation rate below, but close to, 2 per cent over the medium term; without prejudice to the achievement of that objective, the ECB was also enjoined to 'support the general economic policies of the Union' and to contribute to the objectives of full employment and 'balanced economic growth'. Average annual inflation in the 12 years following the introduction of the euro in 1999 was fractionally over 2 per cent.

But that wasn't enough. It did not protect Europe or the euro from shocks that in 2011–12 came close to destroying the entire European Union. There had long been fears that unless there were provisions for enforcing obligations to avoid excessive deficits, the euro could not survive. These original doubts were never dispelled, and there was a clear line leading from this failure to the convulsions of 2010–12. The area's mechanisms for coordination had no teeth. The set-up also lacked an emergency financing facility to provide adjustment assistance to countries in exceptional financial difficulty. On the other hand, if the political will could be found to ensure sufficient centralization of fiscal and debt management policy to put the euro on a firmer footing, would the 'monetarists' have been proved right? The decision by Chancellor Kohl and President Mitterand (and embodied in the Delors Report with its 'three stages' of 1989[7]) to set the launch date at 1999, followed by the successful changeover, the introduction of notes and coins, and a decade of consumer price stability, had made its break-up almost inconceivable – almost, but not quite.

The ECB had also made serious mistakes. It should have acted more promptly to cool the asset boom preceding the bust of 2007–09. Already by 2004 there was considerable evidence of the beginning of a credit bubble. Real estate prices were soaring. Banks were expanding rapidly and leverage increasing. In the euro area money supply measures were rising. Credit and monetary growth from mid-2004 clearly reflected the effect of the low level of interest rates – held unchanged at 2 per cent by the ECB from mid-2003 to the end of 2005. By that time housing bubbles had clearly developed in Spain and France and in smaller countries. So why did the ECB wait so long, and why, even when it finally raised rates, was it only by very small 0.25 per cent steps? Importantly, this slowness was criticized at the time, by, for example, one of Germany's leading economists, Manfred Neumann in an article entitled, 'The case for raising rates faster'. (Neumann, 2006)

Yet here again the mechanism of inflation targeting showed is defects. While several factors explained the ECB's reluctance to raise rates to cool the boom, again exchange rate volatility played a role. Against the US dollar, the euro soared from about $1.00 in 2002 to $1.30 in 2005 and then to $1.40 in 2007. Raising interest rates more quickly and by larger amounts would have caused the euro to rise even further, knocking hopes of recovery. This is another example of how the interaction of floating exchange rates with inflation-targeting central banks misled policy-makers. Indeed, it put them again in the money trap. Even if they had been fully cognizant of the dangers of ignoring the asset price boom, their IT model would not have let them do anything about it; for any action could have made the credit and business cycle even worse. Exchange rate appreciation held down growth, concealed the strength of inflationary pressures and made it inevitable that the central bank should do nothing about the property and asset price boom in many member countries. Thus without attention to external sources of instability, steps to broaden the remit of the monetary authorities, and even moves towards greater fiscal centralization, would not succeed. This was illustrated in the next phase, where again the causes and cures were misconceived: the cause being put down entirely to fiscal indiscipline, and the cure – political union – being out of reach.[8]

How the euro triggered Europe's debt crisis

The euro area's government debt crisis that began in May 2010 represented a highly dangerous and distinct phase of GFC. The background to this crisis was the deterioration of public sector balance sheets after the outbreak of the financial crisis. To stave off the threat of a banking collapse, governments had stepped in to shoulder the costs, and to provide both explicit and implicit guarantees as well as direct injections of capital. Markets soon priced in the cost of implicit guarantees to their ratings of government debt, adding hugely to the real burden of public debt. In addition, the recession triggered by the financial crisis reduced tax revenues and increased social expenditure on unemployment benefits and in other ways, further adding to the debt burden.

One mechanism through which the credit crunch triggered recession was very direct – banks which had funded domestic lending by attracting overseas wholesale deposits found the latter drying up, and then had little option but to cut back, in some cases brutally, on their domestic lending, causing abrupt and disorderly adjustment. The worsening prospects for the real economy in turn undermined the quality of the stock of loans and investment on banks' books, further putting their credit at risk. The credit default swap (CDS) market provided a running 'commentary' on the market's judgement of the risks attached to each bank, which in turn attracted the attentions of short-sellers. This was another aggravating factor: while in normal times, short-selling may add to liquidity and price discovery, at times of incipient banking panic, the ability of hedge funds quickly to marshal vast financial resources and target them on the stocks of vulnerable financial institutions by naked short-selling and speculation in the CDS market meant the prices of some bank stocks collapsed in a few days, further bringing their creditworthiness into question – with knock-on effects on the credits of governments that now stood behind them.[9]

The large sums that then had to be raised on capital markets by governments in turn crowded out banks and other financial institutions in urgent need of capital. Some relief was afforded by the regime of ultra low interest rates which was forced on the ECB, and banks meanwhile widened their lending margins and tightened lending criteria in an effort to reduce bad and doubtful debts and increase risk-adjusted returns – but this would be a long, slow business. Would there be enough time to build up an adequate capital cushion and make further write-downs for the bad debts still on their books before the next wave of defaults? This situation was reminiscent of that in Japan in the 1990s and early years of this century. The softness of the economy and deflationary trends, as well as pressure from government to increase or roll over loans so as to avoid putting borrowers into bankruptcy, had made it very difficult for the Japanese banks to exit from the cycle of high bad-loan losses, falling loan books and dependence on state support, even in an environment of zero or near-zero cost of funds. And once again, the strong exchange rate was an aggravating factor. The eurozone looked to be treading the same path.

Another channel through which external shocks impacted on European banking was through the outstanding loans in foreign currencies that many European banks had on their books. This made the quality of the assets of such banks highly vulnerable to exchange rate risks – again illustrating the heightened risks associated with the fluctuating exchange rate of the euro, especially versus the US dollar. At the same time, direct holdings of poor quality foreign currency securities remained a deadweight on balance sheets. At a time when securitization markets remained largely closed, this damaged the credit supply to the entire eurozone. There were few signs that banks, which had been the main investors in such securities pre-crisis and had been badly burnt as a result, were rediscovering an appetite for this paper. Once again, time was needed to nurse their balance sheets back to health – and that time would be measured in years, not months. But an underlying major factor was once again the impact of the strength of the euro following on the adoption of ultra-loose money policies by the Fed in 2009 and again in the second half of 2010. These bursts of euro strength damaged economic prospects, especially for weaker euro economies, and reduced governments' prospective capacity to service their debts – and the effect was instantaneous as the market wrote down the value of those debts.

The doomed search for a purely European solution

It was a simple matter to list what was wrong with the architecture of the euro – lack of control over sovereign debts, the lack of a mechanism such as exists in every country for automatic fiscal transfers to regions that suffer most in a recession, and the lack of a central financial regulator (which the ECB was remedying through its added responsibilities for financial stability).The argument of this chapter is that such an analysis of the eurozone crisis is incomplete without tracing its connections to the wider international arena, and that its treatment equally needed the involvement of the international community as a whole. A full solution depended on a proper reform of the GFS.

As Kenneth Rogoff, former economic adviser to the IMF, pointed out, the euro area crisis marked a crossroads for the whole GFS.[10] If the euro area managed to sort out its problems, that would give a boost to regional currency arrangements elsewhere – in Asia, North America and the Middle East, and Latin America. Although a long-time advocate of floating exchange rates, he recognized that 'it would make a lot of sense economically to have a smaller number of currencies'. The euro sovereign debt crisis was a 'typical aftershock' of a deep financial crisis.

As already mentioned, another link with the GFS took place through exchange rates. The euro area was suffering from the strong exchange rate versus dollar – Rogoff called it 'ironic' that the euro had been forged to eliminate speculative swings within Europe, but was suffering from being too strong, like the DM before it. Just as the float of the DM did not fully succeed in insulating the German economy in the 1970s and 1980s, nor did the big DM – the euro – insulate the eurozone, which was buffeted by the sporadic weakness of the dollar. Ironically, if Europe did succeed in sorting out the euro problems, that would just worsen its economic prospects, as the euro would rise even further against the dollar, causing recession in export-oriented economies, notably Germany, and prompting a rise in interest rates and possibly a double dip recession in the US. Something was clearly very wrong with the euro's architecture if it could not find the policy tools to protect itself from financial shocks originating in the US; equally, something was very wrong with the GFS if the success of one of its most important poles – the eurozone – in putting its house in order would jeopardize its stability as a whole.

In short, the debate about the sovereign debt and banking crisis in the euro area failed once again to take into account the links between the euro crisis and the outside world. One important link went through the nexus between banking and politics, or more precisely through banking risk and sovereign risk. One result of GFC in both Europe and America was to transfer leverage from financial institutions to the state – as bank liabilities were guaranteed, so the state's debts worsened. A poisonous interaction was set up between banking and political stability. Policy-makers were scared to let borrowers default on their debts and let the private sector take its share of the losses, because that would further weaken the banks which already held so much sovereign debt. There were in principle two ways to break interaction between banking risk and sovereign risk: either to stop exposing sovereigns to banking risk or to stop exposing banks to sovereign risk.

European political leaders were trapped by global markets. At every step, they were brought up short by market reactions to politically motivated initiatives. For example, when at a bilateral meeting at Deauville in France in October 2010, Chancellor Angela Merkel and President Nicolas Sarkozy announced that future rescues of eurozone states should involve losses for private bond-holders, markets cut off funding for weak states. Even Germany's credit was affected. When leaders hastened to repair the damage by drawing up a scheme whereby bond-holders would be forced to take losses but only after 2013, again markets gave it the thumbs down. Indeed, ECB leaders blamed such loose talk for deepening the eurozone crisis, framing this as a conflict between financial markets and public opinion. As Wolfgang Schäuble, Germany's finance minister, said in November 2010, 'While the financial markets want a European responsibility for financial and budgetary policies, public opinion does not.'

The reality was that without a radical reform of the GFS, European politicians would never be masters in their own house. To expand the metaphor further, it was no longer enough for each area and each country to 'put its house in order', as their house could be made untidy by their neighbours.

Euro spokesmen still didn't get it

ECB spokesmen emphasized the difference between monetary union in Europe, which was a good thing, and fixed exchange rates for other people, which were viewed as a bad idea. Inside EMU, any discussion of the possibility that a member state might leave the euro, default or devalue was banned. When discussing the outside world, fixed rates were seen to have no benefits at all. Spokesmen would maintain that European economies needed a common currency. At the global level, however, they insisted that countries stood to benefit instead from the corrective mechanisms of fluctuating exchange. On this topsy-turvy view of the world, the history of international money had been marked by repeated, and often failed, attempts to establish fixed exchange rate regimes – whereas Europe would be triumphantly successful in doing just that. In the outside world, ever since the failed attempt to restore the gold standard in the 1920s, countries were no longer willing to subordinate domestic policies to the stability of the exchange rate; but in the euro zone, they were totally willing to do so (or so the assumption had it). Under Bretton Woods, it was only by moving to flexible rates that some countries were able to avoid the 'Great Inflation' in the US. After the collapse of Bretton Woods, some countries continued to peg to the dollar, often with disastrous results when these led to overvalued rates, according to Jürgen Stark (in a speech made when he was a member of the governing board of the ECB (Stark, 2011)). In the crisis, Stark maintained, fixed rates had caused unbalanced growth and distortions in trade and capital flows, with capital flowing 'uphill' from many emerging markets. Again, Stark claimed, fixing of exchange rates was at the core of the problem.

This build-up was intended to lead to one conclusion: the ECB would join the Bank of England and the Federal Reserve in the western central bankers' concerted attempt to pin the blame on China. Stark dismissed proposed reforms of the monetary regime, such as an increase in SDR allocations and more credit lines from the IMF. The key was excess reserve accumulation, and the way to limit that was greater flexibility of (China's) exchange rate, domestic reforms to (China's) financial insitutions and stimulus to (China's) domestic demand. How very convenient. Yet the euro area had been supposed to provide an island of stability in an uncertain world. How come the neat, affluent Euro house had been shaken by events in poor, faraway China?

It was a shame that a German economist should take this view, because the situation facing China was comparable to the dilemmas faced by West Germany – and indeed continental Europe – after the collapse of Bretton Woods in the 1970s: either fixing, or fully flexible rates. But Stark apparently failed to consider that the way out of its dilemma eventually taken by Europe (when all else had failed) of fixing rates might also be considered an option for a large emerging market in the twenty-first century. Stark's view that fixed exchange rates were good for the eurozone but not for emerging markets rested on the observation that Europe comprised economies 'at similar stages of development', 'a high degree of financial and real integration' and 'largely synchronized business cycles': convergence, integration and synchronization were the buzzwords. But this was a highly dubious assertion, as events of 2010–12 were to show. These events were to demonstrate clearly the great difficulties faced by the particular form of imposed irrevocable fixed exchange rate union adopted in the euro area. They did not undermine the arguments for a global monetary standard. On the contrary, they strengthened them.

From currency zone to a new GFS?

The ECB and euro area governments should be interested in more profound reform of the GFS for the following reasons:

- Wide swings in nominal and real exchange rates between the euro and dollar areas damaged euro area economies, contributing to unemployment, misallocation of investment and a lower level of growth.
- The existing regime did nothing to protect the euro area from destabilizing flows of hot money; indeed, it encouraged speculative financial activities, bandwagon effects in asset prices and overshooting of the effective euro exchange rate in both directions.
- The GFS heightened the risks facing the euro area's banks, by increasing their vulnerability to inflows and outflows of funds, setting up vicious feedback loops between exchange rate, market and interest rate risks.
- Exchange rate risk distorted trade and investment flows – encouraging diversion of such flows to the euro area at the expense of potentially more productive and socially beneficial flows across currency areas.
- Crucially, a good global GFS would make it easier for individual countries to leave the euro area for a time, if they could not keep up with Germany and other core countries, take a rest, and come back in. They would have an alternative, sound and respectable international standard to fall back on.

That would be the best global framework in which a solution to the euro crisis could be sought – though it would of course be no substitute for the necessary reforms to laggard euro area economies that were being put in hand, despite great political difficulties involved. The lesson was that, in addition to such structural reforms, governments and the ECB needed to join in a collective international effort to reform the GFS if they were to produce stability in Europe itself. This was obvious in the case of banking and financial market supervision, for example, where the possibility of the failure of global banks called for agreements or common policies; in practice, these were very far from being realized, but at least their desirability was widely recognized. In monetary policy, however, the need for coordination was strongly denied by the main actors involved – governments and central banks. GFC showed this attitude to be wrong-headed.

For Germany and France in particular, there was now an opportunity to carry the culture of stability that they had sought to embody in the euro into the global arena. Forming EMU had not insulated the European economies in the euro area from disturbances originating abroad; this modern 'euro' version of the Maginot Line was as deceptive as the original had proved to be. Indeed, the creation of the euro had in some ways increased instability. Inside the euro area, it had transformed balance of payments problems into sovereign debt problems, which in some ways were harder to resolve. Internationally, it had split the world monetary regime previously centred on the dollar into parts, weakening the dollar pillar, setting up a see-saw between them and facing third countries and investors globally with a choice of which end of the currency see-saw to jump onto. Some were caught like rabbits in the headlights – paralysed. Others gave a good imitation of Buridan's ass, which starved to death because it was unable to decide between two piles of hay placed at equal distance on either side of it.

The euro area turned out to be an open economy and, like the authorities of much smaller open economies, those of the euro area experienced the same closing-off of policy options, as they were affected by the same constraints. Indeed, the euro currency suffered from many of the same problems as the old DM bloc, without some of the strengths of the bloc had enjoyed in terms of internal cohesion and the leadership of a dominant partner. At critical moments, sudden periods of euro appreciation, as in 2009 and the second half of 2010, triggered crippling debt problems as they weakened the debt-servicing capacity of weaker euro area governments. This underlined the interdependence of Europe and the world economy.

This discussion leads naturally to the subject of the next chapter: the search for reform at the international level. Given the regrettable absence of US leadership, it was tempting to speculate whether euro area governments could join China and possibly other emerging market economies in a push for international monetary reform. After all, European monetary attitudes had much in common with those of emerging economies such as China, with a historic preference for stability over market liberalization. Such an alliance would be strengthened if it could include the UK, host to the world's biggest international financial centre – the element that would be needed to power the engine forward.

The search for an island of stability in Europe could not succeed by internal reforms alone. Paradoxically, it would strengthen the euro if individual countries could have a trusted alternative standard to fall back on. Could the euro be saved only by a broader reform of the GFS?

Notes

1. Fred Hirsch, *Money International*, Penguin Books, 1969, p. 382.
2. 'The intellectual demolition of the gold exchange standard was accomplished as easily by Jacques Rueff as by Robert Triffin,' in Hirsch (1969), p. 380. See also Chapter 12, p. 216.
3. See Otmar Issing, 'Slithering to the Wrong Kind of Union', *Financial Times*, 8 August 2011.
4. As Helmut Schlesinger, former Bundesbank president, put it in 2007, 'The overall political situation in Europe made monetary union both necessary and desirable. If the political will was there, it would have been wrong – and impossible – for the Bundesbank to oppose it. We had good fortune since we could construct the European Central Bank on the Bundesbank model.' (Interview with David Marsh, quoted in Marsh, *The Euro* (2009), p. 176.)
5. Otmar Issing, *The Birth of the Euro* (2008), p. 16.
6. 'Speaking in London earlier this week, Gerald Corrigan, who co-chairs Goldman's risk management committee, said the use of the derivative product was "consistent" with the regulations of the day and were legal at the time. However, the former head of the Federal Reserve Bank of New York went on to admit to the Treasury Select Committee that "with hindsight" the use of the complex derivative should have been more transparent.' James Quinn, *Daily Telegraph*, 25 February 2010. The Greek trades – first reported in detail in *Risk* in 2003 – were cross-currency swaps, which transformed around €10 billion of foreign currency debt into euro-denominated liabilities, but used an off-market exchange rate to do so. As a result, Goldman made an upfront payment to Greece at the deal's inception that would have to be repaid years later. Because it was a currency trade, Greece did not have to disclose this additional liability – in fact, the off-market rate meant the country was able to report a reduction in national debt (Wood and Campbell, 2010).

7. In June 1988, the European Council set up a committee chaired by Jacques Delors, then President of the European Commission, to study and propose concrete stages leading to this union. The committee was composed of the governors of the then European Community (EC) national central banks: Alexandre Lamfalussy, then General Manager of the Bank for International Settlements (BIS); Niels Thygesen, professor of economics, Denmark; and Miguel Boyer, then President of the Banco Exterior de España. The resulting Delors Report proposed that economic and monetary union should be achieved in three discrete but evolutionary steps.

8. At a press conference in August 2011, Jean-Claude Trichet, then coming to the end of his term as president of the ECB, furiously rounded on critics saying that the ECB's record in maintaining price stability had been 'impeccable' and 'better than the Bundesbank's' had been. This may have been true, but as the economist Kenneth Rogoff acidly commented, if the euro collapsed who will remember that in its brief life it kept inflation at 2 per cent? (*Financial Times*, 4 October 2011).

9. Regulators were at a loss how to respond to short-selling. There was no consistent view or policy across the eurozone, let alone internationally. Some regulators tried temporary bans, such as those imposed in August 2011, on naked short-selling but these had little effect in curbing the practice. And the powerful hedge fund industry, with friends in high places, furiously lobbied against such restrictions.

10. Kenneth Rogoff, 'The Global Fallout of a Eurozone Collapse', *Financial Times*, 6 June 2011.

Bibliography

Hirsch, Fred, *Money International*, Penguin Books, 1967; revised edition, 1969.

Issing, Otmar, *The Birth of the Euro*, Cambridge University Press, 2008.

Marsh, David, *The Euro: The Politics of the New Global Currency*, Yale University Press, 2009.

Neumann, Manfred, 'The Case for Raising Rates Faster', *Central Banking*, Vol. 17, No. 2, November 2006.

Rogoff, Kenneth, 'The Global Fallout of a Eurozone Collape', *Financial Times*, 4 October 2011.

Stark, Jürgen, member of the executive board of the ECB, speech at the Institute of Risk and Regulation, Hong Kong, 12 April 2011.

Wood, Duncan, and Alexander Campbell, 'Greek Woes Focus Attention on Role of Eurostat', published online only on Risk.net. Source: *Risk magazine*, 5 March 2010.

7
Money International

Against the backdrop of a fast-changing world economy, this chapter assesses how governments were 'searching for ways out of the trap' by international cooperation.

Consider the sweeping changes transforming economic geography. Assuming recent trends are maintained, between 2011 and the mid 2020s China will grow from being about half the size of the US or eurozone economies to being about the same size as they will be, and the output of emerging markets in aggregate could be twice as large as that of the US or eurozone. Looking further ahead, on current trends, by 2050 India, Brazil, Russia, Mexico and Indonesia will be among the top 10 economies, ahead of Germany and the UK (Brazil overtook the UK in 2012!). Rapid shifts in capital from one part of the world to another will also be sparked by changing perceptions of credit risk, as the government bonds of many western countries lose their hallowed 'risk free' status, and as investment opportunities open up in different parts of the world. The potential for collisions between mutually inconsistent policies during such a period of turbulent change is obvious.

Leadership vacuum

Yet prospects for political leadership to ensure adequate coordination of policies appeared poor. The natural leader, which is still likely to be the US, seemed to be absorbed by what to the rest of the world was political in-fighting, often on arcane domestic issues, and an inability to get its own finances into order. The euro area seemed likely to remain unsettled, to say the least, with the risk of a revival of ancient antipathies. In particular, the growing economic domination and political confidence of a united Germany could easily spark resentment in other countries, especially given its (understandable) determination to ensure adherence to strict budgetary discipline as a quid pro quo for fiscal integration and essential fiscal transfers from the 'northern' euro countries to the less affluent 'Club Med' member states, notably Italy, Greece, Spain and Portugal. There had been a strategic policy vacuum in the midst of turbulent economic transformation. This is what was holding back global demand – a basic lack of confidence in the ability of the global financial system to meet the challenges ahead. As such, it could not be remedied by any amount of pump-priming by central banks, lower taxes or higher public spending. At the same time, central banks might have a vital role to play in facilitating the crucial coordination of policies in key areas, above all monetary and exchange rate policies.

The G20 took stop-gap measures in emergencies, but had no strategic vision. In 2008, faced with a swift collapse of economic activity and trade, governments engineered a coordinated boost to demand and set in motion a longer-term recasting of financial regulation. Recognizing the growing role of large emerging market economies, they also agreed to make the G-20 rather than the old G-7 or G-10 groups of rich countries the prime inter-governmental body to lead the coordination – advised by the IMF. The G20 agreed to institute a review of the international monetary system. It was at least a start. In subsequent meetings, the G20 debated issues such as capital flows, the development of domestic capital markets, the role and composition of the IMF special drawing right (SDR) currency basket, the surveillance function of the IMF, global liquidity and whether a financial safety net was needed to provide liquidity in a future emergency. There was much talk about whether capital controls could be applied in particular circumstances as a last resort. There was discussion of the currency composition of the SDR basket, with a view to including the renmimbi (RMB) in due course, but this was seen as largely symbolic given the minuscule role of the SDR in the system. There was talk also of the need to strengthen IMF 'surveillance' and the mutual assessment programme – but without result. Few observers expected that surveillance could be strengthened sufficiently to become a pillar of the system. Big countries were not willing to allow the IMF greater influence on their policies. Central bank mutual loans – so-called swap lines – were enlarged, though this took place outside the G20 scope, and there were measures to allow more flexible access to IMF resources.

No progress was made in discussing, or even putting on the agenda, the central elements of the international monetary system, namely the rules that governed exchange rate regimes, enforcement of and incentives for fiscal and monetary discipline, and the future of the major reserve currencies. Reform of finance was delegated to bodies of regulators and central bankers, subject to the same pressures and industry lobbying as before and advised by the same groups of academic specialists who had created the regulatory framework that had caused – or at least failed to prevent – GFC.

This was because there was no generally accepted analysis that linked faults in the international monetary system to GFC and the continuing weakness of global demand. The narrative advanced in this book – which links the weakness of the GFS to the regime of flexible exchange rates combined with an excessively elastic supply of credit and a politically influential private financial sector – was not sufficiently widely shared. Yet looking further ahead, given such wrenching upheavals, it was difficult to imagine the world could continue with the existing non-system: that is, with reliance on the US dollar and the euro for their main stores of value and reserve currencies; leaving the issue of global imbalances unresolved; leaving finance cramped by a panoply of new capital and liquidity ratios, but otherwise untamed to cause more trouble. To avoid progressive disintegration it would be vital that the world's major centres of power were linked through common monetary bonds, that they respected the same standards, that they followed compatible rules of the money game, even while not sharing necessarily similar social and political systems or ways of life.

For a time, the idea of a more radical overhaul of the system, going beyond the tinkering that had been the name of the game for many years, seemed to be gaining traction. The IMF started to push ideas that looked towards a sharing of reserves among surplus countries to avoid wasteful duplication. A proposal that the IMF could develop a framework to mutualize or pool reserve holdings was another idea going the rounds. Further factors heightening concern were awareness of the shortage in the supply of safe assets and the implications of the huge growth in cross-border assets and liabilities in different currencies. The first came to the fore with doubts about the credit rating of the US, which could have effects in raising volatility in markets. The second made banks vulnerable to exchange rate shifts – big changes in rates could induce large shifts. This was behind their desperate search for dollar funding when the inter-bank market seized up. Finally, there were fears that the exceptional measures taken by central banks to spur demand, including a massive expansions of their balance sheets, could in future spark a resurgence of global inflation. This highlighted the absence of a mechanism for anchoring the world price level. Central banks were concerned with the domestic measures of inflation that they were expected to keep under control. But this neglected global inflation driven, for example, by rising commodity prices – in turn fuelled by the spillover into the world economy of expansionary monetary policies in the US and Europe. Such commodity inflation had not been an issue in the disinflationary environment of the decade to 2009, but could become more of one, which was probably what prompted Robert Zoellick's surprise proposal (made when he was President of the World Bank) to restore a role for gold. This had the great merit of calling attention to the central issue of how to anchor global money and the price level (Zoellick, 2010). What was lacking was recognition that the prevailing inward-looking monetary regime – floating rates with independent central banks pursuing domestic stability agendas – was not only deeply unpopular in many parts of the world but was also incompatible with full economic integration.

A demand for wider reform

President Sarkozy of France had tried to put reform on the agenda, saying that it would not be possible to emerge from the recession and protect against future turbulence if the economic imbalances that were at the root of the problem were not addressed. 'Countries with trade surpluses must consume more and improve the living standards and social protection of their citizens,' he remarked. 'Countries with deficits must make an effort to consume a little less and repay their debts.' He also asserted that the world's currency regime was central to the issue. Exchange rate instability and the under-valuation of certain currencies lead to unfair trade and competition. 'The prosperity of the post-war era owed a great deal to Bretton Woods, to its rules and its institutions. That is exactly what we need today; we need a new Bretton Woods.' France would, he promised, place the reform of the international monetary system on the agenda when it chaired the G-8 and G20 in 2011 (Sarkozy, 2010).[1] At the same time, widespread disapproval of the type of stimulatory monetary policies pursued by the US – quantitative easing – raised international tensions. The conflict between the US and China on exchange rate policies, the use of capital controls by emerging markets and protectionist measures in the US and Europe all contributed to the unease. Everybody knew that, with the political situation so sensitive in every country, a whiff of protectionism could swiftly lead to retaliation – and raise the spectre of a 1930s-style trade war. This danger had been narrowly averted by the G20 in 2008–9.

Countries also started to build up reserves again (this will be discussed further in Chapter 9), demonstrating an absence of trust in the willingness or ability of the international community – as reflected in the institutions of monetary cooperation – to protect them. Even before GFC, countries had been rapidly building up foreign exchange reserves, which in 2009 amounted to as much as 15 per cent of global GDP, compared to 6 per cent in 2000. Reserve accumulation seemed again to be the only response that many countries were able to give to the credit crunch of 2007–10 and the threat, as they saw it, of quantitative easing (QE). For them, reserve growth was a side effect of policies to prevent their exchange rates from rising and thus damaging export prospects. Politicians in the West often viewed such policies as illegitimate currency manipulation.

The impetus to reform was strengthened by the new willingness of China to flex its financial muscle on the international stage. This followed a call by Zhou Xiaochuan, governor of the People's Bank of China (PBOC), to place international monetary reform on the official agenda (as cited in Chapter 2). The persistence of imbalances had clearly contributed to a shift of financial influence from West to East (including the Middle East as well as East and South Asia). Reformers hoped that China would use its muscle to make good on its pledge to press for international monetary reform. Disappointingly, the G20 could agree only on a pragmatic and limited programme, summed up as 'reform and repair'. It had four pillars: exchange rate flexibility, structural reform, fiscal consolidation and financial sector reform. Implementation would be facilitated by the Mutual Assessment Process (MAP) and Fund surveillance. MAP recognized that external imbalances mattered and that recovery was fragile. Observers pointed out that there was no mechanism to force action on an individual country, especially powerful ones like the US or China. However, it was the best that could be negotiated. Using a set of indicators – monitored by numerous working groups – MAP would monitor changes in internal and external imbalances.

Many governments doubted whether the world needed a new set of international monetary rules at all. They took the view that the world economy had been suffering from bad economic policies, rather than failures of the international monetary system. Countries had followed unsustainable policies. In particular, many governments had persistently followed policies that produced faster growth than was sustainable. It was unrealistic to think that the IMF could be made into a world referee, as in a game of football, and give green, yellow and red cards to the players, when it didn't have the guts to show a red card to the US or to China. The official line of many governments was that GFC had nothing to do with the role of the dollar or the international monetary system but with the lack of sustainable, consistent policies. Unless policies changed, appreciation of an exchange rate (such as the Chinese RMB) would not reduce a country's trade surplus.

The evolution of the system – coping mechanisms

Let us step back for a moment and consider the historical evolution of the international monetary system, usefully portrayed in the following chart from the Bank of Canada (Santor and Schembri, 2010) The positions of various governments can be arranged along a spectrum where the decisive variable is the degree of exchange rate flexibility (GFA stands for the global financial architecture and IT for inflation targeting).

A move towards a more flexible form (to the right of the chart below) would amount to a tinkering with the 'hybrid' system, and rely heavily on what some officials called 'coping mechanisms' – such as allocations of SDRs, or a new substitution account – to deal with shocks. These were

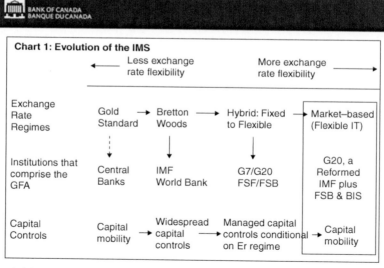

www.bankofcananda.ca

Figure 7.1   Evolution of the IMS

viewed by more radical reformers as treating the symptom of the illness, rather than the problem. However, history suggests that such coping mechanisms often had a better chance of gaining international agreement than did deeper reforms. Under this approach, the dominant role of dollar, and the existing set-up for monetary policies, would be retained.

Beyond such coping mechanisms, the most conservative of the 'systemic' versions of reform would retain the existing paradigm of monetary policy – independent central banks with flexible exchange rates using control over short-term interest rates to achieve price stability – but introduce stronger rules for adjustment and liquidity provision, and a stronger IMF. On this view, the main issue was lack of symmetrical real exchange rate adjustment. The system should permit adjustment to shocks such as China's emergence on the world stage. It should also be able to require real exchange rate changes, so as to avoid unsustainable current account imbalances which in turn produce trade frictions. Economists of this persuasion took the view (challenged in Chapter 8) that payments imbalances were a key factor in GFC and warned that after growth resumed imbalances could re-emerge. The emphasis was on adjustment of the current account. This was a view associated especially with the US and Canada, but it also had supporters elsewhere.

Large countries (and currency areas) should maintain flexible exchange rates and a commitment to price stability. The existing system failed to ensure this because it lacked effective means of adjustment, and created serious vulnerabilities in the world economy. It was a 'hybrid' or 'non-system' with a messy combination of exchange rate regimes and adjustment rules. Some exchange rates were flexible and market-determined; others were heavily managed, often with capital controls, while other economies had fixed rates, or currency boards. Adjustment was not symmetrical; absence of adjustment by surplus countries exerted a deflationary effect on the world economy as deficit countries tried to regain balance by cutting demand. Again and again, surplus countries such as China had thwarted adjustment through intervention. The hybrid system led inevitably to the growth of unsustainable current account imbalances. East Asia's real effective exchange rate had been flat between the 1980s and 2007, whereas Latin America's had risen. The misalignment of China's exchange rate was so large that it was having a huge impact on the global economy. If real exchange rate adjustment was prevented from taking place in one country, it forced other countries to intervene (through managing their exchange rates, reserve accumulation or capital controls).

On this view, the key principles should be as follows: economies should ensure external stability and prevent adverse spillovers; IMF should monitor countries' implementation of timely, orderly and symmetric adjustment, with large countries and blocks adopting flexible exchange rates; market forces should be left scope to organize economic activity and allocate resources. China would be persuaded that it was in its own and the collective interest to let the RMB appreciate substantially. Although many countries had pursued export-led growth in the past, such as Japan, Korea and some other emerging market economies, China was viewed as different because it was so large and there was much more surplus labour to absorb.

Pursuit of such an agenda within the G20 framework was viewed by many officials as the only game in town. G20 members would undertake concerted policy measures to restore growth in the world economy, by fiscal consolidation, structural reforms, increased exchange rate flexibility and financial sector reforms. They would implement a medium-term framework and press on with the mutual assessment process, with the IMF on hand to provide technical advice and encourage commitment. It would be a difficult coordination exercise – the most ambitious ever undertaken in the field of economic policy – which was why the 'mutual assistance programme' was so important. This did not imply, in the view of such officials, continued dominance of the system by the US. The IMF should avoid being dominated by any one country or region and do what was best for the global economy. All systemic countries should adopt inflation-targeting, with flexible exchange rates, sustainable fiscal policies, financial sector reforms and effective macro-prudential policies; and the IMF should reform itself (quotas, governance, surveillance and lending) to become more effective and legitimate.

More radical reformers

Governments that advocated wider reforms agreed with the previous viewpoint that there were flaws in an asymmetrical system. However, they took a different view of what these flaws and asymmetries were. For example, emerging market countries which wanted to move the basis of the system to the SDR usually viewed the main flaw in the system as its reliance on one national currency, the US dollar. This made the system unjust as well as unsustainable. The US enjoyed the privileges of being able to issue its currency to other countries to hold as reserves without assuming responsibility for the proper functioning of the system. American monetary policy was not subject to international discipline. The US used the international monetary system as a vehicle to export its problems to the rest of the world. So it was a matter of major frustration that US international monetary policies reflected a narrow view of America's national interests.

On this view, developing countries were victims of the system. With underdeveloped financial markets, they usually ran currency mismatches, with major holdings of foreign currencies such as the dollar that could be devalued. Developing countries needed stability rather than more flexibility in their exchange rates versus the US dollar. The US and the euro area also printed money in order to devalue their currencies and reduce their debt burdens. The system forced other countries such as China to accumulate reserves and finance the reserve centres, even though the value of these reserves had fallen steeply against gold and in terms of purchasing power.

The US had put pressure on China to appreciate its exchange rate with the excuse of calling for more flexible exchange rates; this revealed the injustice of the post-Bretton Woods system. The US dollar could not meet the domestic needs of the US and play the role of international currency at the same time.

The rise in the gold price illustrated the instability of the system and how much the dollar had depreciated against a neutral benchmark. There was in fact no benchmark for the floating exchange rate regime; so-called floating was actually based on the US dollar, and if the US dollar rate itself was not stable, the system was guaranteed to be 'unsafe at any speed'. Global liquidity was constantly expanding and money creation was excessive in both the US and EU. In 2007–09 broad money in the US and EU expanded from $8 trillion to $10 trillion even though their economies were contracting. This was seen by some as a threat to the system. In their view, the G20 discussions had ignored issues such as America's bad habit of gaining profits at the expense of others. Instead, they should have aimed to replace the role of the dollar, expand the role of the SDR and reduce demand for reserve assets, which were a costly and inefficient way of protecting an economy from volatile capital flows, and produced unsustainable imbalances.

View from the US Treasury

Top American officials said that fixing exchange rates was like shooting messengers because they brought bad news: there was no evidence that the foreign exchange market malfunctioned; it was one of the most efficient markets in the world and worked well throughout the financial crisis and associated currency turmoil, unlike other markets. The dollar's role as a reserve currency had expanded over time because of market demand, not because of official US policy. Relatively, its role had diminished to some extent as the system became multipolar. With regard to more ambitious proposals to reform the system, the US was not ready to subordinate domestic goals to international rules. If an attempt were made to construct such a system in the name of 'discipline' it was unlikely to last – rules could be broken. The Bretton Woods system had been too rigid. The US opposed regular incremental allocations of SDR and saw no appetite in official circles for a substitution account. Were we moving to a more diversified reserve system? It was not clear what commentators meant by this. There was no alternative to floating. The real defect of the system was 'asymmetric bias' – there was no pressure on surplus countries like China to adjust. What needed to be done was clear: the US should increase savings; surplus countries should boost demand. The talks in the G20 were about many aspects of policy in addition to the exchange rate.

To bring reforms about, the international community should make the G20 framework work – in the way the US wanted. Top priority was growth. US spokesmen rejected the criticism that it had wanted the G20 to set current account targets, or caps on current account surpluses, and that it had criticized surplus countries only. The G20 should look rather at indicators of imbalance. The IMF should conduct surveillance over capital flows. IMF credit lines had been extended – it might be a good idea to improve the international safety net, but there was no evidence that this would limit excessive reserve accumulation. Weak surveillance was perhaps the key issue. Reforms to the system and the role of the IMF should be pragmatic and modest; it was important not to confuse the market with vague talk of wider changes. In sum, the US looked to the Fund to conduct rigorous surveillance and provide insurance. Ideas of a supranational currency were undesirable and unrealistic, as was the proposal to make the IMF into an international lender of last resort. In short, the US countered efforts by the IMF staff and countries such as France and China to put more ambitious efforts at reform on the table.

France's perspective

France mounted a somewhat half-hearted challenge to the legitimacy of the system. The international monetary system 'has shown some of its inadequacies in times of crisis', according to Christine Lagarde, when she served as France's finance minister, during a seminar in December 2010 in which she discussed French goals upon taking the G20 presidency: 'Its legitimacy [...] rests on arrangements that go back to 1971 and that has not really been questioned.' Lagarde said that measures taken by the G20 and International Monetary Fund were 'significant but not yet substantial and structural'. France intended to initiate a debate that would lead to 'proposals to make sure that that system serves growth and global coordination more effectively'. 'The world has witnessed major shifts, new economies have emerged on the global stage and we have also experienced intense financial globalization as well as economical globalization,' said Lagarde. 'Even before the crisis started, vulnerabilities were on the rise, as the IMS has failed to prevent global imbalances' (Lagarde, 2010).

A well-functioning system had to meet various tests: fostering growth, meeting the challenges of a multi-polar world and moderating large exchange rate swings. On all these issues, the French pointed to worrying trends. While Paris accepted the need for some currency variations, it complained of the complete disconnect from the real economy and the problems arising from erratic capital flows, economic inefficiencies, contamination and contagion.

According to Christine Lagarde, 'During the crisis [...] there were large capital outflows mainly from emerging countries [which] have been a major factor in spreading the crisis across borders, and given their magnitude and their volatility they continue to be a real threat to global stability [...] The volatility created by the flows clearly limits, hampers their [emerging markets] ability to develop, and it creates a need for self insurance through reserve accumulation, which contributes to worsening the global imbalances.' This was well said.

The role of the dollar as a reserve currency was important because investors held a majority of their assets in dollars, so that action taken by the Federal Reserve had a major impact on emerging markets, especially on those that wanted to peg their exchange rates. This might be acceptable so long as the dollar was stable. But demand for reserves was rising dramatically. More dollar reserves would further heighten global imbalances. Reliance on a single currency fomented economic and financial instability when the exchange rate of that currency against other major currencies was unstable. There was one dominant currency but several economic areas, each of which was exposed to turmoil when that currency was unstable. Disorderly reserve diversification created the risk of disorderly responses – as countries became aware of their vulnerability.

Views from Beijing

As mentioned above, China was also pressing for reform. It needed stability above all to maintain its record-breaking growth rate. Yet the US was in trouble as a reserve currency centre. The Triffin dilemma (see Chapters 9 and 12) had returned: demand for dollars by central banks to hold in reserve created imbalances and US deficits and thus in the long run undermined confidence in the dollar. China feared large losses on its dollar holdings as the dollar depreciated. If the US continued to run a current account deficit, the system could 'snap'. The US economy was having a hard time: with its trade deficit deteriorating again, and an excessive fiscal deficit, the central bank's policy of quantitative easing looked like a desperate measure and in such conditions the currency system could not sustain itself. Although the centre of economic power was shifting to emerging markets and especially to Asia, the renmimbi could not replace the dollar. The only solution would be to share the burden.

When the US was responsible for a large proportion of the world economy, it could pump up demand by itself, but this was no longer the case. The US balance sheet was weak – 'an accident waiting to happen' – and in the absence of a supranational currency the international community would have to manage the current system. If it did not, countries would increasingly resort to barter; China was in fact already doing that, with barter type arrangements with several countries, bypassing the dollar, or only using the dollar to settle net imbalances. China insisted that it would invoice and settle trade in RMB wherever possible. The risk of a trend to disintegration and de-globalization was clear.

Other emerging markets' views

With capital inflows to emerging markets likely to remain volatile, and being countered increasingly by capital controls, tension was growing. Asset managers were in the midst of making a historic shift in their strategic asset allocation to emerging markets. Not many countries responded to the G20's pressure for exchange rates be flexible. In fact, a de facto reform of the international monetary system was taking place, but not in the direction of more flexibility – the reform was characterized more by moves to capital controls and more self-insurance. None of this was welcomed by emerging markets. They were well aware such trends would further increase volatility. Only a few large emerging markets would benefit much from capital inflows.

The G20 falls short

By 2012, the G20 was attempting to push through limited improvements in the existing regime. These were aimed at patching it up, and were conducted by governments who wanted to get back to business as usual. They focused on liquidity provision, safety nets, and limited reforms to governance. Why was there not greater impetus for radical reform? Was everybody waiting for another, bigger, crash? Would another global conflict be needed – as in the past – to beget the visionary ideas and leadership lacking in peacetime?

Such reforms fell far below what was needed. The leaders failed to grasp that it was lack of confidence in the very structure of rules and policy-making models that lay behind continued global economic weakness. Lack of confidence in the ability of any individual government, or the current coordination of policies internationally, held back investment and spending. What was needed at a minimum was evidence that leaders realized this. That was why 'Occupy Wall Street' and other street protests that spread across the world in October– December 2011 were significant.

People were expressing their rage at the corruption of political decision-making, the apparent impotence of governments to do what was necessary, to get their act together, confront the power of finance and forge a better system. A simple announcement that the G20 recognized this, and were instituting talks aimed at a wholesale recasting of the current international monetary system, and that they intended this to lead to a new GFS (taking in the private sector) fit for the twenty-first century, would have done wonders for business confidence, and stimulate recovery of demand. It would have shown that they at last grasped the dimensions of the problem.

Certainly, it was understandable and correct that the immediate response to GFC was to boost demand. In 2010–12 the heart of the implementation of the G20's agenda was a concerted, international $7 trillion boost to demand, to promote growth. This could be done only if all countries joined in. If one country alone had attempted to boost demand, it would have plunged into an unsustainable payments deficit, forcing it to retrench, with little net effect on global demand. The political imperative to reduce unemployment and fend off protectionist pressures made this Keynesian response unavoidable, but it offered no long-term way out of the money trap. It added further to state deficits and debt and risked inflation down the road.

Playing for high stakes

Since the Second World War, the international monetary system has rested on three pillars: first, the undoubted credit of the US; secondly, a competitive, market-based, international money and banking system; and thirdly, a high level of official international cooperation. One way of looking at the challenge facing governments after GFC is to look at its impact on each of these pillars.

Well, they were all still standing, just about, but they had received a battering. The US Treasury bond market, the cornerstone of the entire commercial financial edifice, the benchmark against which yields of securities world-wide had always been measured, was itself at risk from the reduction in the US credit standing and the difficulties of US politicians in getting a handle on its public finances. The free, global, private commercial banking system had been profoundly changed by the crisis; it was not as free, nor as global, nor as private and arguably not as competitive as it had been, with the state taking more direct interest in its activities, banks pulling liquidity back to head offices, and the nationalization of some major banks. A heavy burden of responsibility therefore lay on the third pillar – cooperation among governments. Thankfully, that was holding up, but political pressures were not to be denied. It, too, was under enormous strain.

A great advantage of globalization is that all countries acquire such a major stake in the world economy, are so interdependent, that it has become almost unthinkable for any one of them to uproot and go it alone. Thus, while the world missed US leadership, habits of cooperation persisted. Central banks in particular upheld that tradition, more than a century old, of trusting each other and consulting with each other on outstanding problems. But they too were sometimes elbowed out by political imperatives. In the tense days of 2008, for example, finance ministries suddenly took over negotiations on policies towards large international banks at risk of failure – inevitably, as taxpayer's money was at stake. Matters got ugly very quickly. If there were to be a repeat of that episode, given the even more tightly stretched state of public finances, cooperation would again be tested to the limit. Markets feared that many banks would simply be too big to save. The markets might pick off one sovereign after another, destroy its credit, make the government unable to borrow and then move on to the next victim. Other dangers were easy to spot. The US Congress might decide that what it saw as China's intransigence on exchange rate policy could no longer be tolerated. A breakup of the eurozone would pitch Germany into a dominant position in Europe that neither Berlin nor other capitals wanted, and that some of them would find intolerable. Sino–Japanese relations could deteriorate further, with public opinion on both sides already heated.

If such imminent threats can be avoided, the underlying question remains: how would the shift in geo-political balance power be reflected in changes to international monetary arrangements? Historically, geo-political shifts had always left an imprint on the international monetary system, and the nature of that imprint had reflected the preferences of rising powers and ways of doing things. Thus the British shaped the nature and functioning of the classical gold standard even though they needed to secure cooperation from others to make it work in practice. The 1930s Great Depression was made worse by a total lack of cooperation, as no power was willing to serve as leader. As we saw in Chapter 3, the Bretton Woods system reflected American conceptions of how a capitalist international order should be organized. Similarly, the emergence of the world's second largest currency area, centred on the euro, if it survived, would in time have an influence on the future shape of the system, as would the emergence of India, China, Russia, Brazil, Mexico and others.

It was an uneasy peace.

Part I (Chapters 1–4) portrayed how governments came to be trapped in a dysfunctional GFS and traced the story of how the trap was set from the age of Bretton Woods through the era of monetary experimentation, to GFC. Chapter 3 discussed the conditions likely to be needed for successful reform of the GFS. Part II (Chapters 5–7) reviewed official policies aiming to improve the system. It showed that while these efforts did not address the root causes of the problem they were rescued from total failure by long-standing habits of cooperation and growing interdependence. Yet the analysis demonstrated why muddling through and tinkering are unlikely to be enough. Part III will describe four outstanding issues that added further pressures for change – and that a reformed GFS would have to meet.

Note

1. Speech at the World Economic Forum, January 2010.

Bibliography

Communiqué of Finance Ministers and Central Bank Governors, Washington DC, 14–15 April 2011.

Lagarde, Christine, 'The International Monetary System: Old and New Debates', Address to Workshop of Reinventing Bretton Woods Committee, Paris, 11 December 2010.

Santor, Eric, and Lawrence Schembri, 'A Brave New International Monetary System: Shaping the Future of the International Monetary System', International Department, Bank of Canada, Paper given to conference of National Bank of Poland, 26 May 2010. The paper is published in revised form in the Bank of Canada *Review*, Autumn, 2011 under the title: 'The International Monetary System: An Assessment and Avenue for Reform'.

Sarkozy, Nicolas, Speech at the World Economic Forum, January 2010; published 27 January 2010; English translation at http://www.cfr.org/financial-crises/sarkozys-speech-world-economic-forum-january-2010/p21346

Zoellick, Robert, 'The G20 Must Look beyond Bretton Woods II', published in *Financial Times*, 7 November 2010.

Part III
Four Key Issues

8
Those Global Imbalances

The problem of global imbalances, like the other major challenges facing the GFS – the crisis of reserve currencies, the dysfunctional financial system and its liability to cross-border currency and credit bubbles – added to pressures for systemic change. These challenges are reviewed in the following chapters.

Were global imbalances the cause of GFC?

A remarkable feature of the GFC was that as time passed there was no evidence of an agreement being reached on the underlying causes. Everybody felt it was of great significance for the future of our societies, but there was heated debate about what that 'significance' consisted of. This analytical confusion contrasted with experience after comparable shocks in the previous 50 years. For example, the causes of the developing country debt problem of the 1980s were quickly identified: inflationary monetary policies in leading countries, accompanied by low or even negative real interest rates, had, in the course of the 1970s, stimulated a burst of financial innovation ('syndicated bank lending'), which culminated in a flood of short-term capital to developing countries, followed by a sudden stop after the Federal Reserve raised interest rates abruptly in 1979–80. This hit less developed countries with increases in their interest payments, which some were unable to pay, and so many (starting with Mexico in August 1982) defaulted, threatening to bring down the western banking system. There was much disagreement on what to do about that, but little disagreement on what had happened and why. This was the first big cross-border credit bubble of the post-Bretton Woods global economy, and it set a pattern. The so-called Asian crisis of 1999–2000 was similarly attributable to excess borrowing and lending to emerging markets, encouraged in many cases by expectations that exchange rates would remain fixed. Indeed, most of the booms and busts of the period followed a familiar pattern, as described in such classics as Charles Kindleberger's *Manias, Panics and Crashes* (revised and updated by Robert Aliber, 2011) of a cycle of over-lending and borrowing ending in a crash – usually traceable to a spell of excessively expansionary monetary policies.[1] (For a further analysis of bubbles in currencies and credit see Chapter 11.)

If there was one area of seeming consensus, it was that the growth of China, India and other emerging markets was in some way implicated in the financial crisis. Like most other countries that had gone through the process of industrialization, the emerging markets relied mainly on domestic savings to generate the resources needed for investment. But in contrast to other countries that had preceded them, the current crop of fast-growing developing countries showed a marked reluctance to move into current account deficit, borrow abroad and allow net capital imports. Whereas the 'normal' pattern was for rapidly developing economies to supplement domestic savings by tapping into foreign savings, China and other leading emerging markets generated large payments surpluses, built up huge foreign reserves and exported capital. Many economists considered their excess savings played a decisive role in creating the conditions for GFC. Was this true? If true, how should a future system cope? Even if they cannot be held responsible for the financial crash, weren't their continued surpluses a threat?

A threat to the world economy?

The persistence of global imbalances was at the heart of the whole question of the role of exchange rates and other policy instruments in facilitating a country's adjustment to changing conditions affecting its external payments, and hence to the functioning of the monetary system. To quote a remark by Mervyn King, then the Governor of the Bank of England (press conference, 10 August 2011),

> It is almost exactly four years since the start of the financial crisis. The origins of the crisis lie in the large stocks of indebtedness that resulted from the widening imbalances in the world economy, about which nothing was done for so long.

This chapter argues that, although global current account imbalances did pose threats to the global economy and challenges to policy makers, they were not responsible for GFC, which had much more to do with monetary excess impinging on flawed banking and monetary systems operating within a weak international monetary regime. It was these financial and monetary system failures that made the regime incapable of accommodating large but natural differences in savings and investment behaviour of different peoples around the world. Governments and the IMF responded in the only way they could, given the fact they were unwilling or unable to reform the overall system. They patched it up. As described in Chapter 7, they started on the G20 process – a combination of massive stimulus led by monetary policies, initially also supported by fiscal expansion and a reform of bank regulation. They appeared to meet with some success – the global economy recovered somewhat in 2010 and 2011 – but this was accompanied by the re-emergence of global imbalances, and another stage of the crisis – with a collapse of confidence in the creditworthiness of several countries. As a result, the advanced economies always seemed on the verge of falling back into recession, with a high probability of pulling emerging economies down with them. Essentially, the world economy was in many key respects going back to business as usual – with the US as buyer and banker of last resort, surplus countries increasing exports and the re-emergence of strains: protectionism, capital controls, fragile banks – but with a much worse underlying financial condition, notably severely impaired public and private sector balance sheets. Failure to escape from the doom-loop policy cycle has already been analysed (Chapters 2–5), as has the failure to establish robust regional or international structures (Chapter 6 and 7). We shall argue that these failures, when added to the problems of reserve currencies (see Chapter 9), banking (see Chapter 10) and the possibility of yet another credit boom on the back of the central banks' zero interest rate polices (see Chapter 11), all increased the rational fear of further financial crises.[2]

The subject of this chapter, persistent global imbalances, could be problematic for several reasons – because they encouraged protectionism, for example, and distorted the structure of economies; or they could be natural accompaniments of different savings and investment preferences, which a 'good' GFS should be able to accommodate (by, for example, a mix of private and official financing). So thoughtful commentators have distinguished between 'good' and 'bad' imbalances. Persistent imbalances could be closely linked to other systemic issues, such as the over-extended role of the dollar as discussed in Chapter 9. The best way to manage them is through a monetary order or constitution strong enough to provide a framework within which markets sort out imbalances in savings and investment. Having a concept of the long-term aim that would be in every nation's interests – the public good of international monetary stability – could help to guide and mould short-term managerial responses to the inevitable challenges that governments faced. But, yet again, the capacity to take a long-term view was itself a casualty of the dysfunctional system.

An early test would come as and when the G20 effort to lever up a sustainable global recovery ran into the sands. There was no Plan B. Then, the worst outcome would be to recoil from the probable failure of the G20 consensus strategy by resorting to nationalistic, protectionist policies – and blame emerging markets. Unfortunately by 2012 there were already signs that this was the way things would fall out. Indeed, many firms and markets were already marking or preparing for a retreat from globalization. The retreat would be dressed up under the banner of 'localism' but would amount to a major political as well as an economic setback. It would be another catastrophe caused, like GFC itself, by policy mistakes resulting from a flawed 'official' international monetary regime interacting with a flawed 'private' banking regime. It was unfortunate, to say the least, that central bankers were preparing the intellectual grounds that politicians could use to spin protectionist measures, especially as their analysis was intellectually questionable.

The chances of a cooperative solution were not helped by the ideological splits amongst economists. Already jolted by being linked in the public mind with bankers and politicians as sharing 'blame' for GFC, economists were about to lose further credibility if there were yet another collapse. A first step would be for the Anglo-Saxon-centric school at least to acknowledge the existence of competing views and alternative ways of looking at the world. It is to these rival views that we now turn, after a brief reminder of the dominant view.

Blame Asian and German surpluses?

That view gave China and other 'savings and surplus glut' economies a starring role in creating the conditions that led to the crisis. Ben Bernanke, at a time when he was a governor of the Fed, but before becoming chairman, set the terms of the debate with his influential speech of 10 March 2005, on 'The Global Savings Glut and the US Current Account Deficit', in which he argued that over the previous decade a combination of forces had increased the global supply of saving, helping to explain both the US current account deficit and the low level of long-term interest rates. One aspect of this was that emerging markets had become large net lenders.

Bernanke said it was obvious that in some sense the US had a large trade deficit because US savings had declined, but went on to ask, why this was. This could be in some part a reaction to events outside the US. The counterpart to the US deficit was to be found in emerging markets, which had moved into surplus because of the financial crises those countries had experienced in the previous ten years or so. As a result, these countries had built up their foreign reserves. From 1996 to early in 2000 US attracted vast inflows, especially into equities because of new technologies. This spurred consumption, especially on cheap imports, and strengthened the exchange rate; after the stock market decline from March 2000, the inflow to the US lessened but desired savings in rest of world remained strong, so interest rates fell, causing a fall in US savings, triggering a housing boom.

The special role of the dollar meant that the savings flow out of emerging markets was directed more to dollar assets than to others; but other advanced countries also swung into deficit, and all developed housing booms, except for Germany and Japan, whose payments remained in surplus. This resulted in a global saving glut. Although this change brought some benefits, for the developing world to be lending large sums to the mature economies was, said Bernanke, quite undesirable: 'Basic economic logic thus suggests that, in the longer term, the industrial countries as a group should be running current account surpluses and lending on net to the developing world, not the other way round' (Bernanke, 2005).

What were the policy implications? A reduction in the US budget deficit, though desirable in itself, would not eliminate the current account deficit; what was needed was to help developing countries to re-enter international capital markets as borrowers, rather than as lenders, and to encourage the development of their financial markets. However 'the factors underlying the US current account deficit are likely to unwind only gradually'.

This analysis was enormously influential. Bernanke himself returned to the theme after the crisis had broken out, and his analysis was endorsed by Hank Paulson as Secretary of the US Treasury in November 2008.[3] This approach was elaborated in Martin Wolf's book *Fixing Global Finance* and came to represent the mainstream view of the crisis (Wolf, 2009).[4] The economist Richard Portes argued that global macroeconomic imbalances – in particular, large current account deficits and surpluses – were 'the major underlying cause of the crisis' (Portes et al., 2009, p. 6). In similar vein, Charles Dumas, in *Globalization Fractures*, talked about the 'enormous destructiveness' of the Eurasian savings surplus: 'This surplus has moved like a tidal wave from balance sheet to balance sheet, between businesses, households and government, loading them up with extra debt' (Dumas, 2010, p. 53). The US was forced to follow lax monetary and fiscal policies, and it was 'absurd' to blame Alan Greenspan, at the time head of the Federal Reserve: given the structural surpluses in savings glut countries, which included Germany as well as the Asian surplus countries, would anyone, if chairman of the Fed, deliberately have slowed growth just as a precaution against future debt service problems? The answer, said Dumas, was obviously not. He concluded that the savings glut had caused the financial crisis (2010, p 13). As America slipped back into dependence on debt to restore growth, this, warned Dumas, would lead to a degradation of US credit on which the world's financial system depended. On the latter point he proved prescient.

Where the savings glut/global imbalances theory went wrong

But this approach was analytically questionable and politically dangerous. To deal with the politics first, what was its one-line political message? 'Bash China!' It would be natural if this were resented in Beijing. From the initial opening-up by Deng Xiaoping in 1979, China had taken the system as it found it, and had by-and-large played by the rules, accepting the WTO rulebook, and had succeeded, just like Germany, Japan, South Korea and others before it, by beating the competition, to the benefit of consumers everywhere. To turn to the analytics, this thesis, though dominant, by no means went unchallenged. As Ricardo Caballero pointed out, in the course of a comment on a paper by Murray Obstfeld and Kenneth Rogoff, many economists chose to ignore the inconvenient fact that their widely anticipated worry about global imbalances before the crisis (that they would lead to a collapse of the dollar) in fact played no role in the crisis.[5] Such economists wanted to take the credit for the realization of their forecast of doom, and deeply at heart they still felt that global imbalances were the culprit. So they found a different mechanism. In reality, global imbalances and their feared sudden reversal never played a significant role during this deep crisis. Indeed, the worse things became, the more both domestic and foreign investors ran for cover to US Treasuries. Instead, the largest reallocation of funds was across asset classes, in particular from complex to simple safe instruments.[6] Caballero argued that the real problem was a shortage of safe assets, which emerging markets did not produce, not global imbalances on current account. 'We should not get distracted with secondary illnesses.'

This was a critique more of the mechanism that connected imbalances with the crisis rather than of the basic view that saw excess saving as the problem. A perhaps deeper critique of the global imbalances approach came from Claudio Borio and Piti Disyatat of the BIS.[7] The dominant 'blame China' view emphasised *saving*, a national account concept, whereas what mattered was *financing*. The 'savings glut' approach threw no light on the cross-border flows that financed the credit boom. Indeed, it diverted attention away from the monetary and financial factors that mainly caused the crisis. It was the financial decisions of market participants that determined financing flows, not the *ex post* distribution of savings and investment.

Nor did evidence support the excess savings view. The link between the US current account deficit and global savings appeared to be weak. While the deficit began its trend deterioration in the early 1990s, the world saving rate was actually declining, at least until 2004. At the same time, the cut in US current account deficits after 2006 occurred against the backdrop of an increase in emerging market saving rates. Also, real world long-term interest rates were declining from the early 1990s, irrespective of developments in the global saving rate. The global economic boom from 2003 was 'hard to reconcile with an increase in ex ante global saving', which, assuming nominal rigidities, should depress aggregate demand.

Further, many surplus countries had also had marked credit booms – including China from 1997 to 2000, India from 2001 to 2004, Brazil from 2003 to 2007 and economies in the Middle East. 'Moreover, going further back, the huge credit boom that preceded the banking crisis in Japan had also occurred against the backdrop of a large current account surplus...' (Borio and Disyatat, May 2011, op cit)

Were central banks the real culprits?

On this reading, the roots of the GFC should be traced to a global credit and asset price boom pumped up by central bankers' lax monetary policies and commercial bankers' aggressive risk-taking. The international monetary and financial system lacked 'anchors' to prevent excessive credit growth and to contain the 'elasticity' inherent in global finance. In sum, the main macroeconomic cause of the financial crisis was not 'excess saving' but the 'excess elasticity' of the international monetary and financial system.

The authors anchored their view to an alternative tradition of economics that had, they said, been neglected for too long. This tradition distinguished between market interest rates and equilibrium (or natural) interest rates, and the role played by credit, and went back to John Stuart Mill and Wicksell and those who followed them. The importance of understanding global financial intermediation and its tenuous link to current accounts was also a key theme in Kindleberger (Kindlebeger and Aliber, 2010). In this tradition of economic thought, the true constraint on expenditures was not savings, but financing. Spending can be financed by borrowing and this can determine ex post savings. Agents in the deficit sector require financing to enable them to spend more than their incomes, and it was this very spending that created the corresponding saving in the surplus sector. Similarly, at the global level, countries running current account surpluses were not financing those running current account deficits.

Advocates of the excess-savings-blame-China thesis did not just use the wrong theory. They got the evidence wrong too. The evidence on how the asset boom was financed in the build-up to the crisis did not support the view that it was all the fault of excess savings by some countries. By far the most important source of financing for the credit boom in the US was Europe, not emerging markets. Europe accounted for around one-half of total inflows in 2007. Of this, more than half came from the UK, a country running a current account *deficit*, and roughly one-third from the euro area, a region roughly in balance. Little came from China, Japan or the Middle East From this perspective, the role of Asia – in particular China – and oil exporters in 'funding' the US current account deficit or the credit boom was insignificant.

In other words, to reduce the likelihood and severity of financial crises, the main policy issue was how to address the 'excess elasticity' of the overall system, not whether savings were excessive or not in some countries:

> So long as central banks condition their policy exclusively on domestic developments, global financial conditions may be inappropriate. And in considering the need for cooperation, the effect of a given country's monetary policy is better analysed through the lens of currency areas rather than national boundaries. (Borio and Disyatat, 2011, p. 26)

That is surely right. The authors just cited, senior economists at the central bankers' own think tank, the BIS, recommended that central banks should 'go beyond narrow inflation targeting regimes'. But even such a departure from central banks' model was not a complete answer. Internationally the answer was 'more complex': governments needed to recognize that 'no individual country can be safe unless the world as a whole is safe' (op cit, p. 27). The fundamental weakness was that the GFS lacked anchors to prevent the build-up of unsustainable booms in credit and asset prices leading to serious financial strains, which had derailed the world economy. One implication of this analysis was that even if the scale of current account imbalances were reduced, that would not in itself make the financial system any safer.

...and as de-globalization gathered pace...

Protectionism was on the rise as countries found ways of raising barriers without breaching WTO rules. Countries that suffered a severe banking crisis in 2007–08 accounted for more than half of world output, and the crisis sharply reduced their demand for imports. Their imports were likely to remain depressed for years, even more than their tempered output projections would suggest. The fall of several countries into a sovereign debt crisis, which is often associated with cutbacks in imports, meant that prospects for global import demand darkened further. That was just what happened in the rolling eurozone sovereign debt crisis of 2010–2011. In such circumstances protectionist pressures were likely to increase. Even though governments generally tried to abide by their WTO commitments, gaps in these left ample scope for trade restrictions, and political pressure made it difficult to resist them. A UK government analysis in 2011 of reports by various international bodies and think tanks highlighted continued protectionist pressures arising from unemployment, macroeconomic imbalances and currency tensions, which, it said 'may still risk the consensus in favour of open trade and investment'. It noted that countries had been deterred from using classic 'at the border' trade measures and resorted more to domestic policies like 'buy national' campaigns or subsidies to provide an advantage to their firms.[8]

Clearly, the open global financial and trading regimes remained vulnerable to further shocks – and awareness of this fragility in the environment for business in turn deterred spending and investment. It was likely to be made worse by the way governments resorted to regulations as ways to control banking and protect the public purse from further calls for help. In the US, highly protectionist legislation was repeatedly put before Congress – fortunately usually withdrawn. Yet the threat remained. In the absence of a change in the doom-loop of policy-making, and in the perverse set of incentives facing governments and financiers (which, we insist, was a function of the international monetary disorder), there was little to stop the trade situation deteriorating. Governments, whether bilaterally or through the WTO and the IMF, seemed helpless. This conclusion was supported by a study from the Peterson Institute (Gagnon, 2011), which forecast a return to record current account imbalances on the grounds that the narrowing in 2009–10 mainly reflected the global recession. With US unemployment in 2012 at more than 8 per cent, and double that in some European countries, while China's and India's growth rates were expected to weaken, political tensions were growing.

These tensions were fed by talk of 'currency wars', by the suspicion in the US that foreigners were constantly cheating, by the backlash in Europe against immigration policies, and by events that concentrated minds of people on their domestic scene (such as the devastating earthquake and tsunami in Japan, the horrible massacre by a lone right-wing gunman in Norway in 2011 and populist rhetoric accompanying the presidential election campaigns in France and the US in 2012).

In terms of what to do about such imbalances, the ideological divide was between those who emphasized exchange rate flexibility and those who attached priority to other measures. Long-standing debates about the effectiveness of exchange rate changes in reducing trade and current account imbalances continued without agreement being reached. Occasionally, there had been agreement that a major exchange rate was undervalued or overvalued – for example the Plaza accord of 1985 was possible at the time because there was consensus that the dollar was overvalued. But this attempt at policy coordination proved to be a mistake and in any event no such consensus existed in 2010–12.[9] In the absence of strong supporting policies, current account imbalances could resist even large changes in exchange rates. The structural nature of imbalances required structural policies to address them effectively. That well-worn conclusion was borne out yet again by experiences after the recession, when for example the UK payments deficit showed a pretty feeble response to the massive 25 per cent fall in the value of sterling between mid-2007 and early 2009.[10]

….'quackery' of exchange rate doctors

Unfortunately, the habit of blaming surplus countries persisted. Indeed, it had been such a division of views that had led to the collapse of Bretton Woods system of fixed rates in the first place – in those days the US demanded that Germany revalue; just as half a century later it demanded that China revalue. Thus, how the burden of adjustment should be shared also remained, as in the 1960s, a central issue. Some economists argued that if the world overall were in depression, or suffered from insufficient demand, pressing surplus countries to adjust was sensible. They called for a reduction in official financial outflows, i.e. currency appreciation, in surplus economies.

It was, however, dubious whether surplus countries such as China should boost demand, and mistaken to place so much emphasis on exchange rate policy. It was pie-in-the-sky to imagine that such a boost would spill over into imports and reduced exports – pure expenditure switching – even more so if you do not believe that exchange rates can induce such switching. And look what happened to Japan when it was bullied into expanding demand in the late 1980s – a credit boom and bust from which it had not recovered 20 years later. That kind of sentiment, widely shared and disseminated through the media, showed why it was all the more important to have a correct analysis of the role of payment imbalances in the global economy and as a widely cited cause of the financial crisis. If they had played a major role, then to avoid a future crisis, policies should be directed primarily at reducing payments imbalances and their impact on the financial system. If, however, the main cause of the crisis and recession lay elsewhere – in a malfunctioning financial system, and misguided monetary policies and policy regimes – then policy would naturally focus on these areas. Correct specification of the causes of the financial crisis and of the role of payment imbalances were vital to clear the decks – and to build a consensus round the need to reform the GFS. Too many of the messages that emanated from western governments and central banks amounted to special pleading designed to avert the public's attention from their own past and continuing failings.

My view is that exchange rate changes were the wrong remedy for the wrong disease. For exchange rate depreciation to improve the trade balance, overall domestic spending must fall relative to output, i.e. savings must rise relative to investment. But there's no reason to assume this will take place. In the case of US–China relations, exchange rate volatility would be exceedingly dangerous; a sharp rise in the RMB might deter investment in China, causing a slump, while boosting domestic demand in an already overheated economy was asking for trouble. And the trade surplus might even increase! To quote a recent paper by McKinnon and Schnabl,

China is criticised for keeping its dollar exchange rate fairly stable when it has a large trade (saving) surplus. We argue that this criticism is misplaced in two ways. First, no predictable link exists between the exchange rate and the trade balance of an international creditor economy. Second, since 1995, the stable yuan/dollar rate has anchored China's price level and facilitated counter cyclical fiscal policies that have smoothed its high real GDP growth at a remarkable 9 to 11 percent per year (McKinnon and Schnabl, 2011).

If domestic saving is not affected by exchange rate changes, and so long as domestic savings exceeds domestic investment, China would have a trade surplus that has to be financed by lending abroad. To quote Mundell, writing many years ago,

> The theory that exchange rate changes improve the balance of trade of the country with the depreciating currency is an old fallacy still held by some writers on international economic problems, but not generally subscribed to by any of the great economists. The reality is very different. The exchange rate has relatively little to do with a country's real balance of trade. (1989)

The balance was equal to the difference between a country's production and its spending. There was 'no reason' to think that this relation was determined by the exchange rate or that changes in the exchange rate can bring about shifts in these relationships.The function of the exchange rate was to link the scale of prices in one country with that in another. It had nothing directly to do with the balance of trade, which depended on other factors:

> If we could conceive of trade taking place between two populated planets it would be inconceivable that anyone would concoct the theory that the currencies in which each planet's local trade was conducted would have any effect at all on the planet's balance of trade or interplanetary lending.

The claims made for the benefits of exchange rates changes were, he proclaimed, 'sheer quackery'.

How to contain the risks posed by global imbalances

As a footnote to this diatribe, one consequence of GFC seems to have been that large *depreciations* in exchange rates, such as pursued by the US and UK, had come to be viewed as akin to protectionist measures.

As the British official paper stated disarmingly (seeing as the UK was viewed by many as one of the main culprits),

> The recent economic crisis has put the spotlight on the role of exchange rate policy as a possible distortion of trade, as some countries are thought to be manipulating currencies to gain a competitive advantage. This is a particularly difficult issue, as there is little consensus over what the 'correct' level of a currency might be, and the debate over protectionism has spilled over into sensitive areas such as domestic monetary policy. (UK, 2011)

Notwithstanding the pressure from the US on China's exchange rate policy, there was growing agreement among economists on two points. First, that a narrow focus on exchange rates was misguided. Even if few went all the way with McKinnon and Mundell, there seemed to be a grudging acceptance that exchange rate changes could never address the huge imbalances caused by discrepancies in savings between China and the US. Thus, international negotiations on the payments imbalances between the US and China should not be about the exchange rate. Secondly, there was agreement on another point: that it was wrong to analyse a multilateral system as if it were a bilateral system. China could say, 'we have a deficit with the rest of Asia, do you (the US) really want us to reduce our imports from Asia?' We should learn from Japan's exchange rate experience in the 1980s, as described in several papers by McKnnon.[11]

There were those who thought it might be possible to go back to the Bretton Woods concept of 'fundamental disequilibrium'. If agreement could be reached on how to define it, this would involve a body – presumably the IMF as in the old Bretton Woods era – telling a country running a payments imbalance to take remedial action. But such pressure has already been rejected by numerous countries. So, what should be the focus of action? One approach was to claim that global imbalances were, after all, not a fundamental problem anyway – what damage did they do? If fears of protectionism could be reduced or managed, that point of view had much to be said for it, once it is accepted as it should be that current account imbalances had little to do with the financial crisis. True, there was an argument that they distorted national economies, if they were 'bad' imbalances, resulting for example from subsidies or taxes on consumption. Some economists believed it may be possible, at least in principle, to define a desirable level of imbalance. Yet their common policy remedy, setting target zones for exchange rates, was not appropriate – apart from any other problem, it would require agreement on what is an appropriate level of capital flows. In fact, there was no chance of this vexed issue of global imbalances, with the growing risk of protectionism and dis-integration, being managed satisfactorily within the current international monetary system. It was one more policy area, along with the crisis of the inflation targeting model, zero interest rates, the collapse of a coherent monetary policy, and hopes that tighter regulation would be sufficient to reform banking (see Chapter 10), where the train had hit the buffers.

By contrast, a viable GFS should be able to manage the major challenges facing it. We now turn to the problem of reserve currencies.

Notes

1. See Kindleberger, Charles and Aliber, Robert P., 'Manias, Panics, and Crashes: A History of Financial Crises', Wiley, 6th edition 2010.
2. On the eve of the G20 meeting of finance ministers in Scotland, Andy Haldane, the Bank of England's executive director for financial stability, warned that the relationship between the state and banks represented a 'doom loop' which will keep inflicting crises on the public unless arrested. (Report in *Daily Telegraph* 6 November 2009).
3. See 'A Conversation with Ben Bernanke', Conference at the Council on Foreign Relations. 10 March 2009. www.cfr.org; Hank Paulson, see Statement from the G-20 Summit on Financial Markets and the World Economy. 15 November 2008. www.G20.org
4. In his well-known book, *Faultlines*, Rajan rather desperately recommended that the IMF should as a last resort appeal to the public of countries with large trade imbalances to understand where their real interests lay over the heads of national politicians (Rajan, 2010).
5. Maurice Obstfeld and Kenneth Rogoff argued that, although global imbalances in trade and capital flows didn't cause the crisis, they were generated by the same underlying factors and amplified its magnitude. Excessively stimulatory U.S. monetary policy combined with low global interest rates, credit market distortions, and problematic financial innovations led to a housing bubble. At the same time, exchange rate and other economic policies of emerging market countries such as China helped the US borrow cheaply abroad to finance its bubble. To limit future global imbalances, Obstfeld and Rogoff suggested policies to improve domestic financial market efficiency in less-developed economies, where structural shortcomings tend to boost corporate and household saving rates. Obstfeld, Maurice, and Kenneth Rogoff. 'Global Imbalances and the Financial Crisis: Products of Common Causes.' http://www.frbsf.org/economics/conferences/aepc/2009/09_Obstfeld.pdf
6. See Caballero, Ricardo J., and Arvind Krishnamurthy. 2009. Caballero, Ricardo J., and Pablo Kurlat. 2009. See also Coval, Joshua D., Jakub W. Jurek, and Erik Stafford. 2008.
7. See Borio, Claudio and Piti Disyatat, May 2011.

8. Department for Business Innovation and Skills, paper on 'Protectionism' February 2011.

9. This was an agreement between West Germany, France, Japan, the US and UK to depreciate the US dollar against the yen and DM by intervention in foreign exchange markets. The accord was signed on 22 September 1985 at the Plaza Hotel, New York. The dollar declined by 51 per cent against the yen from 1985 to 1987.

10. The UK share of world exports, weighted by their importance in UK exports, though showing a slight improvement on trend, continued to fall in the period to mid 2011, while non-tourist imports, said the Bank of England, 'do not seem to have responded much to the exchange rate depreciation'; See Foreword by Spenceer Dale, Executive Director, to the Bank of England's Quarterly Bulletin of Q3, 2011, and Kamath and Paul (2011, p. 296); and once again the stimulus seems to have been short-lived – indeed, the UK's current account deficit in the third quarter of 2011 was the highest on record.

11. Go to McKinnon's website at http://www.stanford.edu/~mckinnon/

Bibliography

Bernanke, Ben, 'The Global Savings Glut and the US Current Account Deficit', the Sandridge Lecture, Richmond, 10 March 2005.

Bernanke, Ben, 'A Conversation at the Council on Foreign Relations', 10 March 2009. www.cfr.org; Hank Paulson.

Borio, Claudio and Piti Disyatat, 'Global Imbalances and the Financial Crisis: Link Or No Link?' BIS Working Papers No 346, May 2011.

Caballero, Ricardo J., and Arvind Krishnamurthy, 'Global Imbalances and Financial Fragility,' American Economic Review, May 2009. http://econ-www.mit.edu/files/3662

Caballero, Ricardo J., and Pablo Kurlat, 2009. 'The "Surprising" Origin and Nature of Financial Crises: A Macroeconomic Policy Proposal.' Prepared for the Jackson Hole Symposium on Financial Stability and Macroeconomic Policy, August. http://www.kansascityfed.org/publicat/ sympos/2009/papers/caballeroKurlat.07.29.09.pdf

Coval, Joshua D., Jakub W. Jurek, and Erik Stafford, 2008. 'Economic Catastrophe Bonds.' HBS Finance Working Paper 07–102.

Dumas, Charles, *Globalization Fractures: How Major Nations' Interests Are Now in Conflict*, Profile Books, 2010.

G20 Summit on Financial Markets and the World Economy, Statement of 15 November 2008. www.G20.org

Gagnon, Joseph, 'Current Account Imbalances Coming Back', Working Paper 11.1 Peterson Institute of Economics, 2011.

Genberg, Hans and Alexander Swoboda, 'Old Concepts in New Guises: From fundamental disequilibrium to global imbalances, to the 4 per cent rule', Presentation at the conference organised by the Reinventing Bretton Woods Committee on 'The International Monetary System: Old and New Debates', Paris, 10–11 December 2011.

Hayek, F., *Monetary Theory and the Trade Cycle*, Clifton, New Jersey, 1933. Augustus M Kelly reprint 1966.

IMF, *World Economic Outlook*, September, 2011.

Kindleberger, Charles and Aliber, Robert P., *Manias, Panics, and Crashes: A History of Financial Crises*, Wiley, 6th edition 2010.

King, Mervyn, Speech delivered to the University of Exeter Business Leaders' Forum, 19 January, 2010.

Kamath, Kishore and Paul, Varun, 'Understanding Recent Develpments in UK External Trade', Bank of England Quarterly Bulletin, Q4, 2011.

Laidler, D. *Fabricating the Keynesian Revolution, Studies of the Inter-War Literature on Money, the Cycle, and Unemployment*, Cambridge: Cambridge University Press, 1999.

McKinnon, Ronald and Gunther, Schnabl, 'China and Its Dollar Exchange Rate: A Worldwide Stabilizing Influence?' April 2011.

Mundell, Robert, 'New Deal on Exchange Rates', Nova Economia em Portugal, 1989.

Obstfeld, Maurice, and Kenneth Rogoff, 'Global Imbalances and the Financial Crisis: Products of Common Causes.' http://www.frbsf.org/economics/conferences/aepc/2009/09_Obstfeld.pdf

Paulson, Hank, 'Statement' from the G-20 Summit on Financial Markets and the World Economy, 15 November 2008.

Portes, R. 'Global Imbalances,' Mimeo, 2009, http://pages.stern.nyu.edu/~dbackus/CA/Portes%20imbalances%20Feb%2009.pdfand

Portes, R., 'Global Imbalances', in M. Dewatripont, X. Freixas, and R. Portes (eds), *Macroeconomic Stability and Financial Regulation: Key Issues for the g20.* London: Centre for Economic Policy Research, 2009.

Rajan, Raghuran G, *Fault Lines: How Hidden Fractures still Threaten the World Economy*, Princeton 2010.

UK Department for Business Innovation and Skills, paper on 'Protectionism', February 2011.

Wolf, Martin, *Fixing Global Finance: How to Curb Financial Crises in the 21st Century*, Yale University Press, 2009.

9
The Reserve Currency Overhang

By the second decade of the twenty-first century, the scale of central banks'
holdings of foreign currencies was widely seen as a menace overhanging the
global economy. Yet there was nothing in the existing monetary regime that
set limits to the growth of these reserves.

The natural life of a currency

Reserve currencies play a complex role in international finance. The
'reserve' function itself refers to the fact that assets denominated in
these currencies are held in the official reserves of foreign central
banks. But this reserve function usually grows out of and is closely
connected to the use of the currency – strictly, of assets and instruments denominated in the currency – by the private sector. Its use by
commercial companies, traders and investors leads to its use by foreign
governments and central banks. They all find the services provided by
the reserve currency centre useful in their day-to-day business. At the
same time, the currency serves as the domestic money of residents of a
specific country or region. It is this dual use of a national currency for
international purposes that gives rise to many of its peculiar features.
It also gives rise to difficulties – for example, when the issuing central
bank follows policies that result in an increase in supply running ahead
of demand. For foreign holders, they are assets that must be appropriately managed; for the issuing country, they are liabilities that may be
withdrawn.

The special position of the US dollar in international finance evolved
partly through such market forces and partly by design. As the US overtook the UK as the leading economic power in the late 19th century it
was perhaps predictable that its currency would also become the world's

leading international currency. But in fact this took a long time to be completed; it was only in the mid-1950s that the dollar overtook sterling in terms of its share in foreign exchange reserves and the pound led an active old age as a reserve currency up to the late 1960s (Schenk, 2010); by that time Britain had come to the conclusion that the costs of running a global currency exceeded the benefits. But already at the end of the Second World War the dollar had become the systemic fulcrum when, under the Bretton Woods agreement, all other currencies defined their value in terms of a 'parity' against the US dollar, while only the US dollar itself was convertible into gold. Moreover 'leadership' of world money had passed to the US much earlier – during and immediately following the First World War, a reflection of its determination as well as the dominant political, financial and economic position of the US at the time (see Silber, 2007). But its banks and financial markets looked mainly to the vast US economy for their bread-and-butter business (as they still do, 100 years later) leaving London eventually to reclaim a place as a leading centre – in some ways still the leading international centre. This occurred with the creation by London banks of the euro-dollar market during the 1960s, itself the by-product of US restrictions designed to protect the dollar. Although a few US banks had long been active overseas – notably First National City Bank, Bank of America and then Chase Manhattan – it was really only in the late 1960s that New York began to offer a range of international financial services to rival London.

Some believe there is a natural cycle in the life of a reserve currency. In its 'youth', as it establishes its standing and assuming it is seen as a stable unit of account and store of value – a youngster with good prospects – foreigners increase their balances. As there is a tendency for one currency to become dominant in the world at any time, a growing reserve currency will elbow out other contenders, and chip away at the position of the existing dominant currency. In response to demand, the range of financial markets and ancillary services offered by institutions in the centre naturally increases. Yet every extension of the reserve currency role is associated with a corresponding deficit in the reserve currency country's balance of payments, and eventually this tends to weaken confidence in the currency itself. Maturity gives way, by degree, to dotage.

The first stirrings of concern about the US dollar surfaced only a few decades after it had decisively ejected sterling from its primary position. The spectacular economic recovery of Western Europe and Japan in the decade after the end of the Second World War started making inroads into the dominant US position in international trade as early as the late 1950s and the first bout of market nerves about the dollar came to the surface in 1961. The next 50 years were marked by recurrent bouts of dollar weakness against stronger currencies such as the German mark, Japanese yen and Swiss franc but for much of the time it was reasonably stable. During this time it provided an indispensable benchmark for currency and asset values everywhere, notably for countries that pegged their exchange rates to it – and, during the era of stable exchange rates, an anchor of the world price level as well. A large part of world trade was invoiced and settled in US dollars, traders and investors everywhere maintained bank accounts in dollars, and these private and official balances supported an unprecedented growth in world trade and investment.

From confidence to slump

Thus the reserve role of the dollar expanded throughout the period, providing painless financing of the US current account deficit, despite concern from the 1980s on about the growing net international indebtedness of the US and the illiquidity of its balance sheet (with its assets mostly long-term and its liabilities short term). Indeed, with the rapid export-led growth of emerging economies such as China, Russia, Brazil and India, reserve accumulation grew – and the lion's share went to the US.

Although by the turn of the century, the US had already become the world's largest net debtor, foreign central banks increased their demands for dollars; indeed, there was no slackening in the rate of accumulation of reserves held by other countries in dollars. By the end of 2003, foreign claims on the US exceeded US claims on foreigners by $2.94 trillion, and the US current balance of payments deficit was running at 5% of GDP (Kenen, 2005). Against this background, it was understandable that some economists forecast a loss of confidence leading to a disorderly decline of the role of the dollar. In order to achieve an orderly unwinding, they called for a revaluation of currencies such as the RMB and a substantial cut in the US fiscal deficit in order to bolster the US external position. But in the financial crisis of 2008, far from a flight from the dollar, there was a surge of demand for dollars. The reaction of some European leaders, to the effect that the crisis was 'an American problem' and would cause the US to 'lose its financial superpower status', to quote the then German Finance Minister, Peer Steinbruck, seemed almost comically misplaced, especially in the light of the threatened breakdown of the eurozone (Sieff, 2008).[1] Despite the US debts, the dollar was seen as still a safe haven. But that was not to rule out the possibility that a collapse of confidence in the dollar in future could trigger the *next* financial crisis.

A disorderly adjustment could occur in several ways. For example, as and when central banks diversified from the dollar to the euro, the euro's exchange rate would tend to rise, foreign demand for US treasury bonds would tend to decline and US interest rates rise. As exports from the euro area became more expensive, the euro area would then suffer a deterioration in its trade balance, and slower growth, while the rise in US interest rates would depress the housing market in the US and thus trigger a fall in US spending. The result could be recessions both in Europe and America. That would be a painful and inefficient way to reduce the US current account deficit. Despite the strengthening of the dollar in 2008, GFC showed that these views had some validity. Both euro area and US economies suffered steep recessions, and the improvement in the US balance of payments did come partly from a fall in US demand triggered by a housing and banking crash.

Other factors were also at work to make the reserve currencies come to be seen as a potential source of exchange rate volatility. These included the gigantic scale of reserve assets in relation of countries' GDP, changes in the way in which countries managed their portfolios of reserve assets, and the potential for massive flows of 'hot money' induced by interest rate differentials and exchange rate expectations. The stock of international reserves of emerging markets as a percentage of the GDP of the holders rose from about 15 per cent to 34 per cent from 2001 to 2011 – from about $1 trillion to $6 trillion. As a handful of countries accounted for more than half of total reserve holdings (led by China, Russia, Saudi Arabia, Taiwan and India) large cross-border flows could be triggered by investment decisions taken by only a few people in key centres. The growth of the size of reserves as a proportion of GDP both of reserve centres and reserve holders meant that their disposition became a vital concern for all the countries involved – and for the many other countries which would be affected by the impact of portfolio shifts on exchange and interest rates (Mateos y Lago, 2009). Huge holdings of dollar balances by private agents (such as banks, multinational corporations and fund managers) could become more volatile if they anticipated sales of dollars by official holders. The fear was that, the moment such private agents thought that official holders such as cental banks and sovereign wealth funds were selling dollars, they would dump them on a massive scale, causing a collapse of the dollar itself.

Then there was the euro. In the ten years to 2011, the share of the US dollar in the reserves (of those countries that disclosed the currency distributions) fell from about 70 per cent to about 60 per cent, with the euro as the main beneficiary. From time to time, the fear that large holders would cut their dollar holdings in favour of the euro, or vice versa, fuelled market uncertainty. Whereas, before the introduction of the euro, the second most important currency was the D mark, accounting for only a small share of reserves, after 1999 the euro was immediately a much more credible alternative to the dollar. In the view of many economists, when there are two such assets, the demand for any one of them becomes less certain. In addition, a number of smaller reserve currencies provided alternative options – including the pound sterling, Swiss franc, Australian and Canadian dollars. And then there was gold (see below).

How central banks made the panic worse

Until as late as the 1990s, very few central banks had sophisticated reserve management departments; often staff were rotated from other departments and spent only a short time in the reserve management function. Not surprisingly, their portfolio management skills lagged behind their counterparts in the private sector. But gradually, as central banks learnt from each other and from the plethora of training courses offered by investment bankers, other central banks and specialist providers such as *Central Banking*, skill levels and professional standards improved markedly. This was also a natural reflection of the growing importance of reserve management to the income of many central banks. With that upgrading of status of the function in central banks came more formal statements of objectives (for example, these often detailed the relative weight given to such objectives as liquidity, security and yield), reporting mechanisms and regular review of performance against benchmarks – all the paraphernalia of the typical private sector fund manager. In sum, central banks had adopted a more commercial approach, seeking a combination of yield, safety and liquidity. And central bank boards took a much greater interest in the activities of reserve managers than in the past.

Keeping their portfolios under constant review, central banks became ready to reallocate assets at short notice if needed; and the one thing that scared them more than any other was having to declare a loss, especially if occasioned by default of a counterparty. At the same time, they were under pressure to increase yields. So many of them were tempted to move into higher yielding assets such as securities issued by Fannie Mae and Freddie Mac, the US mortgage giants (financial institutions set up under private ownership yet created by the US Congress with a public mission) as well as mortgage backed securities before the crash in 2007–08. But central banks were quick to scurry back to the safety of US Treasury bonds when the panic was at its height. Central banks that had diversified into euros and other currencies also switched back to the dollar in summer 2008, contributing to the intense global demand for dollars and panic. Sudden shifts in official reserve assets from one institution to another during the panic may even have contributed to the collapse of some financial institutions. For instance, central banks withdrew an estimated $150 billion of unsecured deposits from US banks between August 2007 and August 2008, before Lehman Brothers failed (September 15) and a further $150 billion in the last quarter of 2008. (Pihlman and van Dearborn, 2010). A BIS paper showed that the collateralized borrowings of Morgan Stanley investment bank, for example, shrunk from $1,045 billions at end-November 2007 to $659 billions at end-November 2008 (Allen and Moessner, 2011). True, not all of this was central bank money. But as Hank Paulson, the US Treasury Secretary, later reported, their actions contributed to the squeeze (Paulson, 2010, p. 232). Certainly they drained assets suitable for use as collateral from the market to the central banks that stepped in as lenders of last resort (though not before some banks had failed). This, in turn, worsened a crippling 'collateral squeeze' at the height of the panic. All this applied also to the burgeoning portfolios of fast-growing sovereign wealth funds, that by 2011 were estimated to total about $5 trillion on top of the central bank official reserves of $12 trillion.

Taking all this into account, official portfolios had become a larger and less stable element in the GFS than they had been during the time when they were less actively managed and much smaller in relation to the domestic economies and finances of the countries concerned. While the gross amounts of some $17 trillion controlled by official institutions was dwarfed by private sector portfolios of an estimated $200 trillion, central banks played an important role at the margin (see Roxburgh et al., 2011).

At what point does active, yield-driven portfolio management cross the line into speculation? Most people would regard it as out of order for official bodies to speculate on future movements in currencies or interest rates. They are members of the official international community, bound not only by rules of the IMF but also by a presumption that they should abstain from any actions that might be construed as unfriendly by other central banks or governments. This is especially the case as central banks are privileged 'insiders'. They meet regularly at different levels and exchange views on market movements and, at the level of portfolio managers, they will be able to form a pretty good idea of what other central banks are doing; the temptation to buy or sell assets and currencies with the benefit of such background information might on occasion be too great to resist,. True, there were safeguards. If any central bank trader that was privy to such information was caught taking advantage of it, there would be an uproar and the bank concerned would be cut off from future flows of information. Nevertheless, such disputes would doubtless be conducted on a genteel level and kept within the central bank circles. This risk has indeed led to talk in some circles of whether central bank reserve management should be separated from the governance structure of the rest of the central bank, with Chinese Walls erected to ensure information does not cross boundaries inappropriately.

The ugly currency parade

By the beginning of the twenty-first century, the dollar was beginning to show signs of stress typical of a reserve currency in late middle age. The decline would not be measured by the volume of reserve holdings, which was set to continue to rise for some time, but by more subtle signs. Nobody could tell the timing of its retirement, but the forces pushing it in that direction would not be easily reversed. Foreign holders of dollars worried about three troubling developments.

First, the much-admired institutional structure of US politics seemed to have suffered a dangerous decline in its capacity to deal with pressing economic issues. The compromise reached in the talks to reduce the fiscal deficit and debt in August 2011 narrowly averted a technical default, but left a nasty taste: if American politicians were willing to take it to the brink of defaulting on its debts, political divisions ran so deep that the compromise was likely to unravel under strain. Dollar holders worried that nothing had been done to defuse the debt bomb. They observed that a massive expansion of the Federal government was taking place under President Obama. The US faced a gross debt to GDP ratio at or above 100 per cent for 2011–14 and an increased government role in major areas of the economy including healthcare, automobiles, student loans and financial services. They observed a lack of political will on the part of either party to cut spending. President George W. Bush had vetoed hardly any spending bills while President Obama had expanded spending at a faster rate than any president since Lyndon Johnson.

Secondly, they worried that the Fed, apparently with the full support of the US administration, was following policies aimed at driving the dollar down. A country determined to reduce the value (purchasing power) of its currency cannot hope long to remain a reserve currency centre.

Third, given the concentration of assets in the hands of China and large holdings also of Saudi Arabia, other middle East countries, Russia and other potentially unfriendly or competing powers, some holders also worried about the possibility of a politically inspired run on the dollar.

In these circumstances it was scarcely surprising that large holders of dollar investments such as China, as well as countries like South Korea, Mexico and India, were beginning to buy more gold, as a hedge. Already by end-2010, to judge by a well-known survey of central banks, two-thirds of professional reserve managers expected central banks as a group to be net purchasers of gold in future – a dramatic upturn in gold's fortunes from the pessimism about it expressed by the majority of central bankers 10 years or so previously (Pringle and Carver, 2011, p. 13). Increasingly the dollar was sustained more by the sense that larger holders were locked in by fear of driving the value of the dollar down – and by the absence of viable alternatives – than on its own merits.

The 'killer app' of Asian central banks

Another reason why events often seemed to be on the verge of descending into anarchy was the lack of a mechanism for limiting reserve accumulation. What were the economic and political implications of the concentration of ownership of vast and rapidly rising reserves in a few hands? Would this end up sucking liquidity out of markets, and handing financial control of the world to China? So the scare headlines could run in a few years' time.

Traditionally, economists have not worried too much about such a scenario. They believed that countries that receive inflows of money will have either to appreciate their currencies or experience rising inflation. If a country receiving funds does not intervene in the markets, then people buying its currency have to find a counterparty in the private sector ready to sell; there is no effect on the receiving country's money supply but the exchange rate rises, making the country less competitive. If the country interevenes by selling its currency to the foreign purchaser itself, then this will put more of its currency into the market, increase the money supply and eventually cause inflation, and a decline in the attractiveness of that currency. Either way, these mechanisms will choke off foreign demand. That is how the classical adjustment mechanism was supposed to operate.

However, a number of technical innovations introduced by some official policy makers in recent years have given the scary scenario some verisimilitude. In 2008–10, as emerging markets faced a new flood of hot money fleeing from ultra-low interest rates in the centre economies, governments of countries receiving inflows battled to prevent their exchange rates from rising too far, thus making their economies uncompetitive and threatening recession. So they intervened on a large scale on the foreign exchange markets, taking dollars off the market by official operations – buying dollars in exchange for newly printed domestic money. They had done this for a long time, of course. But in the past it had been difficult for central banks to prevent these operations from causing an increase in the money supply and inflationary pressures. In the short run, so the conventional wisdom had it, they could 'sterilize' the resulting increase in domestic money – 'mopping it up' by issuing more government debt – but in the longer run this was considered to have strict limits.

The killer apps that central banks, especially in Asia, had developed during the previous ten years involved the development and implementation of new instruments – so the central banks issued new kinds of liabilities to absorb local currency funds generated by intervention. These included new central bank bills, and vigorous use of reserve requirements on banks to mop up liquidity. The main aim was to prevent the classical adjustment mechanism from operating. According to some estimates, up to 90 per cent of all accumulation of foreign exchange was sterilized by use of these instruments, which became important tools for reducing the growth in the money supply that would otherwise have resulted from interventions – representing in 2008 an estimated 25 per cent of the broad money supply in China (Greenwood, 2011).

According to John Greenwood (the architect of the famous Hong Kong dollar 'peg' to the US dollar), these sterilization operations were of two types. In type 1 operations, the central bank withdrew the new (excess) reserves created by intervention by selling an equivalent amount of domestic securities; in type 2, the central bank issues and sells an equivalent amount of newly created central bank liabilities, such as central bank bills, bonds and CDs; or it raises the reserves that banks are required to hold with the central bank. All the Asian central banks except for Japan engaged in large-scale sterilization and indeed became adept at it. This represented, Greenwood claimed, a 'dramatic change of approach' in the ten years following the Asian episode of 1997–98. Their motives were to build ample insurance against any future shock (Greenwood, 2011).

If Asian central banks had indeed found effective ways of insulating domestic monetary conditions from reserve accumulation, the traditional limits on their capacity to grow foreign exchange reserves would be further eased. As a result, there would be even less constraint on the growth of global imbalances. Developed countries would be forced to run larger and lager payments deficits to match the surpluses in developing economies operating managed exchange rates with unlimited reserve accumulation. This doomsday machine would surely lead to another boom-bust cycle.

One does not have to follow all these links in the chain of reasoning – for example, as argued in Chapter 8, net current account imbalances were not in our view responsible for the bubble in the US, which was financed largely from Europe anyway – to be impressed by one finding of this analysis: there was nothing to stop the indefinite, unlimited, growth of reserve assets. And every ripple in Western banking and sovereign debt markets merely confirmed emerging markets in their belief that they did need those big foreign currency reserve cushions. But with every doubling of these massive reserve totals – \$12 trillion in 2012, how much in 2020? – the dangers this cancerous growth posed to the world's money also grew more threatening.

Averting meltdown?

Ways would have to be found of reducing the risk of a collapse of confidence in reserve currencies that this presaged. A number of ideas were going the rounds about how to deal with this.

The SDR-based substitution account, proposed originally during a bout of dollar weakness in the late 1970s, was one such idea to receive renewed interest. It would be an off-market mechanism for reserve holders to convert excess reserves into SDR-denominated assets, passing the exchange rate risk onto the account. In the simplest model, participants would deposit foreign exchange (initially dollars) in an account administered by the IMF, in return for SDR-denominated claims. The managers of the account would invest the funds in securities or other asset denominated in dollars and the account would pay interest on the SDR claims.

If properly designed, it could meet some important challenges. In particular, it could help maintain confidence of China and other surplus countries that their interests would be fully taken into account in future reforms. One of the lessons of the 1930s is the need to keep the confidence of major creditors – at that time, the US, now China. Further, the attempt to reach agreement would inaugurate serious international discussions about the overhang of dollar liabilities and the future of the dollar as a reserve currency. The future of the dollar and indeed the euro as reserve currencies would be treated as a matter of international debate. That would be a hard, disagreeable, lump for the US and Euroland to swallow.

However, the substitution account proposal bristled with difficulties. First, there was the critical problem of financing of the deficit in the account if the dollar were to depreciate against the SDR. Secondly, there was also an important issue of making the SDR more liquid and more attractive generally to holders.

On the first issue, the obvious solution remained a risk-sharing arrangement. In the event that the dollar holdings of the account were insufficient to redeem the dollar value of the SDR claims of participants, half of the additional dollars required might be supplied by the US, and the other half by participants. Alternatively, the Fund might make an allocation of SDRs to cover any deficiency. In this way the account would resemble an SDR bank, with its own assets. In the event, as was perhaps predictable, when the original plan came up for discussion in the IMF, the US did not agree to issue any guarantee or even partial guarantee. Would there be any reason to expect a different outcome this time? One difference from 1980 is the presence of the euro. The governments of the euro area might have an incentive to agree to contribute to the risk-sharing needed to make the substitution account solvent. During the 2010–12 upheavals in the eurozone, some non-European central banks switched assets back to the dollar for security, a shock for the euro. This gave the euro managers a taste of what might be in store in future as the market's mood favoured first one reserve currency and then the other. Negotiations would test the feasibility of a bargain on burden sharing between surplus countries and the two major reserve currency centres.

On the second issue, it was widely recognized that the SDR would have to be improved and a market in SDR claims developed to make it more attractive to central banks as a reserve asset. Central bankers, who tended to be particularly sceptical of the substitution account concept, stressed political uncertainties regarding the backing and issuance of the SDR, and the absence of instruments tradable in private markets. A common view was that reserve status is achieved only by market developments and cannot be forced by political will. But some did see potential for a larger role for the SDR, especially if there were changes in the composition of the basket and further improvements in IMF governance.

Negotiate reserve rules?

In addition to the proposed IMF SDR-based substitution account, even before GFC there were also calls for central banks and governments to explore more explicit arrangements for reserve holdings (see Truman and Wong, 2006). These also could trace an ancestry back a long way – they were for example part of the agreements that were made in the early 1970s to arrange 'an orderly reduction in the reserve role of sterling'. Again, during the decline of the dollar in 1978–79, it was feared that potentially disruptive pressures for diversification could erupt at any time and that there would be potential benefits for all parties if agreement could be reached on the way in which reserve holding patterns might develop. This was expressed by a G30 report drafted by the author at the time as follows:

> For example, potential reserve diversifiers might give formal or informal undertakings only to diversify their reserves in line with pre-arranged guidelines…in return for a degree of access to the capital markets of new reserve centres' and currencies. (See Group of Thirty, 1980.)

One proposal echoed this. Richard Cooper argued that the main cause of GFC was a failure of the financial institutions in major financial markets, especially the US and UK (Cooper, 2011). Yet, as he went on to argue, that was no reason not to examine international money – the rules, conventions and practices governing the behaviour of official monetary authorities – and in particular how the adjustment mechanism operated or had failed to. Dismissing the proposal to set targets for current account imbalances, Cooper proposed instead that each country would set a target level for its foreign exchange reserves five years in the future. These targets would be subject to international discussion and review. Each country would be expected to defend its target in discussion with peers, especially if it was unusually high or low. Adjustments would be made to these targets, following which SDRs would be created over the following five years to match the total of adjusted targets. In this fashion supply of reserves would be matched to the demand for reserves, without resort to national currencies. SDRs would be allocated on the basis of their quotas in the IMF – countries with targets greater than their allocations would have to run current account surpluses or borrow. Special arrangements would be made for countries with floating exchange rates. Surveillance by the IMF would, it was hoped, ensure compliance with the targets, which would be interpreted in a medium-term framework – and there could be a scale of sanctions, agreed in advance, for offending countries.

Cooper argued that this proposal could meet three objectives. First, it would introduce a meaningful and objective indicator for balance of payments adjustment in a world with a globalized capital market. Second, it would introduce symmetry into the adjustment process, requiring those with payments surpluses to adjust along with those in deficit. Third, it would provide incremental liquidity to the world economy in the form of an internationally agreed unit, thus reducing dependence on national currencies to play this role. Although aimed primarily at promoting adjustment and dealing with the problem of imbalances (see Chapter 8) this proposal would also, if agreed, provide a structure that could be used to forestall destabilizing portfolio shifts.

A related issue was the provision of liquidity at times of emergency. One would imagine that, with the trillions of dollars in central bank reserves, liquidity was the least of the problems facing the GFS, but the trouble was, liquidity was not always available to the institutions and countries that needed it at the right time and in the right amounts. Central bank swaps helped authorities to gain dollar liquidity during GFC but, as a BIS paper put it, 'the credit crisis will leave behind it a greatly heightened appreciation of liquidity risk' (Allen and Moessner, 2011). Central banks had to go to extraordinary lengths to make liquidity available to their banks, and in the international arena, several countries were saved from serious financial instability only by the willingness of the Federal Reserve to make very large amounts of liquidity available at very short notice. If central banks cannot limit foreign currency liquidity risk sufficiently, they may be led to increase foreign exchange reserves further.

Towards multi-currency reserve holdings

Official agreements or guidelines could serve as stepping stones to the development of a new regime. Official investments in the money and capital markets of emerging markets, denominated in a basket of emerging market currencies, in return for access to these markets for the private sector, could, for example, promote the development of a multiple currency reserve structure, and move towards a Hayekian world of currency competition.

Plainly, the world was becoming multi-polar – or so went the conventional wisdom of the time. True, central bank reserve managers did expect to increase investments in non-traditional currencies. However, the only serious potential reserve currencies were the Australian, Canadian and New Zealand dollars, together with the Norwegian krone and Swedish krona. And although these were all currencies of countries with strong growth potential, strong governance, respect for property rights and developed financial markets, their markets lacked the size and liquidity needed for large trades. Much excitement was generated in 2010 when China started to encourage greater regional use of the RMB and an offshore market was set up in Hong Kong. This was growing at a remarkably rapid rate as investors around the world looked for exposure to the RMB, which was thought bound to appreciate: investors like a one-way bet. But Chinese authorities made clear it would remain a tightly controlled market, that the RMB would remain a non-convertible currency for the foreseeable future and that the border between offshore and onshore markets would remain closely policed. The offshore market and instruments traded on it remained too small to attract major central bank or SWF investments.

On the other hand, there have been examples of countries quickly becoming reserve centres – as the US did in the 10 years following the establishment of the Federal Reserve in 1913 – and of countries winding down their reserve role, as the UK did in the 1970s (though of course markets had relegated it to second league status long before then). So changes can happen quite rapidly. Beijing appeared determined to develop the RMB rapidly and encouraged the growth of liquid markets in Shanghai as well as Hong Kong. Rhetorically, also, it was ready to throw down the gauntlet to the US – disparaging remarks about the dollar coming thick and fast from the mouths of Communist party officials. But investors and traders around the world would hardly take eagerly to large-scale investments in the currency of a Communist country with extensive controls over economic life and, history showed, volatile politics, with no tradition of respect for property rights or an independent judiciary. Predictions that the RMB might overtake the US dollar as the world's major reserve currency by the early 2020s were brushed aside by most reserve managers (though see arguments advanced by Subramanian, 2011).

Given the considerable resources tied up in these reserve hoards – resoures that could be put to better use invested in the emerging market economies themselves – the IMF was not slow to suggest other means of reducing countries' incentives to accumulate them. One was greater surveillance over capital flows. Another was to extend IMF credit lines and make them automatic for countries that may need them. But there was no evidence that such steps would actually limit excessive reserve accumulation – countries tended to say in effect – 'yes, we will have credit AND more owned reserves'. It was easy to say that surveillance of countries' policies should be toughened up, but no sign of key countries actually agreeing to it. Without reform, strains in the reserve currency mechanism and global imbalances could stretch cooperation to its limits. Just as efforts to solve the perceived problem of payment imbalances would not be resolved, either in theory or in practice, by leaning on China to revalue the RMB, nor would the problem of the reserve overhang be overcome by the methods adopted by international organizations.

Time to dismantle the doomsday machine

But what really doomed the hopes of the multi-currency school of reformers was that the foundations of both major reserve currencies were visibly crumbling – that is, their credibility hung by a thread. We all live in credit economies. Trust is of the essence of the credit economy, and nowhere is this more necessary than in international reserves, where one country 'trusts' another to look after its money. It is true that large holders were to some extent locked in; nevertheless, any suspicion that the vulnerable position of holders of dollar and euro balances was being abused by reserve centres would spark a determined search for alternatives that could be deeply destabilizing. The behaviour of both the US and euro area authorities had drained that reservoir of trust without which a multi-currency future could not materialize.

If doubts about reserve assets were to lead surplus countries voluntarily to reduce their surpluses, that might indeed be one positive by-product of such a loss of trust. But official policy, dominated by the leading developed countries, which hoped to reduce the growth of reserves by moving to more flexible exchange rates, was the wrong remedy – and was indeed likely to further erode trust. The push to create insurance mechanisms and safety nets at the international level to reduce the incentive to emerging markets to accumulate reserves was equally doomed to ineffectiveness. As we argued in Chapter 8, pushing surplus countries that were in any case experiencing price inflation, asset and price bubbles to expand demand further was foolish and dangerous, while exchange rate changes would have no lasting effect. The other policies being discussed were merely cosmetic. Structural changes initiated by the surplus countries themselves were the only way in which they would 'buy into' policies to reduce their surpluses, and creditor countries would in their own interests take such action of their own accord in due course. But that would not remove the menace of the $12 trillion reserve overhang. Whichever way governments moved, again they were caught in the money trap.

There is an exit. The aim should be nothing less than the progressive elimination of foreign exchange reserves, but by a completely different route. This should be achieved only by a fundamental reform. At its centre should be the construction of a credible world monetary standard. If there were such a standard, then foreign exchange risk among countries adhering to the standard would be eliminated and there could be no demand for 'foreign exchange' reserves. Existing investments would become claims on the issuers of those instruments – government bonds, equities, bank deposits, ranking *pari passu* with domestic residents claims on those same institutions. Short-term claims could be consolidated through the issue of long-term bonds. Of course this would not remove default risk, or the market risk of fluctuations in the prices of the instruments, but it would remove the foreign exchange risk. Transactions in reserve assets would have no effect on exchange rates. China's SAFE and CIC (the central bank department called State Administration for Foreign Trade and the sovereign wealth fund, China Investment Corporation), which arouse so much passion in US and political circles in other countries, would become just players in the investment game. Each would be smaller than, say, Blackrock asset investment company, which had nearly $4 trillion under management in 2011 – and Blackrock was only one of several large private investment companies operating in global markets.

This is, needless to say, an aim for the long term. But it is precisely the domination of policy by a frantic search for short-term results that dooms it to ineffectiveness. A consequence of such a transformation of 'forex' reserve assets would be to reduce the incentive to hold massive liquid funds abroad by developing countries and emerging market governments. It was an absurd misallocation of resources that in the early twenty-first century emerging economies felt impelled to recycle capital inflows back 'uphill' to the economies of advanced countries, when they needed the resources to invest in their domestic economies.

To be sure, given the productivity of the US economy, the US would be bound to attract a proportion of the new savings generated every year globally – with appropriate shares also going to other developed economies. But the artificial impetus given to such investments by the need to secure protection against exchange rate shocks would be removed.

This fundamental innovation has to be initiated, through a reformed IMF, by the new creditor countries. They have the resources to back a new monetary standard, the incentive to invest in their own economies, and – the muscle to demand action. But it would also absolutely be in the interests of existing reserve centres to have the problem of the reserve currencies 'internationalized'. Of course, this long-term aim would have to be approached in stages. In the first stage, central banks would take the lead in coordinating policies aiming to reduce destabilizing and unhelpful exchange rate volatility between major economies, notably between the euro, dollar, yen and RMB. In the second stage, governments and electorates would finally understand that there are no long-term benefits to be had from floating rates. At this stage, the apparatus of central banks with monetary policies and market operations would be retained but the central banks would have no discretionary monetary policy and no *domestic* open market operations. So the Fed, the ECB, the PBOC – and the central banks of other countries joining the emerging GFS – would progressively abandon domestic market operations and only supply (base) money through foreign exchange operations – intervention in the foreign exchange markets. (For further discussion of the mechanics, see Part IV).

Of course, such a reform would have to meet the test of markets. But if it stood firm, it would deliver what China and other emerging market economies really want – greater stability. In short, the 'time bomb' at the heart of the global trading and currency regime can be defused. This could be accomplished in stages. In the final stage, currencies would peg to new global standard with the elimination of foreign exchange reserves.

Like payments imbalances, the reserve currency conundrum was a time bomb at the centre of the world economy. In the case of the banks, the subject of the next chapter, the bomb had already exploded. It was cleaning up time.

Note

1. See reports by Martin Sieff, UPI, 26 September 2008 and Ambrose Evans-Pritchard, *Daily Telegraph*, 1 October 2008.

Bibliography

Allen William A. and Richhild Moessner, 'The International Propagation of the Financial Crisis of 2008 and a Comparison with 1931', BIS Working Paper No 348, July 2011.

Cooper, R., 'Necessary Reform? The IMF and International Financial Architecture,' *Harvard International Review*, Vol. 30, No. 4, 2009, pp. 52–55.

Cooper, R., 'Reform of the International Monetary System: A Modest Proposal', *Central Banking*, Vol. 21, No. 1, May 2011, pp. 55–60.

Greenwood, John, 'Asian Sterilization: Its Impact on Asian Financial Development and the Global Imbalances', given to the Japan Society of Monetary Economics, 30 May 2011.

Group of 30, 'Towards a Less Unstable international Monetary System', Group of 30, 1980.

Kenen, Peter B., 'Stabilizing the International Monetary System' Contribution to the Roundtable on 'The Dollar, the Euro, and the International Monetary System' at the Annual Meetings of the American Economic Association, Philadelphia, 8 January 2005.

Mateos y Lago, Isabelle, Rupa Duttagupta, and Rishi Goyal, *The Debate on the International Monetary System*, IMS 11 November 2009.

Paulson, Hank *On the Brink*, Headline Publishing Groups, 2010.

Pihlman and Van Dearborn, 'Procyclicality in Central Bank Reserve Management: Evidence from the Crisis', IMF working paper WP 10/150, 2010.3, 2010.

Pringle, Robert and Nick Carver (eds), *RBS Reserve Management Trends*, Central Banking Publications, 2011.

Roxburgh, Charles, Susan Lund, John Piotrowski, *Mapping Global Capital Markets*, McKinsey Global Institute 2011.

Schenk, C. R., *The Decline of Sterling: Managing the Retreat of An International Currency 1945–92*, Cambridge University Press, 2010.

Silber, William L., *When Washington Shut Down Wall Street: The Great Financial Crisis of 1914 and the Origins of America's Monetary Supremacy*, Princeton University Press, 2007.

Steinbruck, Peer, Remarks reported by Martin Sieff, UPI, 26 September 2008 and Ambrose Evans-Pritchard in *Daily Telegraph* 1 October 2008.

Subramanian, Arvind, *Living in the Shadow of China's Dominance*, Petersen Institute, 2011.

Truman, Edwin M. and Anna Wong, *The Case for an International Reserve Diversification Standard*, Petersen Institute, Working Paper 06–2, 2006.

United Nations, 2009, Report of the Commission of Experts of the President of the United Nations General Assembly on Reforms of the International Monetary and Financial System (also known as the Stiglitz Commission report). Available via the Internet at http://www.un.org/ga/econcrisissummit/docs/FinalReport_CoE.pdf

Zhou, X., 2009, 'Reform the International Monetary System' (Beijing: People's Bank of China). Available via the Internet at http://www.china.org.cn/business/news/2009–03/24/content_17490662.htm

10
Can Banks Be Made Safe?

In the last two chapters we critically assessed the policies of the western governments towards the twin issues of global imbalances and reserve currencies. They also faced a third, even more pressing, challenge – the collapse of much of their banking and financial system. How had this disaster happened and what could be done about it?

The disease

During the years leading up to GFC, traditional structures that had held the power of finance in check and channelled it to socially useful purposes lost their grip. Equally, conventional ways of assuring reasonable financial stability – whether by good risk-management, adequate capital, conservative provisioning, or regulatory oversight – had proved to be weak defences against the forces unleashed by globalization, innovation and the over-confidence bred by the long economic boom and ample liquidity.

It was tempting to dismiss calls for yet another group of banking experts to propose yet another set of regulatory reforms – Basel 4, 5 and 6. Not only were crises not going away: they were getting worse. That was why there was an urgent need to re-think the entire basis of finance and its place in the global financial system (GFS). There was equally no sense just in bashing the banks. The only rational way forward was to somehow re-construct a set of standards and rules that would lead financiers in the pursuit of their own interests to serve the public interest as well. Such a system had indeed been in place for generations, at national levels, but had lost force. The internationalization of banking and finance had made it too easy to escape official regulations, while few believed in relying on self-control or self-regulation any more.

The system had developed in such a way as to reward recklessness and short-termism, and to penalize prudence and caution.

This loss of a firm basis for sound banking had disastrous result. At the most obvious level, government spending intended to combat the recession triggered by GFC added greatly to public indebtedness in the countries affected, thus weakening confidence in the sustainability of fiscal policies. This worsened the sovereign debt problems of the euro and the US; but it also meant that governments had less ammunition left to put out the next financial firestorm and stimulate demand. Yet without extra fiscal stimulus, western economies could slip back into recession (having only just emerged gradually from a steep recession); if this happened, bank balance sheets would be further impaired by a new wave of bad and doubtful debts.

Volatile exchange rates between major currency areas contributed to the dangerous mix. Thus when the dollar weakened against the euro, as in 2009–10, prospects for exports and the European economies darkened; markets extrapolated from this, and began to fear weaker economic growth in Europe would increase debt servicing difficulties. Equally, highly stimulative monetary policies in the US raised commodity prices globally, and thus also prospective inflation as import prices rose for European and US consumers and manufacturers. This narrowed the room for monetary policies aiming at stimulating demand. Competition in depreciation – or currency war, as Brazil's finance minister called it – raised acute uncertainties about longer-term inflation prospects. It was a 'competition' from which the emerging markets suffered most as they were exposed to volatile cross-border capital movements. But it was part of the coordinated expansion of demand by fiscal and monetary policies that was the centrepiece of the G20 strategy for exiting from the recession.

The way in which the problems of sovereign debt, banking structures, exchange rate volatility and monetary policy interacted with each other and prevented the world from coming out of recession argued in favour of treating them all as symptoms of one disease, requiring radical surgery. Nevertheless, one cannot do everything at once, so this chapter discusses reforms of the private sector part of the GFS. The key questions were whether the reforms being put in hand in the major currency areas would stabilize banking and finance and make them 'fit for purpose' again. In our view, the answer, unfortunately, was 'No'. Some of the reforms went in the right direction but did not go nearly far enough. They reflected governments' (and banks') desire to patch up a structure that was beyond repair. A new concept of the GFS, and of the relationships between users of financial services, governments and providers, was required.

The impossibility of managing the existing banking system was vividly demonstrated during the critical days in 2008, and in this chapter we look at how crisis management went wrong in both the US and UK. We then move on to medium- and longer-term reform issues. But, first, a word about how the financial institutions of the West evolved to make GFC inevitable.

The diagnosis

As discussed in Chapter 2, the way the institutions had developed in the years before GFC made them appear less risky than they really were. Because of the progressive deregulation of finance (meaning here the abolition of previous demarcation lines between different kinds of banks and financial institutions and official or semi-official controls over deposit and lending rates), following the loss of an international monetary standard, banking had changed its nature. Behind the trusted profiles and familiar high-street names the inner workings of the banks were transformed. No longer were the long-standing traditions of deposit-taking and lending, judging the quality of individual borrowers and the maintenance of adequate liquid assets to meet demands for cash at the heart of the banking business. Instead, trading of securities, securitizing loans, short-term maximizing of monetary returns – first of management rewards and then of shareholder value – and aggressive marketing of services even to small retail customers came to dominate. The legal structures of large banking conglomerates became complex and opaque. Few realized that burgeoning bank profits were being achieved largely by banks using access to low-cost finance to increase the size of their balance sheets, run down their effective capital ratios to dangerously low levels, borrow excessively and engage in a wide range of activities whose risks were poorly understood. In the end huge institutions with hundreds of years of banking experience and honourable traditions were brought down, often by speculative trading activities with a fall in property and collateral values providing the trigger. The episode had shown that the managers charged with controlling these banking behemoths were out of their depth, while being paid very handsomely. As John Kay commented, 'many of the managers of large financial institutions were absurdly well remunerated for duties they failed to perform' (see Kay, *Narrow Banking*, 2009, p. 12).

Was the laissez-faire ideology of the 1990s and early 2000s the driving force behind the 'light touch' regulation? Should we simply blame regulators for being too relaxed? That's too simple. The same period saw the erection of a daunting structure of banking supervision with thousands of pages of detailed guidelines and official regulations. The people who built these structures believed in the case for oversight by public agencies. Few regulators subscribed to this so-called laissez-faire ideology, as anybody who knew them can testify. Yes, there was a mood of over-confidence, even of triumphalism, a belief that 'we' had somehow solved the problems of unruly finance. But this was not a laissez-faire ideology. If policy makers really had believed in letting market forces rip, none of this regulatory superstructure would have been put in place. The forces driving the system were the megalomania of chief executives, supine boards and the greed of bankers and traders determined to find ways round the regulations – all in the context of the rapid globalization of finance. These forces crushed the weak defences society had erected against them. (Central bankers also were responsible for fuelling the boom and failing to insist on action to strengthen banks, as discussed elsewhere in this study – see especially Chapters 2 and 3).

What were the key lessons? One was that the core banks of a country should be designed so that failure of any one could be tolerated and managed without bringing down the others and could be dealt with while maintaining essential public services (the so-called principle of modularity). The public interest required a safe, efficient and trustworthy payments mechanism (no simple matter to ensure in itself) and this should be separated from other risky activities. Another was that the general public should understand better the risk they bear when they entrust their money to a given institution or invest in a given product. A third was that it was probably going to be necessary in future to tolerate mini-recessions to maintain longer-term systemic stability.

Crisis management in the US

Before we get onto the longer-term reform programme, there were several lessons to be learnt from governments' (mis)management of the credit crunch in 2007–08. We refer here to day-to-day decisions, and it should be remembered that these were taken under pressure in the heat of the moment.

The lesson of history was clear: in a bank panic the first priority must be to stem the haemorrhaging of funds and the collapse of confidence in the system. Financial panics are so contagious, and so destructive of the real economy of jobs and companies, that this aim must override everything else. Yet governments and central banks had forgotten this wisdom. In the US, the biggest mistakes were made by someone who should have known better – Hank Paulson, former head of Goldman Sachs and Secretary of the US Treasury from 10 July 2006 to 16 January 2009.

First, he was ill-prepared. It is the job of a good civil service to anticipate and prepare contingency plans for possible eventualities, and Paulson had a full year in his post before the financial earthquake erupted, yet Paulson and the US Treasury were completely wrong-footed when it happened. Stating that 'we' were surprised that the initial shock in August 2007 came from housing, Paulson admits in his memoirs that he had not grasped the way in which financial innovation in the previous few years had 'vastly amplified' the potential damage which losses could inflict on banks and other financial institutions.

It would have been reasonable to expect that as CEO of Goldman Sachs, a firm that took a leading role in these innovations, Paulson would have given more than a passing thought to their possible implications for the economy and the stability of the financial system. Although as Treasury Secretary Paulson kept in close touch with the CEOs of the big Wall Street firms, who were fully aware of the adverse turn in the housing markets as early as 2006 (some firms including Goldman Sachs had been hedging exposures and even placing bets in anticipation of such a change) neither the Treasury staff nor his contacts in the markets had apparently alerted him of the danger – or if they did, he failed to follow up.

Paulson's book, *On the Brink* (essentially his memoirs of the crash) conveys an impression of confusion. As William Isaac, former head of the US Federal Deposit Insurance Corporation (FDIC), a regulator, commented it 'paints a stunning picture of a confused and panicked government without a coherent strategy for getting in front of and containing the crisis'. Here are some choice Paulson quotes (Paulson 2010, and Isaac, February 2011):

> All of this led me in late April 2007 to say ... that subprime mortgage problems were 'largely contained.' I repeated that line of thinking publicly for another couple of months. ... We were just plain wrong. (p. 66)
>
> Lehman's UK bankruptcy administrator, PricewaterhouseCoopers, had frozen [Lehman's] assets in the UK ... a completely unexpected ... jolt. (p. 231)

General Electric...was having problems selling commercial paper. This stunned me. (p. 172)

I'd never expected to hear those troubles spreading like this to the corporate world....(p. 228)

Perhaps I should have foreseen the problems ahead....(p. 314)

I began to seriously doubt that our asset-buying program [TARP] could work. This pained me, as I had sincerely promoted the [toxic asset] purchases to Congress and the public....(p. 385)

Tim Geithner told me that AIG was again bleeding....It astonished me....(p. 342)

AIG would need a massive equity investment. I was shocked and dismayed. (p. 376)

[The] Chairman of Standard Chartered...asked...about Citigroup and GE. 'Are either of those two going down?' he asked. This jolted me. (p. 344)

We had no choice but to fly by the seat of our pants, making it up as we went along. (p. 254)

Is it any surprise that Paulson's decisions showed poor judgment? The decision to nationalize Fannie Mae and Freddie Mac on September 7, 2008, wiping out preferred as well as ordinary shareholders, shocked and destabilized markets. Investors asked, who's next? It encouraged short sales of other bank stocks and was followed immediately by an onslaught on outfits perceived to be vulnerable, notably Lehman Brothers. Eight days later Lehman failed. This had catastrophic results as it sparked a run on banks world wide, and caused an immediate drying up of liquidity in international markets including even basic trade finance; the world economy fell off a cliff.

Paulson's giant missteps

Why was this allowed to happen? Many observers took the view that Lehman was allowed to go bankrupt to punish it for irresponsible behaviour and to make an example of it. Certainly, Lehman had behaved as if it was too big to fail – this was the lesson it had learnt from the official rescue of Bear Stearns the previous March. Paulson himself mentioned this at the press conference on 15 September, the day Lehman filed for bankruptcy: 'Moral hazard is something I don't take lightly', he said. He added that unlike with Bear Stearns, which was taken over at short notice by JP Morgan Chase, there had been no buyer for Lehman. For that reason, 'I never once considered it appropriate to put taxpayers money on the line in resolving Lehman Brothers.' In the book he says he should have been more careful in his choice of words, as some had taken them to mean he didn't care about a Lehman collapse, which was the opposite of the truth. But, as he claimed later, he was unable to state the truth openly – which was that the government had no legal authority to put in capital and a Fed loan would not have been sufficient to prevent bankruptcy. To tell the truth would have brought down the remaining investment banks, including a firm Paulson really cared about:

> Lose Morgan Stanley, and Goldman Sachs would be next in line – if they fell, the financial system might vaporise and with it, the economy. (p. 226)

Paulson was quite ready to discard his free marked ideology when he wanted to. On 19 September, the SEC banned short selling of financial stocks, to give the remaining two investment banks what Paulson called 'a grace period', but this was a temporary measure and Paulson encouraged them to find partners. He also desperately began discussing with the Federal Reserve further ways in which the investment banks could be protected:

> Our rationale was simple: confidence in the business model of investment banks had evaporated, so merging them with commercial banks would reassure markets. (p. 269)

The next misjudgment by the US authorities triggered the most damaging stage of the panic. This was when Paulson and Ben Bernanke appeared before Congress on 23 September to plead for passage of the programme to buy toxic assets from financial institutions (the Troubled Asset Relief Programme, TARP). They argued it was needed to save the financial system and US economy from chaos and financial Armageddon. They said the need was so urgent that Congress should authorize an outlay of $700 billion without hearings, debates or amendments. The markets immediately concluded that the entire US financial system must be on the brink of collapse, and all sources of private finance were closed off. William Isaac was appalled by the Paulson TARP plan. It was 'a plan concocted by Wall Street for the exclusive benefit of Wall Street'. On this view, the market panic could and should have been handled in a much less politicized way through existing institutions, notably the Fed and the FDIC. For example, the FDIC could have promptly issued a broad guarantee of depositors under existing law with approval of the Treasury and Fed – a statement that eventually came only on 13 October.

> Enormous damage was done to the economy and in turn to the financial system by the highly inflammatory rhetoric used by government leaders...to sell the TARP programme to a doubting Congress and public. They got their legislation but scared the wits out of the public in the process. Wallets slammed shut and the economy flatlined in October (see Isaac, 2010, p. 160)

Arguably, TARP did nothing to stabilize the banks that could not have been done without it. The damage was compounded when on 10 February 2009 the new Treasury Secretary, Tim Geithner, announced that the 19 largest TARP recipients would be required to undergo stress tests, a decision one bank CEO called 'asinine'. The Dow Jones index collapsed from 8,200 to 6,500 over the next month.

Paulson's statement that it was only after Lehman failed that the Congress was ready to pass legislation needed to inject capital into the banks looks like yet another post-hoc rationalization. Anyway, it was not capital per se that was needed at that stage, but rather a clear and public commitment that the State stood four-square behind the commercial banking system (see Kaletsky, 2010, pp. 136–37).

Sure, the meltdown could have been even worse. Yet the defence of stability came at excessive, long-term and to some extent avoidable costs. Paulson admits to 'stumbles' on the road to success. But these were giant missteps. As the report of the study by the US Financial Crisis Inquiry Commission made clear, they were partly down to woeful lack of preparation of the Treasury and the Federal Reserve – and, I would add, the fact that Paulson's deepest loyalties were to Wall Street.

Crisis management in the UK

A comparable sorry tale of delays, misjudgments and missed opportunities played out in Britain. During the initial stages of GFC from August 2007 to the start of 2009 ministers said repeatedly that the government's policy was to maintain the stability of the UK banking system. Yet the policies adopted and signals sent to markets were not consistent with this objective.

The background was one of over-confidence. Gordon Brown, Chancellor of the Exchequer from 1997 to 2007, had earned a reputation for 'prudence' during Labour's first terms from 1997 to 2001; orthodox fiscal policies, combined with granting of independence to the Bank of England, created a new and all-too-successful model of economic policy-making – all too successful because it lulled everybody into a dangerous over-confidence. As the long years of apparent prosperity rolled on, Brown's 'prudence' turned into 'pride' which then shaded into 'arrogance'. His *hubris* set the tone for the *hubris* of the City of London. Neglecting the poor state of much of Britain's industry (industrial production was lower in 2001 than in 1997), the government and the Bank of England focussed attention on the growth of services, in the process allowing the economy and tax revenues to become highly dependent on financial services. After 2002, he opened the floodgates of public expenditure; instead of saving all that well-earned credibility and money for a rainy day, he let rip. As his biographer William Keegan had already perceived – Brown's prudence was always 'Prudence for a Purpose' (see Keegan, 2003, p. 333). Listen to Brown and the business cycle was a thing of the past. As the service-driven economy continued to expand year after year, now, Brown thought, was the time to reap the reward and finally realize his socialist and personal ideals. So it was natural that he should have been infuriated by the onset of banking problems only a couple of months after finally becoming prime minister, in June 2007.

Through the rest of 2007 and 2008, as the share prices of UK banks collapsed, British ministers failed to take on board the scale of the problem or deal with it competently. They dithered, unable to accept the fact that the seizing up of the inter-bank market, and the collapse of their shares, threatened all of Britain's major banks. It was understandable that they were frustrated, furious and losing patience. But to make this clear so publicly worsened the loss of confidence. Rows between the government, the central bank and the banks at a time of such fragile confidence and the government's willingness to let talk of possible bank nationalization gain currency opened the door to a share collapse, short-selling and eventually a loss of confidence among bank creditors. At a time when it was essential that banking stability be regained, the aim of maintaining confidence must take priority over everything else. But it plainly did not do so.

When the episode started in August 2007 and the ECB reacted promptly by injecting liquidity on a large scale into the euro banking system, the market looked to the Bank of England for comparable reassuring action; none was forthcoming. Yes, action was eventually taken to save Northern Rock, after the run on it in September, and inject liquidity into the system, but only after Mervyn King, the governor, had warned publicly against the dangers of supporting the banking system as a whole, on the grounds that this could worsen moral hazard (in a letter to the House of Commons Select Committee 16 September 2007). When the Bank eventually offered three month money to the market it was at a very high interest rate which the stronger banks would not accept – and their refusal meant that acceptance by the other banks was an advert of their weakness, so no money was taken.

It was then that the authorities suddenly, it seems, decided that the banks suffered from inadequate capital – and that the world should know it. In January 2008 Mervyn King, governor, called attention publicly to the banks' weak position: 'Uncertainty about the scale and location of losses led to concern about the adequacy of bank capital ... ' This was a misjudgement – perhaps taken to justify the Bank of England's earlier decision not to provide general support for the system. 'The situation must be even worse than we thought' was the natural response of market participants. Following the authorities' squabbling over Northern Rock, talk of nationalization, and now publicly drawing attention to banks' weak capital position – no wonder the hedge funds gloated. During the next eight months, as share prices of British banks skidded down – RBS's shares collapsed by 85 per cent in the year to October 2008 – amid a widening collapse of confidence, the Bank of England was all but invisible. The perception was that nobody was standing behind the UK banking system.[1]

When the government did recognize the need for assistance, the terms imposed on the banks in October 2008 hardly served to strengthen confidence. Recapitalization was made partly by the issue of preference shares to the government earning interest at 12 per cent. This high rate of return was supposed to protect taxpayers' interests. But it was an example of muddled thinking. Taxpayers, who are also depositors, employers and pensioners, wanted above all a functioning banking system. But such 'assistance' made it more difficult for the banks concerned to stand on their own feet, as it was above any likely profit that the banks could earn in the circumstances without taking even bigger risks or exploiting their customers, and so would drain resources and capital from the banking system. Inevitably, bank share prices collapsed again. Against such a sorry background it was absurd for Prime Minister Gordon Brown to claim credit for giving an international lead in the recapitalization of banks. His stumbling record had for a 18 months allowed the collapse of confidence to deepen, with falls in asset values triggering more sales of assets, in a widening downward spiral. He gave the impression that the government hated the banks and out of sheer fury might nationalize the lot.

The official authorities both in the UK and US mismanaged the episode because they added unnecessarily to market uncertainty. Governments and central banks should have followed the basic rules as enunciated by Walter Bagehot (see Bagehot, 1873). In a bank panic, the central bank has to make clear early on that it stands 100 per cent behind the banking system and that it will back this commitment up with unlimited loans against good collateral. Bank managers in charge of banks that need public help should be fired immediately, even if the situation was not 'their fault'; whereas in the US and UK they were, inexcusably, allowed to retire with dignity with their loot. This was against all the rules of the game. Making allowance for differences in banking and regulatory systems, these rules were well understood and applied in practice for several generations. In 2007–08, the UK and US governments and central banks did the opposite of what Bagehot taught; he taught that in a panic you save solvent banks, but punish the bankers; they saved the bankers, but let confidence collapse. This made the losses much worse than they need have been. Their legacy – zombie banks, more dead than alive.

Then came the mismanagement of the eurozone's banking and sovereign debt problems in 2010–11, as described in Chapter 6, to complete the demoralization of markets. In a few short years, bank failures and fear of failures had been allowed to fester until they undermined confidence in all the major centres of finance (Japan, US, UK, the euro area). This would and should change the nature of banking for ever.

But there is a general lesson to be learnt from these stories. The fumbling management of these highly dangerous episodes was an accident waiting to happen. A few short years previously, central banks had been told to focus on price stability (in the US, there was a dual mandate – maximum sustainable employment and price stability). In the UK and some other centres, bank supervision had been taken away from the central bank. These changes had been made to meet the challenges posed by previous problems of the GFS – the bank failures, inflation and other pressures in the 1990s. In the process of these organizational changes, personnel had been switched around, and critical expertise had been lost, or deemed irrelevant, so that the central banks and governments were simply not prepared to deal with GFC. The fact that they did not know what to do was evident to markets. Indeed, the authorities danced to the tune set by the markets – jumping this way and that in their efforts to fend off danger. Instead of the markets adjusting to a solid rule-based structure, it had become their playpen. That was how the players exploited the opportunities open to them.

As one said to the author, 'You can't blame us for taking money off the table.' That was the real reason for the absurd profits of the hedge fund industry. Advised often by former central bankers, they could predict, in any given market situation, which way central banks and other official bodies would jump. That was how the system – the whole GFS – ended up costing the earth.

Structural change

Thus the financial institutions and markets had perversely become risk-magnifiers rather than risk-mitigators, as management had come under pressure to take excessive risks – pressures from shareholders, protected by limited liability, from managers themselves as their bonuses were tied to gross revenues and/or the share price, and from competitors or 'the market'. Further, because of the interconnections between investment banks and the core commercial banks, big investment banks were also in effect too-big-to-fail as they could transmit risks to the financial system generally. Though a major effort was being made by the official regulators to persuade markets that no banks were in fact too big to fail – as shown for example in the document released by the Financial Stability Board in November 2011 listing 29 globally systemically important institutions – the only way they were going to convince the markets that this was for real would be to let the next one that got into trouble fail, with the immediate dismissal and humiliation of the existing senior management and board (see Financial Stability Board, 2011). Don't hold your breath.

The structural reform that offered the best prospects of insulating the core banking system from such 'financial multiplier' effects would be to separate the capital and assets held by different sorts of financial institution and the activities they undertook. This was not about flushing high-risk activity and innovation out of our system. It was about ensuring that the impending failure of a major bank could be managed by the public authorities at acceptable cost without interrupting essential services. It was about getting away from a model where high-street banks strayed into areas of banking in which they had little experience but were insured by the taxpayer. Nor would restructuring be a panacea. Other reforms were needed: to regulation, methods for resolving failing banks, dealing with too-big-to-fail institutions, dealing with cross-border failures. The aim should be to change the culture of banking.

As thoughtful bankers acknowledged, and as explained at the beginning of this chapter and in Chapter 2, gradually over many years, the environment had changed in ways that made banking increasingly irresponsible. For all the talk of advanced risk management techniques, the adoption by most banks of similar business models weakened the system. Whole teams of specialists started to move from one bank to another without any loyalty to a specific institution, encouraging short-termism. The pursuit of short-term shareholder value was taken to extremes. Profit growth was gained through increasing leverage. Shareholders came to see banks as growth stocks, with inflated expectations of returns. But the official sector was equally implicated. Bankers successfully lobbied regulators to relax key safeguards, and to refrain from regulating new instruments such as derivatives. Meanwhile, after successive cycles, central banks, in their efforts to avoid dreaded 'deflation', ended up keeping interest rates too low for too long.

The economists who were in effect running the monetary policies of many countries, including the US and UK, had little interest in, or awareness of, financial stability issues; the possibility that a financial crisis could have extremely adverse real macro-economic effects did not register on their radar screens (at least in the US, as the minutes of the Fed's FOMC meetings for 2005 and 2006 clearly showed when the full transcripts were published). Despite the growth of an international bureaucracy of regulators, with attendant academic advisers, dedicated supposedly to making banking safer, bank instability increased. Central bankers and regulators, who certainly should have accepted their share of the blame, showed an obstinate reluctance to own up, though a few eventually did. With the official sector shirking its duty, why should commercial bankers lead the way in setting an example of self-sacrifice and public responsibility?

To bring back responsibility to banking and finance while retaining sufficient freedom to innovate was the challenge. One key reform was to apply the principle of modularity already referred to. As Paul Volcker, former chairman of the Federal Reserve, often pointed out, the mainstream commercial banks should be seen as serving a special role in society. This reflected the fact that they provided certain indispensable services that people cannot do without even for short periods of time, such as access to cash and payments. As a result, commercial bankers should have duties and privileges. Their duties should involve running the payment system with oversight by the central bank, and providing the usual deposit and lending services of a commercial bank, including corporate lending. They could securitize loans provided they kept a share on their books, and use derivatives when related to customer needs. Their privileges include access to markets supported by lender of last resort facilities from the central banks (see Pringle and Sandeman, 2011).

To give effect to this reform and reduce systemic risk, it was proposed that commercial banks should be barred from engaging in certain activities, including underwriting of securities, proprietary trading and sponsoring hedge funds – the so-called Volcker principles. As discussed below, competition in banking would be increased and to this end new entrants to this sector should be encouraged by the authorities. In addition to market discipline, the banks' asset profile should be regulated to keep risk to a moderate level – so to protect the taxpayer. Of course, higher capital and liquidity rules were also needed, as enshrined in the new Basel III agreement, although they would have to be phased in gradually so as to avoid so far as possible limiting banks' ability to expanding lending and so support economic recovery. These principles were endorsed by the Independent Banking Commission in the UK, and appeared also to be embodied in the Dodd-Frank Act in the US – though that was such an unwieldy, controversial and open-ended piece of legislation that lawyers would dispute what it meant for years, if not generations.

Bank pay

The general public would not readily forgive banks and bankers for their share of responsibility for the credit crunch. Taxpayers knew they would go on funding the results of banks' misjudgments and greed for years through higher taxes and austerity regimes. Bankers were widely seen to have behaved like cowboys – and the remuneration aspect would have to be tackled at its root. It was felt to be outrageous that senior bankers were still taking such a large share of banking revenues with millions of pounds of bonuses each year before tax and dividends.

The action taken in response to the public dismay was clearly inadequate. New rules were brought in that were supposed to limit upfront payment and encourage executives to take a long-term view. An EU law required companies to defer 40 to 60 per cent of bonuses for three years or longer but was vague about who was covered. In the UK, the pay rules applied to senior managers and employees whose activities may have a 'material impact' on the company's risk profile. The higher 60 per cent deferral rate applied only to bonuses over £500,000 (€596,000, $780,000). The FSA also rejected an interpretation of the law put forward by members of the European parliament that would have limited upfront cash to 20 per cent of the total package. Instead, the FSA's revised code said that at least 50 per cent of the total package must be paid in shares or share-linked instruments. However, experts said that the concept of bonus deferral and then payment in shares was likely to be ineffective in its aim to give the bankers and traders an incentive to take a long-term view. In short, the rules failed to put in place adequate incentives for bankers to act in the interests of wider society.

This failure cannot be put down just to bank lobbying. Without wholesale interference in freedom of contract and contract enforcement, it would be very difficult for legislators to curb bankers' pay, however tough they try to be within the existing banking system. There were proposals to make it easier for bank shareholders to complain of excessive management pay. Yet again, these were unlikely to make much difference.

What was so weird – and incomprehensible to the general public – was that even loss-making banks, like RBS in the UK, that had had to be rescued and in which the state had a controlling interest, continued to pay favoured bankers their astounding bonuses. Meanwhile many other banks that had escaped direct state shareholdings continued to reward their senior staff generously, on the grounds that competitive forces obliged them to do so. Given such pliable governments, how long would it take them, under the same pressure of competition, to start taking excessive risks again? If the risks turned sour, they could, once again, dare the government concerned to let them fail. Here we arrive at one of the springs of the money trap.

As somebody who has followed banking for many years and also believes that the City makes a vital contribution to the UK economy (for several years I served as deputy director of a City committee – then called the Committee on Invisible Exports, now called TheCityUK), I have come to the conclusion that payment of bonuses should have no place in High street, commercial banking. This is only rational, as it is impossible to attempt to tie pay to performance. There is no need for an international agreement. Even if one country were to ban bonuses, without any others doing it, that country would not suffer from the feared flight of bankers to other jurisdictions. Others would be appointed to assume their duties, and they would be as likely to do their job as well as their predecessors. It would make no difference to the efficiency with which banking services were provided in that country. The payment of bonuses for regular commercial banking out of gross revenues rather than profits is doubly absurd. The practice is also distorting values and poisoning incentives throughout the public as well as private sectors. One way to achieve this would be to state that banks paying staff bonuses would not be eligible for public support in an emergency.

Integrating banking and monetary reform

Given the above analysis, the question was, even with structural reforms, including reforms to renumeration policies, and even assuming that they were implemented in the key currency centres, and were bolstered by higher capital and liquidity ratios, would these produce sufficient real change? Our answer is, 'no'. Certainly they were worth trying, and better than nothing. Yet the complex overhang of banking problems, in combination with sovereign debt and reserve currency, as well as the vexed relation between states and financial sectors, would probably doom this final attempt to reform. Consider one simple scenario. It was one thing to separate commercial from investment banking, to impose new requirements, and implement the rest of a macro-prudential toolkit; it was another thing to convince markets they were for real. Years after GFC, governments were a long way from having the confidence to do that – to test the market by, for example, letting a big bank fail. The situation was far too delicate to attempt such a rash gesture. We had ended up with the worst of all worlds; with doubts about whether governments had the political and financial *means* to rescue banks (such doubts were reflected in overnight funding problems for banks like Morgan Stanley and Goldman Sachs, as well as for eurozone banks) together with continued moral hazard temptations to management to take excessive risks. To make it all worse, governments were actually pressing big banks to take risks – in the interests of stimulating demand and financing small businesses. This was almost bound to store up further bad debts.

The underlying issue can be put as follows: the public sector had not provided the necessary counterpart for an active private financial sector. Central banks had tried to provide a standard or monetary rule with their inflation targeting and central bank independence (IT+CBI) regimes and under a few exceptional central bankers like Paul Volcker in the US and Karl-Otto Pöhl in Germany (Pöhl was head of the Bundesbank from 1980 to 1991) this had worked for a time. But their achievements had been undone by international capital movements, government meddling, fluctuating exchange rates and excessively elastic credit systems. Finance had not been tamed by regulation and there were doubts about whether it ever could be. Yes, structural reforms, ring-fencing of core banks, higher capital ratios, Volcker rules and bank resolution regimes – supposedly to allow banks to fail safely – were all worth trying. But the political power of the finance interest remained untouched. Under such a 'soft' budget constraint, it would be impossible to restore that sense of personal responsibility for risk-taking that was the essence of good banking. And finance would need a long period of nursing. It would be natural if, despite the public rage, politicians were loath to confront it. After all, apart from any other consideration, financial institutions and individual financiers in countries like the US and UK were large donors to party political funds.

What made the prospect all the more alarming was the weakness of public sector and central bank balance sheets going into what seemed for some countries the prospect of another hiccup in the recovery, if not another recession. This meant the firewall preventing another meltdown of markets and banking structures was itself looking paper thin – and not just in the eurozone.

To the break-up yard?

Given this scary scenario, it was understandable that governments were determined that the big banking groups would never again threaten the viability of public finances. In October 2011 the super-regulator, the Financial Stability Board, which is answerable to the G20 governments, published a list of the world's superbanks – or global systemically important financial institutions. This is it:

Belgium: Dexia
China: Bank of China
France: Banque Populaire, BNP Paribas, Crédit Agricole, Société Générale
Germany: Commerzbank, Deutsche Bank
Italy: Unicredit
Japan: Mitsubishi, Mizuho, Sumitomo Mitsui
Netherlands: ING
Spain: Santander
Sweden: Nordea
Switzerland: Credit Suisse, UBS
UK: Barclays, HSBC, Lloyds, Royal Bank of Scotland
US: Bank of America, Bank of New York Mellon, Citigroup, Goldman Sachs, JP Morgan, Morgan Stanley, State Street, Wells Fargo

These banks would have to comply with a complex new set of rules: a new international standard; requirements for recovery and resolution planning; and additional loss absorption capacity tailored to the impact of their possible default, rising from 1 per cent to 2.5 per cent of risk-weighted assets (with another possible 3.5 per cent to be levied to discourage their efforts to make themselves even more likely to be rescued by growing even bigger, more complex and more inter-connected with each other).

The lesson some market observers took away was simple: these banks were being towed towards the break-up yard. Behind the scenes, they would be told to simplify their structures, so that if they got into trouble their essential services could be kept going while the rest was allowed to fail – at shareholders' and bond holders' expense. But if this was to be for real, and not just a pretend exercise, then they might as well break up in reality. It had become a cliché to say that these banking behemoths had become not only dangerously large, but also too big to manage. Many of them had lost public support for paying their management billions of dollars while relying on state guarantees. Fatally, they did not trust each other, as the continued semi-moribund state of the inter-bank market attested. Once a bank loses the public's trust and that of its peers, its credit is gone. The collapse of credit in banks mirrored the collapse of confidence in credit-based currencies.

There is one thing the public should be aware of. After watching the credit cycle, and how each time round banks are puffed up by the wind of cheap credit, then collapse, bringing down the economy with them, regulators always claim they are learning lessons. Their message is always the same: 'Trust us, we will get it right next time.' The time had come to tell regulators a simple message: your time is up. We do not blame you, but we do not trust you, any more than we trust bankers.

Two options for a new GFS

At the existential level, there are two options. One is to go for state control over the finance sector, or at least of what used to be called its 'commanding heights' – or what would remain after the break-up of the big banks. This would involve nationalization, or at a minimum explicit guidance of credit allocation extended by the big banks and financial institutions, together with controls over cross-border capital and credit flows. Then, at a minimum, finance could be made account-able to government departments and brought within the usual bureau-cratic rules and proceedures governing promotion, pay, and due process.

Remember that, historically, such statist systems have existed for long periods and have served various economies well – continental European economic development was promoted largely by state-dominated banking and central banking systems, as was that of Japan. Such a model is the default position of the superpower of the future, China (as seen by the rapidity with which it reasserts state control over banks at times of stress) and was the basis of the economic development of India and Russia. This was a serious model (though not the kind of thing governments should talk about at the height of a capitalist bank panic!). That would mean giving up the effort to reconcile finance with free markets and, even more basically, with a democratic system of governance and legitimacy. Yet it was the spectre hovering in the background.

The other option was to go for a new model where finance would once again be the servant of the economy. Like many others, Danny Kruger, a former adviser to UK conservative prime minister David Cameron, lamented the dominance of finance over the economy: 'Our economy is not merely powered by finance, as a sailing ship is powered by wind. It is driven before the storm, unable to tack or turn or pause' (Kruger, 2011). Was there, he asked, a destination after the storm? He himself began to sketch one. Real capitalism would put consumers and small business in charge and allow them a view of the future; it would encourage investment as well as spending, quality as well as quantity; it deplored debt piled on debt. The finance 'tail' would no longer wag the economy 'dog' (see also Milne, 2009, pp. 333–8).

Although the reality, in the US, UK and euroland, four years after the onset of GFC, seemed to be of ships lurching in heavy seas, there was hope of reaching dry land. But it was clear that individual governments or even regions could not chart the route to the promised land unaided. What was needed was a collective effort to transform financial intermediation. Banks, as usually understood, could never be made safe enough, even by breaking them up – though that was looking move likely, and even desirable on other grounds (to encourage competition and reduce the political power of the princes of private finance). As some very experienced students of banking observed, many banks collapsing 'in a herd' could be just as bad as one big one going down. But if neither breaking them up, nor nationalizing the lot, would guard society against the risks of banking, what could do so?

My answer is that a new model of financial intermediation will eventually have to be developed, based on a new monetary standard, to reconnect the world of finance with the real economy. Finance could and should be rooted in the real productive assets of the economy. But this kind of reform to banking and finance could be achieved only if made in parallel with reforms to the 'official' international monetary system. It was the absence since the 1970s of a reliable, widely observed, monetary standard, rather than faults in financial regulation, that had produced disaster myopia, the decline in levels of trust, and the shortening of time horizons that in turn created the conditions for GFC.

The GFS was being undermined by yet another deep fault – a result of the interaction between the exchange rate regime, monetary policies and mobile capital. This faultline continually threatened to produce bubbles, asset and currency volatility and crashes. The fact that they come with an international twist makes them especially tricky to resolve, as shown in the next chapter.

Note

1. This does not entirely reflect the benefit of hindsight; the author is on record as having criticized the UK and US authorities at the time on these grounds, in various editorials published by *Central Banking* and CentralBanking.com. See 'Without Proper Incentives We Are Doomed', 8 October 2008, and 'Why We Must Say No to Nationalisation' – Central Banking, January 2009; www.centralbanking.co.uk

Bibliography

Augar, Philip, *The Death of Gentlemanly Capitalism*. London: Penguin Books. 2000, 2001.

Augar, Philip, *Chasing Alpha: How Reckless Growth and Unchecked Ambition Ruined the City's Golden Decade*. London: The Bodley Head. 2009.

Capie, Forrest, *History of Bank of England:1950s to 1979*. Cambridge and New York: Cambridge University Press. 2010.

Cassidy, John, *How Markets Fail: The Logic of Economic Calamities*. London: Allen Lane. 2009.

Davies, Howard, *The Financial Crisis: Who Is to Blame?* London: Polity. 2010.

Financial Services Authority, *Reforming Remuneration Practices in Financial Services. Feedback on CP09/10 and final rules,* August 2009.

Financial Stability Board, *Policy Measures to Address Systemically-Important Financial Institutions,* November 2011.

Independent Commission on Banking, Interim report: April 2011.

Independent Commission on Banking, *Final Report: Recommendations,* September 2011.

Isaac, William, 'Paulson on Paulson', *Forbes,* 2 February 2011. http://blogs.forbes.com/billisaac/ – *Washington Post,* 27 September 2008.

Isaac, William M. with Meyer, Philip C., *Senseless Panic: How Washington Failed America. With a foreword by Paul Volcker.* Hobokem, NJ: John Wiley and Sons Inc. 2010.

Johnson, Simon and Kwak, James, *13 Bankers: The Wall Street Takeover and the Next Financial Meltdown.* Pantheon. London: Allen Lane. 2010.

Kay, John, *Narrow Banking: The Reform of Banking Regulation.* London: CSFI. 2009.

Kaletsky, Anatole, *Capitalism 4.0.* London: Bloomsbury. 2010.

Keegan, William, *The Prudence of Gordon Brown,* London: Wiley, 2003.

Kruger, Danny, 'Cameron Should Work to Return Capitalism to Citizens', *Financial Times,* 3 October 2011.

Milne, Alistair, *The Fall of the House of Credit,* Cambridge University Press, 2009.

Paulson, Hank, *On the Brink.* London: Headline Publishing Group. 2010. Pringle, Robert and Hugh Sandeman, *Response to the ICB's Consultation Questions and Comments on the purpose and Design of a UK Banking Ring-Fence.* Available at: http://bankingcommission.independent.gov.uk/bankingcommission /wp-content/uploads/2011/07/Pringle-Robert-and-Sandeman-Hugh.pdf

Pringle, Robert and Hugh Sandeman, Evidence to Commission 2011: http:// bankingcommission.independent.gov.uk/bankingcommission/wp-content /uploads/2011/01/Robert-Pringle-and-Hugh-Sandeman-Issues-Paper-Response.pdf

Rajan, Raghuram G., *Fault Lines: How Hidden Fractures Still Threaten the World Economy,* Princeton: Princeton University Press. 2010.

Singleton, John, *Central Banking in the Twentieth Century.* Cambridge: Cambridge University Press. 2011.

Skidelsky, Robert, *Keynes: Return of the Master,* Allen Lane, 2009.

Stiglitz, Joseph, *Freefall: Free Markets and the Sinking of the Global Economy.* London: Allen Lane. 2010.

Turner, Adair, Andrew Haldane, Paul Wooley, Sushil Wadhwani, Charles Goodhart, Andrew Smithers, Andrew Large, John Kay, Martin Wolf, Peter Boone, Simon Johnson, Richard Layard, *The Future of Finance – and the Theory That Underpins It.* London: LSE Centre for Economic Performance. 2010.

Underhill, Geoffrey, *Global Financial Integration.* Cambridge: Cambridge University Press. 2010.

11
Markets, States and Bubbles

Repeated cross-border credit and asset price booms and busts caused havoc. Thus, as the debate on the causes of GFC rolled on, there was a natural temptation, especially on the Left, to blame 'the markets'. But this was misguided. They may hold a key to the future.

The new era in perspective

With the onset of GFC in 2007–08, the relationship between the official authorities and the financial markets entered a new era. In large parts of the western world, regulators and financial institutions had failed to take measures to cool the boom in time to avoid the bust. (Those countries that did weather the storm relatively well, such as Australia and many emerging markets, did so mainly because they had suffered crises of their own in the recent past and had strict regulation, and followed conservative fiscal and monetary policies; there had not been time for memories to fade and defences to be lowered.) Because governments and central bankers held inadequate regulation to be responsible, and because the state could not afford to bail out banks again, the pendulum swung towards much tighter state control. Thus the next stage in the evolution of the GFS could easily mark a return to what economists call 'financial repression', that is, state dominance of the financial system with forcible channeling of funds to the state's coffers. That would suit governments in the short term – they needed the money.

To put the changing relationship between the state and financial markets in broader perspective, this chapter looks at the forces that were impacting on it, including public opinion, economists' opinions, financial innovation and the fast-changing markets themselves. The main participants in these markets were the financial institutions and other players as described in Chapters 2 and 10. The markets would be affected in many ways by the governments' responses to the crisis, as discussed in Chapters 5, 6, 7 and 10. Now the markets in which they participated need to be analysed separately. After all, in a market economy it is through the alchemy of market processes that the prices of assets and instruments are determined and scarce resources allocated.

As a preliminary, it is important to keep in mind popular views of the markets. This is because it will be politics, rather than economics, that will decide the future of finance and, given the influence of the mass media, policy-makers will in turn be influenced by popular perceptions. In the popular estimation, bankers, central bankers and the whole financial system had failed society miserably. Markets were the central mechanism of a financial system viewed as unjust, unable to support business or economic growth, rewarding only those sitting at the top of protected institutions and their hangers-on, chronically liable to crises leading to recessions, unemployment and higher taxes, and in the grip of vested interests.

In the media, financial markets were often compared to 'wolf packs' hunting together for prey. They picked the weakest animal in a group – be it a currency, a company or a country – and then ruthlessly hunted it down. Then they would go after the next weakest, and so on. Others preferred the image of a lynch mob: the markets seemed to be easily whipped up by a few rabble-rousers to accuse an innocent party of some crime without due process and then go after him, forcing him to flee or perish. Others use the image of a monster, a huge serpent, which, with a mere flick of its tail, can throw off any restraints mere humans tried to place on it.[1]

Open war

What these colourful images sought to encapsulate was the way in which selling pressure could suddenly build up and bring about a steep fall in the price of an asset, currency or financial instruments, whether it be a company's shares, a government bond or a currency. There were several instances during GFC.

In 2008–09, some famous institutions in finance perished – Lehmans, Washington Mutual in the US – or were forcibly acquired – Merrill Lynch, HBOS (Halifax Bank of Scotland group) – or were saved only by dint of extraordinary state bailouts – AIG in the US, RBS, Lloyds in the UK, UBS in Switzerland, Hypo Real Estate bank in Germany, among others.

The manner in which they were brought down evoked exotic images drawn from the natural world and mythology. After the event, commentators tried to provide rational explanations: this bank had made mistakes lending to property; that one had become too dependent for its funding on fickle wholesale money markets – but these were unsatisfying. Often praised for their vaunted prescience and ability to incorporate information, the markets had given no hint of the impending financial turmoil during the first half of 2007. Worse, markets and banks had been subjected to regular health checks by the authorities. Neither in America nor Europe did markets signal that there was anything seriously wrong with an institution or class, until the last moment.[2]

Then, with banking systems still convalescent, it was the turn of government debt markets. The wolf pack quickly disposed of Iceland and Hungary, before in October 2009 turning their attention to the eurozone, snapping up Ireland as a tasty morsel along the way to Portugal, Greece and Italy. In all instances, governments were sent reeling from the assault, which took the form of large-scale selling of bonds, resulting in a rapid rise in borrowing costs as yields rose. There would be hastily called Cabinet meetings, announcements, declarations, measures, resignations, street protests and then more empty reassurances from 'them' – the authorities. Sometimes the measures brought a brief breathing space. Often governments tried throwing money at the beasts which kept them quiet for a while, but just as often such offerings were contemptuously rejected. Again and again, markets made governments appear fatuous and impotent. Just as statements about the health of the banking system were made to look foolish, attempts to put up defences for the euro – such as bans on certain kind of speculation – were simply brushed aside.

Open war between governments and markets broke out from time to time, as in May 2010 – when tremors hit government bond markets of eurozone countries. This time many commentators blamed governments. The *Financial Times*'s Lex column said on 20 May: 'Angela Merkel (German chancellor) is right: the euro is in danger. The threat comes not from speculators, however, but from policy makers.' The *FT* took the view that the German government's ban on what was called 'naked short selling' of eurozone government bonds was 'the equivalent of taking a wild swing at a straw man'. The *Wall Street Journal* concurred: 'Germany shoots the messenger' ran its headline. In the *Journal*'s view, it was excess government spending, not 'dark market forces', that had caused Europe's debt problems. The article explained that investors who used these markets were not separate from the rest of society and could not be punished for such 'imaginary crimes' without hurting the economy at large.

In an effort to defend the euro, Merkel rushed out a call for closer regulation and a global tax on financial transactions. However, the market reaction was contemptuous – and sellers of the currency promptly pushed the euro's exchange rate to a new low against the dollar. This was a typical instance of how governments were made to look foolish. Other governments were well aware that their turn could come next; indeed, in 2011 the beasts turned their beady eyes on Portugal, Spain, Italy and finally, France. With most currency and government bond markets harbouring weaknesses of their own, no government appeared safe. The US suffered the indignity of seeing its credit downgraded by one agency in August 2011. Even Germany's credit suffered. By early in 2012, with Greek bondholders struggling to reach agreement with the government to limit their losses on holding of Greek government bonds to 70 per cent, the markets turned on Portugal, pushing the yield on its bonds above 17 per cent, a clearly unsustainable level: the message was that the markets expected Portugal also to default within a few years, highlighting the growing risks of contagion throughout the eurozone.

Higher bank taxes and tougher regulation, including gestures to control bankers' pay, were inevitable. Yet, given the fury of the public, it could have been much worse for the banks. The public asked, why weren't more bankers in jail? There were a few prosecutions in the US, though investigations into financial crime were hampered by a shortage of investigators (the FBI having switched staff resources to counter terrorism duties after the attack on the World Trade Center in 2001). Threats to 'break up the big banks' were not carried out, though it seemed that many of them were slowly being towed to the break-up yard (see Chapter 10 for reforms that were being promised or implemented). A few bankers were hounded from office – such as Fred Goodwin, former head of RBS, who in 2012 was also stripped of his knighthood (he had been given this honour in 2004 for 'services to banking' but then went on to drive the bank to the brink of collapse). But most of those who had pushed their banks towards bankruptcy were allowed to retire in their own time with their gains. Some, admittedly, together with shareholders, suffered large declines in their wealth. In the US, according to one observer, 'they all got rich'.[3]

Views from the inside

Whether popular anger was spent as a political force was not clear. It seemed more likely that there was an unsatisfied demand for more radical change than policy-makers had been able to deliver. Indeed, the 'anti-bank' popular demonstrations in many financial centres around the world continued to attract extensive media coverage. For their part, bankers should have been duly grateful that, far from responding to the public's mood, which wanted to see them strung up from the lamp-posts, official regulators decided to protect them. As noted in Chapter 10, lists of systemically important financial institutions were drawn up, the implication being that these would be safeguarded by the state (though whether all states could afford it was another question). The bankers had not only got away with it; they had got the state to erect walls around them and to guard them from the prying eyes of the public. And, above all, the deep waters of the bonus pools remained undisturbed.

Of course, this was not the cover story; regulators claimed that new 'resolution regimes' being adopted by G20 countries would allow them to spread the losses of a bank requiring support across creditors and shareholders while ensuring its vital services continued. But such claims lacked credibility. The reality was that banks throughout the western world were still on life support, with central banks providing the real risk-taking and funding required, especially in the eurozone. Few believed that governments had sorted out how to share the costs of the failure of large cross-border banks and manage the complexities involved. More broadly, it seemed, to say the least, unlikely that governments would be ready to risk advertising to the public that banks were expected to stand on their own feet, when such announcements might actually cause them to collapse. Rigid regulatory requirements, the suppression of finance and, in the last resort, nationalization, seemed more likely to be the solutions adopted by governments rather than a return to the disciplines of market capitalism. But that wouldn't stop them all from pretending to be 'making capitalism work'.

Remarkably few bankers appeared to understand the public's wrath; most just didn't 'get it'. In the run-up to GFC, successful lobbying by the banks had persuaded regulators to relax rules governing the amounts investment banks could borrow relative to their capital (leverage) and not to regulate derivative markets.[4] Credit rating agencies had given the highest credit ratings to instruments that they did not understand. Record profits had been made by fixed income departments of invest-ment banks selling exotic instruments that they knew to be toxic. Some investment bankers had been aware that what they were doing was highly risky, as well as immoral, and went ahead with it all the same. The evidence strongly suggested that some bankers knew the securi-ties they were selling were likely to lose value, and indeed privately bet on this happening while telling purchasers that they were sound. Salesmen liked to talk of 'stuffing the Germans', referring to naive German regional banks eager to purchase any rubbish that the investment banks offered them. It was indeed an era of cynicism, immorality and greed. The somewhat repugnant lifestyles of younger traders were vividly brought to public attention in books written by people on the inside who felt the need to tell their story (see Anderson, 2008, and Freedman, 2009). The fictional story, in which an investment bank sold clients a package of securities containing many that were likely to default, on the advice of a hedge fund manager who was betting that their price would collapse, is told by Tetsuya Ishikawa (see Ishikawa, 2009), a former employee of Goldman Sachs, the US investment bank. Such accounts, together with serious investigations by outsiders, leave no doubt that many people working in the financial sector had become accustomed to operating in a world which they could influence and shape to meet their needs, a world in which you could become a hero inside your institution by misleading clients and ripping them off.[5]

When it all collapsed, the bankers claimed they were as bewildered as everybody else. Often those departments of banks responsible for trading and investing in the financial instruments, and which suffered huge losses, were small parts of large organizations – at least in terms of staff employed. Some of those who were closely involved asked: 'What could we have done to prevent this?' (See Tett, 2009.) All the same, it was shameful that too many senior managers just did not 'get it'. Some of the people in charge of departments that made these huge bets (for example, that a portfolio of securities would default or not) had never understood the instruments or the risks they were taking. As Michael Lewis showed (*The Big Short*, 2010, p. 214), when the crash came, bankers at Deutsche Bank offered Morgan Stanley traders an opportunity to exit from their trades, which were rapidly going sour. But then it dawned on them that the traders had no idea of the risks involved: 'All the way down, the debt collectors at Deutsche Bank sensed the bond traders at Morgan Stanley misunderstood their own trade. They weren't lying; they genuinely failed to understand the nature of the subprime CDO.'

These people were each paid millions of dollars a year. Morgan Stanley allowed the chief trader responsible, Howie Hubler, to resign in October 2007, taking many millions of dollars for himself while leaving his bank with losses reported at $9 billion – at that time the single largest trading loss in the history of Wall Street. The actual experience of the crash was compared to the feeling of being in an earthquake. Lewis describes the day when the bottom fell out of the stock market and great banks veered towards failure, and it was clear only the US government could save them. He quotes Danny Moses, a hedge fund manager who actually stood to make millions because he had successfully shorted bank stocks and subprime securities, four days after the Lehman failure. The stocks of Morgan Stanley and Goldman Sachs were 'tanking', and it was clear that 'nothing short of the US government could save them':

> 'It was the equivalent of the earthquake going off', he said, 'and then, much later the tsunami arrives.' Danny's trading life was man versus man, but this felt like man versus nature. The synthetic CDO had become a synthetic natural disaster. (Lewis, 2010, p. 239)

The blame game

Even with the benefit of hindsight, few senior bankers were ready to express contrition. Sir Andrew Large, a former top regulator and deputy governor of the Bank of England, talking about this in an interview (*Central Banking*, November 2010, p. 62) did say that 'remorse is due from many', and that he shared a 'deep sense of disappointment' with the behaviour of some people in the City of London and on Wall Street. But he emphasized the reasons why it had become difficult to avoid cutting corners. Money was 'left on the table' and 'The pickings to be had became so attractive that the entire machinery of finance swung into that space. So all the mechanisms that had been designed to manage conflicts of interests and govern finance generally in that simpler age – the partnership model, personal liability, and traditional ethics – all were subjected to challenge and in many cases failed at the same time.'

Most bankers found it convenient to pin the blame on politicians for encouraging the property boom, regulators for being asleep at the switch, and central bankers not only for following excessively loose monetary policies but also for failing to ask tough questions about the foundations of financial stability and who should do what. In the UK, many levelled their guns at individual central bankers such as Mervyn King, who was governor from 2003 and deputy governor before that – and at the UK Treasury. King said that he had pointed to growing risks to stability but wished he had shouted louder. Ben Bernanke, chairman of the Federal Reserve, made a half-hearted excuse. But what is certain is that easy money policies were maintained for far too long. Anger on the part of the general public, bewilderment on the part of many bankers, finger-pointing by politicians, were all understandable.

The report of the US Congressional commission into the banking collapse laid the primary blame on government mismanagement.[6] The Bush and Clinton administrations, the current and previous Federal Reserve chairmen, and Tim Geithner, then US Treasury Secretary, all bore some responsibility. Regulators 'had ample power ... and they chose not to use it', said the report. The commission also lambasted 'reckless' Wall Street firms, bankers and homeowners. In a minority report, the six Democrat commissioners emphasized lax oversight of derivatives, poor decisions by credit rating firms, and failures of governance and risk management by banks. The Republican commissioners put the credit bubble, fuelled by accommodative monetary policies, at the head of their list.

Nothing should excuse the breakdown of normal standards of good banking countenanced by the boards and managements of many banks and investment banks. Incompetent risk management and a readiness to allow themselves to be cowed by a dominant CEO were common factors in the worst cases. But it is also true that the system contained insufficient defences against such a breakdown.

So much for the popular narratives, which provided the backdrop to political action. They were couched in moral terms – greed, selfishness, guilt and punishment. What did economists have to say?

How markets make bubbles

There have been several waves of cross-border bubbles since the collapse of Bretton Woods.: the developing country debt bubble of the 1970s, the Japanese property bubble in the second half of the 1980s, which had spillover effects in the Nordic countries; the so-called Asian bubble in the mid-1990s, which also included Russia, Brazil and Argentina; the US stock price bubble of the mid to late 1990s; the Anglo-Saxon property price bubble between 2002 and 2007, which also included Spain, Ireland and Iceland (Aliber, 2011, 134–56).

They can have devastating effects. Take an example of a collapsing bubble from Asia. When the credit-fuelled property and asset bubble in the US, UK and Ireland burst in 2007–08, it set off a tidal wave that battered every country in the world. As the financial tsunami hit Asia, the worst affected countries were those most open to international trade and finance – countries like Singapore, Korea, Thailand and indeed Japan. Although many Asian countries had strengthened their defences against such shocks after the exchange rate and financial collapses of 1997–98 – building up foreign exchange reserves, raising bank capital and tightening supervision – they all proved to be vulnerable. To quote one well-placed observer,

> No matter how strong an economy's fundamentals are, no matter how resilient it is to domestic economic and financial shocks, economic and financial globalization have opened up potent international transmission mechanisms. (Filardo, 2011)

As waves of investor pessimism buffeted the region, normal functioning of trade finance and money markets was severely disrupted, and investment and production fell heavily. There was a severe risk of a downward spiral of asset prices and real economic activity. One of the worst blows was the way so many foreign banks immediately pulled in their horns, abandoning customers in a hasty withdrawal of funds to head offices. This forced central banks to cast aside their inflation targeting rule books and flood the markets with liquidity in attempts to keep them from seizing up. This showed how a bursting bubble generates considerable risks to output, inflation and normal market operations.

Yet very quickly there were signs that the ultra low interest rates and easy monetary policies that central banks pursued in an effort to sustain activity were causing a new rise in asset prices and were laying the seeds for a new self-perpetuating bubble as foreign funds were attracted back in, especially into real estate markets. Every one of the waves of bubbles was set off by an increased availability of money, a capital inflow, rise in the exchange rate (unless it was pegged to another currency) and a rise in asset prices. Exchange rate expectations played a key role (see Aliber, p150).

'There is hardly a more conventional subject in economic literature than financial crises' is the first sentence of Charles Kindleberger's classic study.[7] Despite all the research, including Kindleberger's, when another big bubble comes, it always catches governments on the hop.

Nor were economists any better prepared. In the boom years before GFC there was certainly a sense of unease – this seemed all too good to be true. Yet economists found it hard to say precisely what was wrong. The chief worry was that the dollar would decline in a disorderly way because of the US payments deficit, but this is not what actually happened. Moreover, as people pointed out at the time, the system had withstood many shocks, ranging from the stock market collapse of 1987, through repeated banking crises, the Asian bubble of 1997–98 and the dot.com bubble and bust. Those who cried 'wolf' all the time risked looking foolish. What was the point, for example, of a central bank repeatedly warning the public of the risks that house prices could fall, if they went on rising year after year, so that people who had heeded the central bank's warning and abstained from house purchase, saw friends who had bought a property double their money? The atmosphere of the time is evoked by an article written in April 2007 in the *Wall Street Journal* by Burton Malkiel, professor of economics at Princeton and author of the bestselling book, *A Random Walk Down Wall Street*. The economy would adjust to future shocks:

> Despite the risks and potential problems I have outlined, I remain a cautious optimist. I don't think anyone will make money in the long run betting against the inherent strength of the U.S. economy. (Malkiel, 2007)

He then went on to tell a story that nicely captured the mood of the time. Two rabbis were talking at the time of the creation of the world. One rabbi asked the other whether he was optimistic or pessimistic. 'I'm optimistic,' the second rabbi replied. 'Then why are you frowning?' the first rabbi asked. The answer: 'Because I'm not sure my optimism is justified.'

Investors would have done well to frown: within two years US stocks had lost half their value. Five years later they were still struggling to regain that lost territory.

Economists on bubbles

Apart from the blindingly obvious fact that no economic theory of financial bubbles had been of any use in predicting this one, were there useful insights to be gained from respected economists and schools of thought? After all, in the absence of guidance from scholarship, policy-makers would fall back on pragmatism, leaving them even more open to pressure from politicians, public opinion – and lobbying.

Predictably, economists divided into groups depending on their general attitude to markets – those who viewed the markets as generally benign, those who approached markets with cautious scepticism and those who viewed markets with hostility. Instead of rethinking their positions, supporters of each school of thought took from the episode evidence to strengthen their point of view. Here I will mention the views of a few of the leading schools of thought, notably the Kindleberger–Minsky school, the Marxists, the Austrian School and a couple of contemporary economists.

Kindleberger traces the beginning of a boom to what he calls a 'displacement' – often an exogenous shock that opens new profit opportunities, stimulating investment and production, and drawing in credit finance. Banks and, according to Minsky's elaboration, new sources of credit arise to satisfy the new demands. This is followed by a period of euphoria, when prices seem able only to go up, long-established standards of valuation are abandoned and new standards introduced to justify the price. Agents have a rosy-eyed view of the future, underestimating the downside and building up leveraged positions. Insiders – or just the lucky few – cash in their chips before the crash. Some shock then makes players realize that valuations are grossly inflated and there is a rush for the exit – but not before the crash has started. This is followed by panic, revulsion and withdrawal from the market.

Marxist economists argue that financial bubbles are the capitalist system's means of countering a natural trend towards economic stagnation. But such short-lived bubbles only conceal the underlying economic problems – the class-based nature of the production system – and then inevitably burst. The only recourse of the system is to create new and bigger bubbles, generating a cycle that leads to still greater financial crises and worsening conditions of production – a vicious cycle. This stage of capitalism, known as 'monopoly-finance capital', is accompanied by a casino financial system and promotes extreme social inequality, exploitation of an underclass and corrupt practices. There will be a tendency for such states to engage in foreign aggression and wars, so as to find and protect profitable outlets for corporate savings. Capitalism can keep going only by constant innovation, suggesting that such economists see the only way out of the money trap as lying in a new burst of productivity. While the Marxist approach is often dismissed as just plain wrong, it has strengths that mainstream economics lacks, notably in integrating social forces in the analysis. It has a lively awareness of the restless dynamism of capitalism, and captures its inbuilt tendency to create bubbles. It leads to a clear conclusion: policy will fail unless it is grounded in the structure of society and the economy rather than imposed on it (for a Marxist view of GFC, see Harvey, 2011).

Contemporary bubble theories

'Classical' accounts of credit bubbles miss two important dimensions of contemporary finance and GFC: floating exchange rates and the changed relationship between states and markets. First, economists from Adam Smith to Schumpeter assumed fixed exchange rates with a common currency – the gold standard. Economic fluctuations in one country are transmitted to others through trade and capital flows within a one-world exchange rate system. Central banks have only one aim – to maintain convertibility. Countries could not follow independent monetary policies. Investors faced no *ex ante* exchange rate risk. Central banks cooperated frequently to help each other maintain the fixed exchange rate and gold peg. Investors in foreign bonds in default lost money. And banks could collapse through investing in foreign bonds that defaulted, or through relying on foreign funds that could flee. Governments stood back from financial markets, except as sources of finance. Government spending as a proportion of GDP was small, whereas government currently impinges on all aspects of financial activity.

The financial crises that occurred after the end of Bretton Woods in 1971 took place in a world with floating and big government and acquired a different, and more destructive, character. Volatile exchange rates were an integral part of the build-up to crises and recovery from them. This was not what economists had expected with the advent of floating in the 1970s. On the contrary, many economists thought that floating would, in Kindleberger's words, 'kill off international movements of interest-sensitive capital'. Instead, banks quickly saw that foreign exchange could be a new asset class and an object of speculation – what Kindleberger called a 'displacement' – opening opportunities for speculation, especially as the attitude of the authorities of the leading country, the US, was one of benign neglect of the exchange rate. Moreover, the connections between the state and finance proliferated so extensively that they decisively altered the expectations of markets in ways that were not captured by traditional models.

The Austrian School, which remains vigorous into the twenty-first century, tends to see the management of money by central banks as the source of the disequilibrium. A central bank following an inflation target can easily introduce serious distortions between the market rate, influenced by its policy, and what Austrians call the 'natural' rate. If market rates are pushed below the natural rate, then investment spending will rise excessively and savings will fall – bringing about various forms of 'forced' savings to bridge the gap and eventually causing overheating. This is often signalled by a rapid price rise in at least one major asset, which can lead to a wider credit market bubble. These credit booms lead to 'malinvestments' and have serious long-term economic effects in building up wasteful capacity – as in housing in the boom years before GFC. They arise because of the damaging effect of central bank monetary policies. This is what happened during the later years of the chairmanship of Alan Greenspan (1987–2006) at the Federal Reserve.[8]

This analysis still had salience and persuasive proponents in the early twenty-first century (Brown, 2011). But it had difficulty taking full account of the implications of floating exchange rates and the international dimension more generally for the build-up of credit booms. For this we can turn to theories that have been developed more recently, of which two are notable – those by professors Robert Aliber and Paul Krugman.

Aliber and Krugman

Aliber's account of how bubbles form in an international context integrates exchange rate and interest rate interactions. Bubbles are generated when the flow of money to a country becomes too rapid to be sustained, causing upward pressure on interest rates, as was the case in many emerging markets in 2011; when the rate slackens, it is inevitable that the currency should depreciate and interest rates increase, in part in response to the decline in the supply of credit. Aliber identifies the key factors behind the waves of bubbles over the past 40 years. First, since the early 1970s, a large pool of 'idle money' has been parked with the international banks, available to be tapped by those who believe they can enhance their own returns by taking on credit risk or currency risk. This pool was inflated by the large payments imbalances from the 1970s onwards. The second factor is that there have been a series of shocks at national borders, which either have increased the anticipated returns available on securities in certain countries or increased the scope for cross-border investment by reducing restrictions at the border. The third element is that the early stages of cross-border money flows enhance the returns in countries that receive the money, so that the flows become self-justifying. They feed on themselves.

Another theory was proposed by Paul Krugman in 2008, namely contagion through the balance sheets of financial intermediaries: 'Loosely, when hedge funds lost a lot of money in Russia, they were forced to contract their balance sheets – and that meant cutting off credit to Brazil.' The best way to think about GFC, he argued, was that balance sheet contagion had become pervasive. There had been a major increase in financial globalization, as seen in the growth of international cross-holdings of assets. What stood out was the huge increase in both sides of the US international balance sheet, mainly after 1995. When banks and other asset-holders lost money through defaults in the US, they tended to sell other assets around the world. If they did that, then the international finance multiplier would become more important.

As regards policy implications, Krugman said that this showed that the core problem was shortage of capital, not liquidity. An injection of capital could reduce the financial multiplier effect of the initial shock. It also showed that a bank rescue involving an injection of capital in one country would have great benefits in other countries, suggesting large cross-border externalities. Financial policy coordination, however, was much more important. Capital injections by U.S. fiscal authorities would help Europe, capital injections by European fiscal authorities help alleviate the situation in the US. 'Multilateral Man, come home – we need you!'[9]

Against this, other economists emphasized the failure, as they saw it, of central banks to come promptly to the aid of banks with liquidity support of the traditional kind, as taught by Walter Bagehot in his classic work, *Lombard Street: a Description of the Money Market* (1873). I have discussed this at greater length in Chapter 10, but although I completely agree that major mistakes were made in the day-to-day handling of the credit crunch, and that both the US and UK authorities made a fatal error in failing to make clear in good time that they stood 100 per cent behind their banking systems, it is difficult to believe that a supply of liquidity by itself would have been sufficient on this occasion. It would have reduced the costs of the episode, but not averted the need for capital injection as well (for an alternative analysis of the UK episode, see Congdon, 2011, Essay 18).

Each of these approaches would have differing implications for the relationship between the state and the markets and for lessons to be drawn from the disaster. Krugman would have the state stand by as an emergency lender of capital; Aliber would rely more on making the markets discipline themselves during the build-up to the bubble, with the state staying in the background. Both recognize the changes in the background conditions against which credit and business cycles, as well as asset booms, occur. For Aliber, it is the chronic instability introduced into the finance sector by the exchange rate system itself that needs addressing. Krugman implicitly also recognizes the costs of the system, when floating rates were combined with large cross-border holdings of assets, in his call for the state to inject capital into banks laid low by international strains. In my view, of all the approaches mentioned here, Robert Aliber's comes closest to conceptualizing the day-to-day realities of the interrelationship between markets, exchange rates and official policy.

A mistaken economic ideology?

The fact that the financial earthquake struck at the heart of the global capitalist system rather than at what used to be slightingly called 'the periphery' demolished many myths of the superiority of the western model of banking and financial regulation. It also caused a bout of heart-searching among the dominant schools of 'western' economists: did they have any responsibility for GFC? What lessons did they or the economics discipline have to learn?

Market economists such as Jagdish Bhagwati, professor of economics at Columbia University, defined the issue as one of an inappropriate application of free trade economics to financial markets, which had enabled governments to allow the financial sector to get away with weak regulation, when they should have been aware of its tendency to instability. In his contribution to *The Future of Money* (ed. Oliver Chittenden, Virgin Books, 2010, p. 217), Bhagwati says: 'To carry over the legitimate approbation of freer trade in particular to the altogether more volatile financial sector, which represents the soft underbelly of capitalism, was surely unwarranted.' In his view, this illegitimate extension happened because policy was unduly influenced by Wall Street, which made policy-makers turn a blind eye to the potential of new financial instruments for 'destructive creation' (to adapt Schumpeter's vision of capitalism's gale of 'creative destruction'). According to Bhagwati there was no need to rethink capitalism itself: the notion of capitalism as a collapsed system, requiring invasive surgery, was 'far from compelling'. Instead, it needed to be purged of its excesses; business leaders should behave more responsibly and the dream of 'self-help' should be revived after a period in which social mobility which had been in decline.

Other economists, in contrast, were quick to conclude that capitalism itself was at fault – or at least the version in the ascendant since the Reagan-Thatcher revolution of the 1980s. These views were to the fore at the first meeting of the Institute for New Economic Thinking (INET), the think tank set up by George Soros, at King's College, Cambridge in April 2010. At that meeting, economists such as George Akerlof and Roman Frydman combined to attack a failure of ideas and, in particular, mistaken faith in the rational markets hypothesis as a key factor in the paralysis of policy that allowed the boom before the crash to spiral out of control. But how far were mistaken ideas responsible?

Sadly, many economists are strongly influenced by ideological preferences of one sort or another. When people said the crash reflected 'a failure of ideas' they usually meant that policy-makers were seduced by faith in the self-stabilizing ability of the markets, a belief, they said, that was used to justify light-touch regulation, and a dangerously permissive view of the growth of new financial instruments and markets, which should have been kept under stricter supervision. This in turn meant the authorities took a benign view of asset price bubbles such as that which blew up in the property markets in the US, UK and other countries in 2003–07. But the form of the rational expectations hypothesis espoused by most economists simply meant that people would make the best guess they could about whether to invest or not at prevailing prices, not that 'whatever the market price is, is the right price'.

I agree that there was a tendency to over-emphasize the benefits of financial innovation and neglect social costs. But this was not primarily due to the influence of mistaken economic ideas but rather the lobbying power of the finance industry, together with its seeming ability to produce mega profits year after year and bumper tax contributions to national treasuries, that made the political atmosphere benign for so long for the big beasts of world finance.

In addition to political opinion, and the views of economists, policy directed at reforming the system will also have to take into account the actual evolution of markets on the ground. Here the centre of gravity was moving away from big banks.

Financial innovation continues

Banking has been crippled and will need to spend several years recuperating – if indeed it ever recovers fully. The progressive tightening of restrictions, along with ever higher capital and liquidity requirements, and many other official impositions (see Chapter 10) seem likely to constrain the growth of mainstream banking, at least in developed economies. Restrictions at the national level – requirements, for example, that an international bank incorporates itself as a local subsidiary as a condition of doing business, and keeps sufficient liquidity locally – seem likely to raise costs and take the glamour away from the old banking models.

Where innovation has been proceeding rapidly is in the worlds of asset management, payments systems, equity, bond and commodity markets, mutual funds and investment trusts. In a nutshell, truly global markets have matured in all these areas. Hedge funds and private equity firms cater to the needs of large, professional investors. Yes, there are dangers here also, but they are of a different kind; in any case it is not so much the dangers as the potential that one should look at. Just as the great international banks of the twentieth century – Citigroup, Bank of America, Deutsche Bank, BNP, Barclays, HSBC – pioneered truly global banking, opening up stuffy domestic markets that were usually dominated by a cartel of local banks, so asset managers and other innovators are opening up the world to the potential of international investment.

To begin with some facts, according to the 2011 survey by McKinsey, the world's stock of equity and debt totalled \$212 trillion at the end of 2010. Stocks and shares traded on world's stock markets reached \$54 trillion, government and other public bonds \$41 trillion, bond issues of banks and other financial institutions \$42 trillion, corporate bonds \$10 trillion, securitized loans \$15 trillion and conventional loans \$49 trillion. The volume of assets traded in organized markets globally was put at \$200 trillion. This was about ten times the output of the US (Roxburgh et al. for McKinsey Global Institute, 2011).

These markets have potential systemic significance. Malfunctioning of these markets, shown either in excessive price swings or in a break-down of normal operations, can threaten the continued viability of market players that matter not just for them and their shareholders but for the wider financial and economic system. Some sectors of the markets can also be subject to manipulation by key market players. Nearly all countries have developed such markets, though often in elementary forms. They are essential if modern economies are to continue to function, yet they are unpredictable and depend for their proper working on trust and on confidence. Even when they work poorly, for example when a sector is dominated by only a few players, they are usually to be preferred to other ways of allocating capital – such as by administrative decision, with its normal accompaniment of corruption.

To be clear, these growing markets and institutions cannot replace banking – in the short or medium term. There will, however, be strong regulatory and internal pressures on banks to return to basics – to less complex structures and instruments. Commercial banks will be increasingly ring-fenced, closely monitored and their growth possibly capped – kept in cages to protect the public and the state's finances. High-flyers will tend to flee to less regulated entities and the task of regulators will be to ensure these do not become too big or too inter-connected to fail. Securitized markets will continue to increase their weight in the overall evolution of the system. The emergence of a truly global market in equities and bonds – claims on the productive capacity of the global economy – is a leading feature of the 'new' global financial system.

This will be important when we consider potential reforms of the GFS in later chapters. These are a few of the changes going on, in markets around the world – away from the glare of publicity.

The long view

The GFS has evolved in such a way as to distort incentives of the players, corrupt the relationship between states and markets, and impose unacceptable collateral damage on the real economy. The policy challenge was to reform the GFS so that it could deal with recurrent bubbles and credit cycles without imposing unacceptable costs. Efforts by regulators to keep up with and grasp the challenges involved at the intellectual level were to be applauded, but were they in danger of misleading the public? Was there any solution through regulatory means? Were not the new remedies being offered – time varying regulatory requirements, for example, and the whole macro-prudential toolkit – inherently unconvincing? They would face the same dilemma as previous generations of regulators – the more you regulate, the less responsibility heads of private firms feel for erecting their own safeguards against shocks. Was not Alan Greenspan right in saying that markets had become too complex and too opaque to be adequately regulated?[10]

To sum up, the interaction of governments and markets was predisposed to produce repeated crises when it took place within a system where,

a) major players were too big and inter-connected to fail;
b) monetary policy regimes operated without a reliable long-term anchor;
c) the minimum amount of freedom needed to allow the markets to provide their essential services was also enough to permit destabilizing speculation;
d) regulation was and would remain ineffective because of opacity and complexity of markets; and
e) the political influence of large financial institutions, and their seeming ability to 'select' regulators and politicians, meant that little confidence could be placed in the ability of regulators to make tough decisions affecting the viability and survival of individual firms.

It was also grossly unethical. Because of this, it was storing up political trouble. People had shown great patience. But public opinion could not be expected to put up year after year with such inequitable outcomes, where rewards bore no relation to effort, skill or common sense.

But don't blame the markets: they need boundaries and rules, otherwise they cannot fulfil their role of coordinating and reconciling differing policies and preferences in the common interest. All except a wild fringe of economists have recognized ever since the time of Adam Smith that markets cannot function in a vacuum. Adam Smith took for granted a system of laws governing the acquisition and transfer of property claims, commercial codes, a system of taxation to finance public goods, and the gold standard. He was also fully aware of the key role of ethical behaviour, as shown in his treatise – *The Theory of Moral Sentiments*. The question was, how could a strong framework be developed for international finance in the twenty-first century comparable to that which Adam Smith and the great classical economists had taken for granted in the eighteenth and nineteenth centuries? It should be a system that did not give excessive discretionary powers to the state or its agents (which yet again could be subject to abuse) AND that would be sufficiently robust to contain the powerful forces of international finance.

Part III of this study has examined four controversial areas of international finance – global imbalances, reserve accumulation, financial/regulatory reform and credit-fuelled bubbles. In each case, official policies were based on a faulty analysis. In each case, also, governments were adopting piecemeal, ad hoc *remedies. These did not meet the one test that mattered – restoration of confidence in the direction of policy.*

Notes

1. Niall Ferguson in *The Cash Nexus*, Chapter 10, also asks: are financial markets a power beyond human control?
2. See Fitch Ratings analysis, 'CDS Spreads and Default Risk: A Leading Indicator?' on their website, www.fitchratings.com, May 2011. The analysis concluded that the performance of CDS spreads did not provide leading signals of risks; one year prior to the event, CDS prices of banks that experienced 'credit events' (i.e. defaults or near defaults) had implied a default probability of only 3 per cent. Markets were no better than officials at providing warnings of impending disaster.
3. See Michael Lewis, *The Big Short*, p. 256: 'The CEOs of every major Wall Street firm were also on the wrong side of the gamble. All of them, without exception, either ran their public corporations into bankruptcy or were saved from bankruptcy by the US government. They all got rich, too.'
4. The 1993 report of the Group of 30, *Derivatives: Practices and Principles*, was particularly influential in keeping derivatives off the regulatory agenda. The role played by such 'independent' think tanks would repay further study.

5. As John Plender puts it, 'As for the poor old customer, banking is one of the few industries where people in trading rooms are treated like heroes if they rip off the customer. Retail bankers are less close to the animal kingdom than their trader colleagues, but even there endless mis-selling scandals suggest that the culture remains flawed. And the universal banking model that became the norm after the abolition of the US Glass-Steagall Act in 1999 entrenches conflicts of interest that continue to disadvantage clients'. (Plender, 2011)

6. Report of the Financial Crisis Inquiry Commission (FCIC), January 2011. The FCIC was a commission appointed by the US government with the goal of investigating the causes of the financial crisis.

7. Kindleberger (1978).

8. Steve Hanke (2008) describes the Austrian position in this way: 'With interest rates artificially low, consumers reduce savings in favour of consumption, and entrepreneurs increase their rates of investment spending. Then we have an imbalance between savings and investment. We have an economy on an unsustainable growth path. This, in a nutshell, is the lesson of the Austrian critique of central banking developed in the 1920s and 1930s. Austrian economists warned that price-level stability might be inconsistent with economic stability.'

9. See www.princeton.ed/~pkrugman/finmult.pdf

10. Alan Greenspan, *Financial Times*, 29 March 2011: 'The problem is that regulators, and for that matter everyone else, can never get more than a glimpse at the internal workings of the simplest of modern financial systems. Today's competitive markets, whether we seek to recognize it or not, are driven by an international version of Adam Smith's "invisible hand" that is irredeemably opaque. With notably rare exceptions (2008, for example), the global "invisible hand" has created relatively stable exchange rates, interest rates, prices, and wage rates.' (Obviously the view expressed in the last sentence is not shared by the author.)

Bibliography

Akerlof, George A. and Robert J. Shiller, *Animal Spirits*, Princeton, 2009.

Aliber, Robert Z., 'The Supply of International Reserve Assets, and a Dysfunctional International Monetary Arrangement', paper given at the public investment conferences, sponsored by the BIS, ECB and World Bank, November 2010.

Aliber, Robert Z., *The New International Money Game*, Palgrave Macmillan, 2011.

Anderson, Geraint, *Cityboy: Beer and Loathing in the Square Mile*, Headline Publishing, 2008.

Bagehot, Walter, *Lombard Street: A Description of the Money Market*, first published 1873; new edition with an introduction by Hartley Withers, Smith, Elder & Co, 1912; online source: Johnstone and Hartley Withers (eds), London, Henry S. King and Co. Comments include editorial notes and appendices from the 12th (1906) and the 14th (1915) editions, see http://www.econlib.org

Brown, Brendan, *The Global Curse of the Federal Reserve: Manifesto for a Second Monetarist Revolution*, Palgrave Macmillan, 2011.

Congdon, Tim, *Money in a Free Society*, Encounter Books, 2011.

Ferguson, Niall, *The Cash Nexus: Money and Power in the Modern World 1700–2000*, Allen Lane/ Penguin Press, 2001.

Filardo, Andrew, 'The Impact of the International Financial Crisis on Asia and the Pacific: Highlighting Monetary Policy Challenges from a Negative Asset Price Bubble Perspective', BIS Working Papers, No 356, November 2011.

Financial Crisis Inquiry Commission, *Report*, January 2011, at www.fcic.law.standford.edu

Fitch Ratings, 'Cds Spreads and Default Risk: a Leading Indicator?' www.fitchratings.com, May 2011.

Freedman, Seth, *Binge Trading: The Real Inside Story of Cash, Cocaine and Corruption in the City*, Penguin Books, 2009.

Frydman, Roman and M.D. Goldberg, *Beyond Mechanical Markets*, Princeton, 2011.

Greenspan, Alan, 'Dodd-Frank Fails to Meet Test of Our Times', *Financial Times*, 29 March 2011.

Hanke, Steve, 'Panic Time at the Fed', *Forbes*, 5 May 2008.

Harvey, David, *The Enigma of Capital*, Profile Books, 2011.

Ichikawa, Tetsuya, *How i Caused the Credit Crunch: An Insider's Story of the Financial Meltdown*, Icon Books, 2009.

Kindleberger, Charles, *Manias, Panics and Crashes: A History of Financial Crises*, Macmillan, 1978.

Kindleberger, Charles, and Aliber, Robert P., *Manias, Panics, and Crashes: A History of Financial Crises*, 6th edn, Wiley, 2010.

Krugman, Paul, 'The International Finance Multiplier', cited by Krugman in the *New York Times*, 5 October 2009.

Lewis, Michael, *The Big Short*, Allen Lane/Penguin Press, 2010.

Malkiel, Burton J., 'Irrational Complacency?' *Wall Street Journal*, 30 April 2007.

Smith, Adam, *The Theory of Moral Sentiments*, 1759, Liberty Fund, Oxford University Press, 1976.

Plender, John, 'Star Traders, Rip-Offs and Old-Style Bankers', *Financial Times*, 18 August, 2011.

Roxburgh, Charles, Susan Lund, John Piotrowski, *Mapping Global Capital Markets*, McKinsey Global Institute 2011.

Tett, Gillian, *Fool's Gold: How the Bold Dream of a Small Tribe at J. P. Morgan was Corrupted by Wall Street Greed and Unleashed a Catastrophe*, Free Press, 2009.

Part IV
The Power of Global Finance

12
One Hundred Years of Currency Plans

To get out of the money trap will require a transformation of the GFS. As discussed in Chapter 3, before such a regime change is feasible, intellectual groundwork and consensus-building will be needed. The rich history of thought on monetary reform has much to offer.

From the past to plausible futures

I start by making a few preliminary points.

First, the rationale for aiming reform at the level of the GFS has already been advanced in earlier chapters, and this part of the study takes this as an assumption (it is summed up in the concluding chapter). Only by raising the level at which we tackle these problems can they be resolved – not piece by piece, as governments were doing in the years following GFC, but in an integrated way. This is the lesson from the four issues examined in Part III: they all need solutions that can be effective only at the level of the GFS as a whole. The enormous energies of globalized finance could then again be harnessed for the pubic good.

Second, the broad choice is between 'gold' and 'credit' – gold defined here as representing those regimes built on an impersonal standard, and credit those relying on trust in benevolent discretion: Rules versus Activism. These distinctions are used to help organize the material; readers might bear in mind that the contrasts between these two classes of proposals will run through the presentation and analysis in this concluding part of the book.

Third, what should be the aims of a reform of the GFS? Within the overall aim of chanelling the energies unleashed by markets – the

Power of Global Finance – to the general interest, these are the author's priorities:

- to provide the global public goods of monetary and financial stability;
- to curb the undue influence of commercial (private) financial interests over official policy;
- to provide the authorities of every country or monetary areas and through them every adult citizen with the opportunity to use reliable money, giving them a monetary stake in the future.

Readers may feel that the world economy is changing so quickly that it is unlikely that any reforms proposed in the past could be useful in current circumstances. Yet the underlying issues remain. Focusing just on the international monetary system, as usually understood, there are the classic questions relating to adjustment and liquidity: how should countries adjust to changes in factors affecting their balance of payments? How much time should they be given to adjust? What rules should the international community agree on to govern commercial and financial relations between governments? What powers should international institutions have to monitor and/or enforce such rules? But there is also the prior question which, in my judgement, has been unduly neglected in the more recent discussion: how should the monetary standard be constituted?

Such are the questions that have run through the debates on the monetary system for many decades, even while conditions changed as the world economy evolved. They are likely to remain insistent. It is instructive to go back to the origin of these ideas. One hopes not only for inspiration, but also for help in avoiding repeating the mistakes of the past.

Readers will have noted that we have moved from discussion of the GFS to questions relating to one element – the official international monetary system. To clarify, this chapter summarizes briefly a few of the foundational ideas for international monetary reform and their rationales; Chapter 13 looks at the ideas of some contemporary economists who are interested in the concept of 'the standard'. The final two chapters attempt to integrate proposals for reform of the international monetary system with ongoing changes in banking and money markets into an overall vision for a remodeling of the GFS as a whole (which, to remind readers, is defined to comprise two elements – first, the official international monetary system and, second, profit-making commercial financial institutions, those who use them and the markets in which they interact).

From Fisher to Keynes

Interest in international monetary issues ebbs and flows. One of the intellectual foundation stones of monetary reform ideas, as well as of modern central banking, was laid in 1911 with the publication of *The Purchasing Power of Money*, by Irving Fisher. This suggested a form of 'monetary rule' by which the dollar, which was linked to gold, could be made a unit of constant purchasing power. The real price of gold should be stabilized by altering its dollar price inversely in accordance with changes in a price index; the aim was to stabilize its purchasing power and thus the purchasing power of the dollar. This was the intellectual ancestor of inflation targeting, set within a one-world, fixed exchange rate, gold standard context. One hundred years later, it remains the idea to beat.

High water marks of interest in world money were reached in the 1920s, towards the end of the Second World War (in 1942–45), in the last decade of the Bretton Woods system and in the immediate aftermath of its demise (1960–72), and in the late 1990s during the build up to the launch of the euro. If a rhythm can be discerned in the historical record, episodes of enthusiasm seem to come round only once a generation or so – which is about as long as recent 'monetary systems' have lasted. There was also a steady drumbeat of worry about the longer-term future of the US dollar, the lynchpin of the system, as analysed in Chapter 9. Following GFC several forces have come together that should spur another re-examination: indeed, the money trap resulted from the way in which the problems facing monetary policy, the problems of global imbalances, sovereign debt, reserve currencies and banking and finance had narrowed policy options.

We now summarize briefly the development of ideas about international money in the context of the history of the twentieth century. The first international meeting to consider the future of the international monetary system took place in Genoa in 1922. It was the first that could take account of the implications of the setting up of the Federal Reserve, the resulting claim by the US for parity with Britain, if not leadership of the system, and the fact that countries could not go back to gold at the pre-war level without savage deflation of their economies. One solution to this crisis, as to the crisis at the end of Bretton Woods in 1969–71, would have been to increase the official price of gold (devalue the dollar and sterling and other currencies against gold). But in neither case was this option seriously considered. Another option in the early 1920s was for countries to acknowledge US leadership and peg to the dollar. That was not acceptable to the British. So Genoa was led to give the official seal of approval to a multiple currency reserve system, whereby countries would treat their claims against reserve centers (mainly sterling claims on London) as part of their reserves, in addition to gold. This meant that the world price level would depend on the money supplies in individual countries, set ultimately by their gold holdings and foreign currency reserves. It confronted, but failed to solve, the challenge to international monetary order posed by the creation of the Federal Reserve: who took responsibility for leadership? That question remained unanswered.

In the view of monetary conservatives like Jacques Rueff (see below), the Genoa compromise allowed countries to evade the disciplines of the gold standard and opened the way to an inflationary spiral (Chivvis, p. 64). This in turn was at the root of over-investment in the late 1920s and the downturn of 1929–30. In Mundell's view, if gold had been revalued (against all currencies, not just sterling) in the 1920s this could not only have enabled the gold standard itself to survive, but also have avoided subsequent calamities: 'no Great Depression, no Nazi revolution, and no World War II' (see Mundell, 1999). The stakes in getting decisions about international monetary isssues right are indeed high.

Bancor

Keynes's 1941 plan for an international clearing bank (he called it a clearing union) was designed to combat what he saw as the main international monetary problem of his day, the tendency of the US to accumulate gold reserves, and not recycle or re-lend them out as a true international banker would do. He argued that this imposed deflation on the rest of the world. It is an argument similar to that which has been used ever since (mainly by the US itself!) against countries running big payments surpluses, such as, at various times, Germany, Japan and China.

In its original version, Keynes wrote in 1941:

> the process of adjustment is compulsory for the debtor and voluntary for the creditor. If the creditor does not choose to make, or allow, his share of the adjustment, he suffers no inconvenience. For whilst a country's reserve cannot fall below zero, there is no ceiling which sets an upper limit. The same is true if international loans are to be

the means of adjustment. The debtor must borrow; the creditor is under no such compulsion. (Keynes, 1980, p. 28)

The UK government's white paper of 1943 (which Keynes drafted) showed how far-reaching the changes to the current system had to be to meet this problem. International reserves would consist only of gold and a new international bank money which Keynes called bancor. Bancor would be fixed (but not unalterably) in terms of gold and accepted as the equivalent of gold. This paper gold would be used to settle international payments imbalances. The central banks would keep accounts with the International Clearing Union through which they would be entitled to settle their debts (what the white paper called 'exchange values') with one another in bancors. They would not be allowed to hold national currencies in reserves, though an exception would be made for currency holdings of a member of a group such as the sterling area. The real purpose of the proposals was to discipline surplus countries. Under the plan, surplus countries could be compelled to take 'measures' to reduce their surpluses where necessary:

> Countries having a favourable balance of payments with the rest of the world as a whole would find themselves in possession of a credit account with the Clearing Union, and those having an unfavourable balance would have a debit account. Measures would be necessary... to prevent the piling up of credit and debit balances without limit, and the system would have failed in the long run if it did not possess sufficient capacity for self-equilibrium to secure this. (HMSO, 1943, para 4)

The underlying idea, as the paper explained, was to extend to the world economy the same principle as applied within a closed national banking system – that credits and debits must necessarily be equal. If participants could not transfer credits outside the system but only transfer them within the system, then the international clearing bank would always be able to honour any cheques drawn on it. The clearing bank could lend bancors to any member in any amount it wished, as it would know that the proceeds could be transferred only to the clearing accounts of another member:

> Its sole task is to see to it that its members keep their rules and that the advances made to each of them are prudent and advisable for the Union as a whole. (HMSO, 1943, para 5)

To protect the volume of bancors in the account, convertibility between gold and bancors would be one way – countries could use their gold reserves to purchase bancors but they could not convert bancors back into gold. This provision was not acceptable to the Americans, as the major surplus country, who saw it as a ruse to get them to bankroll the entire system. This was a reflection of the proposed mechanism of adjustment. A country's access to the clearing bank's resources would be governed by its quota, the size of which would be related to the value of its international trade. This quota would not only determine how much a country could borrow but also set a ceiling on its credit balance. A creditor central bank of a country running a payments surplus could keep its balance at the clearing bank within permitted limits by lending bancor to other central banks, building an element of flexibility into the scheme. But when the surplus balance approached the ceiling, then the monetary authority of the Union could require the surplus country to take measures to curb its payments surplus.

This plan outlined a stable exchange rate system while building in a mechanism to provide for both adjustment and an element of credit so that countries could smooth adjustment over time. This would in principle protect the world economy from the deflation that Keynes feared so much. There was provision for devaluation or revaluation of a country's exchange rate. Surplus countries would be required to discuss with the monetary authority measures needed to restore equilibrium in its international balances, including (a) measures to expand domestic credit and demand, (b) appreciation of its currency in terms of bancor, (c) the reduction of tariffs and other barriers to imports and/or (d) increasing international aid. A similar ladder of pressures was to be applied to debtors. However, the US changed the articles to ensure tht it would not be obliged to adjust in the manner originally foreseen.

Triffin

In practice during the Bretton Woods regime from 1945 to 1971 the pressure for adjustment still turned out to be wholly on the deficit countries. The danger of this system leading to deflation and unemployment was avoided because the US alleviated the shortage of dollars by investing and lending on a vast scale overseas, and then by its own move into payments deficit on current account. This growing deficit was then financed 'painlessly' as foreign countries increased their balances of dollars. As it operated in practice, the system turned out to be benign and world economic growth boomed. However, from the start of the 1960s, this created another set of problems.

The Belgian economist Robert Triffin pointed his finger to the fact that the system relied on one national currency, the US dollar, to provide for any increase in reserves for the world as a whole (apart from gold). Such a system would be unstable and susceptible to crises of confidence since the only way surplus countries could accumulate dollars was for the US to remain in overall payments deficit. He predicted that in time this deficit was bound to raise doubts about its credit – i.e. its ability to redeem these liabilities in gold. This contradiction, he said, would eventually bring down the Bretton Woods system.

The aim of Triffin's Plan was similar to that of Keynes's plan as already described. Countries would hold only two forms of international reserve assets – in his plan they would be gold and deposits at the IMF. Countries would be obliged to transfer holding of dollars and other national currencies to the Fund in exchange for deposits. These deposits would be guaranteed in terms of gold. Such deposits would be used by central banks to settle any deficit in their trade with other countries. The IMF could lend to countries in temporary balance of payments difficulties, by crediting their account with a loan, as a bank does to its customers. In this way it would create new deposits, and could regulate their supply just as a central bank regulates the supply of money in a national economy. To prevent the IMF 'bank' from issuing too much money, ceilings would be placed on its ability to expand deposits, and any increase beyond an agreed annual growth rate would need the agreement of a large majority of the Fund's board – representatives of national governments. Over time, the balances of national currencies held by the Fund would be run down – in effect the obligations of reserve currency countries that they represented would be repaid.

The provision that outstanding balances turned into the Fund by reserve centres would be run down would have required the UK and US to run significant current account surpluses – or sell some of their gold. For the reserve centres to run a surplus meant a corresponding deficit in other countries' payments. Admittedly, the period could have been extended over many years, and the Fund could have facilitated the process by temporary lending (as indeed it eventually did to ease the rundown of sterling balances by the UK later in the 1960s). But critics alleged this process might easily cause deflation and recession. Others feared that the Fund's powers to create the equivalent of bank deposits by lending would be abused and lead to inflation. The deposits created by the Fund could be spent by countries receiving them, adding to global demand. If the global economy or merely the economies of the members receiving the additional orders were operating at full stretch then that could increase inflation.

Another weakness in Triffin's plan was the absence of a mechanism for ensuring that global imbalances were reduced. If the Fund was to lend only for short-term purposes, to tide a country over a strictly temporary deficit (as was the Fund's practice), then the broader aims of the Triffin plan, to allow for a regular increase in global reserves (liquidity), would not be attained. Triffin countered that the Fund could always top up the expansion in deposits created by lending with the purchase of securities. But that proposal raised further difficulties. There were only a few countries with developed capital and money markets suitable for such purchases. The US and the UK were the leading international capital markets; it would defeat the purpose of the exercise if the Fund came back to the original reserve centres to help it create reserves needed by the prohibition on the use of national currencies as reserve currencies!

Towards an international central bank

In Triffin's plan, central bank foreign exchange reserves would be centralized in the IMF, allowing it for example to counteract undesirable floods of 'hot money' from one country to another. Although the reformed IMF would stop short of being a full international central bank (for example, the 'money' it created would be available to central banks for use only in transactions with other central banks, not to the general public), it would have many central banking features, and would have marked a giant step towards such an international central bank. On some versions of Triffin's plan, transactions between members could take place entirely in Fund deposits, so that the Fund would act as a central bank, where the ultimate settlement of imbalances takes place on its balance sheet. IMF deposits would be 'backed' by the Fund's investments, which should only be in top-rated securities of developed country governments or international institutions such as the World Bank. Countries would add to their international reserves by acquiring additional deposits at the Fund – either by selling gold to it, or by selling its own currency (up to a ceiling) to the Fund, or by selling the currency of another country to the Fund.

Nobel Prize Laureate James Meade suggested going even further. At a time (the early 1960s) when central bankers viewed any proposal for more flexible exchange rates with horror, he proposed a reform that embraced not only fully floating exchange rates but also a transformation of the

IMF into an international central bank with powers to limit fluctuations between national currencies by intervention as appropriate (Meade, 1961). The Fund would decide how much credit to allow to national governments, to give them time to adjust. To provide overall stability to the system, the Fund would be mandated to keep its unit of account stable in terms of an index of national currencies and against gold. If one currency depreciated in terms of gold, another would appreciate. In such a system, governments would have limited autonomy in terms of domestic economic and monetary policy, while giving up powers over exchange rates to a supranational body. Other authors put forward variants of this proposal over the years. However distant the prospect of realizing the proposal was, given political realities, it seemed at the time to represent the logical destination of the road that the international community had been traveling.

Towards a commodity standard

Other 'classic' proposals would link currencies to a basket of commodities – or to an index of the prices of a number of commodities. These proposals represent a move along the spectrum from 'credit' towards 'gold', with narrowing scope for autonomous national monetary policies.

Among the benefits claimed by proponents of such schemes were, typically, that they would reduce the inflationary tendencies inherent in fiat money controlled by central banks/governments, and that they would tie money to the real side of the economy. Thus the real value of money, and expectations abut the future real value of money, would be stabilized. This would reduce the uncertainty that instability in the unit of account and store of value introduced into business and personal planning and the yield on investments. It would also eliminate the dangers inherent in the granting of power to an international monetary authority or central bank (albeit with accountability to governments) of the kind proposed by Keynes and Triffin.

But such proposals would provide the public good of monetary stability only if leading countries agreed to tie their currencies to a common basket of goods or if one country did so and others tied their currency to that anchor currency. If each country had a different basket – for example – a basket of items that made up its consumer price index – then we would be back in the world of inflation targeting, and there would be nothing to stabilize exchange rates or the system as a whole.

The economists who have favoured such ideas included Friedrich von Hayek and Nicholas Kaldor. Opponents included Milton Friedman (Friedman, 1951). The core insight was put by one of their most enthusiastic proponents, the great American investment guru and founder of 'value investing' – Benjamin Graham:

> Certain key commodities should form a broad connecting bridge between the world of goods on the one hand and the world of money on the other. (quoted in Mehrling, 2007, page 29)

Graham saw financial speculation as the source of the economic depression of the 1930s and his Commodity Reserve Currency set out to do for society what his 'principles of sound investing' could do for the individual investor – afford protection from the evils of speculation. His idea was simple: the state should maintain a buffer stock of commodities financed by the issue of currency that would fluctuate in line with the commodity stocks held. The agency would buy stocks and issue more money when the price fell significantly below the standard price and sell commodities when their price rose significantly above it. He offered this plan in 1933 in a bid to stimulate economic recovery from the Depression. This would, he claimed, put additional purchasing power 'directly in the hands of producers'.

Later he developed the scheme into an alternative to the gold standard. By 1937 he was proposing to replace the Federal Reserve's discretionary monetary policy: the US dollar would be *defined* as equivalent to the commodity unit. He selected 23 commodities for his basket, against which the Fed would issue currency (essentially warehouse receipts). Later Graham extended this and proposed that monetary growth be tied directly to the production of the commodities in the basket – as in a gold standard. He protested against what he saw as the monetary excesses of the New Deal (when, as in 2007–10, the US administration tried everything it could to stimulate the economy through monetary means, but to no avail).

In 1944 Hayek proposed an international version of Graham's commodity reserve plan, and this in turn brought Graham in touch with Keynes. Graham had for years been frustrated by the neglect of his work by academic economists – for which he strongly criticized their narrow mindedness – and he tried hard to insert his ideas into the debate leading up to Bretton Woods. He disapproved of Keynes's ideas for a kind of pure credit system, on the grounds that it applied no adequate constraints on the lending powers of the IMF. He deeply regretted the lack of a more direct link between the world of money and that of production and trade, and he believed there was nothing to tie down the value of international money under the proposals. So he attempted to insert a commodity reserve element into the plan, but this got nowhere (Mehrling, 2011, pp. 28–9).

One common objection to such ideas was that stabilizing the price level of a basket would not stabilize the general price level unless the price of the basket of monetary commodities was constant in relation to the general price level. But as Cooper pointed out (1982 and 1988), if the relationship changed only slowly, then such a commodity standard would at least make the movement in the general price level more predictable.

As a key feature of GFC was precisely such a damaging divorce between the worlds of money and production, it was not surprising that there was somewhat of a revival of interest in commodity monies (see Ussher, 2011). Graham saw that at the heart of financial crises was an excess elasticity of the banking and credit system, a feature identified also by contemporary economists such as Claudio Borio as a key issue in GFC. Graham would have criticized plans to combat such faults by state regulation (macro-prudential policy).

Graham's ideas influenced Nicholas Kaldor, one of Keynes's most important disciples, who with Albert Hart and Jan Tinbergen in 1964 proposed the creation of an international commodity-reserve currency (see Hart et al., 1964 and Ussher, 2011). In a later version, Hart proposed a list of 31 primary commodities that might make up the basket and proposed that the IMF would issue SDRs in exchange. In this way the SDR would be anchored to the real economy. These SDRs would be the principal source of new international reserves; countries would agree not to increase their holdings of gold and foreign currency reserves. At times of deflation or depression, when commodity prices fell, the fund would purchase commodities to any extent necessary to maintain their price in terms of the standard, stimulating new production, and vice versa at times of boom. The basic mechanism would be similar to that familiar from the gold standard, which also put new purchasing power into the hands of gold producers at times of excess demand for gold, but would broaden this to a far greater number of commodities (and exclude gold). The IMF would pay for storage of these commodities and the costs of replacing the perishable commodities in the basket. Once up and running, the scheme would ensure stability in the value of the basket of commodities through purchases and sales of the basket within a margin. The general price level of countries pegging to the SDR would be stabilized to the extent that there was no change in the purchasing power of the basket in terms of other goods – i.e. between the average prices of commodities in the basket and other prices (see Coats, 2011, and Chapter 14). On this point, Kaldor was on the right lines. He believed passionatedly in the need to create a universal reserve mechanism which would command acceptance on account of its evident stability in real value independent of paper money (Hart, Kaldor and Tinbergen, 1964, p. 144).

Hayek

The father of competitive currency plans is Hayek, who as noted, was also attracted for a time to commodity-based currencies. In 1976 the Institute for Economic Affairs published two seminal papers by him on the subject. In the first paper, *Choice in Currency*, he launched an attack on Keynes, branding him as 'a man of great intellect but limited knowledge of economic theory' and explained that he withdrew from the debate about international money when it became clear that even economists he had respected supported the 'wholly Keynesian' Bretton Woods agreement. Writing at the height of the great inflation of the 1970s, he proclaimed that government control of the quantity of money had once again proved fatal:

> With the exception only of the 200-year period of the gold standard, practically all governments of history have used their exclusive power to issue money in order to defraud and plunder the people. (Hayek, *Collected Works* Vol. 6, p. 120)

The pressure for more and cheaper money was an ever-present political force and Keynes had provided those interests with a new rationale:

> There will be no more urgent need that to erect new defences against the onslaught of popular forms of Keynesianism, that is, to replace or restore those restraints which, under the influence of his theory, have been systematically dismantled. (Hayek, op cit p. 119)

It was the main function of such restraints (such as the gold standard, balanced budgets, rules requiring deficit countries to reduce the supply of money, and limitations on the supply of international liquidity) to make it impossible for central banks to capitulate to the constant pressure for more money. Each of these restraints had been swept away.

The world was not in a position to construct a new international monetary order – for example, Hayek said, any attempt to resurrect the gold standard would soon break down under popular pressure. Yet there was no reason to expect that, so long as the people were forced to use the money the government provided, governments would become more trustworthy. The problem was not governments' right to issue money but their right to force people to use it at a particular price. Individuals ought to have the right to decide whether they wanted to use dollars, pounds or ounces of gold. It was governments' power to insist that contracts concluded within their territory be conducted in their currency, and to set the rates at which they should be concluded, that was harmful. With currency freedom, employers would begin offering wages in a currency they trusted and that could be the basis of rational calculation. Governments would lose the power to counteract excessive wage increases and the unemployment they caused by depreciating the currency. Although for convenience most daily transactions would doubtless continue to be carried out in local currency, willingness to hold a depreciating currency would be greatly reduced. Business and capital transactions would switch to a more reliable standard and this would keep national monetary policy on the right path. Hayek dismissed the risk that competition would lead to deflation, and believed people would prefer the currency that was likely to retain its long-term value. He did, however, suspect that in a free competitive environment it was 'not unlikely' that gold would ultimately re-assert its place as 'the universal prize in all countries, in all cultures, in all ages', as Jacob Bronowski put it in his then popular TV series and book *The Ascent of Man* (1973). But in that event the re-emergence of gold would take place through natural evolution, not government direction. Indeed, gold was essentially a free market system.

A few years after these papers were published, most developed countries that had retained the capital controls left over from the immediate post-war world abolished them, so that freedom of currency choice became a reality over most of the developed world. Thereafter there was no compulsion on individuals or companies to maintain more than working balances in pounds or in any currency they expect to depreciate – above the level needed to pay taxes and meet anticipated needs. As a necessary accompaniment, at the same time the leading economies embarked on a sustained anti-inflationary monetary policy, which over the 1980s and 1990s greatly reduced inflation and inflationary expectations. Indeed, there was in most countries a rapid increase in balances held by residents in foreign currencies – but an equally rapid rise in balances in domestic currencies held by foreigners. However, for a variety of reasons there remained a marked bias towards home investment, partly because of inertia and partly because of uncertainty about the future course of exchange rates; investors could never be certain that, when the moment arrived that they needed their money in their home currency, the rate of exchange would be favourable or not. Thus freedom of currency choice came about, but it resulted more in a general and gradual diversification of currency holdings rather than any sudden flight from one currency. Governments also put in place monetary policy regimes that went some way towards 'taking money out of politics' and for the following 25 years or so seemed to offer credible defences against the kind of pressures to which Hayek had pointed. For these reasons, the seeming success of the fight-back against inflation made Hayek's proposals seem irrelevant – until one crisis after another jolted such assumptions. After the monetary demons re-appeared, Hayek's approach was again worth a re-examination.

Hayek's ideas continued to develop: in the paper on 'Denationalization of Money' he advocated the private issue of currency by banks, and in his later essay on 'The Future Unit of Value' he claimed that a semi-automatic regulation of the supplies of the main kinds of money such as he had suggested 'would eliminate *all* the causes of the alternation of inflationary booms and periods of depression and unemployment which have plagued mankind ever since deliberate attempts at a central control of the quantity of money have been made'. After all, he said, the concept of monetary policy was 'a very new idea', and may never do any good:

> The money we now have is not a fully-fledged product of our cultural evolution, but a deformed child…. Our money has been made to serve purposes to which it was not adapted. (*Collected Works*, Vol 6, p 251)

Rueff

The French economist Jacques Rueff (1898–1978) was the leading intellectual champion of the gold standard in the twentieth century and we can now benefit from an excellent account of his career and intellectual development by Christopher Chivvis (see Chivvis, 2010). Rueff reached a coherent political and economic philosophy early in life and remained loyal to it. His criticisms of the gold exchange standard sanctioned by the Genoa Conference and his belief in the virtues of the classical gold standard remained constant. He saw the gold standard as an essential element in a broad liberal order and identified the use of dollars as foreign exchange reserves as being at the heart of the problems of the international monetary system a generation before Triffin made this analysis famous in the Anglo-Saxon world. Rueff was motivated not by nostalgia but by hard-headed realism. The gold standard was needed not in order to return to a lost golden age before the First World War but to deal adequately with the realities of the post First World War period. His call for a return to the gold standard made him 'part of a long tradition of monetary conservatism that had descended from France's negative experience with fiat money', first under John Law in the eighteenth century and then during the inflationary paper money experiment with *assignats* during the French Revolution (see Chapter 6 for the influence of this tradition on France's attitude towards EMU). Like Hayek, he thought that Keynes's analysis appealed to politicians because it gave them a way of avoiding reality, as monetary manipulation could substitute for adjustment:

> On a deeper level still, Rueff thought this weakness was evidence of the growing fragmentation of modern democracies, in which special interests had prevailed on politicians for protection and, in doing so, were destroying social cohesion and economic welfare. (Chivvis, 2010, p. 65)

Keynes and his followers had caved in to special interests as had French politicians who surrendered to the agricultural lobby's pleas for protection.

He carried this analysis through to the problems of the international economy after the Second World War. Both Hayek and Rueff believed that the price mechanism was the key to an efficient allocation of resources both nationally and internationally. To allow the mechanism to function on a global scale required imposing discipline on the world's great powers. Only the gold standard could do that. During the 1960s, Rueff wrote innumerable articles in the Anglo-Saxon media as well as academic papers criticizing Bretton Woods and calling for a return to gold. He agreed with Triffin that the dependence of the system on the US dollar was a critical weakness, and that a continuation of the US payments deficit would trigger a crisis. But whereas Triffin saw the flood of dollars out of the US as necessary to meet the world's growing demand for reserves, Rueff thought it caused an excessive increase in global credit, and was unsustainable: a collapse of confidence in the dollar could easily lead to a global banking panic and deflation. Thus Rueff opposed Triffin's call for the creation of an international reserve asset. He thought it was unnecessary and would be abused.

At the time, Rueff's views remained marginal. De Gaulle trumpeted them and was certainly influenced by them, but Rueff, who was seen as 'a profound friend of the US', was uncomfortable with de Gaulle's confrontational tactics. When in 1966 Rueff called for a doubling of the gold price to allow a restoration of convertibility without a contraction of global credit, his views had no influence on events and in 1967 France abandoned its crusade for gold and agreed to the creation of the SDR. Whatever influence Rueff had exercised – and he was never close to the Banque de France or French ministry of finance – waned further. Rueff then watched Bretton Woods collapse, as he had predicted, and in his last work, *The Monetary Sin of the West* (1972), he attacked the floating exchange regime that followed. This, he asserted, would encourage protectionism, raise uncertainty about international trade and investment and facilitate permissive monetary policies by all countries(instead of just the US), creating throughout the world 'a breeding ground for recession and unemployment'. He foresaw disaster.

Rules or monetary activism?

A fundamental dividing line separates the various schools of monetary reformers. Chivvis quotes a statement that rather movingly shows Rueff's passionate belief in the need for an international order:

> Exchange between nations cannot be left, without danger, to individual decisions unless these are enclosed within the limits of a global level of purchasing power, that ensures at the same time, the stability of internal prices and the equilibrium of international exchange. Only metallic, monetary convertibility can establish such an equilibrium for long periods of time.
>
> If I defended tirelessly for half a century the principle of monetary convertibility, it is not by any attachment to an orthodoxy that, in money matters, would make no sense, but because I love liberty and because I am convinced it is not a free gift. (Chivvis, 2010, p. 176)

Out of touch with the geopolitical realities and economics of his time Rueff may have been, but he has not been forgotten. On the contrary, his works continue to resonate, in the wake of the great crash, perhaps more than at any time since he died. The dollar dilemmas that he laid bare so clearly continue to plague the system and the risks they pose remain as great.

Both Hayek and Rueff were suspicious of activist monetary policies (children of the Keynesian revolution) permitted by the prevailing international monetary system – whether under the gold exchange standard or the post Bretton Woods periods. They saw that the globalizing trading regime was fundamentally at odds with mercantilist monetary and exchange rate policies: one aspired to universality and openness, the other pointed to particularization and separation. More generally, as Hinds and Steil have demonstrated, monetary nationalism, unleashed by the absence of a global standard, is inconsistent with a liberal order (see Hinds and Steil, 2009). They rightly call Rueff 'one of the twentieth century's greatest economists'.

We have traced the restless search for a more stable order back to the pioneering work by Fisher. Many of the greatest economists of the twentieth century made a contribution. The search continues. Keynes's bancor, the Triffin-Meade international central bank, Graham-Kaldor-Tinbergen-Hart on commodity standards, Hayek on competing currencies and Rueff on gold: versions of each of these grand visions of international order continue to be debated.

Some say that the idea of a lofty monetary standard was discredited by the experience of the 1930s. But that was not the lesson drawn by the architects of Bretton Woods. Despite their vivid recent experience, it was the dangers that were posed by what Keynes called 'footloose funds' roaming the world, and the lack of a standard, that impressed them. Everybody agrees that it was a disaster to return to gold in the 1920s at the wrong price. But controversy continues as to whether a rapid devaluation against gold could have avoided all the pain and tragic consequences that followed. In any case we are not discussing here a return to gold, but the need for a contemporary replacement, and the search to find an appropriate one. All the great monetary thinkers took an international approach to securing monetary stability – and it is, above all, that vision that we have lost.

Perhaps any of the ideas outlined in this chapter would be better than what we have: inward-looking, self-referential monetary policies causing frequent monetary shocks to the GFS, leading to destabilizing capital flows, payment imbalances, acrimonious disputes and reversal of globalization. Major monetary mismanagement always leads to political fragmentation. That is another lesson of the last 100 years.

Bibliography

Bernholz, Peter, *Monetary Regimes and Inflation: History, Economic* and *Political Relationships*, Edward Elgar Publishing Ltd , 2006, New edition.

Chivvis, Christopher S., *The Monetary Conservative: Jacques Rueff and 20th Century Free Market Thought*, Northern Illinois University Press, 2010.

Fellner, William, Machlup, Fritz and Triffin, Robert and Associates, *Maintaining and Restoring Balance in International Payments*, Princeton, 1966.

Fisher, Irving, 'A Compensated Dollar', *Quarterly Journal of Economics*, Vol. 27, No. 2, pp. 213–35, 1913.

Fisher, Irving, *The Money Illusion*, Adelphi Company, 1928.

Fisher, Irving, *The Purchasing Power of Money*, The Macmillan Company, 1931 [1911].

Fleming, J. Marcus, Guidelines for Balance of Payments Adjustment under the Par Value System, Princeton, 1968.

Friedman, Milton, 'Commodity-Reserve Currency', *Journal of Political Economy*, Vol. 59, pp. 203–232, 1951.

Graham, Benjamin, *Money as a Pure Commodity*, AER 37 No 2, 304–307 cited by Perry Mehrling in *The Monetary Economics of Benjamin Graham*, 2007, p. 29.

Grubel, Herbert, *World Monetary Reform: Plans and Issues*, Stanford University Press and Oxford University Press, 1963.

Harrod, Sir Roy, *Reforming the World's Money*, Macmillan, 1965.

Hart, A. G., N. Kaldor and J. Tinbergen *The Case for an International Commodity Reserve Currency*, Geneva, UNCTAD, 1964.

Hayek, Friederich von, 'Choice in Currency: A Way to Stop Inflation', Institute of Economic Affairs, London , February,1976; and 'Denationalisation of Money', Hobart Paper, IEA, October ,1976. Reprinted in *The Collected Works, Vol 6: Good Money Part II: The Standard* (ed. S Kresge), University of Chicago Press, 1999.

Hinds, Manuel and Ben Steil, *Money, Markets and Sovereignity*, New York and Yale: Council on Foreign Relations and Yale University Press, 2009.

Hirsch, Fred, *Money International*; with a preface and postscript by Richard N Cooper, Pelican books, London, 1969.

Roy W. Jastram, with updated material by Jill Leyland, *The Golden Constant: The English and American Experience 1560–2007*, Edward Elgar 2009.

Johnson, Harry, *Money, Trade and Economic Growth*, Allen and Unwin, 1964.

Johnson, Harry,'The Taxonomic Approach to Economic Policy', *Economic Journal* December, 1951.

Keynes, J. M., *A Tract on Monetary Reform*, Macmillan, 1923.

Keynes, J. M., *A Treatise on Money Vol II*, Macmillan, 1934.

Keynes, J. M. *Activities: 1940–1944 Shaping the Post-War World: The Clearing Union*, Cambridge, Cambridge University Press, 1980.

Machlup, Fritz, *Plans for Reform of the International Monetary System*, Princeton, 1964.

McKinnon, Ronald I. and Oates, Wallace E., *The Implications of International Economic Integration for Monetary, Fiscal and Exchange-Rate Policy*, Princeton, 1966.

Meade, James, 'The Future of International Payments', *Three Banks Review*, June 1961.

Mehrling, Perry, 'The Monetary Economics of Benjamin Graham', 2007, p. 29. Published in *Journal of the History of Economic Thought*, September 2011.

Mundell, Robert A., *The International Monetary System:Conflict and Reform* ,The Canadian Trade Committee, Private Planning Association of Canada, 1965.

Roosa, Robert V., *Monetary Reform for the World Economy*, Harper and Row, 1965.

Rueff, Jacques, *The Monetary Sin of the West*, 1972.

Rueff, Jacques and Hirsch, Fred, *The Role and the Rule of Gold: An Argument* Princeton, 1965.

Shiller, Robert J., 'Irving Fisher, Debt Deflation and Crises, 'Cowles Foundation Discussion Paper No. 18, 17August 2011.

Shiller, Robert J., Macro Markets: Creating Institutions for Managing Society's Largest Economic Risks, Oxford University Press, 1993.

Shiller, Robert J., *The New Financial Order*, Princeton,, 2003.

Stamp, Maxwell, The Stamp Plan – 1962 Version, *Moorgate and Wall Street*, Autumn 1962.

Stamp, Maxwell, *The Reform of the IMS*, Moorgate and Wall Street, Summer 1965.

Triffin, Robert, *Gold and the Dollar Crisis*, Yale, 1960.

Triffin, Robert, *The Evolution of the IMS*, Princeton, 1964.

Ussher, Leanne J, 'Combining International Monetary Reform with Commodity Buffer Stocks : Keynes, Graham and Kaldor', (Mimeo), 2012.

Williams, J. H., *Post-War Monetary Plans*, Blackwell, 1957.

Williamson, John H., *The Crawling Peg* Princeton, 1965.

Yeager, Leyland B., *International Monetary Relations* Harper and Row, 1966.

Official Publications

Group of Ten: Report of Deputies, July 1964 (Roosa Report) and July 1966 (Emminger Report) Study Group on the Creation of Reserve assets, May 1965 (Ossola Report).

HMSO, 'Proposal for an International Clearing Union', British Government White Paper, CMd 6437. 1943.

13
The Choice of the Standard

The great economists whose ideas were reviewed in the previous chapter all believed that a stable international money is a precondition of wider financial, economic and political stability. To help in the choice of a standard, we consult leading contemporary scholars.

The concept goes back, however, at least as far as Aristotle:

> What money does for us is to act as a guarantee of exchange in the future: that if it is not needed now, it will take place if the need arises; because the bearer of money must be able to obtain what he wants. Of course money is affected in the same way as other commodities, because its purchasing power varies; nevertheless, it tends to be more constant. That is why everything must have its money value fixed, because then there will always be exchange, and if exchange, association.
>
> So there must be some one standard, and that on an agreed basis, which is why money is so called, because this makes all products commensurable, since they can all be measured in terms of money.
>
> *(Nichomachean) Ethics*, Book V, 1133b10–b25

Following Aristotle, we also say that 'there must be some one standard', serving as a unit of account and standard of deferred payment, to act as the essential building block of the emerging GFS. We also follow Aristotle in his broad, humane, ethical idea of the concept. Significantly, Aristotle places these remarks on money in the context of a discussion of justice and proportional reciprocity as the basis of fair exchange. Thus although the term 'monetary standard' may be used to refer to whatever arrangements govern (or 'back') the supply of money, the term 'standard' as used here is intended to evoke also the associations it has in common language – as something worth emulating, a criterion by which performance is assessed, a measure that is expected to endure over time, an ideal. For Aristotle, it is something even more than that – it is a precondition of 'association', of society itself. That also is fundamental – money as the oil of commerce, and commerce as the mechanism by which societies are formed and laws develop. Money should bind people in voluntary associations, not separate them in warring tribes. When Paul Volcker said, 'a global economy needs a global currency' he was indeed echoing Aristotle.

So, leaping nimbly over the next 2,500 years, let us review a few of the ideas that were circulating in the early twenty-first century about the next stage of evolution of the system. Would any of them conjure up plausible worlds? We start with the easy routes – those involving least change in existing arrangements – and then look at the more challenging ones.

The mainstream view is that inflation targeting provides a sufficient standard, as expressed for example by Michael Bordo (2003). He pointed out that since the 1980s there has been renewed emphasis by central banks on low inflation as their primary (if not sole) objective. Although no formal monetary rule has been established, a number of countries have given central banks mandates for price stability:

> In some respects for the US and other major countries there appears to be a return to a rule like the convertibility principle and the fixed nominal anchor of a specie standard.

The argument here is that experience with this so-called rule has not been satisfactory and that the world hankers after a better standard. GFC has led to a loss of public trust, which will not easily be regained. As Mason pointed out as long ago as 1963, the concept of monetary *standards* has been replaced by an emphasis on monetary *policies* (Mason, p. 9). But money is not, and can never be, well adapted to serve the purposes that too many contemporary politicians demand of it. The monetary mechanism should not be burdened with responsibilities it cannot discharge (Mason, p. 114).

There is no prospect of rigid, everlasting stability, nor would it be desirable. The task is to remove the additional unnecessary instability, injustice and opportunities for exploitation introduced by the lack of monetary and banking standards that command respect.

Towards a multi-currency system

Some said that international money would evolve into a fairly stable, multi-polar structure. Therefore, to herald the main discussion of possible and plausible standards, a brief mention could be made of the large group of proposals about reforming the reserve currency system. These have been summed up in various publications (see Stiglitz, 2009, pp. 162–74, also IMF), so there is no need to discuss them in detail.

The notion that the world was moving towards a multiple currency reserve system was perhaps the leading model of 'the future' favoured by economists at the time. Indeed, this did not require any great powers of imagination as in many ways it already existed; in 2010 there were several reserve currencies besides the dollar and euro, as discussed in Chapter 9, notably sterling, the yen and the Swiss franc, with smaller amounts invested in Australian, New Zealand and Canadian dollars, and in Nordic currencies. It was easy to predict that the share of the dollar in reserves would continue to decline, with the share of the euro and that of some other currencies growing, and it was equally easy to predict these would also in time include currencies such as India's rupee and Brazil's real. It would be natural to expect these to be joined by the RMB, if it became fully convertible on current and capital account (see Eichengreen, 2011 pp. 151–52). But all three countries had a long way to go before they developed financial markets, built trust of foreign reserve holders and allowed free access to their markets.

This kind of discussion takes us away, however, from our (and Aristotle's!) central concern with a good monetary standard. Discussions of reforming the reserve currency system, or even proposals for a new global reserve currency, such as that involving regular issues of SDRs, seldom mentioned the qualities of a good international money or monetary standard or showed much interest in this way of looking at the problem.[1] This applies also to the analysis in the Stiglitz report (Stiglitz et al., 2010). Such economists take for granted a Chartalist, fiat money world – a *Weltanschaung* that would have seemed difficult to imagine to anybody before the twentieth century.

In any case the wider use of a growing number of currencies internationally, though largely benign in itself, would not necessarily make for a more stable GFS. Such an evolution would do nothing to reduce the 'excess elasticity' of the global banking and financial system that was one cause of GFC. It would allow more countries to run deficits, so as to meet the world's growing demand for reserves not satisfied by the US – thus potentially exposing more governments to the temptations and risks associated with being international reserve centres. It may even add to instability. If central bank reserve managers and private asset managers 'followed the herd' by changing the composition of their portfolios when exchange rates changed, that would increase volatility in exchange rates. Dislike of this could set up a demand for greater management of exchange rates. Indeed, this might be one route by which the latent demand for greater fixity and certainty in exchange rates eventually comes to be manifested.

Above all, the system would have no anchor other than the prudence of the central banks of the reserve centres. Indeed, it might undermine such prudence by offering them incentives for the wrong kind of coordination of policy – coordinated inflation. The example has been set by the euro and dollar in 2008–10: the central banks of both countries adopted highly stimulative monetary policies that, if each had done it individually, would have caused a collapse of its currency, but because both did it together, it was dismissed in the markets as a 'competition in ugliness' . Which is the worst currency? 'Oh, there's not much to choose between them', was the common refrain.

But one interesting point did come out of the discussion on reform of the reserve system and that was a political one to do with the incentives facing the US. As the UK's experience in the 1960s and early 1970s demonstrated, it is not comfortable to be a reserve centre in decline. Those massive overseas holdings of your currency, which (while they were being built up) had once enabled you to spend comfortably in excess of your means, suddenly come to be seen as a burden. Uncertainty about future demand for the reserve currency, and even more fears of fluctuations in foreigners' demand for it – fluctuations that may be totally unrelated to the performance of the domestic economy – cramp policy making. So the US might well be expected to become more interested in international monetary reform for that reason. And there can be no new GFS without the participation of the US.

Thus although a multi-currency regime would not offer the strong monetary framework that the emerging GFS needs (as discussed in Chapter 11), it could be a stage that the world economy passes through on its way to a better system. To consider the options, we turn to proposals for a more fundamental reform.

A refurbished credit standard

The first set of proposals focuses on establishing a standard based on credit or fiat money, without the need for an international agreement.

Fiat money may be defined as money that 'is not convertible by law into anything other than itself, and has no fixed value in terms of an objective standard' (see Keynes, 1930, p. 7).[2] Here we select two proposals – those we call, first, 'rehabilitating the dollar standard' (Ronald McKinnon) and, secondly, 'a global monetary standard' (Allan Meltzer) . These authors believe in giving fiat money a fresh polish.

Rehabilitating the dollar standard

This view, championed in particular by Ronald McKinnon of Stanford University, emphasizes that the world needs a reliable monetary standard. The best option in practice would be a rehabilitated dollar standard, though McKinnon recognizes that it is 'unloved' by Americans and foreigners. Foreigners still consider it an exorbitant financial privilege of the US, while Americans object to the fact that they cannot set their own exchange rate.

Nevertheless, the dollar standard is a remarkably robust institution that is 'too valuable to lose and too difficult to replace'. The dollar remains a good facilitator of international trade and investment but has become poor as a monetary anchor. Because there is no adequate successor in sight, the best solution would be for the Federal Reserve to take the lead in rehabilitating the dollar standard. This would require the Fed to adopt a more outward-looking monetary policy – one that took into account the effect of its policies on the rest of the world – a move that would also be in the interests also of the US.

Past Fed policy has caused recurrent bouts of dollar weakness – notably in the 1970s, in the late 1980s and again in the 2000s. In 2010–11 the Fed's ultra-loose monetary policy again destabilized the global economy. In all these cases Fed policy triggered huge capital flows out of dollars, a decline in the dollar and exchange rate appreciation in the rest of the world, yet the Fed ignored the warning signs of inflation taking off in countries on the dollar standard's periphery – now mainly in emerging markets such as China and Brazil. When the crash came in each cycle the US economy itself was badly affected.

The US should understand and follow the 'rules of the game' needed to maintain the global dollar standard. The rules are, first, that the US must maintain full convertibility on both current and capital account and secondly, that the US does not attempt to devalue. It cannot, and should not try to have, an exchange rate policy. In a world characterized by a wide variety of exchange rate arrangements, its role is to provide the fulcrum of the system – the benchmark against which other countries and regions orient their policy. The third rule of the game therefore is that the US keeps the dollar sound and stable without domestic inflation – i.e. it recognizes the need to keep the standard respected. This system has worked in the past and can work again, so long as these rules are understood.

So the US should allow other countries to run surpluses, if they wished to, be tolerant of international imbalances and let the pile up of reserves continue. Because of its uniquely easy access to foreign borrowing, however, the US itself must guard against allowing its domestic saving to fall so as to create a perpetual deficit and associated de-industrialization. This danger is best dealt with indirectly by fiscal measures to increase government saving and financial incentives for higher private savings (see McKinnon, 2010).

In many ways the best solution would be for the US to refresh the world dollar standard by adopting an ultra-strict monetary policy, with the Fed either abolished or instructed to follow a money supply rule such as a monetary base target. If the dollar did stabilize due to a change in policy then, again, the option for other countries of fixing to the dollar – or setting up a dollar-based currency board – would become very attractive. If Keynes were alive, he would surely be critical of the US policies at the centre of the world dollar standard that failed to take international repercussions into account. Under Bretton Woods, exchange rates were nominally fixed but in principle adjustable. It hardened into a fixed rate system because countries wanted the link to the dollar to stabilize their own price levels and financial systems. (Britain was an exception in wanting too much macro economic independence which resulted in recurrent balance of payments crises.) It was a good system while it lasted and it can be revived, given the right policies by the US.

A global monetary standard

Allan Meltzer, a leading monetarist and historian of the Federal Reserve, shares the view that the dollar standard has been undermined by the poor record of the Federal Reserve in maintaining the value of money. Meltzer's exhaustive historical analysis shows it has repeatedly chosen to make low unemployment its main policy objective – a defensible position but not an objective that can maintain the dollar standard. The main problem is that the Federal Reserve has authority but no responsibility and no means of being held accountable. As a result it has made many mistakes:

> The Great Depression, the Great Inflation, numerous recessions, the recent financial crisis, and the huge monetary expansion that

spreads inflation around the world are examples of its many failures. (Meltzer, 2011)

Meltzer's proposal aims to internationalize the dollar standard. The monetary authorities of the leading countries or currency areas would follow common monetary policy objectives. For example, the Congress could mandate the Federal Reserve to steer its monetary policy so as to achieve an annual rate of price increase of 0–2 per cent. The ECB and Bank of Japan could then voluntarily adopt similar monetary rules. In each case the central banks would be mandated to support the government's objectives to keep unemployment as low as possible, consistent with maintenance of the inflation objective. Nominal exchange rates would continue to float so as to allow real exchange rates to adjust to changes in tastes and productivity, but the common inflation objective would provide a global standard. Common inflation objectives for major countries would reduce the risk of speculative attacks on currencies.

Other countries could choose voluntarily to peg to one of the major currencies or to a basket of the three. They would regain an opportunity to have fixed exchange rates and import price stability that has been lost since the Bretton Woods System of the 1950s and early 1960s. In turn, the US, the ECB and Japan would gain fixed exchange rates with those countries that chose to adopt them. No meetings or international agreements would be needed to bring this standard about. It would be entirely voluntary but enforced by actions in markets if they saw reason to doubt the commitment to price stability followed by any of the major countries or the fixed exchange rate rule followed by those who adopted that policy (see Meltzer, 2011).

A reformed international credit standard

The second set of proposals again provide for a standard based on credit or fiat money, i.e. money that derives its value by decree of the State, but are distinguished from the first group in that their proposals would require an international agreement or treaties. These include proposals for 'a world monetary union', and 'Bretton Woods II' arrangement without a peg to gold. There are numerous variants on these proposals but the following are chosen to show the main features of this class of reforms (see also, for example, Stiglitz et al. 2010).

A world monetary union (WMU)

Harvard economist Richard Cooper first proposed a currency union formed by the advanced countries issuing important international currencies back in 1984, and revised it in 2008. Members – notably the US, those comprising the euro area, Japan and the UK – should be mature democracies. Countries would replace their national currencies with a common currency issued by the central bank of the union. Other countries would be able on their own initiative to link their currencies to the currency of the WMU. The WMU's central bank might, but need not, have common banknotes. The central bank of each member could continue to issue its own banknotes as at present, but exchange rates among all members of the union would be rigidly fixed. The union would have a single monetary policy managed by a monetary policy committee, operating under a mandate to maintain the stability of the currency. This definition would embrace both financial and price stability. The central bank would aim to stabilize the value of its currency against international wholesale or producer prices, so that rates of change of consumer prices might differ, allowing changes in real exchange rates to take place between the different geographical areas of the union. The international central bank would also be responsible for the oversight and supervision of the financial system (see Cooper, 2008).

Bretton Woods II ex gold

Could the system of par values, where countries declare par values for their exchange rates (with a margin on either side of par) to an anchor currency, such as that which operated from 1945 to 1971, be resurrected? Under the first Bretton Woods system (BWI) the key currency was the US dollar; for all countries in the system other than the US, the primary objective of monetary policy was to maintain the fixed exchange rate with the dollar. For the US monetary authorities, the formal objective was equally clear – to maintain convertibility of dollars to gold at a fixed price for official bodies. In future, either the dollar or the euro could serve as the anchor currency. One option would be to establish such a system of par values without convertibility of the key currency or currencies into gold.

As under Bretton Woods I, the mutual obligations of members of the IMF would be enshrined in international treaties and clothed in a wide range of other rules, conventions and 'codes of good conduct' that provided a well-understood framework for trade and investment.

The essential framework could be inherited from BWI, which would be itself an advantage, though it would need to be adapted for the changed conditions of the twenty-first century. The IMF would resume its former role as the policeman of the exchange rate system and this would give it a position from which to assess the adequacy or otherwise of the economic and monetary policies followed by individual countries. To bring it into the modern world, the governance of the IMF would have to be reformed, so that no country could exercise an effective veto on its decisions.

The main challenge would be to make the system robust against the huge volume of capital flows that could be mobilized to attack par values perceived in the markets to be either under- or over-valued. This might be done by extending the scale of mutual support operations – yet such a course would face difficulties of its own. The familiar Keynesian question of how to ensure sufficient discipline on surplus as well as deficit countries would return – in particular to ensure China and the US would comply with policy recommendations of the IMF. Yet proponents believed China might well agree to such a deal if it promised to bring about a stable international monetary and financial environment. The key for China would be whether the system allowed for a real international influence on US monetary policies.

Composite currency standards

Robert Mundell, who called flexible exchange rates 'an unnecessary evil in a world where each country has achieved price stability' (Mundell, 1999), has made a number of proposals over the years aimed at re-establishing a proper international monetary system.[3] In his 1999 Nobel Prize Memorial Lecture he speculated that although it may be some time off, some kind of monetary union between the dollar, euro and yen areas was conceivable. Then, 'it would not be such a far step toward a reformed international monetary system with a world money of the kind originally proposed back in the days of Bretton Woods.' He developed this idea further in the following years. In 2003, he proposed six steps to bring such an agreement between the big currencies into effect – which he dubbed the DEY, or Dollar, Euro and Yen standard:

1. decide on a common price index;
2. set a target inflation rate;
3. set an upper and lower limit on the exchange rate;

4. establish a joint monetary policy committee to decide on monetary policy;
5. reach agreement on the sharing of seigniorage; and
6. gradually close exchange margins.

A weighted average of the DEY in turn could be used as the anchor for a common global currency, which he called the INTOR; countries and areas would keep their own currencies which would circulate along with INTORS (Mundell 2003).

Fast forward to 2011. In the wake of GFC, Mundell again argued that the two largest currency areas should combine to restore the 'mainstream' of the world economy, recommending fixing the euro-dollar exchange rate at first within wide limits, e.g., €1 = $1.20 and €1 = $1.60. The ECB would defend the dollar at $1.60; the Fed would defend the euro at $1.20. Intervention agreed between the ECB and Fed could also take place within the limits to prevent sudden and unwanted swings. Stabilization of the euro-dollar would benefit third countries that wished to fix to a strong and stable anchor. It would eliminate shocks like the sudden 30 per cent appreciation of the dollar against the euro in the third quarter of 2008 that in Mundell's view nearly destroyed the US financial system.

If successful, the 'Euro-dollar currency area' could be made the core of the SDR. An SDR comprising currencies that were fixed to one another (instead of floating) would be more in the spirit of the SDR when it was first agreed upon in 1967. All the small countries would have a stable anchor to join the system. Countries such as China and the Gulf states that like to fix to the dollar would be in good company; they would not have to adjust to swings in the dollar-euro exchange rate. Both Europe and the US would gain from the stability of the dollar-euro exchange rates. Monetary policy in the US would be more self-correcting. In Mundell's view, had such a system been in place in 2008 the great financial crisis would probably not have occurred. The stabilization of the dollar-euro rate would help China avoid the problems that arise from the instability of the yuan exchange rate with other currency areas, and particularly the euro area. Indeed, China could be made a part of the stabilization if it moved toward a convertible currency and cooperated to reduce its surpluses. If the yuan were made convertible a new and larger monetary area could be created. This would require a collective monetary policy based on monetary stability of a revised DEY area, with the Chinese yuan replacing the Japanese yen. The DEY could then become the central pivot for a restored international monetary system.

Mundell has played from time to time with the idea of linking the DEY (or DEYY, when the yuan will be included) to gold in some way. Thus in June 2011 he suggested that central banks could use gold as an asset to trade among themselves, possibly at a fixed price. However, it would not be possible to start with gold or a gold-convertible currency – a new Bretton Woods – because no country has the position that the US had in 1944. Moreover, the history of Bretton Woods showed that even with the strong US position, gold started to run short, creating the problem of the 1960s. Moreover, there would be the same problem of a lack of a mechanism to keep the dollar price in line with the fixed gold price.

The priority, in Mundell's view, was to persuade the US and Europe to stabilize exchange rates and form a currency area (not necessarily a complete monetary union) that could be the anchor for the world economy. The dollar-euro fix made a lot of sense in view of the common principles of both sides of the Atlantic and the fact that they are part of a successful military alliance. After that stage had been achieved, then, he suggested, a substantial fraction of the world's monetary gold stock could be put into a new supranational institution in exchange for, say, INTORS that would have a value related to the DEY or DEYY. The DEYY would play the role of a new SDR in which the currencies in it are interchangeable, as it was when SDRs were first conceived in 1967. Gold would be held along with currencies as the basic assets of the new World Central Bank (see Mundell, January, March, May and November 2011).

Commodity standards

A real basket

Warren Coats, a former chief of the SDR division in the IMF's finance department, proposed making the SDR into a real currency that would maintain its purchasing power. It would be a development of the SDR, which has considerable 'bureaucratic' attractions as the IMF already has a mandate to develop the SDR (remember that the international community has officially pledged to work towards making the SDR the principal reserve asset). The Real SDR would be tied to the real economy, as its value would be linked to a global basket of goods. The IMF would *define* the currency unit as being equal to so many units of purchasing power as represented by an index of goods and services commonly used throughout the world. The basket of currencies currently used to value the SDR each day would be replaced by a bundle of commodities, ideally 'a globally representative basket of goods' of a typical family, with each good in the basket having an SDR market price.

An international agency such as the BIS or IMF would issue the currency in exchange for financial assets. The supply of the new money would be self-regulating, as the agency would passively respond to demand for the new currency without any attempt to control its supply. This would be entirely determined by demand; in other words the issuer would behave exactly as a currency board does at present. A currency board defines its currency in terms of so many units of the anchor or mother currency and then issues as much of it as customers want at the fixed price, holding assets in the mother country's currency to the equivalent of the currency it issued, so as to assure holders of its ability to convert the currency at any time in any amount if needed.

Although the IMF/BIS would stand ready to issue real SDRs on demand, there would be no compulsory conversion of existing national currencies to the real SDR. Countries could continue with their independent central banks and monetary policies if they wished; or they could simply peg their exchange rates to it. The idea is that countries would voluntarily choose to peg their currencies to the new real SDR because of the advantages it would have – and those benefits would be demonstrated in the market place. Countries anchoring their currencies to it would be assured of stability of their price level with that of the purchasing power of a global indicator of constant purchasing power. In the past this was provided by gold, but the Real SDR would theoretically be superior to gold as an anchor as it would not suffer swings in gold's relative value against other commodities.

Companies or anyone else could obtain or sell ('redeem') Real SDRs in the same way as they now obtain, or deposit, local currencies – through their banks. Banks would have Real SDR accounts with their central banks which would in turn have accounts with the global issuer (BIS or IMF or a new special agency).

This proposal was designed to address specific weaknesses in the existing system of national currencies and independent monetary policies:

- the lack of pressure on deficit countries to adjust;
- the impediment to the free flow of goods and capital and goods erected by volatility of exchange rates;
- the erosion of the dollar's status as a reserve currency, and especially of its traditional feature as a store of value;
- the Triffin dilemma of over-reliance of the system on the dollar;

- absence of more attractive alternative assets, leading to build up of excessive foreign exchange reserves.

Existing, so-called allocated SDRs, which are subject to certain restrictions that tend to hold back their use even among central banks, would in time be abolished so that there would be in effect no distinction between the two kinds of SDRs (see Coats, 2011).

How gold survived the official onslaught

Gold lost ground as official money throughout the twentieth century, the age of State money. When the century opened the gold standard was in full swing; when the century closed, gold had supposedly been banished from all its official monetary functions except as a residual reserve. From being 50–60 per cent of official reserves in the 1960s, by 2000 gold had shrivelled to 14 per cent, and official holdings had fallen by about 5,000 tonnes from the peak to about 33,000 tonnes. A low point for gold was reached in the 1990s, when its demise even as a serious store of value seemed imminent, as it earned no interest, its price had been declining for years and most central bankers regarded it as obsolete (see Pringle, 1993, for a contemporary account). In 1996–99 Gordon Brown, then Britain's Chancellor of the Exchequer, acting on Treasury advice, sold 400 tonnes or one-half of UK's remaining reserves at an average price of about $300 (or about £200) an ounce. This was later seen as a major error, as the gold price (in dollars and pounds) soared fivefold in the next 10 years, but Brown and his Treasury advisers thought it would make him look modern, bold and forward looking at the time.

Under the Bretton Woods system from 1945–71 currencies had par values against the US dollar *and* a defined weight of gold (in the case of sterling, for example, in 1968 it was £1 = 2.13281 grammes, which, at 31.10 grammes an ounce, made an ounce worth £14.11s). But the 'peg' to gold was indirect, as only the US stood ready to convert dollars presented to it into gold – and then only for official holders 'for legitimate monetary purposes'. However, as confidence in the ability of the US to control inflation and thus in the long run to keep to its commitment to convert dollars at $35 an ounce declined, so more countries presented dollars to it for conversion. Private speculators bought gold whenever the dollar was weak and eventually the central banks had to step in to regulate the market through the so-called London gold-pool; they agreed to sell gold when the price rose to $35.20 and buy it back when it sank to $35.08. But after de Gaulle threw down the gauntlet to the US with his call for a return to a full gold standard in 1966, and monetary expansion continued in the US, the days of the old fixed gold price were numbered. Eventually it was a British demand that broke the camel's back and Nixon shocked the world by suspending gold convertibility of the dollar on 16 August 1971.[4]

This move was taken despite protests from the Federal Reserve. The US could have decided to obey the rules of the system (that it had played the leading part in establishing) and tighten monetary policy so as to bring its payments deficit and inflation down and restore confidence in the dollar. Alternatively, it could also have negotiated a rise in the price of gold (devaluation of the dollar against gold). The Europeans had indeed been led to expect that this would happen. Even after the suspension of convertibility, it was widely expected that the fixed rate system would be resumed after a short negotiating interval – with a revaluation of the DM and other surplus countries against the dollar and gold. But as already described (see Chapter 4), differences of view between the Europeans and Americans and the rise of the oil price at the end of 1973 meant the prolonged discussions on this came to nothing. The official international community led by the US then embarked on a campaign to drive all vestiges of gold out of the official system – a task that they thought had been accomplished with the second amendment to the articles of the Fund in 1978.

Governments aimed not only to reduce the role of gold in the international monetary system but also to make the SDR the principal reserve asset. These aims were enshrined in the new articles, which expressly forbade members to maintain the value of their currencies in terms of gold. The IMF was prohibited from choosing gold as the common denominator of a new exchange rate system. The definition of the SDR in terms of gold was abolished, along with any notion of an official price for gold and all obligations on members to make payments to the IMF in gold. The SDR replaced gold as the IMF's unit of account. The Fund also sold part of its gold holdings. Governments came out against gold all guns blazing. The charge was led by the US, which however was careful to keep all its gold.

Gold survived. It was kept in the background, but still used as an official store of value. Whatever the IMF's articles might say, central bankers such as Alan Greenspan admitted that in an emergency, gold would always be acceptable and could be mobilized. An example of such mobilization was provided by its use to facilitate emergency provision of liquidity under swap lines during GFC. Despite the official sector's determined attack on gold, it was not driven out. But governments did succeed in one key respect; to make citizens use their paper monetary units to value goods and services. Almost nobody thought in terms of gold values, only money values. That made it much easier for governments to pick people's pockets.

Gold's revenge

Central bankers had never really given up on gold. By 2011, they had stopped selling and several were buying gold again – the first time since the 1960s that this was being done on a sustained basis. The price reached $1,600, six times its low of $252 an ounce reached after the UK sales in 1999. In real, inflation-adjusted, terms, the gold price had not reached the peak of $800 ($2,300 in inflation-adjusted terms) touched in 1980 but some observers expected it to regain the peak in the light of the extreme monetary injections by the US Fed. And remember that real peak was touched on one day, not on a sustained basis, and was accompanied by global fears of runaway inflation and a collapse of the monetary system. To judge by the gold price, the fears of such a breakdown in 2011 were as bad as they had ever been since 1980.

The foundations for this remarkable rally were laid at the end of 1999 when European central banks announced an agreement to limit annual sales of gold for the next five years, an agreement twice renewed (though varying in the details). This in effect put a floor under the price. There was only one way for gold to go and that was up. At the same time the long period of price disinflation that had started with Paul Volcker's crusade the save the dollar from 1979, when inflation in the US reached 15 per cent (and touched 25 per cent in the UK), had come to an end. During that time inflation had been brought down to 2 per cent and within the next few years had been replaced by fears of deflation. Causes of the remarkable rise in the gold price included the central banks' regime of ultra low interest rates and loose monetary policies, financial market innovations that brought gold buying within the reach of a much larger range of investors, the massive increases in income in emerging markets, notably China, India, Russia and Brazil, which had long had pro-gold cultures and where consumers now could afford to buy much greater quantities for private use, notably jewellery, and towards the end of the period growing fears about the stability of the global economy.

But none of this qualifies gold to resume its role as the monetary standard. In fact, quite the contrary; large price fluctuations are the last thing you want in a standard. What then might qualify gold to be a candidate? There are four main considerations.

First, the evidence is that over the centuries gold has had a remarkable record of maintaining its purchasing power value in the long term; i.e. whatever has happened to the nominal price of gold, its real price shows remarkable constancy. This is brought out in a work of impeccable scholarship, *The Golden Constant* (Jastram, 2004). The wide swings in the price (both nominal and real) during the past 70 years were brought about mainly by official policies: the undervaluation of gold in the 1960s, the inflationary policies of the 1970s, the disinflationary policies of the 1980s and 1990s, and the ultra loose monetary polices during several years in 2003–11. These were exacerbated in the 1990s especially by destabilizing sales of gold by central banks and governments. The evidence suggests that, in the absence of such destabilizing official policies (monetary policies as well as direct intervention in the gold market), the real price of gold tends to be remarkably stable in the long run, while showing considerable fluctuations over periods of up to 30 years.

Second, gold is nobody's liability. Using the currency of any nation as the fulcrum of the international monetary system means relying on the faith and credit of that nation, the integrity of its debt markets, the prudence of its policies – in other words, its willingness and capacity to keep its currency sound. Yet not only is it foolish to rely on such a promise; it introduces a basic inequity at the heart of the system – one country will seem to have an 'exorbitant privilege' of supplying the world's international money, and that country will have a preponderant influence on the global economy.

Third, gold is familiar; it is trusted and admired throughout the world. Every adult knows what gold is. It has been used for thousands of years in nearly all cultures and civilizations and has formed the basis (along with silver) of monetary systems equally for hundreds of years. Nothing else comes close. For money, trust is of the essence.

Fourth, the gold price is forward looking. Because there is such a large amount of gold outstanding and it is widely held by investors, by women in the form of jewellery and by central banks – each group driven by different motives yet all attuned to the gold price – it does not depend on the annual flow of newly mined gold to equilibrate supply and demand. This occurs naturally through the price mechanism; and any factor that might influence the price in the future is immediately reflected in the spot price. Thus it binds the past, present and future together in a chain linking generations that nothing else can do. When

Keynes, in a distant echo of Aristotle, remarked in 1936 that money is 'above all, a subtle device for linking the present to the future', he was reflecting the assumptions and habits of mind built up over generations that money would remain relatively stable in terms of purchasing power. Yet that assumption was only valid so long as it remained based on precious metals; such an assumption has been shown to be without foundation when, partly under the influence of Keynes's own writings, money came to be controlled by governments (Keynes, 1936, p. 294). It was gold – and credit banking on a gold base – that was the basis for the first great age of global economic and financial integration in the 30 years before the First World War. Could it be the basis of the second?

How a new gold standard could work

Its main disadvantages as an anchor are that, as mentioned, the price of gold – relative to other goods – has historically experienced quite large fluctuations over periods of up to 30 years. If the general price level is linked to gold, the economies on the gold standard would suffer periods of prolonged deflation as well as inflation – though the latter would probably be moderate compared to the experience with paper money.

This can take a weak form or a strong form. In the weak form central banks would peg their currencies to the gold price, as expressed in domestic currency. Thus the UK government could declare that as from 1 January 2015 the Bank of England will keep the value of one ounce of gold at, say, £1,000, within a margin of say 5 per cent, with penalties for exceeding the margins (reducing the central bank governors' remuneration, for example, as was required by some countries under the former inflation targeting regime). If the ECB were to move towards this, for example, setting a target in terms of a euro gold price, there would in my judgement be an immediate gain in the credibility of the euro's long-term stability compared with that of the US dollar, which might persuade the US to follow, especially if it brought much lower funding costs for the governments concerned. But there would be no automatic link to domestic money supplies, i.e. no convertibility obligation. As Michael Bordo argued several years ago, gold can serve as an indirect commitment mechanism – 'a way of keeping policymakers honest':

> To the extent that the price of gold, determined in free, world auction markets, is a good harbinger of inflationary trends, gearing policy on the basis of its movements may succeed in achieving low inflation. (Bordo, 1995, p. 27)

In the strong form, as advocated for example by economists such as Kevin Dowd and Lawrence White, a certain mass of gold not only defines the monetary unit but also serves as the ultimate medium of redemption. Issuers of paper currency and checkable deposits make their notes redeemable for gold. The volume of bank notes and deposits is geared to the volume of gold. The quantity of money is thus determined by the forces of supply and demand in the gold market. Payments and surpluses that are not financed through capital flows therefore have to be settled in gold (White, 2008 and Dowd, 2011).

This proposal is designed to secure greater long-term stability of money than is attained under fiat money systems. So there would be a larger market for long-term bonds, for example. Market forces would in the long run automatically tailor the money supply to the economy's demand for money.

Gold bonds and digital gold

The gold bond route

A challenging alternative route to the gold summit is being pioneered by Judy Shelton, economist, author and regular contributor to the *Wall Street Journal's* op-ed pages. Observers are watching her climb from the safety of their look-out points, and every now and then she vanishes in a mist, only to reappear closer to the summit.

The basic idea is that the US issue Treasury notes payable in gold or dollars at the option of investors. The goal is to provide an accessible, gold-linked financial instrument based on straightforward calculations. For example, imagine you have the opportunity today to purchase a debt obligation from the Treasury with a principal amount of $2,400 and a five-year maturity date; at the end of five years, you will have the option to receive either $2,400 or one troy ounce of gold. How much would you be willing to pay for that instrument? In Shelton's words,

> Investors who think the dollar price of gold will likely be higher than the stated principal amount five years from now – because they suspect too many dollars will be printed in the meantime – will pay a premium for Treasury Trust Bonds redeemable in gold. Effectively, they would be purchasing a U.S. government obligation priced like a conventional Treasury bill, for which the rate of interest is inherent in the difference between purchase price and the face amount received at maturity. But they would also be purchasing a call option on gold, so if the dollar price for a troy ounce of gold in five years' time is

higher than $2,400, they can choose instead to exercise the option of receiving payment in the form of physical gold (one troy ounce). (See Shelton, 2011.)

This would be a variation of Treasury Inflation-Protected Securities (TIPS), which the US government has made available to investors since January 1997. A benefit of such a proposal, as Shelton views it, is that the gold price captures not just price inflation but chronic inflation at seemingly benign rates which in the end distort price signals – and can bring about the sort of financial 'panic' that proves most debilitating to whole economies. Auction bidding for annual issuances of gold-backed Treasury Trust Bonds would reveal the level of public confidence in the US Treasury's fiat dollar obligations versus gold, with yield spreads clearly reflecting aggregate expectations of their comparative medium-term values. If market expectations anticipated dollar inflation, i.e. a decline in the future purchasing power of the dollar relative to gold, the bonds would sell at a premium over their face value. By measuring the comparative yields on gold-backed US government obligations against conventional Treasury bonds of the same maturity, it would be possible to glean insights from aggregate investor expectations not limited to consumer prices alone. In short, an instrument that embodied a commitment to maintain the value of the dollar in terms of constant purchasing power relative to gold will function as a barometer on the credibility of the Fed's eventual exit strategy from its lengthy, large-scale quantitative easing operations.

Other countries with large holdings of gold reserves – Japan, Russia, India, Saudi Arabia – could prove their own commitment to monetary stability through the issuance of gold-backed bonds. The rate of convertibility would remain permanent throughout the life of the bond; it effectively defines the gold value of the currency which denominates the instrument. Shelton believes it is conceivable that 'a joint issuance of gold-linked financial contracts by Europe's leading nations – perhaps in response to a U.S. initiative guaranteeing the same – could provide the far-reaching jolt needed to rebuild confidence in a more stable global monetary order.'

As more countries and areas issued gold-backed bonds, governments everywhere could be compelled to follow, creating an international gold-linked network. Although this is not part of Shelton's published work, her proposals could form the basis either for a return to a form of gold standard – with fixed exchange rates – or at least to widespread international use of gold bonds as a check on the issuance of fiat money.

Digital gold

Whereas Shelton's route to the summit starts, in a way, half way up – using tried-and-tested mechanisms for issuing Treasury bonds, and cutting into the existing structure at 'wholesale' level, at the top end of financial hierarchy – there is an even more challenging route. This is for the really serious gold-climber and it starts at the bottom. But in a way that is its big attraction: people are already up and running. As emphasized throughout this study, any proposal for international monetary reform – at the level of the architecture of the system – should go with the grain of the market to stand a chance of success. Yes, political decision-making is often, maybe always, needed. The great turning points in the international monetary system for good or ill have been taken by politicians: Britain's return to gold in 1925, President Roosevelt's fixing of the dollar gold price in 1934, the Bretton Woods agreement, Nixon's closing of the gold window in 1971, the creation of the euro – all were political acts. Yet market realities intrude, unless they are forcibly – and foolishly – repressed as in the former Communist bloc.

This route is being explored by businesses that offer digital gold money services. Digital gold exists. Many firms allow users to exchange currencies for claims to grams of gold, on line. There are teething problems – how would a private credit system be created that did not repeat all the problems of the old system? It would have to allow the creation of credit on a narrow gold base – short of a ridiculously large increase in the gold price. How would that be policed? In particular, how would the liabilities of the US – potential claims on its gold stock – be dealt with? Unfortunately, also, private digital gold companies have been repeatedly subject to fraud, criminal activity, money laundering and other anti-social activities. All that would have to be cleaned up before the public could take digital gold seriously. Yet the history of ordinary commercial banking is also fraught with scandals. If governments continued to undermine public confidence in fiat money, the groundswell movement towards alternatives could become unstoppable. A leading contender is likely to be digital gold (an economist recommending this route, while fully aware it is more of an obstacle course, is Benn Steil; see Hinds and Steil, 2009 and Steil, 2010).

In sum, the proposals outlined in this chapter offer reasonable alternatives to the existing set-up, bringing hope that a stable international monetary order is within reach. It is often forgotten that Keynes himself argued passionately for an international money and believed in a standard. Indeed, all the great classical economists believed in a one-world, international monetary standard, as a precondition of wider economic and political stability..

Which brings us to the topic of the penultimate chapter: The Leap to a New Monetary Order.

Notes

1. There are exceptions. One economist to give serious thought to the features of a good international money is Hans Genberg, who believes there are four main attributes to a true reserve currency – no restrictions on cross-border transfers; use in trade; use in international denomination and invoicing; and a role in international borrowing and lending. But he emphasizes that stable and predictable micro and macro economic policies are important (see Genberg, 2010).
2. The sentence in *A Treatise on Money*, reads as follows: 'Fiat Money is Representative (or token) Money (i.e something the intrinsic value of the material substance of which is divorced from its monetary face value) – now generally made of paper except in the case of small denominations – which is created and issued by the State, but is not convertible by law into anything other than itself, and has no fixed value in terms of an objective standard.'
3. Mundell's first plan for a world currency was made as far back as 1968, when the issue was how to save the fixed exchange rate system (Mundell, 1968).
4. The Bank of England asked the Federal Reserve to cover a part of its dollar holdings by a swap drawing, signalling lack of confidence that the dollar parity could be maintained and was 'anxious to avoid losses on the dollar'; see Harold James, p. 218.

Bibliography

Aristotle, *(Nichomachean) Ethics*, translation by J. A. K. Thomson, with preface by A. C. Grayling, revised edition, Penguin Books, Penguin Classics, 1976.

Bordo, Michael D., *Gold as a Commitment Mechanism: Past, Present and Future*, World Gold Council Research Study Mo 11 1995.

Bordo, Michael D., 'Monetary Standards: An Essay written for the Oxford Encyclopedia of Economic History'. Oxford, 2003.

Coats, Warren, 'A Global Currency for a Global Economy: AReal SDR Currency Board', *Central Banking*, Vol. 22, No. 2, November 2011.

Cooper, Richard N., 'A Monetary System for the Future', *Foreign Affairs*, (Fall 1984), pp. 166–84.

Cooper, Richard, 'Proposal for a Common Currency among Rich Democracies', Working Paper 127, Oesterreichische Nationalbank, 2006.

Dowd, Kevin, 'The End of a Monetary Phenomenon', *Central Banking*, Vol 22, No 2, November 2011.

Eichengreen, Barry *Exorbitant Privilege: The Rise and Fall of the Dollar*, Oxford University Press, 2011.

Genberg, Hans, 'Currency Internationalisation: Analytical and Policy Issues', in Pringle, R and Carver, N (eds) *RBS Reserve Management Trends*, Central Banking Publications, 2010.

Grilli, Enzo and Robert Pringle, 'The Role of Gold in the International Monetary System', in Mundell, Robert, Paul J. Zap and Derek M Schaeffer (eds) *International Monetary Policy after the Euro*, Edward Elgar, 2005.

Hanke, Steve, 'The Dance of the Dollar', Globe Asia, December 20101, available on Cato Institute website www.cato.org

James, Harold, *International Monetary Cooperation since Bretton Woods*, Oxford University Press, 1996.

Jastram, Roy W., with updated material by Jill Leyland, *The Golden Constant*, John Wiley (1997) and Edward Elgar, 2009.

Keynes, J. M., *A Tract on Monetary Reform*, Macmillan, 1923.

Keynes, J. M., 'The Classification of Money', in *A Treatise on Money*. Macmillan & Co Ltd 1965, 1930.

Keynes, J. M., *The General Theory of Employment, Interest, and Money*. Macmillan & Co Ltd 1973, 1936.

Mason, Will E., *Clarification of the Monetary Standard*, The Pennsylvania State University Press, 1963.

McKinnon, Ronald 'Rehabilitating the Unloved Dollar Standard', Heinz W. Arndt Memorial Lecture, Canberra, 15 April 2010.

Meltzer, Allan, 'Towards a Global Monetary Policy', *Central Banking*, Vol. 22, No. 1, August 2011.

Mundell, Robert, 'A Plan for a World Currency', Joint Economic Committee Hearings. Washington 1968.

Mundell, Robert, 'A Reconsideration of the 20th century', Nobel Prize Memorial Lecture, 1999.

Mundell, Robert, 'The International Monetary System and the Case for a World Currency'. Distinguished Lecture Series, Warsaw, October 2003.

Mundell, Robert, 'Is Gold the Answer to Currency Wars and Unstable Exchange Rates?' Asia Society, Hong Kong, 19 January 2011.

Mundell, Robert, Speech on 'International Monetary Reform' China G-20 Seminar, Nanjing PRC, 31 March 2011.

Mundell, Robert, Speech on 'International Monetary Reform: The Next Steps', Astana Forum IV, 3 May 2011.

Mundell, Robert, 'Interview' with Robert Pringle, *Central Banking*, Vol. 22, No. 1, August 2011.

Pringle, Robert, *The Changing Monetary Role of Gold*, World Gold Council Research Study No. 2, June 1993.

Shelton, Judy, 'Getting to Gold: A Bold Proposal for Monetary Reform', *Central Banking*, Vol. 22, No. 2, November 2011.

Sheng, Andrew, 'Central Banking in an Era of QE', *Central Banking*, Vol. 22, No. 1, August 2011.

Steil, Benn and Manuel Hinds, *Money, Markets and Sovereignty*, A Council on Foreign Relations Book, Yale University Press, 2009.

Steil, Benn, 'Asset-Backed and Private Money', paper given to Witherspoon Institute conference on 'Human Flourishing, the Economy, and Monetary Reform'. November 2010.

Stiglitz, Joseph E. and Members of a UN Commission of Financial Experts, *The Stiglitz Report: Reforming the International Monetary and Financial Systems in the Wake of the Global Crisis*, The New Press, 2010.

United Nations, 2009, Report of the Commission of Experts of the President of the United Nations General Assembly on Reforms of the International Monetary and Financial System (also known as the Stiglitz Commission report). Available via the Internet at http://www.un.org/ga/econcrisissummit/docs/FinalReport_CoE.pdf

White, Lawrence H., 'Is the Gold Standard Still the Gold Standard among Monetary Systems?' *Cato Institute Briefing Papers* No 100 February 2008.

14
The Leap to a New Monetary Order

To enable it to serve society properly, money itself should be restored to its true place in a constitutional realm above the cut and thrust of day-to-day politics.

Beyond inflation targeting

'The market will not work effectively with monetary anarchy', states James Buchanan, the Nobel Prize winning economist and a founder of the public choice school; economists should know that such anarchy can 'only generate disorder'. This contrasts with the benefits of a constitutional order:

> Within a regime of stability in property rights, contracts, and money, persons will interact, one with another, to generate an order that will produce and distribute value, as determined by their own choices, which they remain at liberty to take. (Buchanan, 2010, p. 251)

At the global level, we now have a state of monetary anarchy and it is producing the disorder of which Buchanan speaks. He focuses on the need, as he sees it, to 'constitutionalize' the US dollar; if the US did that, then other countries would continue to use the dollar as the international unit of account (p. 258). But his principal argument – insisting on the need to place money in a constitutional realm categorically separate from what he calls the Hobbesian state of anarchy – holds good for any attempt to construct an international standard for money. Sovereignty is exercised at two stages or levels – that which defines and enforces the constraints of a constitution and that which operates within the limits so defined. Buchanan talks of the move from pre-constitutional to post-constitutional stages as a 'leap' from Hobbes's state of nature to a constitutional order. Once such a leap has been made, then, within any set of constitutional constraints, 'the possible range and scope for collective action remains open within broad limits'. We have to pay more attention to the constitutional framework of rules, rather than focus obsessively on day-to-day decisions taken within any given framework.

From such a perspective, modern monetary regimes are essentially mechanisms that attempt to hold central banks accountable for the maintenance of a standard enshrining society's long-term interest in sound money. In this they serve as replacements for the convertibility obligations of previous monetary regimes. But confidence in these mechanisms has been dented by the succession of crises in the 30 years leading up to GFC. When events, markets and political pressures tested their robustness, they developed fault lines. Many central banks started to prioritize objectives other than price stability, such as employment and growth (or in the case of the ECB, supporting the euro area government bond markets); in some instances, governments changed central banks' mandates, and/or gave them more discretion and powers to pursue objectives such as financial stability (itself notoriously difficult to define). There were other defects. The regimes differed from one country to another in their aims, definitions, public acceptance and credibility, so that they did not add up to a coherent international standard. Governments sometimes changed the targets set for the central bank, which undermined public confidence. Central banks themselves varied the time horizon over which they aimed to deliver their price stability mandates. It was clear that the level of inflation in any country was often not under the control of the individual central bank anyway. It proved difficult to make reliable estimates of the output gap (the gap between actual and potential output), an important step in taking decisions on interest rate policy, when business innovation was rapidly transforming the supply side of economies (through supply chain management and other techniques), making them much more flexible. The regimes also contributed to the build up of asset booms and other imbalances in the economy, as apparent success in reducing inflation expectations induced excessive risk-taking. There was no anchor for the world price level. They gave no guide to how to avoid credit booms or manage the subsequent busts.

Even their apparent success in their original mandate during the 'Great Moderation' (the apparent reduction in the amplitude of the business cycle from the early 1990s to GFC) was mainly attributable not

Maynard Keynes (1883–1946) in 1945

Friederich Hayek (1899–1992) in 1983

James Buchanan (b. 1919) in 1986

Robert Mundell (b. 1932) in 2004

to their efforts but to other factors, such as technological progress and globalization, notably the new flood of ultra-cheap goods from China. Meanwhile, the narrow focus of central banks on domestic price stabilization blinded them to broader issues, and meant they were unprepared to deal with a financial panic, especially when it involved cross-border banking problems. The response of trying to bolt on a framework of macro prudential regulation to the monetary regime was an *ad hoc* measure likely to create more fault lines. Central bankers had to juggle price stability, maximum sustainable employment (to use the language of the Fed's mandate), and an indefinable objective to pursue financial stability. As Stephen King, a mainstream economist, put it, 'One of the most important lessons from the crisis is that inflation targeting has not delivered the lasting economic stability we all crave.' (King, 2011)

Not only were there numerous possible conflicts between the objectives but the public would certainly be confused as to what they meant in practice. The decision by the US Federal Open Market Committee in January 2012 to publish the individual interest rate forecasts of its members – showing a wide divergence of views among members – threatened to plunge the whole exercise into farce. At the same time as formally adopting an inflation target of 2%, the Fed was apparently trying to send the message that it would not, necessarily, raise interest rates even if forecast inflation reached such levels, as its immediate concern was to nudge down long-term interest rates. What is clear is that, after 20 years of 'independence', all this had brought central bankers right back into politics. This particular experiment in placing money in a constitutional realm was falling into disrepute.

But if inflation targeting is indeed on the way out, that has profound implications for the whole monetary order. It is very difficult to think of any alternative monetary rule that could replace it within a fiat money system with floating exchange rates and independent central banks. Adding on macro-prudential regulation does nothing to solve the monetary problem itself. This crisis has thrown the whole future of fiat money, of banking and central banking as we have known them into question.

Criteria of a new order

The right solution to such problems of monetary control entails another effort to place money in a special constitutional realm – this time on an international rather than purely national basis. In a globalized economy, an international monetary order is required to maximize the practical freedom of individuals and businesses to conduct their affairs as they wish. It should be wide in scope both geographically and temporally. It should predispose users, and societies as a whole, to take the interests of future generations into account, i.e. a regime that naturally connected past, present and future through a stable standard of value. It should help inhabitants of Planet Earth to feel a shared sense of trusteeship for its resources along with the maximum practical scope for individuality. It would achieve this by the impersonal, decentralized forces of the market, not by state direction. It would recognize that the currency unit was an important public good. Such a system would rest on a framework of rules and norms, underpinned by penalties for infringement and rewards for good behaviour. As argued in preceding chapters, it should include not only a world currency standard but a world banking/financial stability standard. Only when these are in place will the market give the right signals to economic agents.

Let us start by looking at what might be the ideal features of a currency standard and then see how close the world could get to such an idea.

It should mimic the classical gold standard in enabling monetary, commercial and economic unification to take place without requiring political integration. It should rest on consent. The supranational element should be kept to a minimum; certainly it should be able to function without a world government or central bank. Countries should be free to remain fully sovereign if they wished, while also being able to share or pool sovereignty through various political institutions as they saw fit. Thus they should be able to opt out of the world currency standard, just as they could (and did) suspend the gold standard in emergencies, though the attractions and prestige of being a full member of the club would mean that few would wish to do so (few, if any, countries ever left the gold standard voluntarily, before its collapse in the 1930s). At the international as at the national levels, peoples would embrace order to increase practical liberty. It would be a rule of laws and norms rather than of men.

Above all, a new order should serve to re-connect money to the real world. The fracture of that link in the last third of the twentieth century, with the pyramiding of claims by financial institutions on each other, had devastating consequences, as explained in Chapter 10. With a jumble of national currencies and regimes, there was no foundation for long-term expectations about the price level. The standard should be so designed that all citizens naturally feel they have a stake in the global economy. The stake could be represented by the money they hold. Money would ideally be a claim on the world's productive capacity and resources, and its real value would increase with the growth of the world economy. People should be again comfortable holding cash, lending and investing it, and passing it on to their children and grandchildren. They should not have to fear that its real value would be eroded. If the world could move closer to such an ideal, it would not only be much more efficient economically, but beneficial socially and ethically. The end result would be that decision makers would naturally take a longer-term view; many social as well as economic problems have developed out of a tendency for the present financial system to encourage short-termism. Money itself would become the compass guiding decision making by policy makers, business people and individuals.

That is a visionary prospect and may be a long way off. It is certainly a long way from where we were in the second decade of the twenty-first century. But it reminds us of the vital social and public good aspects of money that can easily be lost sight of. As a vision of a possible future, it is worth exploring further.

The monetary unit of account

The unit of account function of money is, like language, a natural monopoly – the more people that use it, the better. This is usually set by the government, just as the government sets the definition of a metre, or yard or which side of the road to drive on. The production and issue of money, by contrast, can be performed in a variety of ways, such as by a currency board, a central bank without a discretionary monetary policy (a model would be the Hong Kong Monetary Authority (HKMA)) or an international organization. Alternatively, it could be left to market competition among private banks. This separation between the definition of the currency unit and the creation of credit was one of the underlying reasons for the success of the gold standard. It also meant that each country could have its national monies – marks, pounds, dollars and so on – while each of the national monies was defined in terms of different quantities of the same thing – gold. The value of gold was independent of the policies of any of these countries, so could not be manipulated by any government. The same should apply to any new international currency unit.

One problem with money is how to define it in such a way that people can know today what an expression such as '$1,000' will mean in 20 or 100 years' time. At present people are unable to say for any currency what it will mean – what it might sell for or buy, or whether it will even exist in 100 years time. Yet it is important both for private and for business life to be able to make plans for the longer-term future – with all its unavoidable risks – without having to worry about the further risk of fluctuations in the measuring rod. It is as if one sets out on a journey of 100 miles long without knowing whether the definition of 'a mile' will be changed as you are driving. So you could end up driving for much longer than you thought – perhaps for ever. The return or profit/loss expected of capital investments with longer-term pay back periods cannot be appraised if the value of the monetary unit in which the investment is made fluctuates unreliably in terms of what it can buy (purchasing power).

The total risk exposure of a group of creditors and debtors depends on the way you measure it – the standard of payment. Some standards create risk between creditors and debtors; others merely distribute a given risk. If the standard by which a loan is expressed itself varies in real terms, then the average risk of both creditors and debtors is greater than if it did not. Similarly with an investment undertaken by a group of shareholders, there is the ordinary business risk that the investment itself may not be profitable, but, if the monetary unit in which the investment is made itself fluctuates in value, there is an additional risk for all parties.

Sound money should not create such additional distributional risk. What criteria should one use to select such a form of money? The best would be that which would be chosen voluntarily by the partners to a contract behind a 'veil of ignorance' where neither knows in advance whether they would be creditors or debtors. Let us assume the debtors borrow in order to invest in real assets. Lenders own financial assets – claims on the debtors. If the value of the financial asset changes during the term of the contract in an unpredictable way, an additional risk is created. As a unit of account, the best money in this case would be one that kept its relative value constant in terms of real assets. That can be represented by the market value of financial claims traded on the market. If the value of the market portfolio were the basis for the monetary standard, then this distribution risk would be zero.

Introducing the *Ikon*[1]

The currency unit could be defined as a fraction of the total of tradable equity claims on real assets in the global economy.[2] It would be, in effect, a globally diversified equity basket, which would in principle include ownership claims on the world's total productive invested assets. This approach centres on the key function of money as a unit of account or calculation rather than the usual focus on money as a means of payment.

As a unit of account over time, the best currency is one that is predictable in value. That would be preferred both by borrowers and investors – whereas with the wide fluctuations in the real value of money, a long-term investment or debt fixed in nominal money is a gamble as much on the future value of the money used as on the objective chances of the project. Further, as a store of value, the most attractive money would be that with the highest return on cash. The smaller the difference between the real return on holding cash and the average real return on other investments or assets, the more attractive cash becomes (that is, notes, coin and current account balances). This would be where the return on cash increases with the real growth of the economy, as reflected in the rise over the long term of the value of claims on the real economy's productive assets. The smaller is the difference between the return on cash and the average yield on risky assets, the more cash will be held.

If money were not only defined in such a way but also convertible on demand into bundles of shares, that would provide money with an anchor to the real economy that could easily be understood and monitored. It would give everybody who holds money an asset with the prospect of rising long-term value, a major incentive to hold money. Indeed, money holdings might under such a standard come close to the level that many distinguished economists have seen as the optimal – when its purchasing power rises with the real rate of interest.[3]

If the currency unit had a fixed value, in terms of the market portfolio, it could be issued by a currency board – just as the Hong Kong Monetary Authority, for example, issues Hong Kong dollars. The HKMA stands ready at all times to buy or sell HK dollars against US dollars at a fixed price (within a narrow margin). The market regulates demand. The same would apply at the global level in the case of the investment currency unit, which we propose to call the Ikon. The market would regulate the supply of such a money, and the issuing agents – say, the IMF or BIS – would stand ready passively to buy and sell (redeem) shares on demand. There would be no need for a world central bank issuing its own money, with all the political complications that would bring – who would control and manage it?

In our utopia, central banks that belonged to the Ikon standard would hold Ikon accounts with the world currency board, which would buy or sell Ikons for eligible assets (such as government debt securities) at the market value of one Ikon. This money would be the reserve base or base money of the world's banking system. One Ikon could be defined as, say, one trillionth of the outstanding value of all equity shares traded on all the world's recognized stock markets. As in the case of the proposed 'real

SDR' described in Chapter 13, arbitrage would ensure that the value of the unit in the market never deviated significantly from its stated official value. The value of national monetary units – dollars, pounds, euros, yen – would be fixed in terms of Ikons.

This account of the functioning of such a currency has already hinted at one benefit of linking money to productive assets. It could reduce the danger that has done so much damage to the world economy and banking systems in the first ten years of the twenty-first century – that of booms and busts caused by market interest rates either (in the first case) falling well below the natural interest rate or (in the second case) rising well above them. (The natural rate is the term Austrian School economists use to describe the equilibrium real rate of interest in the economy, the rate at which there is neither a tendency to start a credit boom nor a contraction.)

Taking the latter case, twice in a relatively short time, central bankers have been trying to combat the feared deflation of economic activity by keeping their policy interest rates at ultra low levels. They did this in 2002–04 and again in 2009–12, when ultra low rates were supplemented by unconventional policies of quantitative or credit easing. But what they really needed was negative real interest rates – very difficult to achieve (when inflation is at low levels) in monetary systems where the nominal market rate cannot go below zero (if it did, everybody would hoard cash – notes and coin) This inability to get economies moving by conventional interest rate policies is what Keynes called the liquidity trap or Austrian economists see as a disequilibrium between market interest rates and the natural rate. If investment opportunities have shrunk, and the natural rate of interest – the equilibrium rate – were to fall to zero, how can market rates be brought below it? Only if market rates are at or below rates that spur investment will they be able to stimulate the economy. As Brendan Brown puts it,

> In the case of zero inflation expectations, then the zero rate trap is operational if indeed market interest rates cannot fall to the equivalent (in nominal terms) of the natural rate – and this is the case if the latter is below zero. (Brown, 2008, p. 193)

Or as expressed in an on-line dictionary, *Economics.About.com*,

> When expected returns from investments in securities or real plant and equipment are low, investment falls, a recession begins, and cash holdings in banks rise. People and businesses then continue to hold

cash because they expect spending and investment to be low. This is a self-fulfilling trap.

But if money were defined to be constant in terms of a diversified portfolio of claims on real assets, money interest rates would move together with the natural rate, so the incentive to invest would be maintained at all times. The nominal rate of interest on risk-free assets would be zero; the real rate on risk-free assets would be positive, as prices declined; and the expected real return would vary according to the risk/return characteristics of the investment. That would also determine the margin between the real return on cash and on other assets. Thus money would move in a pro-cyclical way, which is desirable and stabilizing of goods prices and output. In the long run, if the rate of return on Ikons were constant while output grew, the quantity of money would remain constant and prices would fall, i.e. deflation would take place. But investment would not be hindered by the apparent disappearance of investment opportunities in a slump which is a major cause of depressions, so that deflation of nominal prices would lose its terror.

The only permanent way out of the money trap, and the only escape from the grip of global finance, is to leap into a new monetary order – make a new kind of money – the Ikon. Or, as Buchanan might put it, to leap from Hobbesian anarchy to a constitutional society. That is also, in essence, what market participants have been pleading for. GFC has signalled the end of our old ways of making money. Everybody knows that the advanced economies are in a trap. Economists call it the liquidity trap, after Keynes who first labeled it. Keynes raised the possibility that, after the rate of interest had fallen to a certain level, 'liquidity preference may become virtually absolute in the sense that almost everyone prefers cash to holding a debt which yields so low a rate of interest' (Keynes, 1936, p. 207). Then the central bank would lose control over the interest rate. (He added that while this limiting case might be important in future, he knew of no case of it.)

But now we have a more vicious trap – the money trap itself. It is, in an ironical twist, in part the result of the application of Keynesian-style policies – of the build up of debts, repeated monetary and fiscal injections, credit and quantitative easing. Anybody can see that these measures have recently smacked of desperation. Keynes himself would surely not have been content with them, but would have gone in quest of fresh solutions. For reasons Paul Krugman has explained, they are not being successful; and even if in the next year or two they appear to promise success, hopes will inevitably be dashed once again. Krugman's explanation is that, at a time of general fears of deflation, the central bank cannot reduce real interest sufficiently to spur investment and recovery, as it cannot reduce the market rate below zero: 'The point is that while you can think of things the Fed can do even at the zero lower bound, that lower bound is in practice a major constraint on policy' (Krugman, 2010). Krugman estimated that in 2010 countries accounting for 70% of world GDP were in such a trap – including the US, eurozone, Japan and the UK.

The trap is tightened further when the yield curve is flat out to long maturities. In the past, economies have climbed out of liquidity traps as there was always room for longer-term yields to fall, offering the hope of capital gains, even if short-term rates were very low. But central bank quantitative easing and expectations of low and even declining inflation have produced a situation when throughout much of the developed world not only are yields miniscule but the yield curve is flat. As Bill Gross of PIMCO has explained (in an article significantly entitled 'Zero-based money keeps trapping recovery'):

> What incentive does a US bank have to extend maturity to a two- or three-year term when Treasury rates at that level of the curve are below the 25 basis points available to them overnight from the Fed? What incentive does Pimco or banks have to buy five-year Treasuries at 75bp when the maximum upside capital gain is 2 per cent of par and the downside substantially more? Maturity extension for Treasuries, and then for corporate and private credit alike, becomes riskier. (Gross, 2012)

When interest is at zero across the yield curve, it 'rations credit just as fiercely as it does risk'.

The implications of both kinds of trap are that central banks cannot lower interest rates sufficiently and even printing money does not help. But that is true only in the current monetary system. The way to escape from this money trap is quite different from the way out of the old liquidity trap. This time, it is money that has to be changed – its very definition and content. It has to be endowed with material content, and tied to the real economy. The *Ikon* offers a permanent way out of the money trap. If the value of money is kept constant against a diversified basket of global equities, then investment opportunities can never disappear as long as innovation continues; the yield curve will resume its normal shape, the differing risk-return characteristics of investments can be compared without worrying that the monetary measuring rod will give false signals, and real investment can be made with confidence (though of course the credit default risk always remains). It will tear down the veil of money, which in a recession conceals the future in a mist of uncertainty.

The transition to an Ikon standard could take place in several ways. For example, first, the exchange rates between leading currencies would be managed within an increasingly narrow range, and then fixed. Then, the major powers through the IMF would agree on an anchor for this currency area. This could initially take the form of targeting a common price measure or basket of commodities, or even gold, which will always hold popular appeal. But these anchors would in time be replaced by an agreement, embodied in an international treaty, on the measurement or definition of the world currency unit. Instead of a weight of gold, or a basket of commodities or a price index, the unit would be defined as a fraction of all equity claims traded on recognized exchanges. This proposal uses the technology recently available through the globalization of the world's traded shares and equity exchanges as described in Chapter 11. This would use modern finance technology and the opportunities opened up by global financial market integration to fasten the currency unit to the real economy in a way no other proposal can do.

Other potential benefits of the *Ikon*

Only perhaps gold could compete with such a standard in terms of its attractions to the global public. If the units represented a share in the value of tradable assets, they would over time rise in real value. Prices would gradually fall in line with productivity growth. Nominal wages would on average be stable, and real incomes rise. Nominal interest rates on risk free assets would be zero but positive in real terms. Such a standard could have the potential securely to preserve money's role as a unit of account and store of value and provide expectational stability. When the transition to the Ikon was successfully completed, there would be reason to expect a significant increase in the growth of world output and standards of living.

There are three reasons for expecting such a benefit. First, uncertainty would be reduced. Nobody can know for certain how much spending and investing is currently held back by uncertainty about the future value of money, or relative values of different national currencies, or fear of a sudden regime change, but it seems likely to be substantial. In fact, it may be the key reason for the sluggishness of economic recovery and repeated fears of a relapse into recession. Secondly, the misallocation of resources associated with unanticipated fluctuations in exchange rates and interest rates would be avoided. The savings purely in terms of the unnecessary services of foreign exchange firms and markets would itself be significant. Indeed, large parts of the bloated financial services industry would be redundant. All those investment advisers and firms that charged customers for providing a return that on average only matched the market portfolio would be out of business, as individuals could earn such a return simply by holding cash. Financial services firms would no longer charge depositors for holding their money; instead, they would have to, in effect, pay for the privilege. In one possible further development of this idea, banks as we know them would cease to exist, being transformed into cash machines with 100 per cent reserves on the one hand and organizations for marketing specialized services at users risk on the other (see further explanation on this in the section on banking below). Thirdly, after the period of transition, savings and investment should rise, as investment and savings horizons lengthened. The long-term international fixed interest capital market would reopen to borrowers, as in Victorian times. Investments with long-term anticipated payback periods would become more attractive, and the bias of modern finance and company objectives towards short-term results would be corrected. The real yields on capital investments anywhere in the world could be compared on the same basis, without worrying about changes in the measuring rod used. These would only be some of the benefits of a properly designed global monetary constitution.

The recommendation of a unit to form a global standard draws on the insights of James Buchanan and three other famous economists, who were introduced in the preceding two chapters: Friedrich von Hayek, Maynard Keynes and Robert Mundell. Hayek would, we hope, approve of the proposal to link money to markets through an organic process of development. Buchanan would approve of the elevation of the monetary standard to a constitutional level, a realm beyond the reach of day-to-day politics, something sacrosanct and precious. This enshrines Buchanan's insight into the need to differentiate sharply between two stages of rule-making: the pre-constitutional, and post-constitutional (Much of the discussion of monetary reform continually confuses these stages.) Mundell would, I trust, support the call for a global (not a single) currency and sympathize with the case for a strong anchor. As for Keynes, well, would he not agree with the need to develop new means to coordinate national policies? He believed passionately in a monetary standard, and in the need, admitted by such a reform proposal, for political leaders to come together to put their stamp of approval on a new international monetary order. Knowing financial markets as he did, he would have approved, we trust, efforts to resist undue influence of market players on public policy, and the need for a new GFS.

However, the concept goes far beyond the proposals made by each of them. It departs from Hayek's vision of a competitive denationalization of money, because it reflects the view that the definition of money (though not its production) is a natural monopoly, which is more useful the more people use it, like language. It is unlikely that either Buchanan or Mundell would approve of the notion of a real-asset-based currency – at least of the sort proposed here. Both of them are naturally sceptical of 'new devices', though we would hold that such a currency would merely make use of the technology of modern finance and capital markets to create what would be for the first time a genuinely global standard. The reform has affinities with Mundell's ideal solution of a world currency in which each country would keep its own monetary unit that exchanges at par with the world unit. Keynes would reject presumably the lack of scope for an activist monetary policy. Yet we would suggest that use of such a money could in principle reduce the hazards both of inflation and deflation, eroding the case for a discretionary monetary policy.

Under such a 'utopian' monetary constitution, money can be a stake in the future growth of the global economy, in its growth dividend so to speak. With the currency unit being defined as an indirect claim on global output, it would naturally grow in value with the growth of the world economy. In some versions of the proposal, central banks and regulators would continue to monitor the solvency of the issuing banks and the integrity of markets. The currency units could still be called by familiar names – euros, dollars, pounds, but, as under the gold standard, they would be defined in terms of a common denominator. Countries could suspend membership of the area from time to time if they so wished, in case of emergency, as they did under the gold standard.

A real currency

How would this compare with the other anchors for world money considered in previous chapters? A currency board arrangement with self-regulating money supply could have, as anchors, a basket of goods, the global CPI index, gold, a basket of currencies, or a 'Real' basket (see accounts of each of these in Chapter 13). So the question comes down to whether an equity basket is a better anchor to money than these other anchors. Although the proposal naturally calls for research, it should not be dismissed as a 'casino currency'. It could help to solve a wide variety of the problems identified in Chapters 8 to 11: global imbalances, the reserve currency overhang, the reform of banking and the problem of international cross-border flows leading to wide exchange rate swings and bubbles would all be contained within such a standard. There would be no compulsion or supranational governmental body – except an issuing agency; that is a key advantage. Comparisons with the problems of the euro would be misplaced. No centralized fiscal union would be needed because countries would only join *if they were prepared of their own free will to make the sacrifices and adjustments required* to remain members of the Ikon club. That would be the best route to global monetary integration. Because the exchange rate between national currencies linked to the *Ikon* would be expected to be stable, capital flows would be equilibrating, as they were under the gold standard. With the greater flexibility of economies introduced by technological revolutions in supply-side management and flexibility in real wages and prices, and the benefits of the new monetary standard, the advantages would outweigh any disadvantages.

Money exists to serve the real economy and to facilitate the fulfilment of the needs of individual consumers. That is best achieved if money is insulated from political interference. If people naturally feel they and their firms and institutions should adjust to money – as should their governments – because it will be in their long-term interests to do so, the world would be a healthier place. The Ikon would be seen as part of the natural landscape. In 50 years, people would look back on the early twenty-first century and exclaim how odd it was that those people ran around with so many national currencies, most of them quite worthless, and all of them getting in the way of business, travel, social intercourse and the full enjoyment of life in a global community.

Giving nations and individuals a chance to hook up to an international monetary standard, as described in Chapter 13, could quickly change attitudes, especially if combined with a radical reform of banking and finance as proposed in the next section. It would give individuals, not just governments, a common measure of value, linking past, present and future, and across space as well as time. People would realize that a complicated network of dozens of currencies did little to promote individual well-being. That network had given power and money to the elites that controlled these national monies. It had divided the people of the world into separate tribes loyal to separate currencies. The remedy was to pool sovereignty. To quote Mundell,

> The benefits from a world currency would be enormous. Prices all over the world would be denominated in the same unit and would be kept equal in different parts of the world to the extent that the law of one price was allowed to work itself out. Apart from tariffs and controls, trade between countries would be as easy as it is between states of the US. It would lead to an enormous increase in the gains from trade and real incomes of all countries including the US.[4]

More broadly, with one money people could again focus on the more important things in life, rather than spend time gambling on how fast money would lose value in relation to alternative assets like real estate, stock market investments, art objects or gold. They would lose the money illusion that confused them – which had been a chimera. By strengthening confidence in the longer-term future, a good monetary system could also help societies get off the growth *carousel* – if that was what people wanted. There would be less pressure to chase after growth at all costs.[5]

Binding banking to the real economy

Given the objectives stated at the outset of this chapter, and following the conclusions reached in Chapter 10, I would opt also for a comparable evolution of banking systems. This could be promoted under the existing international monetary system with its dozens of national currencies or accompany adoption of a common currency unit as described in previous paragraphs. They are designed to deal with the recurrent and seemingly insoluble problems created by the existing organization of banking.Remember the memorable remark of Mervyn King, as governor of the Bank of England: 'Of all the many ways of organizing banking, the worst is the one we have today' (King, 2010).

The key change would be to convert bank assets into investments in securities held by unit trusts (known as mutual funds in the US); their assets would be direct investments in the real economy and their liabilities 'shares' where the risks are borne by the investor (depositor). It can be readily admitted that such systems (there are several variants) would have inefficiencies compared with banking, but these have to be compared with the frightening, open-ended costs imposed by successive bank crises. There are several variants of this basic idea which embody the principles mentioned above. There is only space for a brief account – with references to a selection of the available literature on the topic. Two such proposals may be briefly outlined.

Mutual fund (unit trust) banking

Bank deposits would be converted into claims on the portfolio of assets held by the bank (mutual fund), and so their value may change; as owners, their depositors would earn a return tied to the performance of the portfolio. Making a payment from such an account would require the transfer of a varying amount of units, depending on the value of the fund at the time. (This system will be familiar to those who have accounts with money market funds.) As with unit trusts, managers would normally be compensated with a percentage of the fund's assets. Depositors would select the portfolios in which they wished to invest from a range of options. It would be essential that the mutual fund disclosed fully its portfolio of underlying securities. Critics have been quick to point out snags. There would still, for example be the possibility of a run on cash funds, as was seen in the run on some US money market mutual funds at the height of the panic in 2008. But this would be reflected in a decline in the price of deposit shares. In contrast to traditional banks, such a bank could not fail if the value of its assets declined. The incentive to withdraw funds at par before the bank closes would disappear with the possibility of non-par clearing. The equity nature of the liabilities eliminates the sources of instability associated with traditional banking (see Cowen and Kroszner, p. 227 citation on p. 289). So the answer to sceptics who say that attempts to confine banking may result in moving the problems elsewhere is surely not to step back but to go to more radical reforms.

Limited purpose banking

A scheme by the name of 'limited purpose banking' has been proposed by the American economist Laurence Kotlikoff (Kotlikoff, 2010). Under this scheme banks would be dismantled and turned into consultancies or marketing firms. These firms would sell mutual funds, which could include real estate funds, private equity funds, commercial paper funds, residential mortgage funds, small and medium size enterprise funds, inflation-indexed funds and so on. Banks would not be allowed to own any financial assets or borrow (except for those specific assets they needed to run their unit trusts, such as furniture and buildings, computers and so on). Loans would be transformed into securities. The real problem with the subprime episode was not securitization itself but that the sellers of these mortgage were lying about what was in the securities. There was no adequate disclosure. Thus Kotlikoff insists on the need for a super-regulator to check, verify and independently rate all the assets of the unit trusts (formerly banks). So banks would be splintered into large numbers of small mutual fund companies, each holding specific assets. When companies want to borrow, for example, they would go to a bank and apply for a loan; the application would be checked by a regulator responsible for ensuring the accuracy of the information disclosed by the borrower, and then the bank would auction it to a mutual fund company specializing in business loans. Brokers would no longer be allowed to take positions as principals in trading activities, which has been necessary to provide liquidity and make the market function, because it has been found to be impossible to stop them from gambling at public expense; they would be transformed into online exchanges where each seller is matched with a buyer electronically; brokers would not be allowed to have risk exposures. Cash would be accessed through cash mutual funds, which would hold only cash assets – in effect, balances at the central bank.

Kotlikoff is driven by a passion for stopping financiers at all costs from swindling the public. Sadly, although most banks throughout the world were for many generations run by decent, prudent bankers maintaining high ethical standards, as explained in previous chapters (see Chapters 1, 2 and 10) the system developed in such a way as to push these bankers to the sidelines, and thousands were made redundant when the passion for marketing and cross-selling services, as well as the pursuit of growth, size and maximum return on equity took hold of bank management and investors. Under his proposal, banks would only be middlemen – financial companies would be specifically prohibited from borrowing and lending. Mutual funds would be at all times marked to market. Owners of cash mutual funds would be free to write cheques against their holdings, use debit cards or access cash from ATM machines – these cash funds would represent the demand deposits services offered by existing banks. But as investos, they would bear the intermediation (credit) risk.

Kotlikoff's proposal is framed in terms of one country's banking system, and would leave its central bank free to pursue an independent monetary policy (it would have full control over narrow money held in its cash mutual funds), with a floating exchange rate, but could easily be extended to fit with the global monetary standard – a Real SDR or an *Ikon* investment currency – as outlined in previous sections of this chapter.

True, this scheme has been criticized on several grounds, notably for its reliance on a super official regulator to monitor and rate every security. This could be a bureaucratic nightmare. The super agency would also need to be empowered to pry into personal details of every borrower, and put them online. Much debate would be needed on these and other issues, but the scheme should not be dismissed as impracticable. Again, what we have to compare such schemes with is the existing dysfunctional monetary and banking system with its unacceptable costs – and the absence of any convincing remedy within the existing paradigm.

In conclusion, it may be seen that, referring back to the argument advanced in Chapter 10, banking can be made safe – by eliminating banks. If the world's biggest financial institutions are indeed on their way to the break-up yard, and if even the resulting bits and pieces would continue to pose a threat to society, something has to be done. Laurence Kotlikoff is the first to admit that his plan is not perfect but it shows that alternatives to banks are conceivable: 'Limited purpose banking is, I'm convinced, the best and simplest solution to our horrendous and, unfortunately, ongoing financial plague' (Kotlikoff, p. 124). The world can manage without banks as we have known them, especially if money itself was put onto a new basis as described earlier in this chapter and reconnected with the real world.[6]

People are aware when they invest in unit trusts (mutual funds) that it is at their risk. There seems no compelling reason why this principle and this culture should not be extended to much of what is usually known as banking (and in fact, the trend of finance for decades has been to usurp the banks' traditional role as the centre of the financial system). This could be effected by transforming existing bank loans into securities or by a form of narrow banking, as already discussed and as will be mentioned in the next chapter. For those who despair of ever being able to organize banking in a way that does not impose intolerable costs on society, such schemes offer possible solutions.[7]

The best way forward for the GFS involves not just another arrangement for exchange rates between fiat currencies, but rather the re-establishment at the constitutional level of proper global monetary and banking standards. As Buchanan puts it, the need is for 'the value of the monetary unit be made one of the rules of the game, within which economic interaction takes place, rather than being used as a counter in the strategy of play' within the rules. Buchanan himself refers to Hayek, in calling for money to be part of the 'higher law'. Such a vision informed the thinking of the Founding fathers of the US – just as Congress should fix weights and measures, so it should fix the measuring rod of money.

Like other standards, it should remain unchallenged (Buchanan, p. 256). The same line of thought should apply to the framers of the future monetary constitution of the world.

These are the building blocks of a strong constitutional, global, monetary structure for the GFS that would, once it were in place, harness the power of global finance. Its consequences would be dramatic and far-reaching. Firstly, it would facilitate and promote exchange between the different peoples of the earth, rather than (as present arrangements do) call attention to and accentuate their separateness. Secondly, it would reconnect the world of finance with the real economy. Thirdly, it would encourage decision makers, including governments, business corporations, investors and consumers, to take longer-term time horizons.

Is this a pipe dream? Well, it would be, if it were not for the breakdown in trust in the existing GFS, high unemployment, fears of a relapse into another, possibly deeper, recession and the absence of credible remedies.

Notes

1. An Ikon is defined as 'an image', 'a representation', 'an important and enduring symbol', a 'picture on a screen'; see The Free Dictionary at www.thefreedictionary.com
2. This section develops ideas discussed during the 1970s, especially in Germany; see for example Engels, 1981.
3. According to Milton Friedman, money holdings are optimal (for fiat money which is costless to produce) when its marginal utility is zero, thus it should earn the real rate of interest, as would the Ikon (Friedman, 1969).
4. http://robertmundell.net/economic-policies/world-currency/
5. On this, see Diane Coyle, *The Economics of Enough: How to run the Economy as if the Future Really Matters*, Princeton University Press, 2011.
6. Internet-based services are already by passing banks by putting leaders in touch with potential borrowers and look set to transform the full gamut of financial services.
7. The financial sector reforms urged in this section are in line with those proposed by Sebastian Mallaby (2010). Policy-makers should if possible drive financial risk towards institutions that impose fewer costs on the taxpayers (than banks have done). As he states:

   That means encouraging the proliferation of firms that are not too big to fail, so reducing the share of risk taking in the financial system that must be backstopped by the government. It also means favoring institutions where the incentives to control risk are relatively strong and therefore where regulatory scrutiny assumes less of the burden. (p 380)

   Mallaby refers to hedge funds, but the recommendation could apply equally to other types of asset managers, with the safeguard and caveats he mentions, such as ensuring that none of them become too big to fail.

Bibliography

Brown, Brendan, *Bubbles in Credit and Currency: How Hot Markets Cool Down*, Palgrave Macmillan, 2008.

Buchanan, James, 'The Constitutionalization of Money', *Cato Journal*, Vol. 30, No. 2 (Spring/Summer 2010). Copyright © Cato Institute.

Coyle, Diane, *The Economics of Enough: How to Run the Economy as if the Future Really Matters*, Princeton University Press, 2011.

Engels, Wolfram, 'The Optimal Monetary Unity: Real Asset Currency, State Monopoly Sovereignty and the Private Issue of Bank Notes', Campus Verlag, 1981.

Friedman, Milton, *The Optimum Quantity of Money: And Other Essays*, Aldine Transactions, 1969.

Gross, Bill, 'Zero-based money keeps trapping recovery', *Financial Times*, 6 February 2012.

Keynes, J. M., *The General Theory of Employment, Interest, and Money*. Macmillan & Co Ltd 1973, 1936.

King, Mervyn, 'Banking: From Bagehot to Basel and Back Again', 25 October 2010.

King, Stephen, 'It's Time to Re-Examine Inflation Targeting', *Financial Times*, 13 February 2011.

Kotlikoff, Lawrence, *Jimmy Stewart Is Dead – Ending the World's Ongoing Financial Plague with Limited Purpose Banking*. John Wiley and Sons, 2010.

Krugman, Paul, 'How Much of the World is in a Liquidity Trap?' *New York Times*, 17 March 2010.

Mallaby, Sebastian, *More Money than God*, Bloomsbury, 2010.

15
The Emerging Global Financial System

The future of the global financial system will be shaped both by organic, market-driven evolution and by political action. The opportunity to move to a better system must not be wasted.

Policies by which governments attempted to steer their economies out of recession, balancing plans for medium- and longer-term fiscal consolidation with short-term fiscal and monetary stimuli, met with only limited success in the years following GFC. Austerity for ever was out of the question on political grounds; a bigger fiscal boost was ruled out in most advanced countries by fears of market reaction to public indebtedness.[1] Structural changes to cut unemployment – such as policies to free up markets, raise levels of skills, increase competition and ease restrictions in product markets – would take years to show results. Central banks had reached – some would say they had exceeded – the limits of what they could do without running unacceptable risks of further, even bigger, credit-fuelled booms and busts. Meanwhile, the uncertainty gripping financial markets could at any time erupt in further turbulence that would again set back hopes of a full recovery. It was uncertain whether fast-growing emerging market economies could continue their rates of growth in the face of weak demand in most advanced economies. The US, as usual, seemed to be a bright spot, but longer-term prospects there too were uncertain. Policy-makers around the world lived in fear.

This was a different kind of crisis. Not only did it point to deep-seated faults in the structure of the GFS, there were fears it could erode the springs of capitalism itself. To quote Nobel prize winner Edmund Phelps,

A capitalist system dogged by frequent crisis and fears of crisis may levy a toll not only on people's comforts and sense of security but also on the generation of innovation itself. (Phelps 2009 a)

And even more tellingly,

> Much is dysfunctional in the US and the UK: a financial sector that turned away from the business sector, then caused its self-destruction, and a business sector beset by short-termism. (Phelps 2009b)

In this book, I have argued that the sources of these faults – of the money trap, as described in Chapters 1–4 – lie in a dysfunctional banking/finance system interacting with an excessively pliable international monetary/ regulatory system. Whatever the reader's views on the remedies outlined, the analysis leads to the conclusion that a far-reaching restructuring of the institutional and ethical framework of the financial system is required.

Pressures for change

Pressures are building up for more radical change than the reforms that governments were putting in place or contemplating after the crash. The following paragraphs outline some of these pressures.

Dysfunctional banking and finance

Unacceptable social costs have been incurred as a result of the structure and activities of banks in leading centres, including the UK, US, the euro area and Japan. The costs to public finances and the nagging worry that further injections of public funds might be needed in future raised doubts about whether governments had the political and financial *means* to rescue banks, short of imposing even higher taxes on future generations. Yet, as discussed in Chapter 10, the measures proposed to make banking more stable, even if implemented in full, would not remove the incentives to take excessive risks.

Lack of confidence in regulation

The approach to financial regulation that has been followed so far, known as the Basel process, has been shown to be deeply flawed. We know the rules have been adapted to suit the industry, and have been exploited by the banks for their private interest (this is also the testimony given to the author by several senior officials who have been personally involved in rule making under Basel). The fact that nobody understands or can understand the system except a few bank lawyers is itself a sufficient condemnation (to move from Basel to another milestone of post-GFC reform, the Dodd-Frank Act, this is 2,600 pages long, and in October 2011 more than 100 committees were at work drafting 243 new rules to give effect to it, upon which more than 25,000 written comments had been made) (Tett, 2011). (See Chapters 2, 4, 5 and 10 for more detailed analysis of financial regulation).

Uncontrollable capital flows

Cross-border capital movements driven by diverse monetary policies and diverse expectations about future exchange rates have been a source of periodic booms and busts. Financial flows often dominated. Claims of proponents of floating in the 1970s that exchange rate changes would be gradual, and that they would correspond to differences in national inflation rates, proved to be misplaced. Uncertainty made it difficult for companies to plan future international investment rationally, distorting the allocation of resources. Speculation was destabilizing when there was no international monetary standard around which expectations of yield, equilibrium exchange rates and purchasing power could cluster (see Chapters 2–5 and 11).

Systemic bias against emerging markets

When the US and/or the euro area adopted expansionary monetary policies, funds flowed out around the world, frequently overwhelming local defences against financial instability. The answer given by the US and Europe – that emerging markets and other so-called peripheral countries should let their currencies appreciate – is politically difficult and often impractical in countries with fragile banking and finance systems. Moreover, it is unrealistic to expect them to be able to strengthen their markets in the short term. That is one reason for the chronic instability of finance, with five major cross-border asset bubbles and crashes in the years between 1980 and 2010. As discussed in previous chapters, the GFS also has a bias favouring the centre countries. That was a reason why China, Brazil, Russia and many 'peripheral' countries pushed for a fairer, more symmetrical regime. They were on the receiving end of current arrangements and suffered from their side-effects, including high volatility of commodity prices, notably oil, as well as the patronizing attitudes of governments of reserve centres. The G20 process was not likely to reduce this instability in any significant way (see Chapters 4, 7 and 11).

Over-extended reserve centres

The arrangements did not serve the long-term needs of the reserve centres either (see Chapter 9). For example, the US suffered from the over-extension of the role of dollar as a reserve currency – as one economist put it, the rest of the world gave the US the rope with which to hang itself.[2]

Lack of adequate adjustment mechanism

Flexible exchange rates contained no mechanism by which to bring the current accounts of the balance of payments into equilibrium. As the late Tommaso Padoa-Schioppa, an economist, stated,

> It is an illusion to think that a flexible exchange rate would effectively enforce discipline on national economic policies and ensure the rapid correction of imbalances, both because the market is not always 'right', and because its signals are in any case insufficient to trigger 'good responses' from economic policy. (Padoa-Schioppa, 2010)

Nor would political arm-twisting make up for the systemic absence of an adjustment mechanism. For example, there was next to no chance that US pressure on China to revalue was going to produce results likely to satisfy the US. On the other hand, the US would not be prepared to break up the world's trading and currency system (by imposing trade and exchange controls, for instance) just to make a point to Beijing. So the result was a dangerous stalemate that satisfied nobody.

The absurd reserves mountain

Every cycle caused an increased appetite for reserves as a cushion against future shocks. Everybody agreed this was irrational; but demand for reserves from emerging economies increased further after GFC as it did after the Asian bubble 10 years earlier. Countries became allergic to allowing even a temporary drop in reserves, for fear that the market would pounce on them; Russia was one case, Mexico another. Mexico had $90 billion at the start of 2008, which on a rational view was at the time fully adequate to cushion any probable shock, but it was feared that the market might judge that to be insufficient, so Mexico started accumulating further reserves as well as arranging 'swap' lines with Fed and access to IMF facilities.

Yet at the same time, given the deterioration in the US balance sheet, there was also a growing fear of *a flight from the dollar*, as discussed in Chapter 9.

Nationalism on the rise

The lack of an international standard encourages economic nationalism, inducing politicians into catering to the satisfaction of short-term national needs, if necessary at the cost of international cooperation, agreed rules of good behaviour and their longer-term interests. One leading economist accused President Obama of delivering 'body blows to the world trading system, which his pedecessos had built up over decades of US leadership' (Bhagwati, 2012). As discussed at several points in preceding chapters, pandering to protectionist impulses allowed policy makers to avoid facing up to the unpalatable truth that full monetary sovereignty was incompatible with reaping the benefits of globalization (see below).

The euro–dollar seesaw

One additional pressure for reform of the GFS came from the launch of the euro, which worsened the dilemmas facing third countries, torn between the dollar and the euro areas. If a country fixed to either of them, but traded with both, it ran into difficulties when the dollar-euro rate fluctuated. In the 2007–08 panic, the dollar initially depreciated against the euro but then, in the second half of 2008, before and imme- diately after the Lehman collapse, the dollar soared, bringing huge difficulties for many countries (mostly small ones) fixed to the dollar. Equally, when the euro soared against the dollar, areas like the CFA franc and other countries tied to the euro suffered, as well as the coun- tries of the euro area itself.[3] As argued in Chapter 6, the eurozone itself desperately needed a more stable international system and monetary standard if it was to survive. The troubles of the euro zone then tested the fabric of wider international cooperation, as both the US and UK leadership blamed euro area leaders for failing to come to grips with its crisis, thus dragging down the wider world economy (see also Chapters 6, 9 and 11).

Weak central bank and public sector balance sheets

Chances of reviving confidence in national currencies were badly damaged by the weakness of the balance sheets of many leading central banks and of the governments that ultimately stood behind them. A fiat currency is ultimately 'backed' by the taxing power of the sovereign. (The Roman Empire and its currency were brought down by the erosion of its tax base as much as by the debasement of its coinage or its debts.) Central banks of many emerging market countries as well as of the reserve centres were severely affected by GFC. Reserve-centre central banks' balance sheets were damaged by the inclusion of poor-quality assets, the huge increase in assets and liabilities as they pumped up the supply of base money in an effort to sustain overall monetary expansion in the face of a collapse of bank lending, and (in the case of the ECB) the purchase of the bonds of weak member countries. Many emerging market central bank balance sheets were damaged by the appreciation of their domestic currencies against the currencies in which their foreign reserves were denominated, such as the dollar; on a mark-to-market basis, some were technically insolvent. At the same time the public finances of the sovereigns that ultimately supplied the capital to central banks as needed to refinance the rescues of other sovereigns (in the case of the ECB) or banks (in the case of the Fed, Bank of England and ECB), threw doubt on their long-term capacity to recapitalize their central banks – and in the case of the euro, their political will to do so. In the case of the ECB, it had no 'sovereign' with the power to tax standing behind it.

The US at risk

But the eurozone was not the only reserve centre spreading fear around the world. So was the US. Never before had a reserve centre pursued so blatantly a policy likely to undermine confidence in its currency. Under the Obama administration, it seemed evident that the US Treasury's (undeclared) policy was to drive down the value of the dollar and that this was supported by the entire cabinet. As discussed in Chapter 11, a regime where the centre country feels that circumstances oblige it to resort to such unilateral policies is unsustainable. Moreover, the US budget deficit was coming close to the level at which, according to a leading student of historical inflations, rapid inflation becomes a probability. When a government borrows to cover 40% or more of its fiscal expenditures it can slide into hyperinflation (Bernholz, 2003). At the time of writing, the markets were giving the US the benefit of the doubt; they were preoccupied gorging on easy meat – the carcass of the euro sovereign debt markets. But if the political stalemate over fiscal consolidation in the US were to continue, it would not be long before the markets turned their attention to the big elephant in the room. Suddenly, it looked vulnerable.

'Time is running out'

All this made confident predictions about a smooth transition to a multi-currency, multi-polar world appear highly suspect. There could be no assurance whatsoever that a multicurrency reserve system would be stable, especially if some of the key currencies were undermined by the forces outlined in the previous paragraphs. To assume that this could be managed by central bank cooperation, swap lines or even guidelines covering reserve portfolio diversification flies in the face of the evidence. Pessimism was being increasingly voiced in official circles. For example, although the IMF's default mode is one of cautious optimism, by September 2011 it had recognized, in effect, that policies were in a trap:

> Time is running out to address existing vulnerabilities. The set of policy choices that are both economically viable and politically feasible is shrinking as the crisis shifts into a new, more political phase. Negative surprises and the intensification of risks have raised the urgency of prompt policy action to strengthen the global financial system. (IMF *Global Financial Stability Report*, September, 2011).

With 'time running out' (recall the diagram in the Introduction) the search for a better financial framework was 'heightened by the limited room to deploy further fiscal and monetary policy stimulus'.

Gold

Is gold the answer? Should governments flunk real reform, gold-centred proposals such as those reviewed in the previous chapter could attract increasing popular support. The function of the gold market for the next few years will be to signal the strength of market pressures facing policymakers. If they let matters slide too far, as eurozone leaders did in 2011 in failing to act decisively to quell market suspicions about the future of the euro, market anxieties could lead to panics, which would be signalled in a soaring gold price. If central banks add to market nervousness by themselves purchasing gold on a large scale (in 2011 central bank purchases were already at a 40-year high), they could lead a wider stampede into hard assets and a flight from paper. The return of gold to a monetary role of some kind – for example, as part of a commodity basket or redefined SDR – might then become difficult to avoid, even if less rational than alternatives. If central banks themselves show more confidence in gold than in paper, others would follow. If governments were to get on top of the situation, the price of gold may well decline. The problem for governments is that gold is a universally understood and trusted monetary asset. Central bankers have conducted a campaign for one hundred years – their hundred years' war – to persuade the public that their paper is as good as gold and they are at present losing. Gold has defects as an anchor, notably quite large swings in its real value, and we should be able to design a better anchor, but 'time is running out'.

The domestic politics of change

Given that all these forces were progressively undermining the cred-ibility of existing arrangements, where will the impetus for political action come from? Obvious candidates are the rising creditor powers, notably China, India and Russia (see the next section). Pressures nearer home could reinforce their demands. Judy Shelton has described how fear of losing the dollar as a meaningful unit of account has forged a confluence of interest in monetary reform among disparate parties – among those who used the dollar because it was America's legal tender and those who relied on the dollar as the world's reserve currency. Within these groups there were 'decidedly mixed feelings' about the continued monetary hegemony of the US:

> This makes for an unexpected coalition for monetary reform. The decline of the dollar is linking the economic anxieties of Americans – on Main Street and Wall Street – with profound concern elsewhere in the world over whether America will continue to exercise global leadership. (Shelton, 2011)

The demand for bankers to be put in their place was evident at the domestic political level. The feeling of unfairness was manifest in the widespread 'Occupy Wall Street' protests in the US and similar demon-strations in other countries, as well as the riots against austerity meas-ures in eurozone countries and the widespread sense that policy-makers had lost touch with public opinion. Moreover, there were signs that this popular demand for a change was being focussed on the call to reclaim money from the control of the elite rather than a general anti-busi-ness protest. This was shown for example in the programme of the Tea Party movement and calls for a return to gold; whereas before GFC such calls were voiced by a small minority, after it they were no longer being laughed out of court. Younger people, in particular, felt short-changed, inheriting a fragile economy built by their parents and grandparents on unsustainable levels of debt (Hyman, 2011; Coggan, 2011).

Now for a bit more background on the perspectives of two other groups of critics: the rising creditor nations and operators at the heart of western finance.

How major emerging market governments viewed the system

While remembering my promise, made in the Introduction, not to discuss the 'decline of the West', it is nevertheless necessary to take into account how the West was viewed by other countries, as that had become an influence on the evolution of the system. As seen from the outside, the West was undergoing not only a relative 'decline', but also a loss of trust in its institutions, and notably its institutions for economic and monetary policy making. Included in this indictment were the still western-dominated institutions for international cooperation, such as the IMF. This criticism stood in sharp contrast to the satisfaction and pride with which western leaders regarded their institutions. In the West, the major institutions of policy making, notably the central banks and finance ministries, were seen by some mainstream economists as well as governments as having performed well, as had the international monetary system. Its resilience was much praised.

But in developing countries, as amongst domestic critics, there were insistent demands for a change. The institutional underpinnings of the western model were viewed as unsound. There was also a clear desire for the international institutions to allow countries to follow their own models, and a resistance to 'globalization' as defined in the West, which too often meant persuading people in the rest of the world to adapt their institutions and norms to western concepts. In East Asia, the history of the way the West opened up the region to trade – the British forcing trade, and opium, on to China in the mid nineteenth century and the US forcing the opening up of Japan through Commander Perry's mission with the menacing Black Ships in Tokyo Bay in 1853 – are regularly brought up in conversations in Beijing and Tokyo. Students are taught about them at school. Yet European and American leaders visit East Asia often without any understanding of the way that such traumatic historical experiences and resentments still smoulder beneath the surface.

Contrary to the perception in the West, Beijing tended to feel that China was being asked to shoulder too much of the burden of adjustment. China's twelfth five-year plan (2011–15) assumed that China's propensity to consume was limited while the need for investment, especially to raise low incomes in rural areas, would remain strong. The plan did not even mention the great bogeyman of the west – its foreign exchange rate regime. Indeed, there were all the makings of further friction, especially with the US, given China's strong resistance to a move to a flexible exchange rate regime, or to a large, one-off revaluation. Instead, Beijing called for the US and Europe to stabilize the dollar and the euro. Parallels were drawn between the dilemmas facing China's exchange rate policy today and Germany's in the 1960s, which led to repeated currency crises and eventually to the breakdown of Bretton Woods. Beijing was clearly encouraging greater international use of the RMB, but this was designed more to reduce China's vulnerability to the dollar rather than as an endorsement of the current monetary system or its evolution towards a multipolar system. China had its own agenda for reform, and it was centred on the objectives of stability and discipline, twin pillars of its growing geo-political presence.

In New Delhi also the view of the Western plight was clear: finance got out of hand, regulators were complacent and the tendency of its leaders to lecture others on how to run their affairs exposed as hypocrisy. There may be less tension between India and the West because India had a more balanced economy than China's, had not accumulated excess reserves and had therefore not been at the receiving end of political pressure to let its currency appreciate, switch more resources to domestic growth, and hence help to re-balance the world economy. But the views of its political and business leaders were no less critical. Y. V. Reddy, a much-respected former governor of the Reserve Bank of India (RBI), published a book in 2009 called *India and the Global Financial Crisis*, which showed his initial critical reactions to the credit crunch, and these views were broadly representative of sentiment among the country's leaders.

...and a perspective from the City of London

Even Western bankers had given up defending the system. Indeed, many thought the global financial system appeared to be on the verge of disintegrating. As noted by seasoned observers in the very heart of the City of London, markets were often paralysed by fear. Nothing was working as it should, as participants waited to see where the losses would fall – how many more skeletons were going to fall out of cupboards. Increasingly, it was realized that a large part of the claims (loans and investments), built up gradually over many years on over-optimistic assumptions of future growth, would never be repaid. How would the unavoidable losses be shared? Would the world decline into another recession before government and private sector finances had recovered from the last one? There was, said Stephen King, chief economist of

HSBC, one of the world's biggest banks, 'a loss of faith in the entire financial system' (King, 2011).

A long-term evolutionary process

In sum, strong political as well as economic forces reinforce the pressures likely to transform both the main elements of the GFS: the official international monetary system and the commercial financial system. The sooner that leading governments can bring themselves to recognize that, and take the lead in shaping the direction of change, the sooner will private sector confidence revive, leading to greater willingness to spend and invest, and improved prospects for long-term economic development.

This book has linked the failures of the existing GFS model to three underlying factors: the excessive influence of 'the finance interest', which added muscle to the 'too-big-to-fail' problem; lack of an agreed and workable international adjustment mechanism bearing on both deficit and surplus countries; and, linked to this, the absence of an international monetary standard. What is needed is a standard that linked the (official) monetary system properly to the (still nominally private though in effect part nationalized) financial sector. That is why it is necessary to integrate discussions on the future of banking, and reform of financial regulation and structures on the one hand, with debate on the future of the international monetary system on the other. Many of the problems originated in domestic banking and finance but the solutions can only be international. Only a strong GFS would make it safe to deploy expansionary fiscal or monetary policies. Governments would be forced to strengthen the policy framework to enable more resolute use of stabilization policies – and such strengthening could only be done internationally. That is the missing link in the official strategy for sustainable recovery and growth. An apparent loss of sovereignty is the political pill they would have to swallow.

They would have to tackle the banks. Again and again, the *banking problem* has been at the core of financial and economic disasters: the Icelandic and Irish economic collapses, the eurozone sovereign debt debacle, the collapse of Nordic banks, the Japanese decade of deflation, Latin America's lost decade, the US and British collapses, many other episodes of systemic banking and currency turmoil in emerging markets – banking failures each and every time. Each time, the public bore a large part of the cost. Each time, regulators and central bankers would say 'We are learning, we will do better next time', or, my favourite, 'The search is on. ...' for a solution.

An alternative future for banking

Changes to the structure of banking analysed in Chapter 10 in the UK and US, such as ring-fencing retail banks, pointed in the right direction, and were certainly worth implementing in full. If bankers could again of their own will reinvent a culture of banking prudence, on the model of Sweden's successful Handelsbanken, which has for years operated without any bonuses, and deliberately resisted the temptations of quick profits that have brought nearly all other banks down, that would be even better (see Kroner, 2009, for a description of the bank's management policies, which, says the author 'are diametrically opposed to so-called best practice in the industry' in avoiding what he calls the 'seven deadly sins' of modern banking).

However, these are weak defences to pit against the forces making for chronic instability in banking and the finance sector as a whole, as analysed in Chapter 10. My own conclusion is that it is not possible to make finance safe within the existing GFS, short of draconian regulation on the one hand or a quasi-religious conversion of the financial community to an ethic of public service on the other.[4] I have come to the view that nothing short of the transformation of finance as we know it will be sufficient to remove the threat that the existing organization of banks still poses to the economy – even, given their political clout, to democracy. Applying the principles mentioned above, and outlined in Chapter 14, this would involve converting bank assets into investments in securities held by unit trusts (known as mutual funds in the US); their assets would be direct investments in the real economy and their liabilities 'shares' where the risks are borne by the investor (depositor). Two options for such a reform have been outlined. The so-called globally systemically important banks may break up under regulatory and commercial pressures anyway; yet even that would not solve the systemic problems of banking, as shown in Chapter 10. (See Cowen and Krozner, 1990, and Kotlikoff, 2010.)

I am well aware that such a finance structure would introduce many inefficiencies into the system, and that it will be difficult to manage without banks as we have known them – at least for a transitional period. But the costs of continuing as we are are likely to be even higher.

... and a new international currency unit

Such a transformation of banking would sit well with the establishment of a new international monetary standard of the kind outlined previously. For example, a convertible asset-based currency as described in Chapter 14 offers one way forward. A global investment currency standard, together with mutual fund banking, would banish bank failures. We cannot banish the real risks of economic uncertainty, so customers, deposit holders, would bear the risks of a fluctuation in the value of the currency, but we can banish unnecessary risks that arise from the measuring rod we use and from the way in which financial intermediation is organized.

As outlined in Chapter 14, such a monetary standard could be developed using the technology available as a result of the progressive globalization of capital markets. The key step is for major governments to agree not on a common currency but on a common monetary unit of account in which citizens can have confidence. Further steps would be needed to realize the potential of such a reform, but it would open up the prospect of bringing the public good of international monetary stability back to the world economy for the first time in 100 years. The currency unit could be defined in a number of ways; I suggest defining it as a fraction of the global equity market portfolio, so that its value would increase with the growth in productivity. Money would become a claim on the future of the world economy, giving every citizen a stake in it. As it would increase in real value with the rise in productivity, cash would be in high demand as a means of payment and store of value. The supply of money defined in this way could be self-regulating, as the supply of money is at present under currency board arrangements. A global currency board would passively issue money defined in this way on demand, just as the Hong Kong Monetary Authority issues Hong Kong dollars. There would be no need for a global central bank with a discretionary monetary policy. It would be a wholly voluntary standard. There are other ways of defining the unit of account – such as indexing it to a global basket of representative commodities. The point is that it would provide a benchmark against which individual national currencies – which would continue to exist – would be measured against and eventually aligned with, all on a purely voluntary basis.

The opportunity

So much for a vision of the long-term evolution of money and the financial architecture. I realize this is not likely to be realized any time soon. What of the more immediate steps that might be taken to revive confidence in the direction of policy? In Part II of this book, we reviewed the search for ways out of the money trap already taking place at national, regional and international levels. Unless we can make the leap to a new

order and bring about the transformation of global monetary arrangements and banking that is needed, we shall be driven back onto the
measures being pursued at those levels (see Chapters 5, 6 and 7). We
now review additional steps that could be taken to realize some of the
benefits of a one-world system without the total transformation of the
GFS outlined above.

A path to reform of the GFS

Even at this less utopian level, the debate about objectives needs to be
wide-ranging. The principal objective of reforms should in my view
be 'expectational stability', not growth. It is essential to stabilize the
expectations of individuals, companies, financial institutions and
governments with regard to key financial parameters – the financial
environment in which they make plans for investment, aid flows,
long-term strategic planning and inter-governmental cooperation. But
what should one make of insistent demands that economies 'had' to
grow faster if we were to repair damaged balance sheets and get out
of the debt trap? Though true enough in narrow accounting terms –
was this not a kind of bullying? It could be viewed as psychological
warfare waged by the elite against the common sense of the people.
Why, people wondered, indeed should 'we' – or our children and grandchildren – all work harder and 'grow' economies faster to pay down
debts that 'they' – the bankers, governments and central bankers – had
played a large part in piling up? (True, all who borrowed excessively
were also partly responsible, but the leaders had set the tone.) 'Growth'
was not within the gift of governments anyway; and illusions about
future growth had been one of the contributory causes of the credit
binge than preceded the crash. It was time to get off that carousel.[5]
What governments could and should provide was a robust framework,
a money and banking standard, and rules of the game. Money itself can
be the compass. Then growth might develop of its own accord – or it
might not.

This is not to deny the value of technological and entrepreneurial
innovation, which is the wellspring of economic progress, or that for
many decades emerging markets will need to grow rapidly to absorb
the flow of new entrants to their workforces and raise living standards.
There would be nothing in the international financial architecture
proposed here to prevent that. But there should be no compulsion to
grow. If that implies that many advanced countries will not be able
to service their debts, then mechanisms for orderly default will need

to be developed, and are likely in my view to be needed and used. Alternatively, high rates of inflation will need to be deliberately engineered – putting another nail in the coffin of fiat money.

With greater expectational stability as the aim, how could the international monetary system be reformed to help achieve it? In the next few sections, we recognize that the world will not jump immediately to the revolutionary monetary plans of the kind sketched above and described in previous chapters. The next section focuses on bold political initiatives that might be considered and that go in the direction of the desirable long-term recasting of monetary arrangements. They both go to the overriding theme of this book – the need for an international monetary standard.

Two major strategic options will be considered: a *North Atlantic Currency Area* and a *New Creditor Standard*.

A North Atlantic currency area

While new creditor countries will doubtless lead the push for reform, their efforts will continue to focus on the existing monetary arrangements, featuring existing reserve currencies. They could seek either to *reform* or to *replace* them. Reform efforts could look towards a grand bargain between Europe and North America designed to address the four great challenges facing the system (as examined in Chapters 8–11).

The most practicable way of starting would be by close cooperation between the US, Canada and the Europe Union (rather than the euro area), aiming in the first instance at jointly managed exchange rates. This would recognize that, as all governments of the North Atlantic area followed policies aimed at similar objectives, those aims would best be achieved by establishing a common monetary area (as outlined for example in Allan Meltzer's proposal mentioned in Chapter 13). These talks would be aimed to convert the existing system of inward-looking policies into an outward-looking approach. This would be designed to facilitate solutions to the problems of global imbalances, the reserve currency overhang, financial sector reform and credit bubbles. A new North Atlantic monetary standard, to which the US and Canadian dollars, as well as the euro and pound sterling, would belong, would make further reserve accumulation by emerging markets unnecessary, and currency diversification pointless. This would remove a major incentive to run payment surpluses, and so lead in time to greater self-discipline on both deficit and surplus countries (see also Mundell, 2011, citations p. 243).

In the euro area countries, the UK and the US, such monetary cooperation would support efforts to bring public finances under control – the essential condition of greater monetary stability more widely. If the euro area were to break up or be restructured, then close monetary cooperation between the both sides of the Atlantic – US, Germany and the UK, for example – would of course be even more vital. The main point is that such an international reform effort cannot wait for the euro area or the US to 'clean up its act'. For each country or for the euro area to ease the grip of global finance – to escape from the money trap – policy coordination along with internal reform are needed.

This would amount to a joint effort to procure the global public good of international monetary stability by establishing a voluntary common standard (and it should not be seen as the US 'joining' the euro, or the euro countries 'joining' the dollar area). Monetary policies would be dedicated to serving the long-term interests of all nation states in a stable international order. Fiscal policies would still be available for stabilization purposes. The emphasis of domestic policies would switch to structural reforms. The rewards could be far-reaching. Credible evidence of closer cooperation between the world's dominant monetary domains would produce a surge in business confidence. This is because it would signal to business that the major powers had learnt the true lesson of GFC; it will put in place what had been missing in their response to the crisis. The feeling that leading authorities were united in wanting to see reform happen, and that it was for real, would inject much-needed adrenalin into the world's comatose financial system. Once European and US authorities got together, it would also be much easier to deal with wayward financial markets. It would indeed necessitate agreement on common rules for banking and finance. It would make redundant the resources currently engaged in what should be the socially useless task of betting on exchange rate fluctuations. It would permit all parties – governments, businesses and individuals – to have a clearer view of their long-term prospects and interests.

Countries that currently peg either to the dollar or the euro would benefit from having a large, more stable, currency area to which they could link their currencies. Most of them are uncomfortable with, or will never be ready for, floating, but many have been torn between the dollar and the euro, especially when their exchange rates diverge, causing wrenching adjustments in their economies as the relative profitability of exports and price of imports from these areas veers unpredictably and causing big fluctuations also in income from services such as tourism as well as transfers, such as remittances by immigrants. As the US, Canada and EU account for about 50 per cent of world output, one of the main sources of financial and economic instability in the world economy would then have been excised.

Or a creditor *Putsch*?

Another possibility would be for the emerging creditor nations, disillusioned with the bad debts and resistance to change they encounter in the West, to aim to *replace* existing arrangements and seize control of world money – a creditor *putsch*. There are precedents. The US did it by establishing the Federal Reserve in 1913 – a move that, combined with the seizing of financial leadership from the City of London during the First World War, and the determined policies of successive US administrations over the following half century, succeeded in replacing sterling-gold standard by the dollar-gold standard (France then conducted the funeral rights for sterling's international role by insisting Britain dismantle the sterling area as a condition of joining the EU, or EEC, as it then was, in 1973). It may be noted, however, that the dollar needed to walk on golden crutches for the first few decades of its reign – with its fixed gold price – and hasn't done so well since it discarded them. Perhaps such creditors would insist on a link to gold, as the UK and US did when they were top nations.

Following the example of the US one hundred years earlier, China is building up its gold reserves, buying in the markets as well as adding undisclosed sums to various official reserve funds from its domestic production. It is already the largest gold producer in the world. In 2011 its officially disclosed reserves totalled 1,054 tonnes of gold, the sixth largest in the world, but these accounted for only 1.6% of its reserves (valuing gold at market prices), demonstrating the huge scope for gradually accumulating more gold in furtherance of its geo-political aims (see Hale and Hale, 2011). With the expertise it has been acquiring in managing offshore RMB markets, currently mainly in Hong Kong, it hopes to be able to develop international use of its currency without losing control of its domestic economy. This is a common fear of new reserve centres – Germany and Japan both fought against becoming reserve centres because they were historically used to development models in which the state took the lead, and even when fully industrialized, it went against the grain of their histories and traditions to give too free rein to markets. Foreigners depositing funds in DM or in yen never felt absolutely comfortable about doing it, as the authorities seemed to take an unnecessarily close interest in why they were holding funds there, and what they might do with them. They didn't develop the international banking habit of lending out their surpluses, of allowing foreigners to build up huge liquid assets, and they didn't exactly encourage the development of all the ancillary services that go to make a financial centre – such as international insurance, accounting, legal and other professional services – many of which will best be provided by foreign enterprises.

But China, with the benefit of Hong Kong, could outsource much of its international financial business, while it is also promoting the growing financial onshore centre in Shanghai, and loosen controls on international transactions by residents. Although political differences probably rule out an alliance with the other great creditor country of East Asia, Japan, they would make a formidable couple – the world's two biggest international creditors – if they could arrange a 'marriage of convenience'. China could also reach out to the other Asian superpower, India, and indeed to Europe, including the City of London, which could provide all the offshore markets and expertise that China needs. The new creditor countries could then discuss with the US a winding down of the dollar area, with its extended overhang of dollar liabilities, and a handover of the reserve currency role to the New Creditor Standard. As long as the conditions were not onerous, with the residual liabilities transferred to the international community, this would be greatly to the advantage of the US.

Promoting policy coordination

With inflation at low rates throughout the industrialized countries, monetary cooperation between large currency areas to produce the public good of stable *international* money would open the door to closer policy coordination on a wide range of other issues. Under existing arrangements, little or no progress has been made in addressing the problems of global imbalances and excess reserves, and in 2012 no progress seemed in sight. Indeed, ad hoc cooperation that breaks down under pressure may intensify friction, as the examples show. The G20 focus on developing indicators of payments imbalances is, in reality, a façade – just a way for the US to bring pressure on China. The Chinese authorities are aware of this, and the chances for a successful outcome using this approach appear to be low. The big problems facing the world economy outlined in Part III – global imbalances, the reserves overhang, financial instability and cross-border asset price bubbles – would be easier to address jointly once there was an international standard provided by two or more major powers or currency areas. This would provide a core to the system, and reduce the fear of regime change. The IMF would then naturally assume a much more central role in negotiations on such outstanding issues, which currently are left to fester without a solution. Developing countries, the vast majority of which prefer pegging their exchange rates to floating (most of the world outside Europe is on a *de facto* dollar standard) would much prefer such a system. Coordination should focus instead on objectives that are in the interests of all countries, including stable exchange rates. Over time, this would facilitate a return to a more stable, rules-based, international monetary system.

Don't forget the anchor

Whatever the choice of the standard, it should be anchored in something other than the will of governments. As Bernholz' exhaustive study of world inflations has shown, that is the lesson of history, however painful it may be for governments to recognize it (Bernholz, 2003). Monetary and exchange rate cooperation – even the formation of a common North Atlantic monetary area – would not be enough. Having observed over the past 40 years many very able people trying to manage a pure credit or fiat monetary system, and being given the tools to achieve it – whatever tools they thought they needed – as well as full operational independence – my verdict is negative. Indeed, the verdict was delivered by GFC: human ingenuity is not up to the task of developing institutions that can maintain the value of money and deliver reasonable financial stability under a pure credit system with competitive banks and money markets. To imagine that its faults can be remedied by tweaking financial regulation or by macro- prudential policies is as utopian as to dream of a global currency. Experience shows that to provide financial stability under fiat money requires the imposition of extensive state controls over finance, banking and international money, with restrictions on personal freedoms that should be unacceptable. Unless we grasp the opportunity to reform opened by this unprecedented financial crisis to establish new international monetary and financial stability standards, banking and the financial sector will become so highly regulated that they will be unable to finance economic growth or support the growth of small firms or technological innovation. Bankers are quite right to point this out. Again, this is the money trap in action. There is no credible recipe for financial stability under the existing GFS.

That is why an anchor, such as those discussed in Chapters 12 through 14, should be attached to the international monetary standard. Nobody should be under any illusions that it would lead the world to a promised land of financial stability any time soon. But if leaders were willing to start on the path, that itself would give heart to the troops. Business confidence would start to revive once the financial establishment showed it understood the issues.

Robert Skidelsky has recommended a 'super-sovereign reserve currency' as the central aim of structural reform of the world's monetary system. I agree. I also agree when he says it should be part of a wider package and should include agreement on a more stable system of exchange rates. Both were wanted by East Asian countries:

> There is justice in the American insistence that China expand its domestic demand; but also in China's insistence that America learn to live within its means. This rebalancing of global demand would underpin a balanced monetary system. It is also fully in line with the evolution towards a more plural world order. (Skidelsky, 2010)

The proposals summarized in Chapter 13, as well as those advocated in Chapter 14, draw on the analysis that has been developed throughout this book – though the validity of the analysis – how we got caught in the money trap – should be judged independently of the policy proposals made.

The proposals reviewed and assessed in Chapters 12 and 13 share certain key characteristics. First, the authors understand the importance of a monetary standard, which from Aristotle to Keynes has been seen as a classic feature of a good money, though one generally neglected in contemporary debate. Secondly, they all tie money, albeit in different ways and through different connections, to the real side of the economy. Thirdly, they would all, if put into effect, make redundant a significant part of the financial 'service' industry as presently constituted, along with much of its regulatory apparatus, releasing resources for other employment. Fourthly, they all challenge belief in, and reliance on, money illusion – the assumption that you can fool most of the people most of the time. The insistence that people learn was a fundamental insight of the monetarist counter-revolution of the 1970s led by Milton Friedman. Remember that the big idea behind giving central banks independence was to make them responsible ultimately to the people rather than the government, but unfortunately it didn't work out as intended. In that sense also, these proposals represent a return to the ideas of those pioneering monetarists, but in a one-world context suitable for a globalized economy. It would put money into a quasi-constitutional realm above the cut and thrust of day-to-day politics.

Yet rational discussion is drowned out by the weight of propaganda from the establishment. Despite the evidence of disintegration and looming anarchy, governments cling to credit money. Pliable money suits many interests – not just governments, but also top bankers, financial middlemen, the fixers, the brokers, the agents, the advisers, all who cream off that little, almost imperceptible, percentage of the public's money, whether in commissions, taxes, inflation or default. Newspaper revenues depend on them. Governments bow the knee to them. Academics advise them. Central banks and international institutions use public money to employ them. Universities court them. And, above all, the public has been persuaded to value things in terms of official money.

There is another way. There are traditions of thought, including contributions from some of the world's most respected economists, going back a hundred years or more, that insist: it does not have to be like this. We don't need to reinvent the wheel. We need to study what has been written and said before, and adapt it to our needs. We must resist the insidious propaganda from all sides that says there is no alternative to Knappian money.[6] That is why we should appeal to the testimony of the great economists, few of whom believed in purely national, fiat money. Keynes himself passionately believed in the case for an international currency. The purpose of the options reviewed here is to encourage readers to resist current official propaganda. The manipulators and regulators of money have been given the benefit of the doubt long enough.

As regards the political chances of reform, politicians are well aware of the anxiety at the spectre of continued high unemployment, especially among young people, and the anger at the moneyed classes and the finance interest. While it may be difficult for politicians, especially in countries like the US and UK, to acknowledge that acceptance of full globalization involves a loss of nominal monetary autonomy, measures that would involve such an acceptance while seizing control of money back from the bankers could pay electoral dividends.

The near-death experiences that many economies have experienced in recent years may return. Next time, the entire global economy will be at risk. This is because many countries have run out of rope – the financial means to repair their balance sheets. They may not find the resources – financial, political or perhaps spiritual – required to rebuild their defences against further onslaughts. Yet, in the absence of the needed transformation of banking and monetary arrangements, turbulence could become chronic. All the benefits the world has derived from the growth of globalization over the past two generations are at risk. We should go forward to full economic integration not back to state planning and state rivalry. The overuse of monetary tools has become the main obstacle to progress. Money is not properly used as a weapon of social control. When it is over-used for such statist ends, it loses, over time, its more basic functions in society.[7] It is time for people to tell governments: give us back our money. We don't trust you to look after it for us.[8] It is time to try another route. The restoration of money to the people would be the best foundation of a better global financial order.

Notes

1. The tortured language used by official bodies in an effort to reconcile fiscal consolidation with stimulus is illustrated by the following from the OECD: 'Given the downward risks to growth, it is important to anchor expectations about medium- and long-term fiscal discipline in a manner that allows for a temporary easing of the fiscal stance to buffer unexpected weakness' (OECD, 2011).
2. An image used by Barry Eichengreen; see Book Discussion Event, 19 October 2011, http://www.imf.org/external/mmedia/view.aspx?vid=1227160773001
3. This had been a factor in previous crises: In the late 1970s, when the dollar was depreciating, countries fixing to the dollar suffered surpluses and inflationary pressure. But when US policy shifted and the dollar soared in the early 1980s, countries fixed to the dollar suffered deflationary shock and debt insolvency. This was the real cause of the international debt crisis that erupted in 1982. Another example was in the late 1990s, when the IT revolution lifted US productivity requiring real dollar appreciation.This created deflation (albeit mild) in the countries tied to the dollar, including China, Hong Kong, Panama and the Gulf countries.
4. British economist Charles Goodhart conducted a thorough review of all macro-prudential policy candidates for a new 'blueprint' for financial stability, concluding in effect that there isn't one within the existing GFS; we will just have to live with crises, managing impending cross-border failures of large financial institutions on a case-by-case basis. (Goodhart, 2011). On the ethics of banking, see Judt (2010).
5. Here the concept of 'stall speed' is instructive. The western world on this view is 'condemned to grow' faster than stall speed. At only 2 per cent average annual growth, economies will demonstrate an inability to behave like the historical capitalistic model should. Corporations lose incentives to invest because profit growth stagnates, unemployed workers are not rehired and the standard cyclical model of seasonal rebirth is jeopardized (see Gross, 2011).
6. Named after Georg Friederich Knapp (1842–1926), author of *'The State Theory of Money'*. For a discussion of the Chartalist (Knappian) versus Metallic historical concepts of money, see Bell and Nell (eds), 2003.

7. This may be viewed as a generalization of Goodhart's law, which states that whenever a monetary aggregate or other economic indicator is made a target of policy, it loses the attributes that qualify is to play such a role.

8. For a devastating critique of contemporary *mores* and the implications of the decline of trust, see Tony Judt, 2010: 'As recently as the 1970s, the idea that the point of life was to get rich and that governments existed to facilitate this would have been ridiculed' (p. 39). See also Sedlacek (2011), who criticizes economics for having lost touch with the moral principles on which the discipline was built and 'on which it should stand'. 'Learning from the crisis appears to be our only hope…. The truth appears in a crisis, frequently in its unpleasant nakedness…but in all its vehemency' (p. 322).

Bibliography

Bell, Stephanie A and Edward J. Nell (eds), *The State, the Market and the Euro: Chartalism versus Metallism in the Theory of Money*, Edward Elgar, 2003.

Bernholz, Peter, *Monetary Regimes and Inflation: History, Economic and Political Relationships*, Edward Elgar, 2004.

Bhagwati, Jagdish, 'Shame on You, Mr Obama, for Pandering on Trade', *Financial Times*, 7 February, 2012.

Coggan, Philip, *Paper Promises: Money, Debt and the New World Order*, Penguin Books, 2011.

Cowen, Tyler and Randall Kroszner, 'Mutual Fund Banking: A Market Approach', *Cato Journal*, Vol. 10, No. 1, Spring/Summer 1990.

Goodhart, Charles, 'The Emerging New Architecture of Financial Regulation', in *Monetary Policy and Financial Stability in the Post-crisis Era*, South African Reserve Bank 90th Anniversary, South African Reserve Bank, 2011, pp. 1–54.

Gross, Bill, 'Developed world cannot thrive at "stall speed"' *Financial Times*, 11 July 2011.

Hale, David and Lyric Hughes Hale, *What's Next? Unconventional Wisdom on the Future of the World Economy*, Yale University Press, 2011.

Hyman, Louis, *Debtor Nation: The History of America in Red Ink*, Princeton University Press, 2011.

Independent Commission on Banking, Final Report, UK, 2011.

Judt , Tony, *Ill Fares the Land*, Penguin Books, 2010.

Kay, John, *Narrow Banking* CSFI. 2010.

Kay, John, 'Europe's Elite Is Fighting Reality and Will Lose', *Financial Times*, 25 October 2011.

King, Stephen, 'I Can't Hear the Markets But I Can Smell Fear', *Financial Times*, 8 September 2011.

Kotlikoff, Lawrence, *Jimmy Stewart Is Dead: Ending the World's ongoing Financial Plague with Limited Purpose Banking* John Wiley, 2010.

Kroner, Niels, *A Blueprint for Better Banking: Svenska Handelsbanken and a Proven Model for Post-Crash Banking*, Harriman House, 2009.

OECD, 'Special Briefing Note by the Secretary General of the OECD Ahead of the Cannes Summit', 31 October 2011, OECD, 2011.

Padoa-Schioppa, Tommaso 'The Econonic Crisis and Global Monetary Disorder', Louvain-la-Neuve, 15 February 2011.

Phelps, Edmund S., 'Refounding Capitalism', *Capitalism and Society*, Article 2, Vol. 4, No. 3, 2009(a).

Phelps, Edmund S., 'Uncertainty bedevils the best system', *Financial Times*, April 14, 2009(b).

Sedlacek Tomas, *Economics of Good and Evil*, Oxford University Press, 2011.

Shelton, Judy 'Gold Standard or Bust', *The Weekly Standard*, Vol 16, No. 43, 1 August 2011.

Skidelsky, Robert, 'A Golden Opportunity for Monetary Reform', *Financial Times*, 9 November 2010.

Tett, Gillian, 'Dodd Frank's Long-Distance Paper Chase', *Financial Times*, 28 October 2011.

Index

Note: Page references in italics refer to portraits.

Printed and bound by CPI Group (UK) Ltd, Croydon, CR0 4YY